Acknowledgements and disclaimer

In researching and writing this 12th edition of The Complete Guide to Buying a Property in Spain, I have once again been advised and helped by a good many people. Many prefer to remain in the background; but you know who you are, and I thank you greatly for your patience and professional insights.

I acknowledge the considerable advice and input of María José Cobos Mayorga, an accountant and *Gestor* in Nerja; the notary in Nerja; Banco Sabadell bank; insurers MAPFRE; property sales and rental specialists Teamstar Holiday Rentals, part of Team Group; the Ayuntamiento de Nerja, my local Town Hall; the local property rates office Recaudación Provincial de Málaga; the local water board; electricity supplier Endesa; and telephone company Movistar, a brand of Telefónica. All provided information knowing that while this book might cite examples from their experience, products and services, it does not endorse anyone or any company in particular.

Most of all, I would like to thank my wife who has had to put up with me working on yet another edition of this guide after a period when a flurry of market and legislative changes left the previous Complete Guide in need of significant revision.

Great care has been taken in updating information, but any errors will be of my own making, and should not reflect on anyone else. Every effort has been made to check accuracy, but the information herein should not be regarded as investment advice or, indeed, as any other form of financial or legal advice. It is your responsibility to seek proper legal and other expert advice before purchasing or selling property in Spain.

Buying in Spain? Read this first...

This guide aims to help purchasers avoid problems when buying property in Spain. I also offer an 'after-sales' service. During 35 years of living and working in the property market in Spain, I have established a network of trusted estate agents and other professionals in popular areas: Costa del Sol, Costa Blanca, Costa de la Luz, and the Balearic and Canary Islands. I can ask agents to send you information, to meet you on arrival if you plan to visit, and to arrange accommodation during your house-hunting trip. You may contact me in Nerja, Málaga province, Spain through the following channels:

A I Foster
Calle Granada 23
Pasaje Granada - Local 3
29780 Nerja
Málaga
Spain

Telephone: +34 95 252 3695
Mobile: +34 629 577445
To speak to me personally, call between 17.00 and 19.30 hours United Kingdom time (18.00-20.30 CET), Monday to Friday.
Email me at tonyfoster@live.com

Order additional copies of this book from your local bookshop, or from online retailers including Amazon, through which a Kindle version e-book is also available. For bulk orders, email me directly.

Y013355

The item should be returned or renewed
by the last date stamped below.

By Anthony I Foster

CREATIVE MEDIA ASSOCIATES SPAIN 2016

The Complete Guide to Buying a Property in Spain
by Anthony I Foster

First published in paperback September 1994
12th edition published September 2016

CMAS
Plaza Chaparil 8
Edificio Peñaflor II-2A
29780 Nerja
Málaga
Spain

ISBN: 978-84-940270-3-1

Printed in the United Kingdom by
Lightning Source UK Ltd
Milton Keynes, MK11 3LW

CONTENTS

NOTES

Figures

In Spain, one hundred thousand Euros and fifty Euro cents would be written as: **100.000,50 Euros**

In this book, we use the United Kingdom and US convention, under which the same figure would written as: **100,000.50 Euros**

01: Introduction

So you are in sunny Spain and about to search for your dream home. As you sip your first chilled drink, heed a few words of well-meant advice from an old pro, so to speak.

Do not leave your brains in the left-luggage locker at the airport! Many did just that and lived to regret it. Many more by far have heeded the warning and avoided numerous pitfalls to settle into new homes and fulfilling, sun-drenched lives with minimum fuss.

You may have read tragic stories about people who sought a Spanish Shangri-La, only to lose life savings through the wiles of unscrupulous developers or estate agents. Maybe they met someone in a bar who had property for sale, only to discover too late that the friendly local did not own it, or there were enormous debts on the property.

You may have seen poignant pictures of a retired British couple in tears as bulldozers moved in to demolish their Almeria province home, which they had every reason to believe was built legally.

In the Costa del Sol town of Marbella, thousands of homes were declared illegal after decades of unlawful construction sanctioned by local politicians and bureaucrats in cahoots with developers. Even the Hollywood star Antonio Banderas, an honoured son of Málaga province, ran into planning difficulties with a home there.

With more than 35 years' experience, I am acutely aware of what can happen, which is why I first wrote this guide in 1994 and revise it regularly to keep up with changing laws, practices, trends and events.

By summer 2016, Spain's housing market was showing modest but sustained signs of revival. It remains a good time to find bargains. Plenty of savvy investors and nesters are doing just that.

Hundreds of thousands of expatriate home owners have already bought trouble-free throughout Spain. I aim to help you join their satisfied ranks.

Here are some first thoughts to fix firmly in mind...

Everyone is selling or knows someone who is. Just about everyone you meet professes to be an expert and apparently does a bit of property selling. Mention your interest, and the waiter will tell you of a friend with something at a very good price, or knows someone who will help.

Maybe you get into conversation with a local or a waiter in a bar, who may try to sell you their own property, or they know somebody who wants to sell. Do not jump into a deal. If it goes wrong, and it probably will, you will have no comeback.

Also, **everyone is an expert.** Spain is just full of bar-room lawyers who profess to know it all. Ignore them!

Scout around. Unless on an inspection flight with a reputable agency and being met by their agents, spend time looking round. Find areas you like, note 'For Sale' signs, and contact agencies handling the sale. Ring the number on the sign; they will almost certainly speak English, and maybe Swedish, German or French.

Check out the estate agent. You may develop a feeling about their trustworthiness, but it is still a good idea to ask if they are 'API registered'. If so, they are registered with the province's professional body, the *Colegio de Agentes de la Propiedad Inmobiliaria.* They should have deposited a financial bond with this institution, giving you some protection if things go wrong. Or they may be 'GIPE-registered' with *La Asociación Profesional de Gestores Intermediarios en Promociones de Edificaciones,* in which case you should ask to see their registration certificate with this professional association.

There is **no law regulating estate agents in Spain.** It is difficult to hold an agent responsible if things go wrong. If you deal with an API- or GIPE-registered agent, you are at least using someone who passed exams set by a professional body. Details of their registration and relevant number should be on a sign outside the office, on the exterior, or in the window display. Look for a three- or four-figure number, and ask for proof. If they cannot show it, just walk away.

The absence of a 'For Sale' sign does not necessarily mean it is not for sale. Ask an API- or GIPE-registered estate agency if it has anything in your preferred area.

Hire a lawyer and pick the right one. Even dealing with a registered estate agent does not mean you are 100% safe. You simply must employ a lawyer. If possible, use one recommended by someone who previously used them to buy property successfully. Even then, refer to this book to check that your lawyer is doing the job properly and reviewing, asking for, and arranging for all required and authorised documentation to be available when needed.

Check in advance **what fees the lawyer will charge.** As a rule of thumb, it will be 1% to 1.5% of the purchase price. Query it if it is higher. Bear in mind that you will also pay property transfer taxes, IVA (value added tax), and notary and Land Registry fees (chapter 6).

What happens next?

You have found what you want to buy, and the first thing to understand is that the Spanish system is probably very different from you own country's way of doing things. In Spain, all deeds for properties are drawn up by government-appointed public notaries, *Notarios*.

These experienced, specialist lawyers are responsible for legalising documents such as an *Escritura* (property title deeds) and a *Poder Notarial* (Power of Attorney, or PoA).

For property, a *Contrato de CompraVenta*, contract of purchase and sale, is drawn up and a deposit is paid. This fixes the price, so **you cannot be outbid at the last minute.**

The contract is binding on both parties. It stipulates the date of the final payment and of the signing of the public *Escritura*. This is signed in the notary's office, witnessed by the *notario*, whose signature legalises the transaction. All parties involved must be present to sign the *Escritura,* or must have appointed people with Power of Attorney to act on their behalf.

For example, if a property is owned jointly by a husband and wife, and you and your wife are joint purchasers, all four must either be present or represented by persons with PoAs drawn up in Spanish and notarised so that, say, a husband can sign for an absent wife or vice versa.

If a buyer or seller is having a PoA made up in their home country, they will need to provide a photocopy of their ID card, or of the page in their passport with their photograph on, to the person who will be using the PoA in Spain to sign the contracts and *Escritura*. A copy of your ID card or your passport's photograph page must be scanned into the Spanish notary's computer database.

You have probably spent half a lifetime building up to this monumental decision. You are excited at the prospect of owning your very own place in the sun. So please do not spoil it for yourself.

Give it plenty of thought before you proceed, and tread carefully. If you follow the guidelines laid down in this book, you should not go wrong. Happy Home Hunting!

02: First Steps

Spain has a reputation for bureaucracy. If you are buying property and/or intending to live or work in the country, taking four key steps on arrival will help to avoid grief later. Open a Spanish bank account. Obtain a foreigner identification/tax number. Establish proof of residency, and get listed on the local electoral register.

Key step 1: bank account

You need a *Cuenta Bancaria*, Spanish bank account, to pay in Euros for property, and to cover standing orders for electricity, community fees, water, and property rates (IBI). It is easy to open one, particularly in coastal areas and islands where most banks have multilingual staff. To satisfy anti-money laundering rules, present your passport, NIE certificate (see below), proof of your address in your own country – your driving licence, for example – proof of earnings, e.g. your most recent wage slip showing what you were paid for that period, your contract of employment, and your annual income. Sign the contracts, and deposit a small sum.

Order a cheque book, a *Talonario*, at the same time. These come from head office and normally take up to four days. Request a 'hole-in-the-wall' cash machine card too; Spanish banks normally close after 14.00 hrs on weekdays, and are closed at weekends.

To speed money transfers, ask for the full title of the Spanish bank, its postal address, IBAN number (this normally has the letters ES and two numbers), the ten digits of the 'Sort Code', the ten digits of the account number, and the Swift Telex Code.

Most Spanish banks offer **internet banking**. To speed matters, you can open an account as a non-resident then convert to a resident's account if you move to Spain.

My strong advice is to shop around before opening an account in Spain, as banks here do not follow the custom that applies, for example, in the UK, where a fixed charge is levied on Bank Drafts. All banks in Spain charge a percentage of the amount of the Bank Draft. This charge can be anything up to 0.5%, which can add up to a considerable amount when the Draft is for a large sum of money. You will of course need the Bank Draft to make the final payment at the notary's when you go to sign the *Escritura* title deeds.

You should also ask what the cost would be to transfer funds to your home country if or when you decide to sell your property, as banks normally charge a percentage for these transfers as well.

Key step 2: NIE

The *Número de Identificación de Extranjero* (NIE) identification number is your ID number as a foreigner (*Extranjero*). It needs to be registered with the Spanish tax authorities to pay taxes in Spain: for this purpose, it also becomes your NIF (*Número de Identificación Fiscal*). These taxes may include, among others, transfer tax on purchasing property, and non-resident taxes later.

Apply for your NIE as soon as possible, as it can take some time to process. Armed with all the necessary documents, your lawyer or estate agent should take you to the nearest National Police station with a *Departamento de Extranjeros*, foreigners department.

Or you should give Power of Attorney to your lawyer or estate agent to do so on your behalf (but see 'Note well' on page 12). It is highly unlikely that a *Departmento de Extranjeros* will deal with you in any other language than Spanish; you are warned!

There, you present a completed application, a photocopy of it, and a form known as a Modelo 790. To pay for the NIE certificate, you or your lawyer should previously have taken the Modelo 790 to the bank to pay 9.45 Euros per application. This fee may change or could vary throughout Spain, so please regard the figure that I have provided as being only as a guide.

You will also need your passport, and a photocopy of the passport page that bears your photograph. Your lawyer or estate agent should be able to supply all these forms. If giving a lawyer or estate agent

Power of Attorney to obtain your NIE number/s, you need your passports photocopied on official notary's paper. This can be done at the notary when you sign the Power of Attorney. The notary signs these and stamps them as authorised copies for a fee of about four Euros per passport.

Note well: If arranging an NIE from another country, check with your lawyer in Spain to see if he really can do this with a Power of Attorney, as rules change and can vary locally. At the time of writing, the Spanish government was reviewing this issue.

Where I live, a lawyer can certainly apply locally for your NIE certificate, but only if a photocopy of your passport is attached to the Power of Attorney and then sent, in the case of the United Kingdom, to the UK Foreign Office to have an *Apostille*, a legal validation, attached to legalise this document in Spain. You send this document to your lawyer in Spain to apply for your NIE.

Alternatively, you may apply for an NIE at a Spanish embassy or consulate in your own country of residence.

You should understand, though, that this takes longer than applying in Spain because they send application forms to Madrid, who later post the NIE certificates to your home address. When applying for an NIE through a Spanish consulate, allow at least two months for delivery.

Note: it is very important to keep at least a copy of the NIE certificate, because you may need to produce a copy of this at some future date.

To register your NIE with the tax authorities, you may have to visit them. Or, when you have signed the *Escritura* title deeds, you may be able to sign an authorisation form for either your lawyer, your *Gestoría*, or the notary's office to register the NIE for you.

Key steps 3 & 4: Residencia/Empadronamiento

If you plan to live for more than 183 days per year, or to work in Spain, you must obtain *Residencia*, residency, and register on the electoral register of the city, town or village where you will be living.

What you need

The process is comparatively simple for **citizens of** EU member states. You will need the following documents and forms, which can be obtained from a *Gestoría*, who will also fill them in for you to avoid errors that might otherwise cause delays:

- An application form for each person and a photocopy of each application form;
- A Tax Form (Modelo 790). When it is filled in you must pay 10.60 Euros for each person applying. This is in Málaga province, and may vary elsewhere, so ask your lawyer;
- One passport photograph for each applicant – the photos must be on a white background;
- The passports of each applicant, and a photocopy of each;
- And a *Certificado de Empadronamiento* for each applicant.

If working as an employee or self-employed, you should need only to present a certificate from the *Tesorería General de la Seguridad Social* (Social Security office), which proves that you are currently working and registered with the Social Security authorities in Spain.

If you are employed, your employer should obtain this for you. If self-employed, ask your Gestoría to get the certificate. If you are of retirement age, see chapter 10.

If you are under retirement age and planning to take up permanent residence in Spain, but you do not intend to work and will not be paying contributions to the Spanish social security system, obtaining your *Residencia* depends on being able to prove that you have sufficient funds to live on, and that you are covered by private medical insurance.

You will need to prove as an individual that you have an annual income of around 5,200 Euros. At the start of 2016, for example, the actual amount was 5,136 Euros. If you are a couple with children, ask a Gestoría what is the minimum income you must prove for the whole family. For the adults, it is more than, though not as much as double, the amount required for a single person; and there is a pro-rata figure for the children.

Sadly, the Spanish authorities no longer issue an ID card such as a Spaniard would have. This is a pity, as these cards show a photograph and a fingerprint, easy proofs of identity.

Instead, the authorities now provide you with only a green Residencia card. It shows your personal details and NIE number, but bears neither a photograph nor a fingerprint. So, legally, you must carry some other proof of identity.

For UK citizens in Spain, this means carrying your passport with you at all times. This would be necessary, for example, if you were stopped by Guardia Civil traffic control when driving, or if you had to prove identity to pay by credit card or cheque in at a hotel.

To save you having to carry your passport, I advise going to the nearest notary's office to **get the notary to photocopy it onto official notarial paper.** They will sign it to say that it is a copy of the original. The cost recently was approximately four Euros per passport where I live.

This copy should be accepted by the National Police, Municipal Police, and the Guardia Civil. It should also be accepted when paying with a credit card.

Where to apply: If you are an **EU national coming to work or to live in Spain for more than 183 days a year**, apply for the *Residencia* certificate at the *Departamento de Extranjeros*, foreigners' department, at the same National Police offices where you may previously have applied for your NIE number.

You can do so at the same time as applying for the NIE if you do not yet have one. Your lawyer, or the estate agent you are dealing with, will undoubtedly be able to advise you on this.

If you feel that going on your own will be difficult, maybe because you do not speak Spanish well, contact a *Gestoría Administrativa* to send someone along with you to apply for *Residencia*. Your lawyer or estate agent can put you in touch with a *Gestoría Administrativa*, or may themselves take you to obtain your *Residencia*.

Before going to the foreigners department at the national police station, you must register on the electoral register (*Padrón*) at your local Town Hall. You will need to present a copy of your *Escritura* title deeds for the home you have purchased, or a property rental contract, along with your passport and NIE certificate.

Once you have registered on the *Padrón*, you must request a *Certificado de Empadronamiento* (certificate of registration on the electoral register), which you will need to obtain your *Residencia*.

The Town Hall may well tell you that that the *Policía Municipal*, the local police, will call personally at your property to ensure that you are indeed living at this address.

Registering on the *Padrón* adds to the town's official head count, so more public money comes its way. **If you have *Residencia* in Spain, registering on the *Padrón* is obligatory.**

The foreigners department at the national police station may prepare your *Residencia* while you wait, which is certainly the case where I live; but in other locations you may well have to return at a later date.

When you collect the green *Residencia* card, you must present the document showing that you have paid for it, along with your completed *Residencia* application form.

03: Buying a Resale Property

Resale properties, i.e. second-hand, are the most common type of housing purchase. Typically, a *Contrato de CompraVenta* **contract of purchase and sale** is drawn up, a deposit is paid - normally 10% of the agreed sale price - and the contract is signed by vendor and purchaser.

Customs vary. I live in Nerja, Málaga province, where estate agents have been in the habit of requesting a 'reservation payment' of 3,000 Euros towards that 10% deposit.

In such cases, a **'reservation contract'** is signed by both parties when the 3,000 Euros is paid. The property is thus reserved exclusively at the agreed price while your lawyer conducts searches, or to give sufficient time to arrange a mortgage.

If all goes to plan, the full *Contrato de CompraVenta* is drawn up and the balance of the 10% deposit becomes due in 15 to 21 days.

If you do not pay the balance by the deadline, you forfeit the 3,000 Euros unless there was a legal obstacle to completion, or if no mortgage was available.

Any **deposit should be held by your lawyer** until he is sure everything is in order with the property before releasing funds to the vendor. Both the Reservation Contract and the *Contrato de CompraVenta* should be drawn up by the estate agent or your lawyer. If by the agent, it is vital that your lawyer vets the contract before you sign and part with deposit money.

It is better to know about all **immediate and future expenses** before you buy. So before signing a *Contrato de CompraVenta*, find out:

- The annual community fees, *Gastos de la Comunidad*. On some *Urbanizaciones* (complexes, housing estates) or *Edificios* (apartment blocks), these can be up to 2,000 Euros or more.
- *The Inmuebles y Bienes Inmobiliarias* (IBI), the local Town Hall's annual rates (levy) on your chosen property

- Approximate costs involved in the drawing up, completion, signing, copying and registering of the *Escritura* title deeds for the property, and any other incidental charges.

Before signing contracts and paying a deposit, your lawyer must see:

- The *Escritura* title deeds to check that the people selling the property really are its owners
- A *Nota Simple* Land Registry document showing the legal owners and mortgages or other encumbrances on a property. This has a full description – bedrooms, bathrooms etcetera - and the surface area. These should match those on the *Escritura*. Otherwise it may mean any, some, or all of the following: sellers are not the owners; they have extended or altered property without permission; they failed to register a change, albeit approved; or the *Escritura* could not be registered.

Once your lawyer is satisfied, you move on to the *Contrato de CompraVenta* contract of purchase and sale. Before signing and paying a deposit you must ensure that all the following issues are covered in the contract.

I   Price and payment terms.

II   Since June 1, 2013, vendors of a property must register its **Energy Certificate** (*Certificado Energético de Edificio Existente*) with the *Delegación de Industria*. This indicates how energy-efficient the property is. The Estate Agent must get the certificate when receiving instructions to offer a property for sale, and must state the energy rating for each property in their publicity or their window displays. Your lawyer should get this document to present at the notary's when you go to sign the *Escritura*. **Property with an official, built-area of less than 50 square metres does not need this certificate.**

III   **Purchasers are responsible for debts on the property** only from the day of the signing of the *Escritura* and receiving the keys. Your lawyer must see proof that any outstanding debts associated with a property have been paid up-to-date before signing the *Escritura* and making final payment. All debts in Spain are on the property, not the person. Charges to look out for include community fees, electricity, telephone, water - though this may be included in community fees - and IBI property rates.

IV The **description of the property** in the *Contrato de CompraVenta* contract of purchase and sale must match those in the *Escritura* and the *Nota Simple*. If not, the owners must show your lawyer a valid building licence for any extensions or alterations. They must accept, in writing in the contract, responsibility for the costs of declaring changes at the notary's office, including Land Registry fees. If there is no planning permission, your lawyer must ask the *Ayuntamiento* (Town Hall) to ascertain if the work can be legalised. If it can, the current owners will be responsible for all of the costs.

V   The *Contrato de CompraVenta* contract of purchase and sale should show **full registration details from the Land Registry.** These include the *Finca* Number (The Land Registration No.); the book Number; and all other details. This information can be had from either the *Escritura* or the *Nota Simple*.

VI *Situación Catastral* (the catastral situation) – the registration reference number on the Registro Catastral, which is the annual rates registry.

VII A section in the contract of purchase and sale should be headed *Cargas,* charges, and should declare the property to be **'Free of Charges and Encumbrances'**. Any outstanding mortgage should show here. If you do not wish to take over the mortgage but want it paid off, take this up in the Conditions of Payment section of the contract as follows…

VIII If there is a mortgage on the property, the amount owed on the **existing mortgage**, including all cancellation costs, will be deducted from final payment. On the day the sale completes, your lawyer or estate agent will obtain the amount owed to the bank, and the cancellation costs for the notary and Land Registry fees. The lawyer or agent will arrange for a bank representative to be at the notary's to sign a deed cancelling the mortgage. This normally happens on the same day, just before you sign the title deeds. The cancellation must be signed by the notary prior to you signing the *Escritura.*

IX There should be a clause headed *Arrendamiento,* covering any **tenants**, in the *Contrato de CompraVenta* contract of purchase and sale. This should declare the property free of sitting tenants.

X If property is **sold furnished**, which is normally the case for a resale, a complete inventory should be drawn up, signed by both parties, and annexed to the *CompraVenta*. This avoids nasty surprises when you return to sign the *Escritura* and, on checking the property, find no furniture. If vendors are Spanish, the property may well be sold unfurnished. If so, ask for a list of what is being taken. I have had cases where property was sold unfurnished and vendors took not only furniture, curtains and light fittings, but also kitchen units, cooker, hob, refrigerator and washing machine. Visit the property just prior to completion to see what has been left as agreed.

XI Spanish tax laws generally oblige purchasers to **retain 3% of the sale value** declared on the *Escritura* to pass to the taxman. But if sellers are Spanish nationals, or foreigners with *Residencia,* the retention does not apply. There are local variations. In some, there is no retention if vendors present a current *Residencia* card. In others, notaries insist that vendors also present a certificate from the local tax office showing them to be tax-resident in Spain, i.e. declaring all their taxes in Spain and not just filing tax returns of property taxes as a non-resident would. Your lawyer will advise if you must retain the 3% or not. This is fully discussed in chapter 14.

XII The *Contrato de CompraVenta* contract of purchase and sale has a **double penalty clause** stating that if buyers do not complete the purchase on the date stated, they will lose the deposit paid, while vendors may put the property back on sale. If vendors do not complete on the date stated, they must pay purchasers double the deposit paid. This ensures both parties are locked in and have considered all implications.

XIII   One party may be taken **seriously ill just prior to completion.** In my view it would be harsh to impose penalties in such a case. So I would suggest that a further clause is inserted stating that, under Civil Code 1.105 of Spanish law, it would not be considered a breach of contract if delays were caused by accidents or Acts of God. In Spanish, this would read: *No supondrá incumplimiento de los plazos previstos en este contrato los retrasos producidos, por caso fortuito o fuerza mayor de los recogidos en el artículo 1.105 del Código Civil.* This would extend the completion date until the unwell person was able to attend the notary's to sign the *Escritura,* or a Power of Attorney was in place for someone to sign on their behalf. For this clause to be effective there must of course be, in the case of a serious illness, medical proof that this is the reason for invoking this clause.

XIV   The vendors are responsible for the payment of the **Plusvalía** (chapter 6), and this obligation must of course be reflected in the wording of the *CompraVenta* and the *Escritura* title deeds.

XV   If property was built within the last five to six years, seek proof that a **building licence was obtained** and that a **building completion certificate**, *Certificado de Final de Obra,* and a licence of first occupation, *Licencia de Primera Ocupación,* were issued. If vendors do not have these, your lawyer gets copies from the Town Hall. You could have difficulties if these have not been obtained and paid for.

Declaring a price

It has been common in Spain to under-declare a sale price because of high transfer taxes on resale property. In Andalucía, for example, the transfer tax was 8% for resale property in early 2016, while 10% value added tax applied to new property. Transfer taxes vary regionally (see Appendix A), so check with your lawyer.

It has been common in Spain to **under-declare the sale price** of a resale property. For example, a property may be sold for 200,000 Euros, but the sale price on the *Escritura* deeds will maybe show as 150,000 Euros.

The taxman is now much stricter. My firm advice is to **declare the actual price being paid** to avoid potentially high capital gains taxes when you later sell.

Even so, with average property prices now much lower than in 2008, you may honestly declare the actual amount paid, only to find the authorities assign a higher value to the home and tax you accordingly. The way they calculate this varies regionally. Where I live, tax authorities set a minimum declared value of twice the *Valor Catastral* rateable value in 2004. In 2005, this so-called 'coefficient' was 2.2, rising to 2.7 in 2008, but was only 1.73 in 2016.

The result is that **tax can be higher than the sale price would imply**. Also bear in mind that the authorities have four years to check the declared price. If they value it higher, they can issue a *Complimentario*, a supplementary charge, and may impose fines.

Your lawyer can advise on the **minimum value** that the taxman will likely put on the property. In this way, you will avoid facing a supplementary charge between 6% and 10% – depending on the *Transmisiones Patrimoniales* that apply when you are buying – on the difference between the declared purchase price and the valuation the tax authorities put on it. You also want to avoid fines.

Be guided by your lawyer on declared value, which should be agreed with vendors before signing contracts and paying the deposit.

Before you sign your Escritura, the notary needs a copy of your NIE certificate as this must be included in the Escritura. Your lawyer will also need a copy of the NIE certificate to present, along with your Escritura, at the Land Registry office to pay relevant taxes and for the office to register the property in your name/s.

You will also need your NIE certificate to transfer the contract for the electricity and water, to insure the property and, of course, to pay your annual property taxes in future.

Before going to the notary's to sign the *Escritura,* your lawyer should obtain a **certificate from the** *Recaudación Provincial,* the local property Rates Office, stating that there are no outstanding rates owed on the property. This is presented to the notary's office when preparing your *Escritura* for signing. The notary needs the reference number from this certificate in order to prepare the *Escritura* title deeds, and to obtain a certificate from the Rates Office.

As for **Annual Community Fees**, your lawyer or estate agent should obtain a certificate from the *Administrador de Fincas,* the administrator of the community where you will be living, showing that fees on the property you are purchasing have been paid up to date. This certificate is then taken up in the *Escritura* title deeds, stating that there are no such outstanding fees.

I usually obtained a *Nota Simple* from the Land Registry on the day of the *Escritura* signing. This ensured that no debts or mortgages had been registered on the property since the initial search was made, contracts drawn up, and the deposit paid.

This precaution is no longer necessary as the **notary is obliged to obtain, by fax, a** *Nota Simple* from the Land Registry showing any debts or encumbrances registered against the property. Your lawyer or estate agent should organise this with the notary at least three days before the signing and, at the same time, present all relevant documentation that the notary needs to prepare the *Escritura.*

If the property you are buying is being sold in Euros, ask your Spanish bank to issue a Banker's Draft for the final payment. In this case, make sure you allow enough time for funds to be transferred to your Spanish account for the completion.

If the property is foreign-owned, the vendors may want payment in their country's currency, for example in British Pounds or US Dollars. This is perfectly legal. In this case, I suggest you agree an exchange rate against the Euro before signing the Contrato de CompraVenta contract of purchase and sale, and have this rate stipulated in the contract. If final payment is being made in one of these currencies, you will need a Banker's Draft from your bank to take to Spain for signing the Escritura deeds. The currency website xe.com is one widely used and well regarded source for latest rates.

A Banker's Draft, known as a Cashier's Check in the USA, is a cheque guaranteed by your bank. The funds are removed from your account when the draft is issued, thus ensuring payment to the person or persons to whom the cheque is made payable. In my experience, this is the easiest and safest way to make final payment. Similarly, if you are paying the balance in Euros, you simply ask your Spanish bank to issue a Banker's Draft before going to the notary to sign the *Escritura* deeds.

Remember! Before handing over the Banker's Draft to the vendors at the notary, the estate agent or your lawyer should have obtained the **last receipts for electricity and telephone, and for water** if these are not included in the community fees. Clearly, this is to ensure that there are no outstanding debts, and to deal with the transfer of these utilities to your name.

When you go to the notary, you present your passport/s, your NIE certificate/s and the Banker's Draft/s. The staff will scan your passport/s into their computer and photocopy the draft/s on official notarial paper.
If the sale is in a different currency, they will still photocopy the drafts on to official notarial paper, but will need to know the exchange rate used against the Euro to show the Euro amount on the *Escritura* so that they can calculate transfer taxes etc. Your lawyer or estate agent will no doubt advise you on this matter.

You will recall that if it is a resale property and the vendors are either not Spanish nationals, or are foreign nationals not fiscally resident in Spain, **you must retain 3% of the sale price** declared on the *Escritura,* which you deduct from the outstanding balance. Or to put it another way, the vendor only gets 97% of the declared price. The 3% withheld must be paid to the local tax authorities within 30 days of signing the Escritura. This retention acts as a deposit against the vendor's assumed capital gains tax.

Effectively, you are acting for the tax man to collect some of the vendors' assumed capital gains on the deal. Under normal circumstances your lawyer will deal with paying the retained 3% to the tax authorities on your behalf.

Beware though! If final payment is in British Pounds, for example, you must still transfer funds to Spain to cover payments in Euros of the 3% retention, if that applies, plus notary and Land Registry fees etc. Transfer such funds at least 10 working days prior to completion date to ensure that they are sent in good time.

So you have now signed the *Escritura* deeds, handed over the Banker's Drafts, and are happy legal owners of a home in Spain. Well done! But there is still a little more to deal with.

You must now pay the costs of the *Escritura* and obtain a ***Copia Simple,*** a simple copy of your *Escritura*. In some cases, the notary may be able to prepare your *Copia Simple* immediately and let you know the costs; or you or your lawyer may have to return in a few days to collect it and pay the charges.

If these taxes and other fees are unpaid within 28 days of signing the *Escritura,* fines are levied. There is normally a longer period allowed for the *Plusvalía* tax to be paid, but a copy of your *Escritura* must be presented at the local Town Hall **within one month of the signing**. My advice is to avoid any problems by paying these costs as soon as you know them.

After making the payments, to your lawyer or to the notary's office, they will take a first copy of the original of your *Escritura* to the Land Registry for them to register the document.

After some two to three months, your *Escritura* will be collected by your lawyer or the notary's office and you can then pick up the first copy of the original. If collecting the *Escritura* from the notary's office, present your *Copia Simple* and proof of identity, then take away your registered *Escritura*.

Congratulations! You have safely negotiated the Spanish property maze with help from your trusted professional advisors. You may even get a pleasant surprise in the form of a small refund from the money you deposited with your lawyer or the notary to cover costs for registering the *Escritura* at the Land Registry. They will normally overestimate these costs, because they prefer to make a refund rather than request further money from you.

If you lose what is classed as 'the original' of your *Escritura,* do not worry. The so-called First Copy of the *Escritura,* minus your signature, goes to the Land Registry, and this is what you receive when it is returned to the notary with all registration details. This document is what is commonly known as 'the original', even if it is not. The notary retains the true original that you all signed. Once you have your *Copia Simple* of the *Escritura,* you or your lawyer will need to **take a few photocopies**. These are to:

- Pay *Plusvalía* tax at the local Town Hall
- Change the *Contribuciones IBI* (annual rates) to your name
- Transfer the electricity contract to your name
- Transfer the water contract to your name
- Give to the administrator of the community of owners

The relevant forms will have to be filled in and signed. This may not be easy for you but, as explained in chapter 6 on *Escritura Costs,* the agent you are buying the property through, or your lawyer, should make the necessary photocopies for you. They will either accompany you to the various offices, or will visit these on your behalf.

Your lawyer, or the estate agent you are buying the property through, should go with you to the local office of the electricity company to change the name on the contract. The same applies to water if it is not included in the community fees.

To provide some idea of **fees when transferring the contract** to your name: if it is for the same number of kilowatts (kW) of installed capacity as the previous owner, the cost will be around 26 Euros to 32 Euros.

If you want more power, it will cost you 65 Euros for each increase in the number of kWs contracted. So if you want to boost the supply from 2.22 kW to 3.45 kW, the charge would be 65 Euros for increasing the wattage, and 26 to 32 Euros to switch it into your name: grand total 91 to 97 Euros.

This was an example from Nerja near Málaga. It may be different where you are buying.

Depending on the property's age, you may be obliged to install **a new trip-switch system** and replace wiring from the trip-switch box to the electricity meter. If so, this must be done by an **approved electrician**, who will then obtain a *Boletín de Instalación*, a certificate approving the installation. You will not be able to transfer the electricity to your name without this.

The **cost of all this can vary enormously**, but you really do need to know that it can currently (2016) range from around 600 Euros to 1,500 Euros depending on the work involved.

You, or your lawyer or estate agent, need to present the *Boletín de Instalación* and copies of your *Escritura*, your NIE certificate and the previous owner's electricity bill, which shows the reference number of the electricity meter.

It can be an old bill from the vendors, though the last one they received would be better. This is because if the estate agency does its job properly, when its gets the meter reading the day before signing at the notary's, the agent knows how much electricity has been consumed since the last bill, and can calculate the outstanding amount owed for power.

The electricity company will need a telephone number so it can send an engineer to check the installation and to fit an ICP, a **circuit breaker** to stop you using more kWs than you contracted for.

You will need to be at home for the engineer, or to leave keys with the estate agent. The electricity company is unlikely to specify a precise time. It is usually as vague as 'morning, 'afternoon' or 'evening', and even that timetable can slip. The water company also **charges to switch a meter to your name**. The fee where I live is 125 to 150 Euros, and you leave a deposit of 95 Euros for the meter, a sum that should be returned to your bank account by the water company if you subsequently sell the property.

The electricity and water companies will need your bank account details to set up a standing order for your regular payments to them.

Your estate agent or lawyer should also advise the **administrator of your residential community** of the change of ownership and go to the *Recaudación Provincial* local rates office to transfer to your name the **responsibility for paying IBI**, the annual levies on property.

I deal with transferring the electricity, water, community and annual rates for clients as I believe it should be part of the service the estate agency offers, or should be part of the work of your lawyer, and that there should be no extra charges.

Costs involved in the *Escritura* are explained in chapter 6.

04: New Property or a Plot of Land

This chapter deals with buying new property within four categories:

- To be built from a developer's plan – 'buying off plan'
- Already under construction
- Recently completed but never lived in
- Buying land then having you own property built.

Buying off plan

This is quite complicated. Documentation is extensive, and even more care is needed than for buying resale or completed property. However, you may decide that the advantages of having a home built to your own specification outweigh any downside. Either way, use a lawyer, and preferably one that comes recommended.

Before paying a deposit and signing a contract, your lawyer will obtain a *Nota Simple* from the Land Registry as proof that the seller really does own the land, and that there are no mortgages or encumbrances on it. Your lawyer must see proof that a building licence was obtained from the local Town Hall and paid for.

If the property is near the beach, your lawyer should ensure that development is approved by the *Jefatura de Costas*, the Coastal Authority, as well as the *Ayuntamiento*, Town Hall. The *Ley de Costas*, Law of the Coasts, which came into force in 1998, restricts building within 100 metres of the high-tide mark.

If a planning application was submitted to the Town Hall after May 5, 2000, the developer is obliged to have an insurance policy called *Seguro Decenal*. This guarantees the foundations and structure for 10 years. It does not currently cover the quality of other building materials used, though it is anticipated that these will be included at some later date. Details of the policy must be included in the contracts for the property; so without a

Seguro Decenal, the *Escritura* title deeds cannot be created. To obtain this policy, an approved and registered company must first carry out a geological survey. Test-drillings establish what foundations are required. Laboratory analysis examines the quality of the reinforced concrete being used for the foundations and structure.

Before signing and paying a deposit, ask your lawyer to give you a breakdown of approximate *Escritura* costs. This should state who is responsible for paying *Plusvalía* tax – it should be the seller – and this applies to all categories of property in this chapter.

When buying from a developer or builder, they will almost certainly try to persuade you to declare in the *Escritura* a much lower purchase price than you are actually paying. It has been common practice in Spain to under-declare, but my strong advice is to state the true price (page 22).

You will need a bank account (page 11) in Spain to pay the deposit, to make stage payments for the property, and to later pay standing orders for electricity bills, community fees, water, annual property rates (IBI) and annual property taxes.

Remember, **when transferring funds to your Spanish bank**, the details must show it is for the purchase of the property you are buying. It is imperative that all payments are made to the developer or builder by your Spanish bank, because you will need a certificate or certificates from your bank in Spain for the notary's office, showing that funds to purchase have been imported legally.

So let us assume that **you have chosen the plot, have seen the plans, and that contracts are now being drawn up**. It is vital that all the following details are included in the purchase and sale contract:

I   The total square metres of the land/plot; the square metres of the house/villa/apartment; and the total price when the building is completed and ready for you to move into.

II The **deposit**, which is normally 25% of the total price; and the stage payments, normally 25% on completion of the roof, 25% on tiling the bathroom and kitchen and plastering the walls, and 25% on the completion of the building, the signing of the *Escritura* and the handing over of keys. As you are initially paying a considerable sum on signing the contracts, and in future stage payments, it is imperative that your lawyer has checked everything thoroughly before signing contracts.

III Your bank will release stage payments to the developer or builder only on receipt of an Architect's Certificate, stating that each stage has been completed. If you are not in Spain during building, and will not be around to make stage payments yourself, then you must leave instructions with your Spanish bank to release money only on receipt of these certificates. **I really must stress how important this is.**

IV The developer/builder is responsible for obtaining and paying for: the *Seguro Decenal* 10-year insurance policy for foundations and structure (page 29); the *Licencia de Obra* building licence from the local town hall; the architect and surveyor fees for the entire building project and when it is completed; the *Certificado de Final de Obra* and *Licencia de Primera Ocupación* – the building completion certificate and the licence of first occupation; and the *Boletín de Instalación* – certificate of installation issued by the *Delegación de Industria* (Delegation of Industry) for electricity and water. You need copies to obtain electric and water meters.

V All **registration details** of the land where your property is being built must be included: the *Finca No.* (The registered land number at the Land Registry), the Book No., and so on. Your lawyer should extract this information from either the *Escritura* of the land/plot, or from the *Nota Simple*, which is the registration document from the Land Registry.

VI **A detailed plan** showing the square metres, specifications of the building and, if applicable, prices per square metre of floor and wall tiles. A very detailed specification of the building and installations is required to ensure no hidden extras appear during construction. Plans and specifications are annexed to the contracts and signed by all parties. In Spanish, this is called a *Memoria de Calidades*.

VII If a **kitchen is being installed**, then a detailed plan must be prepared showing exactly what is being fitted and what domestic appliances are included. It should also make clear that taps and plumbing connections are included. This should also be annexed to the contract and signed by all parties.

VIII If you are having a gas cooker or hob, or the water heating is gas fired, **gas installation** should be included. The inspection and contract for the gas supply, and payment, which is the responsibility of the developer or builder, should be reflected either in the contract or specification. If there is no mains gas and you need gas cylinders, as is often the case in small towns or villages, the developer or builder must supply you with the contract to obtain these.

IX The developer or builder is responsible for obtaining and paying for the **certificates for installation** of the electricity and water so that you can have meters installed. You should be responsible only for payment for the installation of electricity and water meters.

X If the **garden is being landscaped**, as is the norm in Spain, this should also be specified in the contract or the building specification.

XI It should be clearly specified in the contract what your 'quota of participation' (page 61) in the Community of Owners will be. If the Community has not yet been formed, at least you will know what percentage you will have to pay towards the fees. If the Community has already been formed, ask what your fees will be, as these can often be anything up to **2,000 Euros or more annually** depending on the services and facilities included.

XII The developer or builder is responsible for the payment of all **debts on the land**, i.e. *IBI* (Annual Rates) and any other charges up until the time that you take possession of the property.

XIII A **penalty clause** will doubtless be included in the contract to the effect that if you fail to meet the payments agreed, it becomes null and void and you lose what is already paid. The developer or builder will also likely be free to offer your property for sale to another party. So, as in buying a resale property (chapter 3), you must be sure that you will be able to meet these payments when they become due.

XIV A further penalty clause should be included in the contract to state that if the building is not completed on the date agreed, then the developer or builder must pay an **indemnity for each day after the completion date**. The sum per day must be negotiated with the developer or builder and reflected in the contract. It should be enough to cover, for example, the cost of a daily rate for you and your family to stay in a hotel until such time as the building is completed. As you can see, if you proceed in the correct way with a property purchase, you are well protected should anything go slightly awry.

XV The **final payment and the signing of the** *Escritura* will be made on completion of the building and presentation of the *Certificado de Final de Obra* (building completion certificate) and the *Licencia de Primera Ocupación* (Licence of First Occupation).

XVI It should be made clear in the contract that you are **responsible only for the payment of the costs of the** *Escritura* **for the sale and purchase of the property,** but not for the segregation of your plot from the rest of the land *(Segregación)*, the declaration of a new building *(Declaración de Obra Nueva)*, or the Horizontal Division *(División Horizontal)* in the case of an apartment. The costs of the *Segregación* (segregating your plot from the rest of the *Urbanización)*, the *Declaración de Obra Nueva* (declaring the new building) and, in the case of an apartment, the *División Horizontal* (horizontal division) are the responsibility of the developer or builder. It should also state who is responsible for the payment of the *Plusvalía* value-added tax. This should be paid by the seller (chapter 6 has more details of this tax) and of course must be reflected in the *Escritura* when you go to sign at the notary's office.

XVII Your lawyer should check if the land is **registered for Annual Rates** (*Contribuciones* IBI). If so, your lawyer must obtain a certificate showing that IBI has been paid up to date. Once completed, the building must also be registered with the *Recaudación Provincial* rates office (pages 37).

If you request any **alterations or additions to the property** under construction, you must always ask for a **written quotation**. This should be signed by both parties to prevent any disputes on 'extras' when the building is completed. Any major alterations or additions may also extend the completion date of the building. If this is the case, a new completion date should be agreed in writing and signed by both parties, as this will obviously affect the contract's penalty clause covering late completion.

The following applies to all types of purchase covered in this chapter...

You must obtain an NIE (page 12). When you have your NIE certificate, you or your lawyer must take photocopies to the notary's office when you go to sign your *Escritura* for the property. This is because the notary must include your NIE number in the *Escritura*.

Your lawyer will also need a copy of the NIE certificate to present, along with your *Escritura*, at the Land Registry office to pay relevant taxes, and for the office to register the property in your name/s.

Please take note that **fines for late payment** will be levied if these taxes and other fees are not paid within 28 days of the signing of the *Escritura* title deeds.

A longer period is usually allowed to pay the *Plusvalía* tax, but a copy of your *Escritura* title deeds must be presented at the *Ayuntamiento*, Town Hall, within one month of the signing. My advice is to pay these costs as soon as you know them. Note that IVA (Spanish value added tax) due on the declared purchase price on the *Escritura* must be paid to the developer before the *Escritura* is signed. The fact that you have paid the IVA must be recorded in the *Escritura*.

You also need your NIE to insure the property, for the installation of the electricity meter, the water meter, and in future to pay the annual taxes on the property. These are fully explained in chapter 16.

So you have now signed the *Escritura,* have handed over final payment, and are now the happy legal owners of your property in Spain. Well done! But there is still a little more to deal with.

You must now pay the costs of the *Escritura* and obtain a *Copia Simple,* a simple copy of your *Escritura.* In some cases, the notary may be able to prepare your *Copia Simple* immediately and let you know the costs, or you or your lawyer may have to return in a few days to collect it and pay the charges involved.

If these taxes and other fees are not paid within 28 days of signing the *Escritura,* fines for late payment will be levied. A longer period is usually allowed for payment of *Plusvalía* tax, but a copy of your *Escritura* must be presented at the local *Ayuntamiento,* Town Hall, within one month of the signing. My advice is to avoid any problems by paying these costs as soon as you know how much they are.

After making the payments to your lawyer or to the notary's office, they will take a first copy of the original of your *Escritura* to the Land Registry to register the document. After about two to three months, your *Escritura* will be collected by either your lawyer or the notary's office, and you can pick up the first copy of the original.

If collecting the *Escritura* from the notary, you present your *Copia Simple* and proof of identity, then take away your registered *Escritura.*

Congratulations! You have safely negotiated the Spanish property maze with a little help from your trusted professional advisors. You may even receive a small refund from the registration of your *Escritura*, as the amount held by your lawyer or the notary for the Land Registry is a deposit, and they normally ask for more than is needed to cover this fee.

If you ever lose what is classed as 'the original' of your *Escritura*, it is not a disaster for reasons already explained earlier (page 26).

Once you have a *Copia Simple* of your *Escritura*, your lawyer will need to take a few photocopies. These are to:

- Register for the *Plusvalía* tax at the Town Hall
- Register you for annual *Contribuciones* IBI, property rates
- Contract the electricity meter
- Get a water meter if not already installed.

The relevant forms have to be filled in and signed. The estate agent that you are buying the property through, or your lawyer, should make the necessary photocopies for you. These advisors will either go with you to the various offices, or do so on your behalf. Costs for obtaining the *Escritura* are set out in chapter 6.

All the documents mentioned are crucial. Without the *Certificado de Final de Obra*, the *Licencia de Primera Ocupación*, and the *Seguro Decenal* to prove that there is a 10-year insurance policy for the building, you will be unable to sign the title deeds at the notary's. Nor will you be able to get an electricity or water meter, which means no electricity or water supply.

The *Certificado de Final de Obra*, building completion certificate, is issued by the architect and a copy is presented to the planning department of the local *Ayuntamiento*, Town Hall.

This document informs the authorities that your home has been finished in line with the plans presented in the original application. The planning department then sends an inspector to measure the building to see if it does match these plans. All being well, the department issues the *Licencia de Primera Ocupación*, the licence of first occupation. If the property has *not* been built in accordance with the plans submitted to the planning department, they will *not* issue the *Licencia de Primera Ocupación*. Hence the importance of obtaining this document from the developer/builder before making the final payment and signing the *Escritura* title deeds.

You should also receive a copy of the *Certificado de Final de Obra*, building completion certificate, supplied by the architect, and the original of the *Licencia de Primera Ocupación*, licence of first occupation.

When buying a new property that is being built for you, it is very important that, when the building is completed, the developer/builder **registers your property** with *Recaudación Provincial*, the local property rates office. This is also something that could be included in the contract, so that the developer/builder commits to do this on completion of the building.

Indeed, many town halls in Spain and her islands will not issue the *Licencia de Primera Ocupación* without seeing proof that the property built has been registered with *Recaudación Provincial*. Of course, without the *Licencia de Primera Ocupación*, you will neither be able to sign the *Escritura* title deeds nor obtain your electricity or water meters.

A property already under construction

Buying unfinished property is less complicated than having it built from plans, but there can be pitfalls. Before a contract with the developer/builder is drawn up and signed, your lawyer should see proof that the seller is the legal owner of the land.

The lawyer should ask to see a copy of the *Escritura* title deeds and a *Nota Simple* copy of the Land Registry document as proof of ownership and validation that there are no encumbrances on the land.

Assuming that the property is **already constructed to roof level**, the following items should be in the contract with the developer/builder:

I   Just as is the case for the purchase an off-plan property from a developer/builder, they must have obtained and paid for the *Licencia de Obra*, building licence, from the local *Ayuntamiento*, Town Hall. The details of this licence must be reflected in the *Contrato de CompraVenta* contract of purchase and sale. The developer/builder should also have obtained and paid for the *Seguro Decenal* 10-year insurance policy if this applies (see bullet point II below). On completion of the building, the builder/developer is responsible for the obtaining and paying for the *Certificado de Final de Obra*, building completion certificate, which is supplied by the architect; the *Licencia de Primera Ocupación*, licence of first occupation, issued by the local Town Hall; and the *Boletín de Instalación*, certificate of installation, issued by the *Delegación de Industria*, industry delegation, for both the electricity and water installations. You will need copies of both these *Boletines*, and also one of the *Licencia de Primera Ocupación*, to obtain your electricity and water meters.

II If the planning application for building was presented at the local *Ayuntamiento*, Town Hall, after the watershed date of May 5, 2000, the builder/developer must by law have a *Seguro Decenal* 10-year insurance policy for the property under construction to guarantee the foundations and structure for that period. It does not currently cover the quality of other building materials used, though it is anticipated that these will be included at a later date. To obtain a *Seguro Decenal*, an approved and registered company must do a geological survey of the land. Test drillings study the type of foundations required. Laboratory tests assess the quality of the reinforced concrete for the foundations and structure. If the builder/developer does not have this insurance, you cannot obtain the *Escritura* title deeds. So it is very important that the details of this policy are reflected in the contracts.

III The total square metres of the land/plot and the total built area of the property and its terraces.

IV Full registration details of the land/plot; for example, the *Finca* number, which is the registration number of the land/plot, the book number etc. These are obtained from either the *Escritura* or the *Nota Simple,* the copy of the Land Registry document.

V The price for the property should be clearly stated, and the payment structure/stages shown in detail. Under normal circumstances, it is possible that because the building is technically already half-built, the developer/builder may ask you for 50% as a deposit, with the balance to be paid on completion of the construction and the handing over to the purchasers of the keys and the corresponding *Escritura* title deeds.

VI A detailed plan of the property showing the square metres, the specifications of the building, and the prices per square metre of floor and wall tiles if applicable. A highly detailed specification of the building and installations is required specifically to ensure that no hidden extras appear during construction. The plans and the specification should be annexed to the contracts, and must be signed by all parties. In Spanish, this annexed detail is known as a *Memoria de Calidades.*

VII If a kitchen is to be installed, a detailed plan should show what is being fitted and what domestic appliances are included. It should also be made clear that taps and plumbing connections are included. This should be annexed to the contract, and must be signed by all parties involved in the purchase and sale.

VIII If you are having a gas cooker or hob, or the water heating is gas-fired, then the gas installation should be included. The inspection and the contract for the gas supply, payment for which is the responsibility of the developer/builder, should also be reflected either in the contract or specification. If there is no piped gas supply and you have to have gas cylinders, as is often the case in small towns or villages, the developer/builder must supply you with the contract to obtain these.

IX Electricity, water and sewerage is connected to the property and there are no connection charges. You should only pay for installation of the electricity and water meters, and for any gas cylinders that are being supplied.

X If the garden is being landscaped, this should also be reflected in the contract or specification.

XI Your 'quota of participation' (page 61), *Cuota*, in the Community of Owners should be clearly specified in the contract.

XII There will likely be a **penalty clause** stating that if you do not meet payments as specified, the contract becomes null and void and you lose whatever you have already paid, leaving the developer/builder free to offer the property for sale again. So be sure before signing the contract that you can pay as agreed.

XIII A **penalty clause** should be included stating that if building is not completed on the agreed date, then the developer/builder should pay you as an indemnity a fixed sum for each day after the completion date. It should be enough to cover you and your family's hotel costs until the building is completed.

XIV The final payment and the signing of the *Escritura* will be made on completion of the building and presentation of the *Certificado de Final de Obra,* building completion certificate, and the *Licencia de Primera Ocupación,* licence of first occupation.

XV When the *Escritura* title deeds are drawn up, you should be responsible only for the costs for the *CompraVenta*, purchase and sale document. You should not be responsible for the declaration of the new building; the *Segregación de la Finca,* segregation of the land; nor, in the case of an apartment, for the *División Horizontal,* horizontal division. All of this should be clearly stated in the contract with the developer/builder, which should also specify that the vendor should pay the *Plusvalía* tax (chapter 6). This responsibility must be reflected in the *Escritura* title deeds when you go to sign at the notary's office.

XVI The developer/builder is responsible for all debts on the property until the handing over of the keys and signing of the *Escritura.*

Remember that before signing contracts with the developer/builder and paying the deposit, it is a good idea to ascertain what the approximate costs of the eventual *Escritura* title deeds will be. This avoids a nasty surprise when you go to pay for it at the notary's office on completion. Ask your lawyer to give you an approximate breakdown of these costs.

You will need a bank account (page 11) in Spain to pay for property and then to pay standing orders for electricity, community fees, water and IBI property rates.

When transferring any funds internationally to your Spanish bank, **the documentation must show that it is for the purchase of the property that you are buying**. It is imperative that all payments are made to the developer/builder by your Spanish bank, because you will need one or more certificates from this bank to show the notary's office that the funds for the purchase have been imported legally.

If you request **any alterations or additions to the property under construction**, you must always ask for a written quotation. This should be signed by both parties to save any disputes over 'extras' when the building is completed. Any major alterations or additions may also extend the completion date. If so, a new completion date should be agreed in writing and signed by both parties, as this will obviously affect the contract's penalty clause for late completion.

All the documents mentioned above are crucial. Without the *Certificado de Final de Obra,* building completion certificate, the *Licencia de Primera Ocupación,* licence of first occupation, and the *Seguro Decenal* 10-year insurance policy for the building, you will be unable to sign the *Escritura* title deeds at the notary's office. Nor will you be able to get an electricity or water meter, which means no electricity or water supply.

The *Certificado de Final de Obra,* building completion certificate, is issued by the architect and a copy is presented to the planning department of the local Town Hall. This document informs the authorities that the building has been finished in accordance with plans presented when the original application was made.

The planning department sends an inspector to measure the building to see if it really does match these plans. All being well, the department then issues the *Licencia de Primera Ocupación.* However, if the property has *not* been built according to submitted plans, the department will *not* issue the *Licencia de Primera Ocupación.* Hence the importance of obtaining this document from the developer/builder before making the final payment and signing the *Escritura.*

You should also receive a copy of the *Certificado de Final de Obra,* building completion certificate, which is supplied by the architect, and the original of the *Licencia de Primera Ocupación,* the licence of first occupation. It should be clearly stated in the contract that the developer/builder is not only responsible for obtaining these documents, but also for paying for them.

When buying a new property under construction, it is vital that the developer/builder registers the new building with *Recaudación Provincial,* the local property rates office.

This responsibility should be reflected in the contract, because many town halls in Spain and her islands will not issue the *Licencia de Primera Ocupación* without first seeing proof that the property has been registered with *Recaudación Provincial.*

Property recently completed, but never lived in

Buying an uninhabited, ready-built new property is the least complicated purchase option here. Yet before signing contracts and paying a deposit, your agent or lawyer should request a *Nota Simple* from the Land Registry showing that the developer/builder is the registered owner of the land built on, and that it is free of encumbrances.

The *CompraVenta* contract of purchase and sale for the recently completed property that has never been lived in must show:

I   A building licence has been issued and also paid for; and details of planning approval should be included.

II   If a planning application was submitted after the date May 5, 2000, the developer must have *Seguro Decenal* insurance guaranteeing the foundations and structure for 10-years (page 29).

III   The certificates from the architect and the Town Hall have been obtained: the *Certificado de Final de Obra* building completion certificate; the *Licencia de Primera Ocupación* licence of first occupation; and the *Boletín de Instalación* installation certificate issued by the *Delegación de Industria* industry delegation for the installation of the electricity and water. You need copies of these *Boletines* to get your electricity and water meters. The contract should reflect the fact that the developer/builder has these documents, and that they have been paid for.

IV   All the registration details must be included: i.e. the *Finca No.*, which is the plot/land registration number; the book number; and so on. This information can be obtained from the *Escritura* title deeds or the *Nota Simple* registration document from the Land Registry.

V   The total square metres of the plot/land and the total constructed area of the property and its terraces should also be included.

VI   There are no connection charges for electricity, water or sewerage, and you are responsible only for paying for installation of electric and water meters if not already installed. The developer/builder should supply you with the gas contract to obtain gas cylinders if gas appliances are installed but no piped gas available.

VII   Your quota of participation (page 61) in the Community of Owners is clearly stated.

VIII   The developer/builder is responsible for all debts on the property up to the date of the signing of the *Escritura* and handing over the keys.

IX The price and payments to be made are clearly stated in the contract.

X There will likely be a **penalty clause**. If so, it means that if you do not meet the payments as specified, the contract becomes null and void and you lose whatever you have already paid, leaving the developer/builder free to offer the property for sale again. So you must be sure before signing the contract that you will be able to make the payments as agreed.

XI When the *Escritura* title deeds are drawn up, you should be responsible only for the costs for the *CompraVenta* contract of purchase and sale, and not for the Declaration of a New Building, or the *Segregación de la Finca,* segregation of the land, or the *División Horizontal,* horizontal division in the case of an apartment. This should be clearly stated in the contract as should responsibility for the payment of the *Plusvalía* tax, which should be paid by the vendor (please refer to chapter 6) and be reflected in the *Escritura* when you go to sign at the notary's.

XII The final payment and the signing of the *Escritura* will be made on presentation of the *Licencia de Primera Ocupación.*

XIII Before you sign the contract, your lawyer must have obtained a *Nota Simple* from the Land Registry proving that the person you are buying the property from is the registered legal owner and that there are no mortgages or encumbrances on the property.

XIV Before signing the contract and paying the deposit, ask your lawyer for an itemised breakdown of approximate costs involved in obtaining the *Escritura.* This will avoid surprises when you go to the notary's to pay for the title deeds. The *Escritura* should state that the vendor pays the *Plusvalía* tax.

XV If the Community has already been formed, ask for proof that the annual IBI property rates and community fees are paid up to date. Do this before making final payment and signing the *Escritura.*

You will need a bank account (Page 11) in Spain to pay for property and then to pay standing orders for electricity, community fees, water and IBI property rates. When transferring funds to your Spanish bank, the documentation must show that it is for the purchase of the property that you are buying.

All payments to the developer/builder must be made through your Spanish bank, as you will need one or more certificates from this bank to show the notary's office that the funds for the purchase have been imported legally.

Note well: All the documents mentioned are crucial. You will be unable to sign the Escritura title deeds at the notary's office unless you have the *Certificado de Final de Obra* building completion certificate; the *Licencia de Primera Ocupación* licence of first occupation; and the *Seguro Decenal* (page 29) showing there is a 10-year insurance policy for the building. Nor will you be able to get an electricity or water meter, which means no electricity or water supply.

The *Certificado de Final de Obra* building completion certificate is issued by the architect, and a copy is presented to the planning department of the local Town Hall. This document informs the authorities that the building has been finished in accordance with plans presented when the original application was made.

The planning department sends an inspector to measure the building to see if it really does match these plans and, all being well, issues the *Licencia de Primera Ocupación,* licence of first occupation.

If the property has not been built in accordance with the plans submitted to the planning department at the Town Hall, they will not issue the *Licencia de Primera Ocupación.*

Hence the importance of obtaining this document from the developer/builder before making the final payment and signing the Escritura title deeds. You should also receive a copy of the building completion certificate from the architect, and the original licence of first occupation.

Remember also that the contract should clearly state that the developer/builder is not only responsible for obtaining these documents, but also for their payment.

When buying a newly completed property, it is vital that the developer/builder registers the new building with the *Recaudación Provincial* property rates office.

This responsibility should be reflected in the contract as many town halls will not issue the *Licencia de Primera Ocupación* without first seeing proof that the property has been registered. Without the *Licencia de Primera Ocupación*, you will be unable either to sign the *Escritura* title deeds or to obtain your electricity or water meter.

Buying land then having you own property built

If you are thinking of buying land to build your own home, tread very carefully. **Use a lawyer** because the process is fraught with danger.

First ensure that the local *Ayuntamiento*, Town Hall, will give **planning permission,** and how many square metres of built property, including sun terraces, they will allow.

The agent or person with whom you are negotiating to buy land may in all good faith state that you can build, for example, a three- or four-bedroom villa with a double garage.

Then the Town Hall may say you can build only a small, two-bedroom house with no garage, or you cannot build at all because the land is zoned for agricultural use only, or is simply not large enough.

To avoid costly disappointment, you or your lawyer should obtain a document called an *Informe Urbanístico* from the Town Hall, and the same document from the *Junta* regional government, as a safeguard.

This states exactly what the planners will authorise you to build, the total square metres that you can construct, and the maximum height of the building.

So if you really can build your dream home, you now need an architect and a builder with good reputations.

Finding an architect is easy, and he or she can help you deal with planning approval. For some idea of fees, I asked a local architect for a ballpark figure for a property of 120 square metres. He estimated that the total cost, including a surveyor's fees, would be in the region of 5,500 Euros including value added tax.

The estimate of building costs is presented to the Town Hall by your architect along with the project details. The Town Hall uses the estimated build-cost to levy a charge for a building licence. In 2016, the Town Hall where I live was charging 7.6% of the figure quoted by the architect for the cost of building. This will likely vary from one town to another, so use this purely as a guide.

On top of these costs, you are legally obliged to have a Seguro Decenal insurance policy guaranteeing the quality of the foundations and structure of the property for 10 years. This does not currently cover the quality of other building materials used, though it is anticipated that these will be included at some later date. If the builder does not have this insurance policy, you cannot obtain the *Escritura* title deeds.

In our example, the cost of this policy for our 120 square metre property would be around 7,900 Euros. You must use an insurance agency specialising in *Seguro Decenal.* Your architect will likely contact an appropriate agency and give you a quotation for costs.

Beware! When paying an architect for the project/plans, you will normally pay only 70% of his or her total fees initially. The remaining 30% falls due for payment when the building is finished. Unfortunately, when people receive the first account from the architect, they often think they have paid the fees in full.

Once the building is completed, the architect issues a *Certificado de Final de Obra* building completion certificate, and presents it to the *Ayuntamiento* on your behalf. The Town Hall inspects the property to check that it has been built in accordance with the plans presented. If all is in order, they issue the *Licencia de Primera Ocupación,* licence of first occupation which you need this to make the *Declaración de Obra Nueva,* the declaration of a new building, at the notary's office.

You simply must find a good builder, which is not always easy.

There are 'cowboy' builders in every country, but just imagine how much more difficult it is going to be in a foreign one. Ask people who already live in your target area if they know of a good builder: there is nothing like personal recommendations.

Once you have found one, your lawyer should draw up a complete specification for the building work reflecting, for example, the cost per square metre for tiles, the models and types of sanitary fittings, taps, doors, windows etcetera. A completion date should be fixed, with a penalty clause for late completion (see points XII and XIII on page 40). This document is a contract and should be signed by all concerned.

If you still want to build property, be aware that the **cost may be much greater than first imagined**, even when buying from a developer/builder; you will always want extras as work progresses. If you request any such alterations or additions, ask for a written quotation. This should be signed by both parties to prevent disputes on building completion.

Major alterations or additions may extend completion. If so, a new date should be agreed in writing and signed by both parties, as this will affect the penalty clause for late completion.

Spend as much time as possible on site when your property is being built. This is to ensure that everything is in accordance with the plans, and also to be on hand to request changes, such as having an arch rather than a square opening between rooms.

You may choose tiles, or may tell the electrician where you want sockets or wall lights. If you are on site, things can be dealt with on the spot rather than receiving phone calls or e-mails, which can slow things considerably.

When building on your own land, the electrician and plumber must obtain a *Boletín de Instalación* certificate of installation from the *Delegación de Industria* industry delegation, which approved the installation.

You will need these certificates to get your electricity and water meters. They can be obtained only by registered electricians and plumbers who are members of the *Asociación Provincial de Instaladores*.

You must pay for the land through your Spanish bank account, as you will need a certificate from the bank proving that the funds have been imported legally from your country of origin. Payments to the builder must also be made through a Spanish bank account and identified clearly as payments for the building of your villa. This is most important as you will also need a certificate/s from your Spanish bank proving the funds were imported to pay your builder.

You will need these certificates for the notary when you go to sign for the land that you are buying, and later on when you go back to make the *Declaración de Obra Nueva* declaration of a new building.

You must also **register the new building** with the *Recaudación Provincial* property rates office, which is normally in the capital of the province that you are buying in. Your lawyer or architect should be able to deal with this for you.

Registering your property with the rates office is vital because many town halls in Spain will not issue the *Licencia de Primera Ocupación,* licence of first occupation, without first seeing proof that the new building has been registered with *Recaudación Provincial.* Without this licence, you will be unable to declare the new building at the notary's.

If you do buy land and a purchase contract is drawn up, follow much the same course of action as for buying resale property (chapter 3) when it comes to documentation and what should be included in the contract.

If you are buying land and building a property, then you will technically be making two *Escrituras.* When you pay the balance owing for the land, you will make the *Escritura* for the land, and will later return to the notary's to declare the new building on your land once the property is completed.

Please refer to chapter 6 for fuller details of these costs.

05: Rural and Inherited Property

Here we deal with buying a *Finca Rústica* (or just *Finca)*, farmland; a *Cortijo,* farmhouse; or a house in a *Pueblo,* a Spanish village. If the *Finca* or village house is very old and has been handed down through generations, there may be no *Escritura* title deeds for it. You must tread very carefully, and will definitely need the help of a Spanish lawyer.

Remove any rose-tinted spectacles when looking at farm properties. Living there may not be as idyllic as it first appears. In hilly and mountainous areas, such properties are up dirt tracks, very often a considerable distance from a tarmacadam road. When the winter rains come – often as torrential, tropical-style storms - tracks can become impassable. In such cases, you would almost certainly need a four-wheel drive vehicle (4WD) to get to and from your property.

There is often no electricity supply, and connecting one can be very expensive even if it is possible. Shops and facilities are not on your doorstep, and what if someone is taken ill? Think country by all means, but go into it with your eyes wide open and with a full understanding of the pros and cons.

There are legal restrictions on whether you can build or extend properties on farmland, depending on what use the land is classified for and on its extent. Farmland in Spain falls into two categories: *Terreno de Regadío* (irrigated farmland) and *Terreno de Secano* (dry land). You will often hear people say they have a Finca, meaning they have a country house with land. If you are allowed to build, you would be able to construct more square metres on irrigated land than on dry.

For either category of farmland, your lawyer should check with the Town Hall to see if building is permitted at all and, if so, what are the minimum square metres of land that the plot must have to obtain planning permission. This minimum figure can vary tremendously, even within the same municipal area.

If there is no building on the *Finca* land and you plan a new house, your lawyer must obtain an *Informe Urbanístico* from the *Ayuntamiento,* Town Hall, to see what if anything you may be authorised to build: notably the total square metres that you might build, and if you would be allowed more than one storey.

Your lawyer/architect must also establish if authorisation is needed from the regional government offices, often known as the *Junta,* allowing you to build on this land.

Some regional governments have overruled local town halls that have authorised building in rural areas. In some cases, these *Juntas* are banning building regardless of the extent of the land. So your lawyer/architect must get authorisation from both *Junta* and A*yuntamiento* before you proceed with the purchase and pay deposits.

If there is a *Cortijo,* farmhouse, on land that you are buying, and you wish to alter or extend existing property, or to demolish it and build a new house, your lawyer/architect must obtain the same information - an *Informe Urbanístico* and possibly authorisation from the *Junta.* This is in case you may not be able to extend the existing structure, only to renovate what is already there.

You may not be able to demolish an existing building and build a new house. If you can demolish the existing property, you may be allowed to rebuild a home covering only the same number of square metres as did the previous building.

You will of course need planning permission to extend or demolish the existing property and build a new house, which means you will need plans drawn up by an architect, and you are legally obliged to obtain a *Seguro Decenal* insurance policy (point II, page 38). For more details on new build matters refer to chapter 4.

Remember, you must use the services of a recommended lawyer when buying one of these types of property. He or she should be consulted before signing any contracts and handing over any deposits.

If the property you are buying is Spanish-owned, or the sellers are foreign but have *Residencia*, residency status, and can prove that they are fiscally resident in Spain, then payments to them must be made through your Spanish bank account. This is because you will need certificates for the notary proving that the funds for the purchase have been imported legally into Spain from a foreign country.

It is vital to reflect the **exact square metres** of the *Finca* in the *CompraVenta* contract of purchase and sale. I know cases where purchasers were told there were 5,000 square metres, which was not reflected in the contract, only to discover when the *Escritura* was signed that there were only 1,500.

In addition, the square metres, number of bedrooms, and other relevant details should be checked against the *Escritura* title deeds, as the present owners may have extended the property without declaring the new building work at the notary's office.

If this is the case, and they have had planning permission from the local Town Hall and also have both a *Declaración de Final de Obra* building completion certificate and a *Licencia de Primera Ocupación* licence of first occupation, they must make a *Declaración de Obra Nueva*, declaration of a new building, at the notary's before you buy.

If planning permission has not been granted for building extensions, your lawyer needs to know if it can be legalised and what the costs would be, which of course should be paid by the present owners. Your lawyer should advise you on this.

Rights of Way

It is important to have rights of way and water rights included in the *Escritura* title deeds: water is normally supplied from a shared well in the countryside. I recommend that you ask your lawyer to get a certificate, the *Certificado Descriptivo y Gráfico con Linderos* from the *Catastral* offices, which are normally in the main city of the province where the property is situated. This plan of the land shows the boundaries, exact square metres, and the square metres constructed. Your lawyer can download this online and should produce it along with all other documentation at the notary's office when you sign the *Escritura* title deeds. He should also contact the owner of the well to find out how much water has been contracted for.

With these plans, you could then have a topographical survey made to clearly mark the boundaries of your land. When you are being shown land, it is quite customary for the owner, or whoever is showing it to you, to tell you that the boundary is such and such an olive tree. Or they might pick up a stone and throw it, saying that where it falls is roughly where the boundary is. This makes for a colourful anecdote to tell your friends, but having a clearly marked boundary and plans could prevent future disputes erupting. It always makes good sense to be prepared.

You will need a bank account (page11) in Spain to pay if the vendor is selling in Euros, and then to pay standing orders for electricity, community fees, water and IBI property rates.

A longer period is usually allowed to pay *Plusvalía* tax, but a copy of your *Escritura* must be presented at the *Ayuntamiento*, Town Hall, within one month of the signing. My advice is to pay these costs as soon as you know them.

You will also need a copy of your NIE identification and fiscal number certificate for the notary when you: go to sign the *Escritura;* insure the property; transfer the electricity meter, the water meter; and, in future, pay the annual taxes on the property. These issues are fully explained in chapters 14 and 16.

So you have signed the *Escritura,* made final payment, and are now the happy legal owners of your land/house in Spain. Well done! But there is still a little more to deal with.

You must now pay the costs of the *Escritura* and obtain a *Copia Simple,* a simple copy of your *Escritura.* The notary may be able to prepare this immediately and let you know the costs, or you or your lawyer may have to return in a few days to collect it and pay. If the relevant taxes and fees are not paid within 28 days of signing the *Escritura,* you will be fined. A longer period is normally allowed for paying *Plusvalía,* but a copy of the *Escritura* must be presented at the local Town Hall (*Ayuntamiento*) within one month of the signing. Avoid hassle by paying these all of these costs as soon as you know them.

After making the payments to your lawyer or the notary, they take a first copy of the original *Escritura* and register it at the Land Registry.

After two to three months, your *Escritura* will be collected by your lawyer or the notary, and you pick up the first copy of the original. To collect the registered *Escritura* from the notary, present your *Copia Simple* and proof of your identity.

You may receive a small refund from the registration of your *Escritura,* as the amount held by your lawyer or the notary for the Land Registry is a deposit, and they normally ask for more than is needed.

If you should lose what is classed as 'the original' of your *Escritura,* it is not a disaster.

As you have learned, the so-called First Copy of the *Escritura,* minus your signature, is sent to the Land Registry and this is what you receive when it is returned to the notary with registration details.

This document is commonly known as 'the original' even if it is not really that. Happily, the notary retains the true, signed original.

Once you have a *Copia Simple* of the *Escritura,* your lawyer needs to make a few photocopies to:

- Register for *Plusvalía* tax at the Town Hall
- Register in your name for the IBI *Contribuciones* annual property rates/tax
- Transfer the electric meter to your name
- Transfer the water meter to your name if your water is supplied by the local water board.

If there are no title deeds, ask a lawyer to get you a document called an *Expediente de Dominio,* Proof of Domination, proving ownership.

This was previously dealt with by the courts but, under July 2015 legislation, a public notary can now handle it for you.

This means that an *Expediente de Dominio* can now be obtained in a much shorter time than before, when courts would have taken up to two years to issue one. I understand from my local notary that if the situation is uncomplicated – i.e. if it is clear that the seller is the rightful owner – then it should all be completed within about three months.

Any complications could means it taking take up to five months, assuming that the problems are not insurmountable. In brief, a search is made to prove ownership of the land; people neighbouring the property are contacted; and a notice is placed in the *Boletín Oficial del Estado*, the official state-bulletin, to give anyone who may have claims on the property the chance to come forward. Your lawyer will advise on exact procedures.

Be aware that you will not be able to get a mortgage until the *Expediente de Dominio* is registered at the Land Registry.

After your lawyer has prepared the *CompraVenta* sale and purchase contract, you pay a deposit on signing it.

To protect you, your lawyer should hold this deposit until confirming that the *Expediente de Dominio* can be signed, at which time the rest of the purchase price will be paid to the seller.

If the property has been inherited, and the deceased owner had a Will & Testament leaving it to the present owner, you or your lawyer must ask to see proof that an *Escritura* has been made in the name of the inheritor, and that any death duties have been paid.

This is important, because if the property remains in the name of the deceased, you cannot obtain an *Escritura* in your name.

You could also inherit problems over unpaid death duties. My advice in these cases is to consult a Spanish lawyer.

As regards **contracts for the purchase of a rural or inherited property**, follow the procedures in chapter 3 for buying resale dwellings.

06: Costs for *Escritura* Title Deeds

Costs for an *Escritura* vary according to the property value. Transfer taxes are set by provincial governments (Málaga, Murcia, Valencia, Madrid, Canary Islands, Alicante etcetera). See Appendix A (page 135) for different regional transfer taxes.

It was once the custom to under-declare purchase price, commonly by about 30%; in which case a property sold for 200,000 Euros would appear to have changed hands for only 140,000 Euros.

Aware of this, tax authorities have been valuing properties at much higher 'official' levels for the purposes of calculating various charges. So although a seller may press you to under-declare the price, my advice is to declare the full amount.

Honesty is the best policy because the Land Registry compares the value declared on your title deeds against official tables of values for properties of this type in your area. If the declared value is lower than the Registry's valuation, it can demand a supplementary charge on the difference, as well as administration charges, postage and fines.

For example: you declare a sales price of 140,000 Euros on a house, but the Registry values it at 200,000 Euros. If relevant local taxes add up to 10%, you can be charged an additional 6,000 Euros on the 60,000 Euros difference, as well as administration charges and postage. It will be more if these taxes are greater than 10%.

Spanish house prices have dropped dramatically since 2008, so even if you declare the true amount paid, the tax authorities may still place a higher value on the property.

In a recent example: a Málaga property was declared at 45,076 Euros but the *Junta de Andalucía* valued it at 81,137 Euros. The tax on the difference, and a hefty fine imposed on top, added up to 7,212 Euros. Had the correct amount been declared, the total cost for the difference would have been only 2,524 Euros.

You need to be aware too that if the declared value is 50% less than the official valuation, you can be forced to sell the property to the authorities for the declared value. It would be a heavy punishment and, as far as I know, this has never actually happened. But it pays to seek advice from either your lawyer or the notary to avoid your own story becoming a celebrated case study!

As an example of how the Land Registry values property, the tax authorities where I live set a minimum declared value in 2004 of 2.0 times the *Valor Catastral*, the rateable value of the property. This multiplier can go up or down each year. In 2005 it rose to 2.2, stayed the same in 2006, jumped to 2.7 in 2008, and was down again to 1.8 in 2012. There may also be regional variations. For example, they may well use different calculations in the provinces of Murcia and Valencia, so be advised by your lawyer.

As a rule-of-thumb, on a resale property *Escritura* costs will be equivalent to around 9% of the total price of the property, but check with your lawyer and/or estate agent. So for our 200,000 Euros house, you might expect *Escritura* costs in the region of 18,000 Euros.

On a property being built for you, these costs may be greatly increased if you also pay for the *Escritura* for the land purchase, the administrative segregation of your plot from the rest of the land, and the official declaration of a new building at the notary's office.

Costs for an *Escritura de CompraVenta* for various property types are.

For resale property

When buying a resale property, the *Escritura* costs are:

- Transfer tax (*Transmisiones Patrimoniales*) on the declared value varies regionally (see Appendix A, page 135). Before signing contracts, ask your lawyer for a breakdown of this and other costs.
- Notary fees for preparing and legalising the *Escritura* depend on declared value and the number of pages

- The Land Registry deposit – about 0.5% of declared property value
- *Plusvalía* value-added tax levied by the *Ayuntamiento*, Town Hall, based on the increase in land value between the previous owner buying the property and then selling it to you. Usually, the longer the seller owned the property, the greater this tax will be. Legally, the seller should pay the *Plusvalía*; but to ensure that it really is paid, I would suggest that the amount owing for the *Plusvalía* should be retained by your lawyer from the final payment to the vendor. One reason for this is that if the property is foreign-owned and the sellers are returning to their country after the signing, what guarantee do you have that the *Plusvalía* will be paid? Under recent legislation, the local Town Hall can embargo the property purchased if the *Plusvalía* tax is unpaid, even if it was previously agreed that the vendor would pay this.

For a new property

When buying off-plan from a developer/builder, or a property under construction, or a new property which is finished but has never been inhabited, the *Escritura* costs are:

- IVA at 10% (4.5% in the Canary Islands) of declared value is paid to the developer/builder before signing the *Escritura*.
- Stamp duty (*Actos Jurídicos Documentados*) of 1.5 % on declared value
- A deposit for the Land Registry: about 0.5% of declared value
- *Plusvalía* tax as detailed above for a resale property.

A rule-of-thumb for new property is that *Escritura* costs are 3.5% more than for resale property. So they could be around 24,000 Euros (12.0%) for our 200,000 Euros house.

The figures above also apply to garages in the same place as the dwelling and purchased on the same date. However, if the garage you are buying is in a different place, or is purchased on a different day, you pay 21% IVA and not 10%.

The 21% IVA rate also applies to buying commercial premises. In all cases though, you will pay much more if you have not previously agreed that the developer/builder is responsible for the costs of the *Segregación*, segregation; the *Declaración de Obra Nueva*, declaration of a new building; the *División Horizontal*, horizontal division, for an apartment; and the *Plusvalía* tax.

It is important that this is made clear in the *Contrato de CompraVenta* contract of purchase and sale.

Buying land and building your own property

Escritura costs here are greater because you are technically making two title deeds - one for the land and, later, one for the new building. However, total costs are lower than for buying a resale or new property purchased from a developer/builder. This is because you pay 8% transfer tax on the land value, but only 1.5% tax for the building, which is much higher value than the land.

The breakdown is:

- Transfer tax (*Transmisiones Patrimoniales*). In Andalucía, this is 8% for a property sold for up to 400,000 Euros, and 9% if the purchase price exceeds that figure. The rate varies across regions; ask your lawyer for details where you are buying.
- Notary fees for preparing/legalising the *Escritura* – these fees depend on the number of pages and on the declared land value.
- Deposit for the Land Registry – about 0.5% of declared value
- *Plusvalía* tax as detailed earlier in this chapter.
- *The Declaración de Obra Nueva*, declaration of a new building, to be made at the notary once building is complete. The costs for this *Escritura* are: stamp duty (*Actos Juridicos documentados*) of 1.5% on the declared value of the new building; notary fees for preparing and legalising the document depend on the declared value of the building; a deposit for the Land Registry – about 0.5% of declared value.

You normally have 30 days after signing the *Escritura* to pay all costs. If you do not meet this deadline, there is normally a fine of 10% on the amount outstanding up to three months after the date of signing. Once three months have elapsed, the fine increases to 50%, so beware!

Note, by the way, that there is no *Plusvalía* tax paid on the declaration of a new building.

To avoid problems, it is a good idea to deposit funds for *Escritura* costs with your lawyer to pay on your behalf. You should obviously ask the lawyer for an account and receipts of payments.

Remember that if you do not speak Spanish, are a foreigner in the country, and do not know how the system works, you need to have employed a lawyer or registered *Gestoría*.

07: Community of Owners

In the United Kingdom and some other countries, local authorities are responsible for maintaining roads, green areas, and street lighting on a housing estate, or around an apartment block.

In Spain, the apartment block or the *Urbanización*, housing estate, is completely private, and all the owners are responsible for its upkeep. The law requires that a community of owners is formed, and that each owner contributes towards shared costs according to a formula that means some pay more than others.

The *Comunidad de Propietarios*, the Community of Owners, is made up of all owners of villas, apartments and business premises in the development complex.

They are responsible for paying for the maintenance of zones and items of common ownership, such as lighting in hallways in apartment blocks, communal gardens, swimming pools, and so on. Taxes payable by the community are divided up among owners. The *Comunidad* must also promote harmony among its members.

An *Administrador de Fincas*, Administrator of Properties, is appointed by the community to deal with shared payments. The *Administrador* prepares annual accounts for community annual general meetings.

The amount that each owner pays in community fees is established according to a 'quota of participation' in the community, and by the services that are included.

This quota is determined by the size of your property. For example, someone with a three-bedroom property will most likely have a higher quota, and therefore a higher community fee, than a neighbour with a one-bedroom property.

Your quota is stated in the *Escritura* title deeds, so you can easily check if the correct amount of participation has been applied when assessing your community fees.

Some community fees cover the painting of the exterior of the apartment block, or of all the villas/houses on a complex, every two or three years. If so, the community fees would be higher than on an equivalent complex where this is not included. If painting exteriors is included, the cost is normally spread over the two- or three-year period.

At the AGM, annual general meeting, which should be notified to you well in advance, owners elect a president, treasurer and secretary from among themselves. They can also at his time change or reappoint the *Administrador* of the community.

Complaints and suggestions must be presented in writing to the *Administrador* a reasonable length of time before the AGM for these issues to be voted on at the meeting.

It is very important for all owners to make an effort to attend the AGM, because all decisions taken at these meetings have legal force and will affect everyone in the community. If you are unable to attend, you should give somebody your proxy to vote on your behalf.

It is very important that all owners keep their community payments up to date. Failure to pay can result in your property being embargoed by the community of owners, who may subsequently auction it at a knock-down price to recover outstanding debts.

Payment dates for community fees vary. You may find the community requests payments half-yearly or annually in advance.

If you are not resident in Spain, the most sensible course is to set up a standing order from your Spanish bank to pay on your behalf. Find out when payments are to be made, so that you have enough in your account to cover them when due.

Check what the community fees are before you sign contracts, so that you can estimate annual outgoings. Some community fees can be a considerable sum.

In addition, you should get a copy of the statutes of the community so that you can gain a clear understanding of the rules and regulations that are binding on all owners before you become one. Your estate agent or lawyer should be able to help you do this.

Why bother? Well, say you plan to live permanently in Spain and have a dog, but the community rules do not allow pets: it would be quite a problem if you had bought while not knowing this.

It is also very important to establish if you need authorisation from the community to carry out any building work on or in the property, quite apart from requiring a building licence from the Town Hall.

I have had cases where people obtained a building permit from the Town Hall and started work, only to be stopped by the community, which insisted on its own rules being followed.

08: Power of Attorney

A *Poder Notarial*, Power of Attorney (PoA), is required if you or a joint purchaser cannot be in Spain to sign the *Escritura* title deeds.

Due to the relatively low cost of making a PoA in Spain, it makes sense to sign one while you are in the country – when you are signing purchase and sale contracts, for example. That way, a PoA is already in place if you cannot attend the notary's for signing the *Escritura*.

To do this, go along to the local notary's office in Spain, provide personal and passport details, and tell them what you want the PoA for and to whom you are giving power of attorney.

The cost of a Special PoA is 70 to 80 Euros depending on the number of pages. A Special PoA will authorise a named person only to buy or sell a specified property for you, nothing more.

If you make a General PoA, costing around 90 to 120 Euros depending on the number of pages, this authorises a designated person to do almost anything on your behalf: buy or sell property, apply for loans, obtain a mortgage, whatever. In my opinion, and in the majority of cases, it is sufficient to make a Special PoA.

If you lack time to sign the PoA while in Spain, you need a solicitor or public notary to prepare the PoA in Spanish and your own language. For this to be accepted in Spain, it must be in Spanish. Ensure that the PoA being drawn up includes authorisation to obtain NIE foreigner identification numbers for you if need be.

If you are making the PoA in your country of residence then, once it is signed, the public notary must obtain an Apostille certificate (from the Foreign & Commonwealth Office in the case of the United Kingdom).

This is an official certificate allowing documents to be recognised in all EU member states without further legal certification. The Apostille should be attached to the PoA to authenticate the latter for use in Spain.

Your notary will likely send the PoA to the Foreign & Commonwealth Office in the UK, or its equivalent elsewhere, for the Apostille to be attached for you. However, you should allow some time for this process to be completed.

However, if you make the PoA at a Spanish Consulate in your country of residence, there is no need for an Apostille. It is regarded as being the same as if you had signed the document in Spain.

If you have to make the PoA in the UK and have no idea where to go, contact the nearest Spanish Consulate and ask for the name, address and telephone number of either a lawyer who can prepare the PoA in Spanish and English, or a public notary in your area. Or contact one of the UK law firms listed at the back of this book (Appendix B).

If the person that you are sending the PoA to – most likely a lawyer or estate agent – does not have copies of your passport or NIE certificate, you must enclose a copy of each. Your representative in Spain will need these when signing the *Escritura* title deeds at the notary's office.

The cost of preparing a PoA in the UK or elsewhere will be considerably more than in Spain, in the region of 200–400 British pounds (280-560 Euros) plus the notary fees and the cost of the Apostille. It is also much more complicated.

Remember that if a UK citizen or citizens give Power of Attorney to someone in Spain to sign *Escritura* title deeds as property sellers or buyers, then that representative must present the notary with copies of the passport or passports of the people involved.

09: Spanish Wills and Inheritance Tax

It is always sensible to make a Will & Testament governing what happens to your assets if you die. If you are buying a property in Spain, I would argue that it is absolutely essential for your long-term peace of mind, and that of your family.

Under Spanish law, a third of the property automatically passes to the children on the death of either the husband or wife. However, your own country's laws normally override Spanish law, and you may leave your estate according to your national laws.

A recent EU directive, now in force in Spain, means that anyone with property in Spain, but who has not made a Spanish Will & Testament, will be subject to Spanish laws of succession. To put it another way for absolute clarity, a Will & Testament made in your country of origin will not override Spanish law on this. So if you have property in Spain, it is of vital importance that you make a Spanish Will & Testament.

When the Spanish Will & Testament is drawn up, the notary should include a clause stating that it is your wish that the present norms and dispositions of your country and nationality apply to this testament. This will mean that your country's laws of succession are applied in settling your own estate.

In Spanish, this clause would read: *'Declerando que es su voluntad que sean aplicadas las normas sucesorias del país de su nacionalidad a las presentes disposiciones testamentaria.'*

When you make a Will & Testament in Spain, it includes a further clause to the effect that this does not affect any that you may have made in your country of origin. This is obviously important, because the Spanish one would otherwise cancel those in your home nation.

Even so, there is potentially a problem. If you do not make a Will & Testament in Spain, the one that you have made in your country of origin would suffice, but your country's law would, in legal terms, need to be 'proved'.

This would create a Probate situation, entailing further costs and aggravation for your surviving beneficiaries.

I once sold a property owned by a husband and wife, and their two sons. A contract of purchase and sale had been signed and a deposit paid, but the mother died before the *Escritura* title deeds were signed, and did not have a Will & Testament in Spain.

I put them in touch with a very good lawyer in London who got all the documentation together reasonably rapidly to deal with the Probate situation which had been created, and within six months the family were able to sign their acceptance of the inheritance document.

There was considerable delay beyond the original completion date for the sale, but the very understanding purchasers were prepared to wait for the situation to be resolved so that we could make the *Escritura* in their names. We were fortunate that they were patient, but it demonstrates why I stress the importance of making a Will & Testament in Spain.

I had a further case recently where the wife of a client died, and neither had made a Spanish Will. It had to go to Probate in England, which not only took time but also added to total costs the sum of 2,500 British pounds for solicitors' fees in the UK.

If you wished, the estate agent or lawyer you are dealing with will be able to arrange for a Will or Wills to be drawn up for signing at the same time as you sign the *Escritura*. Or it could be done when signing the contracts of purchase and sale, assuming there is enough time to prepare your Will/s.

In Spain, Wills are now prepared in two columns: one in Spanish and the second in your own language. The translation should in theory be done by an official translator; but generally speaking, the notary's office will accept a translation made by someone known by them to have a good command of both languages.

If you are **buying in joint names**, you both need to make Wills. Each will cost approximately 200 Euros to cover translation and the notary fees for preparing the Wills, presiding over the signing, and legalising them. After signing, you receive a *Copia Simple,* a simple copy of each original, but without signatures. The original signed-copies of the Wills must remain in the notary's office.

The notary sends a document to a central registry with details of the reference numbers of the Wills, the signing dates, your names, and at what time they were signed. No details of the contents are divulged.

If single or joint owners should die in a country other than Spain, the surviving partner or children will need to have an Apostille attached to the Death Certificate.

In the United Kingdom, an Apostille is obtained from the central government's Foreign & Commonwealth Office. The certificate and Apostille are then sent or handed to the lawyer or *Gestoría Administrativa* dealing with the inheritance in Spain, along with a copy of the deceased person's Will & Testament. On receipt of the death certificate with the Apostille attached, an official translation of the death certificate can be made. This will almost certainly be cheaper than having it translated in your own country.

You can avoid this time and expense. If you can get a multilingual International Death Certificate (IDC), then there is no need for an official translation in Spain.

Your *Gestoría* or lawyer will present the last Will & Testament to the notary's office, asking them to request a certificate of *Ultimas Voluntades* (the last registered Will & Testament) from the central register. When the notary receives this certificate, your *Gestoría* or lawyer can then present the death certificate, duly translated, and a copy of the *Escritura* title deeds of the deceased person's property. This allows the notary's office to prepare the new *Escritura* in the name of the inheritors.

You have a maximum of six months to present the necessary documents to the tax authorities, and you will of course have to pay death duties on the inheritance. The amount to pay, and the discounts allowed, are complex, as are the inheritance taxes that are applied in Spain.

As a rough idea though, if the person or persons inheriting are husband/wife or children of the deceased, they may inherit 15,957 Euros per person free of tax. You will also be able to deduct funeral costs. The amount that can be inherited free of tax by a person who is permanently disabled is much greater than the figure quoted, however you would need to check with your *Gestor* regarding this. The percentage of tax payable on the taxable balance is on a complicated scale ranging from 7.65% to 34.00%. Best consult either your lawyer, *Gestoría* or fiscal advisor.

In Andalucía region, covering almost all Southern Spain, there have been recent major inheritance tax changes for residents. Until recently, direct family members who held valid *Residencias* and inherited an estate valued at no more than 175,000 Euros per person were probably not liable for inheritance tax. However, direct family members without valid *Residencias* were not entitled to this allowance.

Due to a recent EU directive, the Spanish government is now obliged to apply the same inheritance tax allowances for both residents and non-residents, and across the whole of Spain. At the time of writing, the 175,000 Euros allowance still applied in Andalucía, but may well have varied among regions of Spain. So do check with a *Gestoría*/fiscal advisor in the region where you are buying.

Death does not come cheap in Spain. In addition to inheritance taxes, you have the lawyer's or *Gestoría's* fees for presenting and paying these taxes, and also costs for making a new *Escritura* for the property.

One way of avoiding death duties is to put the property in the name/s of your child/children. This tactic is called *Usufructo* in Spanish law, and your child/children would have to sign the contracts of *CompraVenta* purchase and sale contract.

The notary must also be advised of this when preparing the *Escritura* title deeds. If you do buy in your child/children's names, but with you having *Usufructo* rights of use, your child/children must either sign the *Escritura* with you or give you or your lawyer a Power of Attorney to sign on their behalf.

By retaining lifelong rights of use, you cannot be refused access to the property, and a child, or children, cannot sell it without your signature/s appearing on the *Escritura*. You are entitled to rent the property and receive the income.

Once you have made a Will & Testament in Spain, there is no need to make a fresh one if you sell a property and buy another. This is because the Will states that it covers anything you own in Spain at the time of death: property, stocks and shares, cash at the bank, and so on.

The Will & Testament that you make in Spain is purely for Spanish territory - the mainland, the Balearic & the Canary Islands - and does not affect Wills made in the UK or other countries.

If you make a Will in Spain, then make a new one or change your existing Will in your country of residence or any other country, you must add a proviso that the new Will does not affect any Wills made outside of that country, otherwise it would cancel your Spanish Will.

Usually, a Will made in Spain leaves the estate to a husband/wife and, on the death of both, to any children and, on the death of the children, to grandchildren. So the only time you need a new Will is if you wish to alter the beneficiaries or what they will inherit.

10: Retiring, Residency and Working

If you plan to live permanently in Spain, you should obtain *Residencia* (residency) and also get a *Certificado de Empadronamiento* by having your name put on the electoral register, *Padrón*, at your Town Hall. You need to do this to register for free care under the Spanish Health Service.

If you are not of retirement age, please see page 14 for details of how to obtain *Residencia* (residency) and become *Empadronado*, enrolled on the electoral register.

If you are of retirement age, you qualify for an S1, previously known as an E121, with which you can register with the Spanish health authorities and receive reciprocal free healthcare under the Spanish social security system. If you are a pensioner, you will also receive other benefits, such as reduced fares on public transport.

If you are of **retirement age and a citizen of the UK**, contact the Pensions Service in Newcastle (tel: +44 (0)191 218 7777) to see if you qualify for an S1. Previously, it would have been sufficient to have been paying your UK National Insurance (NI) contributions for a specified period. Now, you must be of retirement age.

Give them your UK NI number, and tell them you are taking up permanent residence in Spain. If you qualify for an S1, then when you have purchased property in Spain you contact the UK Pensions Service again, giving them your address to send the S1 to you.

Ask them for an S1 that covers all dependents that will be living with you in Spain, as they will also be entitled to reciprocal health care.

If you are of **another nationality but part of the EU**, contact the pension authorities in your own country about the S1 document.

On receipt of the S1, and armed also with your *Residencia, Empadronamiento,* passport, and copies of all these documents, go to the nearest offices of *Seguridad Social,* social security, and register yourself with the Spanish Health Service.

Once you have registered your S1, *Residencia,* passport and *Certificado de Empadronamiento,* take all the relevant documents to your nearest *Ambulatorio,* the local state-run health clinic, to register with a doctor.

The *Ambulatorio* will then give you a plastic card called a *Tarjeta Sanitaria Individual* – personal health card – with your Social Security Number on it. You use this card to make appointments with your doctor, or on admission to a hospital.

You would probably find this daunting to deal with yourself, particularly if you do not speak Spanish. I advise asking a registered *Gestoría* to handle it for you.

Health care cover commences from the day you register your S1. In some circumstances, registration may take several months. So you should:

- Present the S1 as soon as possible; do not wait until you need treatment, as you may be charged and these costs may not be refunded.
- Ask the Spanish authorities to apply to your home country's health authorities for S1 cover if you have dependent family members living with you.

If you are from a EU country and are holidaying in Spain, but are not staying for more than 183 days and do not intend taking up *Residencia,* you can obtain an EHIC card (European Health Insurance Card), previously known as an E111.

UK citizens can do this either through the online option found at **www.nhs.uk/healthcareabroad,** or by ringing the Pensions Service on +44 (0)191 218 7777 – or 0845 6050707 within the UK – to apply for the EHIC. It is similar in size to a credit card, and valid for five years. You will need one for each family member. This gives temporary medical cover while you are in Spain or any other EU country.

If you are from another EU member state, contact the authorities in your home country to obtain the EHIC card.

If you are not of legal retirement age and therefore do not qualify for an S1 from the UK, or you are not employed or self-employed, you will of course need private health insurance (PHI). Or it may be that you are working or self-employed and would anyhow like the added cover that PHI brings.

Various schemes are available in Spain, and your policy should cover all aspects of healthcare, to include doctors, hospitalisation, etc.

For some idea of PHI costs, I asked my local office of Mapfre, one of the largest insurance companies in Spain.

Costs vary with age and whether an individual, couple or whole family are being insured. It is impossible to cover all age groups and families, but here are some typical quotes, rounded up to the nearest Euro, for some standard PHI policies.

- Man, age 34: 59 Euros per month (p/m)
- Woman, age 26: 69 Euros p/m
- Joint PHI for husband, age 32, and wife, age 28: 133 Euros p/m
- Family cover for man, age 32, wife, age 30, and children, ages three and five: 248 Euros p/m
- Family cover for man, 42, wife 40, and their children, ages 10 and 14: 246 Euros p/m
- Family cover for man, age 51, wife, age 53, son, age 22: 246 Euros p/m

If you have PHI cover in your own country, check to see if this does or can cover you in Spain. Many PHI companies have Spanish subsidiaries, so you may well be able to transfer the policy to Spain.

If so, ask them to supply you with a document/certificate translated into Spanish, and which confirms that this covers you for private health care while in Spain.

You will need to have the policy translated into Spanish to obtain your *Residencia* if your status requires you to prove that you have both sufficient income and also PHI.

Working as an employee - *Cuenta Ajena*

If you are working in Spain, whether employed or self-employed, you must apply for *Residencia*. **If you are an employee**, see page 14 for a description of the documentation needed to obtain your *Residencia*.

You must get a *Número de Identificación de Extranjero* (NIE), the foreigner identification number which is also your tax number in Spain. If you are going to apply for *Residencia,* you do not need to apply for the NIE separately, as this will be issued along with your *Residencia.* So it makes sense to apply for the *Residencia* immediately (page 13).

Where you obtain the *Residencia* and NIE from varies from one town to another. It is normally the *Departamento de Extranjeros,* foreigners' department, at a National Police Station.

Your employer's *Gestoría Administrativa* should also be prepared to take you to apply for the *Residencia* and your NIE, which can be applied for at the same time. They will probably make a small charge for doing so, but it can save you a lot of frustration.

You will need to fill in an application form and present it to the bank with a photocopy and a form known as a Modelo 790. You will pay the bank around 10.60 Euros per application prior to presenting the Modelo 790 to pay for your *Residencia* and NIE.

This fee could change or vary from one part of Spain to another, so please take it simply as a guide. You will also need your passport, a photocopy of the passport page that has your photograph on it, and a *Certificado de Empadronamiento,* a certificate from the local Town Hall showing you are registered on the electoral register. Your *Gestoría Administrativa* can supply you with the application and tax forms.

Your employer must give you a copy of the contract you have both signed, detailing terms and conditions of employment. The company or person employing you, or their *Gestoría Administrativa*, should help you register with Social Security. When you get your Social Security card, go to the *Ambulatorio* to register with a doctor.

Self-employed (*Cuenta Propia*)

If you plan to start up in business then you need to register with the tax authorities and Social Security and get an NIE number. You will need the help of a *Gestoría Administrativa/Graduado Social* to deal with registering you and then to deal with your own social security payments and tax returns. A *Graduado Social* is a specialist in Spain's social security and labour laws.

Look for the 'GA' sign outside the *Gestoría's* door. You will also need their help with contracts, payroll and social security for any staff that you plan to employ.

If you are self-employed, see page 14 for a description of the documentation needed to obtain your *Residencia*.

Looking for work

Looking for work in Spain? Then go to a local office of the *Instituto Nacional de Empleo* (INEM) to register as *demandante de empleo*, seeking employment. They advise of anything available. If you find employment without INEM's help, you must let them know so they can remove you from their database.

11: Business Premises

Many people holiday in Spain and imagine it would be great living there. They think: 'We could buy a little bar, spend time on the beach, take it easy, with no stress like we have back home.'

The reality of running any business in Spain is far removed from this dream of the good life, particularly when the economy is still recovering from the recessions of the past decade.

Take the bar trade. In summer, a bar in a holiday hotspot often needs to be open seven days a week, and all hours of the day and night, to produce enough profit to see owners through usually much-slower winter months. Competition is fierce too: there are just so many bars, cafeterias and restaurants fighting for custom.

Take unscheduled days off to go to the beach instead of opening regularly, and you will soon wonder where all your trade went. So think very carefully before buying this type of business.

You can certainly expect little leeway from landlords if you run into trouble. Commercial rents just seem to go up and up. They are rarely cut. Many Spanish landlords would rather see a property lie empty than accept a rent that means they return to a low base for future rent negotiations. In popular areas, there is usually someone who will pay the higher rent if you will not.

Also, many town and village properties are owned by individuals or families rather than commercial landlords with large portfolios. So the family's income that is used to house, feed, educate, heal and entertain itself, and pay its debts, is likely to come in large or significant part from the rent that you are paying. If they have high costs, they need to cover them from the rent on their commercial property, particularly when unemployment remains high, jobs insecure and wages low in Spain.

If you really do plan to start a business, do not rush. Take time to see what you think is lacking in the area where you plan to live, then set up a business that you think has a fair chance of being successful.

Once you have found premises to rent or buy – and it may be an existing business - you will certainly need the help of a recommended lawyer to deal with the contracts. You will also require the services of a *Gestoría Administrativa*, fiscal advisor, to handle paperwork, opening licences, registering with the tax authorities, social security, and so on.

The lease is normally for one year, renewable up to a maximum of five years. The price of a lease varies depending on size, location and type of activity – it is a free market. You could be investing a considerable sum; so negotiate as long a lease as possible.

Rent is typically reviewed each year, when it should increase only by the percentage rise in the official measure of the cost of living. This index is published each January in the *Boletín del Estado,* the official state bulletin.

Before committing to purchase a lease, you and your lawyer/*Gestoría,* should meet the landlord and the leaseholder of the premises to negotiate the rent, terms and conditions of the new contract.

The contract should give the tenant the right to resell the business in the premises to a third party, as you may wish to do that at a later date.

The landlord is normally entitled to receive as much as 30% of what the lease is sold for. It therefore makes sense to negotiate a lower percentage if possible, and this agreed figure should be included in the contracts.

Remember that the landlord may well want to renegotiate the rent with the new owners of the business, so this may affect what you might reasonably say to prospective buyers when marketing the business for sale.

Your lawyer should also get agreement that at the end of the term of the lease, you have a right to renew the lease; but you would need to renegotiate the rent at that time.

To summarise all of this, the contract for the lease should cover the following terms and conditions:

- The price of the lease and form of payment
- The length of the lease
- The rent
- Your right to sell to a third party
- The percentage to be paid to the landlord if and when the lease is sold to a third party.
- Rent can be increased only in line with the rise in the official cost of living index, published each January by the government.

Before you commit to signing contracts, your lawyer or *Gestoría Administrativa* should also check out what type of business opening-licence has been issued by the *Ayuntamiento,* Town Hall.

I have come across a case, for example, where the premises had an opening licence only for a supermarket, yet the landlord/owners had converted them into a bar and sold the freehold or lease at an attractively low price.

The person who bought it discovered too late that the Town Hall would only authorise use as a supermarket. They had no choice but to convert it back to a supermarket, which cost a lot of money and time. So tread very carefully and, I repeat, use the services of a recommended lawyer.

The lawyer should also check that the opening-licence can be transferred to your name.

If you are renting/leasing premises, you must retain 19% of the rental paid to the owner. This retention, which you pay instead to the tax authorities, may well have been introduced originally because many landlords/owners were not declaring rental income.

If the premises already have an opening-licence, it may be that you can simply transfer this to your name at the Town Hall. Even this can take time though, and different local authorities have varying views on whether you can run the business in the interim.

If the premises you are leasing/renting/buying are new, or you are altering them, you need detailed plans drawn up by an *Ingeniero Técnico Industrial,* industrial technical engineer.

These must be stamped and approved by the *Colegio Oficial de Ingenieros Industriales,* the professional body for these specialists.

You present these plans to the *Ayuntamiento* and pay for the licence. Your lawyer or *Gestoría Administrativa* will deal with the transfer of the opening licence or organise the *Ingeniero Técnico Industrial* to do the necessary work to draw up the plans and arrange for them to be approved by the *Colegio.*

You must also obtain an NIE number and a *Licencia Fiscal,* fiscal licence, registering you with the tax authorities, and must also register with the *Seguridad Social,* Social Security, and make social security payments.

You will need a *Gestoría Administrativa* and fiscal advisor to deal with these issues, and your lawyer should be able to recommend who to use.

If you have a rental contract for the premises, your lawyer or *Gestor* should also ensure that it is registered in the *Cámara de la Propiedad,* registry of rented property, and stamped as registered.

If your business involves handling food – a café, restaurant or gastro-pub maybe - you must sit an **examination on dealing with food**. This is known as a food handling licence.

This examination is not difficult to pass. Most of it is good common sense. But you should prepare thoroughly for it, and will receive a certificate for your successful efforts.

If buying the freehold on a business property, the documentation and the clauses in the contracts should be pretty much the same as for buying a resale property, as outlined in chapter 3.

Again, you would be well advised to use the services of a recommended lawyer to deal with the contracts and to ensure that the premises have the correct licences for the business that you are intending to set up.

12: Spanish Driving Licences

If you plan to drive while temporarily in Spain, take your current driving licence with you.

If you intend to live permanently in Spain, and will apply for *Residencia,* you must exchange your country's driving licence to a Spanish one within two years of the date on your *Residencia.*

Note that if your licence is valid for less than two years, you must renew it before you can exchange it for a Spanish one, as this process requires there to be a minimum of two years left on your current licence. If you do not do so, you could face a heavy fine. Your new, Spanish licence will be valid up to 10 years if you are younger than 65, or up to five years if you are 65 or older.

When applying for your Spanish licence, you will need: your current driving licence; two passport-size photographs or yourself; and also a *Certificado de Empadronamiento* from your local Town Hall stating that you are registered on the *Padrón* electoral register proving that this is indeed your permanent residence in Spain.

If you move home, even within the same town or village, but not in the same street, you will need a new *Certificado de Empadronamiento* from your local Town Hall proving your new address. You must then present this document at the *Tráfico* office, advising them of your address change.

If you decide to deal with the Spanish driving licence application yourself, you should make an appointment with the *Tráfico* office before going there. However, my advice is to contact a *Gestoría Administrativa* to deal with it for you, even if you are pretty fluent in Spanish. Dealing with *Tráfico* can be lengthy and complicated – even Spaniards are wary about it.

Renewing a driving licence

For people **aged 18 to 65 years**, the licence is renewed every 10 years. From **65 years of age**, it is renewed every 5 years. Be aware that *Tráfico* does not send out reminders that a licence is about to expire; so you should keep a diary note of the date, and be sure that you act in good time.

To renew your licence, go to a registered medical centre and make an appointment for a check-up. You will need to present:

- Your current driving licence
- Your *Residencia* (residency) document
- Your passport.

Your simple medical examination will include an eye test. If you need glasses to pass this, you must also wear glasses on the passport-size photographs that you present. If you need glasses for driving, you must always carry a spare set in the car, and may be fined if you do not do so.

During the examination, they will take your photograph, prepare the medical certificate, and send all necessary documents to *Tráfico*. The fee for the medical certificate and driving licence will be around 50 Euros. If you are older than 70 when renewing your licence, you pay only for the medical certificate, about 27 Euros, as there is no charge for the driving licence for over 70s.

It is advisable to take a photocopy of your old licence to carry with you until you receive the new one, just in case the renewal gets lost in the post. If stopped by the police, you could show them the renewal form and a copy of your old licence.

You can go yourself to *Tráfico's* offices to renew your licence, but my advice is do it by post or ask a *Gestoría Administrativa* to handle it.

If you lose your licence, or it is stolen, you must report this to the *Guardia Civil* as soon as possible. They will prepare what is called a *Denuncia*, a formal report, which you should then present to *Tráfico* in your area.

Again, my advice is to get your *Gestoría Administrativa* to deal with this for you.

General Obligations for Drivers

In general, private cars may not travel faster than 50 kilometres per hour (kph) in urban areas and 120 kph on motorways and dual-carriageways. However, you will encounter even lower limits – such as 20, 30 and 40 kph – in many built-up and residential areas.

It is obligatory to have the following documents in the car when driving:

- A driving licence
- Valid comprehensive or third party insurance
- Proof of payment of the insurance
- Original identification documents for the vehicle, namely the technical inspection card and traffic permit.

Photocopies of these documents are admissible only if certified by a notary at a cost of approximately six Euros per page, or by the Municipal Police, *Tráfico* itself, or some banks. These documents must be carried at all times when you are driving.

It is obligatory to wear a seat belt in both the front and rear of a car, and a crash helmet when on a motorbike, scooter or moped.

You must have two red triangles in the boot of the car. In the event of a breakdown on a single carriageway, one is to be placed in front of the vehicle, and the other behind at a distance of about 10 metres, from where it must be visible from 100 metres. If the breakdown is on a dual carriageway, such as a motorway, you need only place the triangle that goes behind the vehicle.

You are also obliged to have two authorised, reflective vests in the car. These must be put on before leaving the vehicle if it breaks down.

If you commit a breach of traffic regulations outside the urban area and you receive a fine, such as for speeding, you will have a 20% discount if you pay it within 20 days. Serious fines do not qualify for this discount. Payment of fines is made at the *Tráfico* offices, usually in the main city of the province, or at Banco Santander.

13: Mortgages

Mortgages are available in Spain. Most Spanish home owners have variable rate loans where the interest rate changes annually. There are also fixed-rate mortgages, which could be worth considering with the basic level of interest rates currently low by historical standards.

There is a wide range, but to give you and an idea of what was on offer recently, I went to my local branch of Banco Sabadell.

I choose it as an example because it specialises in non-resident mortgages, mainly through its Banco Sabadell branches, though it also offers home loans to residents, and all SabadellSolbank branches throughout Spain have multilingual staff. Of course, their offer also covers day-to-day banking, finance for non-resident customers, and all the financial needs of Spanish residents.

Banco Sabadell lends up to 70% of either the bank's valuation of the property or of the purchase price, whichever is lower, with a maximum term of 40 years and subject to financial status. You need to be older than 18, have a regular stable income, and be able to show that you can afford the mortgage.

The basic types of mortgage types include **variable-rate**, **fixed-rate**, and **mixed-rate**.

Variable-rate mortgage

The rate is adjusted every 12 months to match market rates. This lets you take advantage of falling rates, but costs more when rates rise. Monthly repayments are a fixed amount, and are adjusted just once a year.

Be aware that the maximum loan-term for this particular type of mortgage is 40 years; while the oldest you can be at the end of the mortgage repayment period is 75.

The interest rate applied may depend on the Euribor, the European

Interbank Offered Rate, at which banks lend to each other in the short term. It is published by the European Central Bank.

Prepayment fee (% of prepaid amount): 0.50% during the first 5 years of the mortgage, 0.25% the remaining years.

Bonus Mortgage: If you would like interest rate discounts you may open a Prestige Care Account and entrust the bank with your home and life insurance; but **please note** that the insurance policy is available only to residents of the European Economic Area and Russia.

Fixed-rate mortgage

This assures constant monthly payments over the life of the loan. The maximum term is 30 years. The oldest you can be at the end of the mortgage period is 75. However, if you wish to benefit from lower repayments during the initial years, Banco Sabadell's '**Different Mortgage**' may fit your needs

Prepayment Fee (% of prepaid amount): 0.50% during the first five years of the mortgage, 0.25% in the remaining years. If early repayment of the entire remaining loan causes a loss to the lender, whose initial calculations were based on the expected term of the mortgage, an interest rate risk fee of 4% is charged.

Mixed-rate mortgage

This may be the solution if you want to avoid possible interest rate rises during the initial years of a mortgage, but are prepared to accept adjustments longer-term.

The maximum term is 40 years. The oldest you can be at the end of the mortgage period is 75. Monthly payments are made at a fixed interest rate for the first four years. After that, the rate is adjusted annually.

Prepayment fee (% of prepaid amount): 0.50% during the first five years, 0.25% in the remaining years. If early repayment of the mortgage causes a financial loss to the lender, an interest rate risk fee of 4% is charged.

MORTGAGE PAYMENT CALCULATOR						
Rate (%)	10 Years	15 Years	20 Years	25 Years	30 Years	35 Years	40 Years
3.00	9.66	6.91	5.55	4.74	4.22	3.85	3.58
3.25	9.77	7.03	5.67	4.87	4.35	3.99	3.73
3.50	9.89	7.15	5.80	5.01	4.49	4.13	3.87
3.75	10.01	7.27	5.93	5.14	4.63	4.28	4.03
4.00	10.12	7.40	6.06	5.28	4.77	4.43	4.18
4.25	10.24	7.52	6.19	5.42	4.92	4.58	4.34
4.50	10.36	7.65	6.33	5.56	5.07	4.73	4.50
4.75	10.48	7.78	6.46	5.70	5.22	4.89	4.66
5.00	10.61	7.91	6.60	5.85	5.37	5.05	4.82
5.25	10.73	8.04	6.74	5.99	5.52	5.21	4.99
5.50	10.85	8.17	6.88	6.14	5.68	5.37	5.16
5.75	10.98	8.30	7.02	6.29	5.84	5.54	5.33
6.00	11.10	8.44	7.16	6.44	6.00	5.70	5.50
6.25	11.23	8.57	7.31	6.60	6.16	5.87	5.68
6.50	11.35	8.71	7.46	6.75	6.32	6.04	5.85
6.75	11.48	8.85	7.60	6.91	6.49	6.21	6.03

How to use the table: In the first column, find the annual interest rate offered. Move along that row to find the monthly repayment for the term of the loan. This is the monthly repayment for each 1,000 Euros that you wish to borrow. For instance a 200,000 Euros mortgage loan at 6% for 10 years means a monthly repayment of approximately 2,220 Euros (11.10 x 200). I say 'approximately' because I have rounded monthly repayments in the table to the nearest Euro cent to make it easier to read. The actual repayment in this example would be 2,220.41 Euros (11.102050 x 200).

Get a quote: Lenders should provide a free, fully-detailed quotation of the mortgage payments and your loan and purchase expenses. Ask for this at a branch in Spain or by calling a mortgage centre. In Banco Sabadell's case, the mortgage centre telephone is +34 902 343 999 and the web page is at: **bancsabadell.com/en**

Documentation

Original documents must be shown before signing a mortgage or property purchase contract. The bank will need the following documentation:

- Identity card or passport, and NIE certificate
- If you are employed, your last two pay-slips, income statement, and a letter from your employer stating the type of contract that you have, your seniority, annual salary and your position
- Your last income tax return (Form P60 in the UK, or the equivalent tax statement elsewhere)
- If you are self-employed, an accountant's letter indicating the name of your company or that you trade under, the sector in which it operates and its registry details; confirmation of turnover and profits for the last two years; and salary, dividends and bonuses that you have received
- A banking reference
- Property related documents: the private purchase contract for a new property, or the *Escritura* title deeds for a resale property
- An Experian file or other credit report

Your application and queries should be handled quickly and efficiently. In Banco Sabadell's case, they promise a response within 48 hours.

Self-build mortgage

Mortgages may be available to self-build a home. For example, Banco Sabadell lends up to 70% of project costs, to draw down in stages. The minimum age of the borrower at the start of the loan is 18. The oldest you can be when the mortgage expires is 75. The loan must be drawn in full, and construction completed, within about 18 months of first draw-down. A surveyor acceptable to the bank monitors and approves construction stages. Staged draw-downs are released on receipt of relevant certification from this surveyor. Completed property is re-valued by a bank appointed valuer.

Non-banking expenses

Costs incurred before you apply for a mortgage include the **valuation fee** and assorted **additional costs and legal fees**.

Valuation fee

The maximum amount of loan depends on the property value, so the bank needs a *Tasación*, a valuation by a bank-approved valuer.

Additional costs and legal fees

When you buy property with or without a mortgage loan, Spanish Law stipulates compulsory costs to ensure no problems when the final transaction is made. There is also the tax office to satisfy. These expenses and taxes have nothing to do with the bank, and are usually equivalent to 11% of the purchase price (7% transfer tax or IVA for the purchase itself, 3% for any mortgage needed, notary and Land Registry fees). Include these in your budget to avoid any unpleasant surprises. They include the following:

- Your own legal fees
- The bank's legal fees
- Resale property transfer tax, payable on the purchase and the mortgage
- New-build property IVA (equivalent to Value Added Tax in the UK)
- Land Registry fees payable on both the purchase and the mortgage
- Notary fees payable on the purchase and the mortgage
- Valuation fees
- Arrangement fees

Ensure that your lawyer provides a detailed breakdown of all costs prior to commencing the transaction.

Bank fees

Banco Sabadell charges an arrangement fee of 1% to 1.5% of the mortgage – subject to a minimum of 750 Euros - depending on the acquisition of other Banco Sabadell products and services. Valuation fees and a fixed-rate reservation fee will also apply. The bank can of course provide further details.

Legal advice

Use a lawyer to bring together all the documentation at the appropriate time. The lawyer will advise on obtaining legal title to the property, and is responsible for providing a detailed breakdown of purchase costs, which are separate to mortgage arrangement charges.

Insurance and protection

Fire insurance is compulsory for property used as collateral for a mortgage, but banks recommend considering at least two other policies. A Home Protection Plan is a comprehensive insurance for your property, while mortgage-related life insurance will cancel outstanding mortgage debt in the unfortunate event of your death or, optionally, permanent disability.

Securing a loan

A first charge over the property is required as security for the loan.

Signature

Once a bank has approved your mortgage application, you provide documentation for them to take care of all the rest.

If you are buying a **new home from a property developer** and applying for a mortgage on the property, the bank is going to need a 'New Building Certificate' (*Licencia de Primera Ocupación*) from the developer, and will also require from you a photocopy of the private purchase contract or letter of offer. In the event that you are buying **an existing home** and applying for a mortgage, the bank will need a photocopy of the present owner's *Escritura* title deeds. If you are planning to **build your own home**, then the bank will need the following documents:

- A photocopy of the deeds of the land or plot
- A building project (*Un Proyecto de un Arquitecto*) stamped by the Architects' Association
- The planning permission from the *Ayuntamiento*, Town Hall
- The compulsory *Seguro Decenal* 10-year construction insurance.

All banks add **disclaimers** to their mortgage offers telling you where their responsibility stops and what you may and may not do.

Check these carefully. Banco Sabadell, just as one example, stipulates that in providing the services that I have tried to outline accurately, the bank is not in any way acting as legal, tax and/or other professional advisors or giving legal, tax and/or other professional advice.

The bank strongly recommends that you obtain independent legal, tax and/or other professional tax advice as appropriate.

Also, their services are not offered to any person in any jurisdiction where their advertisement, offer or sale is restricted by law or regulation, or where they are not appropriately licensed.

Offers apply only to people aged over 18, and are subject to an applicant's status and conditions. Security is required on Spanish property. Written quotations are available.

Calls to bank staff may be recorded. Internet e-mails are not necessarily secure as information may be intercepted, lost or destroyed. So please do not e-mail account or other confidential information.

Your home may be repossessed if you do not keep up mortgage repayments. Check that a mortgage will meet your needs if you want to move or sell your home, or if you want your family to inherit it. If you are in any doubt, seek independent advice. Changes in exchange rates may increase the value of your debt in currencies other than the Euro. For variable-rate mortgages, there is a risk that the total sum payable may increase significantly as interest rates rise.

14: Spanish Property Taxes

The only certainties in life are death and taxes. **So this chapter is required reading**, and you really would be best using a *Gestoría Administrativa*, an *Economista* (chartered accountant), or an *Abogado* (lawyer) to handle all relevant tax issues.

I deal here almost exclusively with property-related taxes. If you are tax-resident in Spain, your income tax liabilities are beyond the scope of this book and you should contact a recommended, registered professional.

Tax law for non-residents

Real Decreto Legislativo 5/2004 of the 5ᵗʰ March and *Real Decreto 1776/2004* of July 20, 2004, remain the most recent laws containing all changes at the time this book was published; but as tax laws constantly change, you must check with your tax advisor.

Tax identification number (NIE)

All individuals and companies must have a fiscal identification number (*Número de Identificación Fiscal, NIF)* for tax purposes. There is no discrimination between Spanish nationals or foreigners.

For foreign owners of Spanish property, this is the same number as the *Número de Identificación de Extranjero* (NIE) issued by the foreigners' department at the nearest National Police station, or by any Spanish Consulate. The procedure is in First Steps (page 12).

To register your NIE with the tax authorities, you may need to visit them personally. Alternatively, you may be able to sign an authorisation for your lawyer, your *Gestoría*, or the notary's office when you have signed the *Escritura* title deeds, to do so on your behalf.

Once registered with the taxman, the NIE also becomes your NIF. For foreign-owned companies, the fiscal identification number is the *Código de Identificación Fiscal* (CIF) number issued by the Spanish Tax Office.

A photocopy of the original NIE certificate must be presented at the notary's office when signing the *Escritura* title deeds, because the NIE is also your tax number in Spain. Without the certificate to prove that it really is your number, property transfer taxes cannot be paid when the *Escritura* is lodged at the Land Registry, so the title deeds cannot be registered.

Fiscal representatives

Non-resident owners are obliged by law to have a registered fiscal representative in the following cases:

- When a non-resident has a permanent base of activity in Spain
- When the Spanish tax office requests that a non-resident appoints a fiscal representative because of the level of income that the individual is obtaining from Spain
- For non-resident companies in all cases.

The fiscal representative should be a qualified professional such as a *Gestoría Administrativa, Economista,* or a lawyer.

A number of individuals act as fiscal representatives in Spain, but you should deal only with people registered with the relevant professional college. There should be a plaque outside their office showing their college registration number.

Non-resident owners of property in Spain

Here I discuss properties that are not rented out; rented out; or rented out for only part of the year.

Properties that are not rented out

Every individual owning a property in Spain is liable for non-resident income tax based on the *Valor Catastral* (Rateable Value). If there is no *Valor Catastral,* then 50% of the value stated in the *Escritura* title deeds will be used as the basis for taxation. **The tax form that you will need is known as a 210-I.** Each owner on the *Escritura* title deeds pays a proportional share of the tax. The tax must be paid during the following year. For example you will be paying the tax in 2017 for the year 2016. The tax year in Spain runs from January 1 to December 31.

The town or village that your property is in will determine the percentage of tax that you must pay.

If your Town Hall **has revised or modified the** *Valor Catastral* within the last 10 years, the tax base is 1.1% of this value.
If your Town Hall **has not revised or modified the** *Valor Catastral* during the previous 10 years the tax base is 2% of this value.

The tax rate on the December 31, 2015, for residents of the EU, Iceland and Norway was 19% of the tax base. For residents of all other countries the rate was 24%.

For example: if the *Valor Catastral* where I live was 50,000 Euros in 2015, and had not changed since December 31, 2005, income tax payable in 2016 would be 190 Euros, which is 19% of the tax base of 1,000 Euros (2% of 50,000).

Rented-out properties

Properties rented out short term

Tax is based on the rental income, and must be paid quarterly as follows:

- Pay January, February and March between April 1 and 20
- Pay April, May and June between July 1 and 20
- Pay July, August and September between October 1 and 20
- Pay October, November and December between January 1 and 20 the following year.

The **Tax Form is 210-R** and the rate is 19.5% as of December 31, 2015, for residents of the EU, Iceland and Norway, but it is 24% for residents of other countries.

If the property is rented by a company, for example an estate agency or rental company, the non-resident taxes will be retained at source by that company and paid to the tax authorities on your behalf. The same non-resident income taxes apply. You pay taxes on the proportional part of the *Valor Catastral* for the number of days that the property has not been rented, and use Tax Form 210-I for this.

For the number of days that the property has been rented out, you pay taxes based on the rental income and use Tax Form 210-R.

Properties rented out long term

If a property is rented out on a long-term contract with all the rent paid in advance, then tax must be paid according to the same timetable as for short-term rentals.

For example, if the long-term rental was paid in full in February, tax on the rental income must be paid between April 1 and 20. If rent is paid monthly, tax is due according to the payment schedule outlined above for properties rented out short term.

Rented out by non-resident EU, Icelandic and Norwegian citizens

EU owners of Spanish property who are non-resident in Spain but are renting out their Spanish property can offset expenses against the rental income, just like Spanish tax residents can.

Deductible expenses are: interest paid on a mortgage; IBI property rates; community fees; insurance; electricity; water; maintenance; and, if applicable, the collection of refuse/garbage.

To be able to deduct these expenses, you must present an official certificate of residency from your own country of residence. To stress this point another way, without this certificate you cannot deduct these expenses. Applying for a refund of expenses for non-resident taxes withheld at source by a company can be done for up to four years.

Please note that there is no 'double taxation' agreement with Denmark, and the Republic of Cyprus is classed in Spain as 'a fiscal. paradise', an offshore tax haven.

Non-resident companies' special taxes

All non-resident-owned companies are liable to special taxes, which are 3% of the *Valor Catastral* per annum and must be paid in January of the following year. Use **Tax Form 213**. Exemptions from this special tax are translated literally as follows:

- Foreign States or Public or International Institutions
- Organisations with the right to apply an agreement with an information-exchange clause, provided that the individuals who own the property are resident in Spain or in a country with an agreement of this type
- Organisations that carry out financial operations other than simple building tenancy or rental
- Companies listed in the officially-recognised secondary securities markets
- Non-profit organisations complying with legal requirements.

Non-resident property sellers

Any non-resident individual or company selling property will have 3% of the sale price retained by the purchaser as a deposit against assumed capital gains on the property.

The purchaser must pay this retention to the Tax Office within one month from the *Escritura* date. If it is not paid, this sum becomes an encumbrance on the property purchased.

Non-resident property vendor/s are obliged to pay any outstanding Capital Gains Tax (CGT) four months from the date of the sale.

For a non-resident vendor, the CGT rate is normally 19%, though from 2012 through 2014 it was 21%. In 2015, it was between 19.5% and 20%. 2016 started with the rate at 19%.

Profit will be the difference between the declared purchase price and the declared value when sold. **Use Tax Form 210-H.**

For a non-resident vendor who has not made a gain at the time of selling, there is the possibility of recovering the 3% retained. For this use **Tax Form 210-H.**

If you are a vendor wishing to reclaim any or all of the 3% of the sale price retained by the purchaser, you must have paid your annual taxes. If you have not made tax returns each year since you bought your property, the authorities in Spain will deduct them from the amount you are claiming and also levy fines for late payment. So you could well find that you will get nothing back.

You can therefore see that it is really is **very important to make tax returns each year.**

Resident in Spain for tax purposes

If an individual (Spanish National or foreigner) stays in Spain for more than **183 days** in any calendar year, or if the **principal base** of their business and professional activities or economic interests are in Spain, then the tax authorities will assume, unless it is proved otherwise, that he or she is **tax-resident in Spain.**

This assumption will be extended to a wife or husband, provided there is no legal separation or divorce. Any children who are underage and depend on you will also be deemed to live in Spain.

Temporary absences are taken into account in determining the period of your stay in Spain, unless you can prove that you habitually live in another country during 183 days of the calendar year.

Anyone else is considered **non-resident in Spain.**

All individuals that are tax-resident in Spain are liable for income tax on their worldwide income and assets. This means declaring all properties owned, though a permanent home will be exempt from wealth taxes. Second and further properties will have to be declared, including any in another country. If they are not rented out, they will be taxed on their rateable value. They will be taxed on profits if they are rented out.

Company tax-residency

A company is considered resident in Spain for tax purposes if it is constituted under Spanish law, or has registered offices in Spain, or has a head office in Spain.

Foreign residents selling a property

When signing a sale, foreign residents selling property in Spain must prove they have tax-resident status in Spain by presenting to the notary the certificate issued by the Spanish Tax Office.

A resident selling property in Spain must make a tax return regardless of whether a profit or loss has been made on the sale. There is an exemption from CGT for tax-resident sellers over 65 years of age on selling their home.

Resident sellers over 65 years of age selling their home need to know that 'home' is defined as the property where the vendor has been **living for at least the previous three years** up to the date of the sale. A *Certificado de Empadronamiento* (page 14) showing that you registered on the electoral register at the Town Hall is sufficient proof.

Residents **under the age of 65 may also qualify for relief on CGT** on sale of a home, but only if all proceeds are rolled over into purchasing another property. This option may also be exercised to a lesser degree by re-investing only part of the proceeds, in which case the exemption will apply only to that proportion of the money.

CGT on second or further properties sold by tax residents is charged on profit calculated by taking the sale price then deducting the original purchase price and the costs and taxes involved in the acquisition.

CGT tariffs for 2016:

- On profit up to 6,000 Euros – 19%
- On profit from 6,000.01 to 50,000 Euros – 21%.
- On profit more than 50,000 Euros – 23%

Wealth tax and property value

For the purposes of assessing *Patrimonio*, a property's value is understood to be the higher of: the *Valor Catastral* (rateable value); the value on the last change of ownership; or the value that the Administration has assigned to the property for any reason.

The Administration can make valuations on the following basis:

- Supplementary tax demands on the last transfer of ownership are based on the difference between the value the purchaser declared to have been paid on the *Escritura* title deeds when buying and the value according to the tax authorities.
- Payment of tax on inheritance or donations of property.

Remember: If your personal assets exceed an official threshold in a particular year, you will be liable for wealth tax for that year. For example, this threshold was 700,000 Euros for tax year 2015.

Double Taxation

Countries with which Spain has double taxation agreements on income tax include: Austria, Belgium, Brazil, Canada, Czechoslovakia, Finland, France, Germany, Holland, Hungary, Italy, Japan, Luxembourg, Morocco, Norway, Poland, Portugal, Romania, Russia, Sweden, Switzerland, Tunisia, United Kingdom, USA.

These treaties applied as of April 2012. Please note that there is no double taxation agreement with Denmark. The Republic of Cyprus is classed in Spain as 'a fiscal paradise', an offshore tax haven.

The information in this book cannot be invoked as a basis for appeals. You should always check the latest regulations for yourself if you are living or working across national borders. The information on taxes was prepared after consulting Maria Jose Cobos Mayorga who is both a college registered *Gestoría Administrativa* and *Economista* in the town where I live – Nerja, Málaga province.

The opinions expressed here, and the information provided, are in good faith, but it is always advisable to check all tax liabilities and concessions with a registered *Gestoría Administrativa* or *Economista* in Spain as tax laws are constantly changing. Understanding how the system works, and who to talk to at the tax office, is important.

15: Selling Property

You have decided to sell your property in Spain. Maybe your children have grown up, so you do not need such a large property to spend holidays in. Or maybe you plan to live permanently in Spain, and want a bigger property. Whatever the reason, here is what you need to know about selling, and about ensuring that you know the cost of repatriating the proceeds, if that is what you intend to do.

Many who have sold agree that it is not worth the trouble of trying to sell it yourself: using an estate agent is much easier. If you give an agent the exclusive right to sell, they should be prepared to reduce commission rates. The flip-side is that offering property through various agents increases the possibility of a sale.

Agents should know market values in your area, and will advise on both the asking price and realistic sale price. Another advantage of using multiple agents is that a realistic valuation is more likely.

You may feel that your property is worth more than the suggested valuation. It is your call, but you could price yourself out of the market. Be guided by agents, particularly in a buyers' market.

The agents will take photographs of your property to display online and in their window. They will also send details to potential buyers and their overseas agents.

Once the agent has a buyer and a price has been agreed, they will request from the purchaser a holding deposit of 3,000 Euros. A *Contrato de Reserva*, reservation contract, will be drawn up, with the balance of the full 10% deposit being due within 15 to 21 days. This commits purchasers to the sale, gives them time to arrange a mortgage, and allows their lawyer time for necessary legal searches.

If the searches are satisfactory and/or they have an offer of a mortgage, but do not pay the balance of the 10% by the agreed date, they lose the reservation deposit.

If they proceed as agreed, they then pay the balance of the 10% deposit and a full *CompraVenta* purchase and sale contract will be then be drawn up and signed by sellers and buyers. One variation is that the agent may instead request the full 10% deposit on the signing of the *CompraVenta*. This commits both parties to the purchase and sale, and to the price and conditions agreed.

Whichever type of contract is signed - *Contrato de Reserva* or *CompraVenta* - a price is fixed, as well as penalty clauses and the date on which final payment must be made.

The contract will normally contain a double penalty-clause stating that if the buyer does not complete the purchase on time, they will lose the deposit to the vendor, who will then be free to offer the property for sale to someone else.

A very important points is that if vendors do not complete on the date agreed, they must pay the disappointed purchaser double the amount that was lodged as a deposit! This ensures that all parties are locked into the contract and have considered all implications.

However, there is always the possibility of either the seller or buyer being taken seriously ill just prior to the completion date of the contract. Under these circumstances, it would be harsh to impose penalties if they were unable to complete on the agreed date.

I once handled just such a situation and now suggest that a further clause is inserted to cover this eventuality. It is based on Spanish Civil Code 1.105, which states that it would not be considered a breach of contract if delays are caused by accidents or so-called Acts of God.

In Spanish, this would read: *No supondrá incumplimiento de los plazos previstos en este contrato los retrasos producidos, por caso fortuito o fuerza mayor de los recogidos en el artículo 1.105 del Código Civil.*
This would extend the completion date until the afflicted person could attend the notary's to sign the *Escritura* title deeds, or until a Power of Attorney was made for someone to sign for them. Please note that medical

proof of the illness involved is required to invoke this 'get out' clause once it is the contract.

The contract will state that the vendor is responsible for all payments of electricity bills, community fees, annual property rates, water (if this applies) and any other encumbrances on the property up until the signing of the *Escritura*.

The seller must also pay *Plusvalía* tax levied by the *Ayuntamiento*, Town Hall, on the increase in the land value since it was last purchased. Depending on how long you have had the property, the *Plusvalía* can be a considerable sum. Ask either your lawyer or estate agent to obtain the figure before signing the contracts of purchase and sale.

When your property is sold, unless you have a valid *Residencia* residence permit, and can also prove by way of a certificate from the Spanish tax authorities that you are paying your annual taxes as a resident in Spain, 3% of the declared sale value will be kept by the purchasers as a 'retention'.

If you reside in Spain, you must anyhow obtain a certificate from the Spanish tax authorities stating that you are fiscally resident there. To do this, you may have to present: a certificate of *Empadronamiento* from your local *Ayuntamiento*, stating that you are registered on the electoral register; and a copy of your NIE certificate or *Residencia* (pages 12 to 16).

Ask your *Gestoría Administrativa* to deal with this; you may find it daunting to do yourself. This document must then be presented along with all the others needed at the notary's office before you go to sign the *Escritura*. However, do check with your lawyer/*Gestoría Administrativa* to see whether you need the tax certificate or if your *Residencia* will be sufficient to avoid the 3% retention.

If the 3% retention applies, the purchasers must deposit this with the tax authorities in Spain within one month of the signing of the *Escritura* title deeds. The 3% is a deposit against your possible capital gains tax (CGT) on the property.

CGT is described more fully in chapter 14 along with details of how you may be able to avoid paying some or any CGT. You should ask your advisor if you can reclaim either part of the 3% retention or the whole amount less costs such as the *Gestoría's* fees.

Even if your agent has a buyer for your property, you should under no circumstances allow them possession until the *Escritura* has been signed and full and total payment has been made.

If you allow the purchaser earlier possession, there is a danger that they may decide they do not want to buy the property, but refuse to leave. You then have the problem of getting them out.

In a sticky market, your agent will maybe have someone who wants to rent your property for six months or a year, with an option to buy at the end of this period.

My advice is to refuse, as it can be fraught with danger. They may pay the rent for two months and then stop paying and refuse to leave, and may have had no intention of buying in the first place.

Where does this leave you? As they have both rental and option-to-purchase contracts, it will take time and money to get them out of the property. You are meanwhile unable to offer it to anyone else until the situation is resolved. It is a worst-case scenario, but it can and, indeed, has happened in my experience.

If you do decide to risk agreeing to a rental and option-to-purchase contract, get a lawyer to draw up the contracts and to ask for a substantial sum for the option-to-purchase.

The amount paid for this option is deductible from the total selling price if the option is taken up, but is forfeited if the option is not exercised. In the latter case, you at least have some compensation for the length of time that your property has been off the market.

With regard to the final payment for your property, the best way to deal with this is to insist that it be made through a Banker's Draft, made payable to you in the currency agreed, and handed over to you at the signing of the

Escritura at the notary's. It may well be suggested that final payment is made by way of a transfer to your bank on the day of the signing of the *Escritura*. I would say that this is a lot more complicated, and it is so much easier for both parties for it to be dealt with by using a Banker's Draft.

When you put your property up for sale, if you feel you may not be able to get back to Spain for the signing of the *Escritura* to complete on the sale of your property, it makes sense to give Power of Attorney to your lawyer or somebody that you trust in Spain, to deal with it on your behalf. For full details see chapter 8.

Remember that if you are a UK citizen or citizens giving Power of Attorney to someone in Spain to sign the *Escritura*, then your representative in Spain must present the notary with copies of the passport or passports of all sellers named on the *Escritura*.

Whether or not you grant someone Power of Attorney, the Banker's Draft for final payment should be made payable to you, then either forwarded to your address if you want the funds in your home country, or paid into your Spanish bank.

If you do want to repatriate the funds, ask your bank what it will cost. As banks charge a percentage for transferring funds to a foreign country. For example, for up to 50,000 Euros, some currently charge approximately 150 Euros, while transfers greater than 50,000 Euros are sometimes charged at 0.4% to 0.6%. In my view, this is extremely high; so check in advance, shop around, and try to negotiate a lower cost.

What your estate agent will need

Estate agents handling the sale will doubtless ask for photocopies of:

- Your *Escritura* title deeds
- The last receipt for payment of IBI annual property rates
- The last electricity bill
- The last receipt for payment of community fees if this applies

- The last water bill if this applies
- The last telephone bill if this applies
- Your passport and NIE certificate.

Some people are reluctant to leave a copy of their *Escritura*, but there is no need to worry about giving agents this; it is of no value to them. They need either this copy, or at least the land registration details, as they are now obliged to obtain from the Land Registry a *Nota Simple*.

This document shows you are the registered owner and that there are no encumbrances on your property. The estate agent also needs to know the annual community fees and IBI, as these costs must be included in the advertising of your property.

The agent will also ask you to sign a document authorising them to offer your property for sale at the price agreed, as well as their commission for selling the property.

They will clearly need a set of keys for the property, to be able to show prospective buyers around. If you are getting keys cut for this, please check that they will open the locks before handing them over to the agent. People have often left me keys that were so badly cut that I could not get into their properties when required.

When your property is sold – i.e. when a contract is signed and a deposit paid – advise any other agents with whom you placed the property, and arrange to collect keys from them.

You would be amazed at the number of people who neglect to do this. As these other agents are unaware that the property has been sold, they may continue to show it to prospective renters, which can create somewhat embarrassing situations.

Renting out property

If you are not living permanently in Spain, you may want to rent out your home when not using it. Many agencies are more than happy to do that for you. They generally take 10% to 20% of the rent as commission. They may deal not only with the renting, but also with cleaning, and the laundering of bed linen. They charge separately for cleaning, laundry, gas cylinders and other costs that they may incur. The agency should issue an annual statement of your account, showing rental income and expenses.

'Cowboy' agencies, the disreputable ones, are to be avoided at all costs. Be sure to get a solid recommendation before entering into anything. Ask people who already rent out their properties to recommend an agency. The agent through which you bought your property may very well offer a rental/management service as well. If not, they should at least be able to recommend someone else.

What owners want

I asked a long established and reputable estate agent where I live, and with which I have dealt for many years, for some idea of what owners expect from renting out property, and what potential renters want. Their replies provide an idea of services and charges that you might expect or even demand from similarly well-run letting agencies.

Owners want the highest rental income with the lowest costs and least hassle. The rental agent I spoke to takes 20% commission and shares it 50:50 with its collaborators around the world so they can source bookings throughout the year round rather than being reliant on any particular holiday season.

They charge owners only when the agency actually does anything, for example a fee for securing a rental, a cleaning charge when they clean, a laundry charge when they change the laundry, a pool-maintenance charge per visit, a gardening charge per visit. This way, there is complete transparency on fees.

They do not believe in yearly or monthly management charges, or key-holding charges, as they believe this can sometimes be difficult to substantiate, particularly if the property in question has not rented well. If they do rent out the property on their books, they would naturally hold the keys, so why make a charge?

Like many better agents, this one has 'inherited' a large number of property owners who had bad experiences with so-called 'mama and papa agents' who conduct business from home or the local bar.

The most frequent complaints about bad agents is that the owners never know if their property is being rented out or not, nor what rent is being charged. So they have no idea what money they are due, and sometimes suspect that they are not told about all the rentals.

This same rental agent has invested heavily in an automated booking system that sends notification to property owners as soon as the agent takes the booking. This way, owners know at all times whether the property is occupied or not.

This agent does not pay owners by cash in a bar, but produces official invoices with IVA (value added tax) applied and transfers money into owners' bank accounts.

Their entire rental team is employed, registered and insured. So everything is above board and on the right side of Spanish tax and accounting rules for the sake of both owners and the agency.

They can also show owners the projected and actual percentages of occupancy, so owners can predict yield.

They do not call 'a mate who knows a mate' to fix electrical faults, but send their own qualified electrician, and receive a report which is passed on to the owners.

They do not ask a neighbour to do 'a quick clean', but instead have a professional cleaning team equipped with smartphones so they can also check inventories and report damage as well as sending photos to back up their reports.

This allows them to debit a holidaymaker's credit card as per terms and conditions so that the agent can replace or repair whatever was damaged.

They do not accept the notion that it is just bad luck when something breaks. They fix it, supported by that photographic evidence to show why the expenditure was needed.

What holidaymakers want

High-profile frauds have made some holidaymakers nervous about booking properties in Spain by internet.

Unsuspecting holidaymakers have made reservations and paid online only to discover on reaching the resort that neither the agent nor the property exist.

Rental agents tell me they are often asked: 'How do I know you exist? How do I know the property is yours to rent? How do I know my money is not just going in to your back pocket?'

Having a physical presence benefits the agency as holidaymakers already in the resort can visit these offices maybe seven days a week, 365 days a year, or call them around the clock for help and advice. The result is that they have been getting 58% repeat business, high by industry standards.

So quite apart from the efficient housekeeping services that they like to see in their rented accommodation, holidaymakers feel safer with a completely legal, fully-registered and insured agent in the centre of town and available around the clock.

I just need someone to look after my property

If you do not rent out, but want someone to look after your property in your absence, approach a reliable agency, or ask the locals if they can recommend someone to manage the dwelling.

As a bare minimum, this should include a weekly visit; airing the property; watering your plants; and checking for signs of damp and any water leaks. I personally believe that these services are worthwhile paying for, and can be invaluable.

To help you judge for yourself, I asked one of the local agencies where I live to provide some ballpark figures for the cost of a management-only contract. It quoted the following approximate annual charges: 250 Euros for a one-bedroom property; 300 Euros for a two-bedroom property; and 350 Euros for a three-bedroom property.

Now compare the monthly costs of such contracts with the considerable sums that could be involved if repairs and maintenance are not carried out in good time.

Management costs may be minimal if the contractor also rents out the property. They would be checking it anyhow if rented, so a management charge should apply only if it was empty for a reasonable period.

16: General Information

There are aspects of looking after your property, and of life in Spain, that are useful to know about. Hopefully, there is just enough here to make things easier as you start to settle-in permanently, or visit more frequently and for longer.

Insurance

Insuring property is important, particularly when you own an apartment. Under Spanish Law, you are responsible for any damage to property below or next to you if there is a water leak or something similar.

To give you some idea of insurance costs, I visited a local office of MAPFRE, one of Spain's largest insurers.

Depending on whether the property was a holiday home, a permanent home, and rented or not, the approximate annual insurance figures they quoted me were:

- 1 bedroom apartment, 45 square metres (m^2), contents up to 20,000 Euros, holiday home or rented out – 187 Euros.
- 1 bedroom apartment, 45 m^2, contents up to 20,000 Euros, permanent residence – 184 Euros.
- 2 bedroom apartment, 70 m^2, contents up to 20,000 Euros, holiday home or rented out - 215 Euros.
- 2 bedroom apartment, 70 m^2, contents up to 20,000 Euros, permanent residence- 208 Euros
- 2/3 bedroom townhouse,90 m^2, contents up to 28,000 Euros, holiday home or rented out – 274 Euros.
- 2/3 bedroom townhouse, 90 m^2, contents up to 28,000 Euros, permanent residence – 263 Euros.
- 3 bedroom detached villa with pool, 120 m^2, contents up to 30,000 Euros, holiday home or rented out – 359 Euros
- 3 bedroom detached villa with pool, 120 m^2, contents up to 30,000 Euros, permanent residence – 342 Euros

Check that insurance is valid if the property is not being used for long periods, and whether you have to advise the insurers if it is being left empty for any length of time. The insurance agent may ask if the windows have *rejas,* iron bars, and if there is an alarm system, which should reduce the premiums. They will need a separate list of items of value such as jewellery, as normal insurance would not cover these.

Before signing the agreement, ensure that you understand fully what is and what is not covered by the policy. Standard policies cover Acts of God (such as lightning, flooding etcetera) as well as robbery, but many will limit the amount insured. For example, your cover may be quite restricted if rainfall of more than 40 litres per square metre is recorded, winds greater than 90 kilometres per hour, of if there is hail and snow. Check the fine print!

You should have no problem getting insurance. Ask for recommendations from the agent you bought your property from and/or speak to others who have bought property in the same area.

Parking signs

I am often exasperated by the lack of information about parking restrictions. Spanish delight in towing away cars then slapping on hefty fines to retrieve them from the vehicle-pound. Often the 'culprit' is none the wiser for his misdeed. Here is an attempt to make understanding signs a little easier.

No Parking: A red-bordered circle with a red X on a blue background. Normally on a metal pole at kerbside, or against the wall if on a pathway.

Stop only for a few minutes: A red-bordered circle with a single red diagonal line on a navy blue background.

Pay and display: A red-bordered, square white sign with a single red diagonal line against a navy blue background. Look for the ticket machine where you pay. Leave the ticket visible in the car.

No parking this side of road from 1-15 or 16-31 of month: A red-bordered circle with a single red diagonal line on a navy blue background with 1-15 written in white. On the opposite side of the road, there will be an identical sign, but with the dates 16-31.

A box underneath each of these signs will state either **MES IMPAR**, meaning that on the side of the street that has odd building numbers there is No Parking on the specified days in the months of Enero (January), Marzo (March), Mayo (May), Julio (July), Septiembre (September) and Noviembre (November).

On the other side of the road, this box will read **MES PAR**, meaning that on the side of the street with even building numbers there is No Parking on the specified days in the months Febrero (February), Abril (April), Junio (June), Agosto (August), Octubre (October) and Diciembre (December).

Other parking restrictions: You might find a yellow line painted on the edge of the kerb, with a sign similar to the No Parking type and bearing one diagonal line and the words **Excepto Carga y Descarga 8h a 14h.**
   This means that you cannot park during the hours of 08.00 to 14.00 because this is a loading and unloading area. You are, however, allowed to park there before and after these times.

Key point: If in doubt, park where there are no signs. If your vehicle is taken away by the *grua* tow truck and impounded by the police, it will cost a lot to get it back!

Traffic Department - Tráfico

The Traffic Department's procedures are complex. You can do it yourself: I advise using a *Gestoría Administrativa* to deal with them.

Buying a car

To buy a car in Spain, you need to present:

- A copy of your NIE certificate. One issue you may encounter is that, technically speaking, an NIE certificate is valid for only three months, and states so at the foot of the document. In my experience, all public authorities except *Tráfico* tend to accept the certificate no matter how old it is. However, *Tráfico* insists that you renew the certificate so that it is still within a three-month validity period, even though you NIE number does not change between renewals. Check with your own lawyer/*Gestoría*.
- A rental contract for an apartment/house for a minimum of one year, or the *Escritura* title deeds, or a valid *Residencia*.

For **new cars**, the dealer will normally register the vehicle in your name at a cost of approximately 300 Euros, but you also pay registration tax, which varies according to engine size and the price of the car. For **used cars**, you need the following documents so that your *Gestoría Administrativa* can transfer a second-hand vehicle to your name:

- The *Inspección Técnica de Vehículos* (ITV) card – i.e. the vehicle's logbook – and a current ITV certificate (like 'the MOT' in the UK)
- The *Permiso de Circulación,* a white registration card to be signed by the vehicle's seller to authorise transfer to your name
- A certificate from *Recaudación Provincial* showing no outstanding *Impuestos de Circulación* fines or annual road tax payments.

Contract of sale for a vehicle

This can be made up by the interested party and needs to show:

- The buyer's and seller's names and addresses and the identification numbers from their valid passports and *NIE/Residencia* or *DNI*
- The vehicle model and registration number
- The sale price and form of payment
- That the vehicle is free of charges
- Date of contract, and the signatures of buyer and seller.

The seller, buyer or their *Gestoría* will have to present to *Tráfico* the original contract and a photocopy, along with copies of passports and NIE certificates/*Residencias* in the case of foreign sellers/buyers, or their DNI (document of identification) if they are Spanish. *Tráfico* will stamp the copy presented. At this point, the seller will be exempt of any responsibility for fines, accidents or traffic taxes in later years.

The seller or their *Gestoría* should present this stamped copy to the Town Hall's *Rentas* department so that no future requests for payment of vehicle tax are made to him or her.

Things you need to know as a vehicle seller

Transfer of previous title to the new owner: The seller is responsible for this, and should do so before handing over the car or motorcycle. To avoid unnecessary journeys and having to make the appropriate transactions in the offices of *Tráfico*, I advise asking a *Gestoría Administrativa* to deal with this on your behalf. Dealing with *Tráfico* can be a nightmare. The *Gestoría's* fees for this will likely be around 60 Euros plus IVA value-added tax.

The transfer tax on selling a vehicle depends on the age and the cylinder capacity of the vehicle. As a rough guide, a five-year old Opel Corsa would be approximately 180 Euros, and a two-year old motorcycle of 250cc some 114 Euros. To transfer the vehicle to a buyer's name you need the following:

- A photocopy of the buyer's passport, NIE/*Residencia* certificate or DNI
- Proof of address, i.e. *Escritura*, rental contract or *Certificado de Empadronamiento*
- A photocopy of the seller's passport, NIE/*Residencia* certificate or DNI
- The transfer document signed by both parties
- The *Tarjeta de Inspección Técnica* card showing that the vehicle has a current ITV (MOT in the UK) certificate
- The white *Permiso de Circulación* card.

I cannot stress enough how important it is to transfer ownership of the vehicle to the buyer's name. Otherwise, road tax, any fines and accident expenses will continue to be sent out in your name, and you will be responsible for these payments until ownership is transferred officially.

To ensure the transfer is made, sellers should pay the *Gestoría's* fees to deal with it. If you sell but then receive such payment demands, maybe the vehicle was not transferred to the buyer's name. Options to resolve this are:

- Pay all outstanding taxes at the *Oficina de Recaudación* tax office and deregister the vehicle at the *Tráfico* offices, presenting the last paid receipt. Then present a copy of the deregistration to the Town Hall's *Rentas* department to annul future vehicle receipts
- If your car was not sold, but you no longer possess either the vehicle or the documents, go to the Town Hall's *Rentas* department to cancel the Road Tax demands. If you are still receiving demands for road tax, or possibly fines, contact your *Gestoría Administrativa* immediately and ask to get the car cancelled on the *Tráfico* computer system. Until this is dealt with, you are liable for these debts, and interest charges will be added on a daily basis. Bank accounts may also be embargoed until payment is made.

Buying a motorcycle or moped

New

- **Up to 49 cc:** Once purchased, get the registration from *Tráfico*. This is often dealt with by the dealer.
- **More than 49 cc:** Same procedure as for a car.

Second-hand

- **Up to 49 cc:** Deal with the transfer of ownership at *Tráfico*. Better to ask a *Gestoría Administrativa* about documents and cost.
- **More than 49 cc:** Same procedure as for a car.

ITV Technical Inspection of Vehicles

All cars, vans, mopeds and motorcycles must be inspected periodically. It is illegal to buy, sell or insure a vehicle lacking a current *Inspección Técnica de Vehículos* (ITV) certificate. At the nearest ITV test centre, you must present the vehicle's white *Permiso de Circulación* circulation permit and its *Tarjeta de Inspección Técnica de Vehículos* technical inspection card. ITV costs quoted here are for guidance; these figures were for Andalucía, the Southern region of Spain, and can vary from one province to another.

Cars

A **new car** must be inspected after **four** years. A car of **four to ten years** must be inspected every **two** years. A car of **more than ten years** must be inspected **annually**. Recently, ITV charges were nearly **37 Euros for a petrol car** and **42 Euros for a diesel one.**

Vans

New vans must be inspected after two years. Vans of more than six years must go through the ITV annually. Vans more than 10 years old must be inspected every six months. Recently, ITV charges are around 40 Euros for a petrol van and 45 Euros for a diesel one.

Mopeds, motorcycles and scooters

A new moped or motorcycle of **up to 49 cc** engine capacity is inspected after three years at a modest cost of nearly 22 Euros for the moped, and almost 33 Euros for a motorcycle. A new motorcycle or moped/scooter of **more than 49 cc** is inspected after three years at a cost of nearly 33 Euros for either.

Vehicles with foreign registration

These can stay in Spain for **only six months** in each calendar year. Beyond this limit, the car must leave Spain or must re-registered with a Spanish plate, a *Matricula*. It is possible to request an **extension of six months** if an owner can prove sufficient economic means for that period.

Registering an imported car in Spain is a complex procedure, and best handled by a *Gestoría Administrativa*. Fees are around 300 Euros for the *Gestoría* as well as charges made by *Tráfico* for the *Certificado Técnica*, the *Impuestos de Circulación* road tax, and the *Matricula* registration number plate. The cost of all this documentation is around 400 Euros in addition to the *Gestoría's* fees. You take these documents and the number plate along with the vehicle to have an ITV (the equivalent of a UK MOT) costing about 110 to 130 Euros. High import taxes and registration costs mean that –unless your vehicle is virtually new - my advice is to sell before you leave your country and then purchase a car in Spain.

Also, if the vehicle is right-hand drive, it will bring its own problems when trying to overtake on single-carriage roads, and the headlights will need adjusting for driving on the right-hand side of the road.

Road taxes - *Impuestos de Circulación*

All vehicle owners pay. Annual tariffs vary by location. Mine are roughly:

Cars

- Up to 7.99 Horse Power (HP): 22.20 Euros
- From 8HP to 11.99 HP: 60.10 Euros
- From 13HP to 15.99: 134.30 Euros
- From 16HP to 19.99 HP: 167.30 Euros
- 19.99 HP to 1,000 HP: 209.10 Euros

Motorcycles

Up to 125cc: 7.80 Euros
126cc to 250cc: 13.40 Euros
251cc to 500cc: 26.70 Euros
501cc to 1,000cc: 53.40 Euros
>1,000cc: 106.80 Euros

Mopeds

7.66 Euros

Garage entrance - *Entrada de Vehículos*

Anyone who owns a garage or an entrance, such as gates, from the roadway giving vehicle access to a house or a building is subject to this tax. For illustration, local annual tariffs where I live depend on whether they apply to an individual or communal garage, and are approximately:

Individual garage

Up to 3 metres of frontage: 83 Euros
Each metre of additional frontage: 18.03 Euros

Communal garage

For garages each up to 3 metres of frontage:

- With 2 parking places: 51.20 Euros for each parking place
- With 3 parking places: 34.40 Euros each
- With 4 parking places: 25.60 Euros each
- With 5 or more: 20.70 Euros each
- For each metre of additional frontage, shared proportionally among the garages: 30.70 Euros each.

Each vehicle entrance must display a **Vado Permanente** sign (entrance permanently in use) so that people do not park in front of it. Then if a vehicle obstructs the entrance, you can call the tow truck *(Grua)* to take the obstacle away. Where I live, this sign costs about 46 Euros. It is payable only once and should be requested at the *Rentas* department of the *Ayuntamiento*, Town Hall. Each Town Hall sets its own Road Tax and Garage Entrance Tax, so **figures could vary widely by location.**

Building permit - *Licencia de Construcción*

Permission is needed for any building work in or outside property. For example, to re-tile a bathroom or terrace, or to replace windows, you need a *Licencia de Construcción* from the local *Ayuntamiento*, Town Hall.

Go to the *Departamento de Urbanismo,* planning department, and complete a form requesting a licence for *Obra Menor*, minor building work. You will need the address of your property, details of the work planned, and an estimate of the cost. The price of the licence is fairly low, but fines for building without permission can be quite high.

If you plan something more ambitious, say an extension to add another bedroom, check if the *Departamento de Urbanismo* will allow it. If so, you present architect's plans, building costs and the address. A licence for works of this type costs much more than for minor work or refurbishing.

The budget that you present should include the costs of materials and labour, carpentry, electricity etc. Even if the work is to be carried out by the owner, this must be quoted at a professional rate.

You may also need authorisation from your *Comunidad*, community of owners for building work in or outside your property.

Requesting a Permit

All works must be licensed before start-up. A licence may be requested by the owner, their representative, or the builder. If you cannot present the application personally, you need to give your representative or the builder a notarised *Poder Notarial*, a Power of Attorney, to do so on your behalf.

The cost of a *Poder Notarial*, if made in Spain, is approximately 65 Euros. If it is made outside of Spain, the cost could be considerably higher, and it must be in a bilingual Spanish/own language format with an *Apostille* attached to legalise it for use in Spain (chapter 8).

Licence charges for minor building works

Alterations to existing buildings are *Obra Menor*, minor work. For example:

- Re-tiling floors
- Re-tiling kitchen or bathroom walls
- Building or removing interior partitions
- Re-placing or removing doors, windows, gratings
- Tiling a garden or terrace
- Decorative girders/pergolas for garden or terrace
- Raising garden walls.

Such works do not need plans. After payment, the permit is normally granted within a couple of weeks. Where I live, the cost of a licence for *Obra Menor* is 7.1% up to a building-work value of 60,000 Euros, above which it becomes 7.6%. 3.3% is paid on applying for the licence, the rest when it is issued. If the work is valued at more than 60,000 Euros, 3.8% is paid on application, the balance when the licence is issued. There is a minimum charge of 31.10 Euros. Check local charges at your own Town Hall, or ask your advisor to do this for you, before launching any work.

Licence charges for major building works

The extension or construction of a new house is considered *Obra Mayor*, major work. For example: building a new house; extensions, roofs, garages; an additional floor/storey; roofing-over a terrace or garden. These works need plans approved by the College of Architects. The **architect's fees** vary around 5% to 10% of the value of the work, and do not include the cost of the building permit. The cost of a *Licencia de Obra Mayor* where I live is currently 7.6% of the building cost quotation.

Requirements for carrying out any work

The Town Hall, grants a permit only if the following conditions are met:

- The house is in a legal urbanisation or approved building zone
- The square meterage involved complies with building regulations limiting how much area can be built on
- It is approved by the planning department.

Completed work will be **surveyed by the architect's office** in the *Ayuntamiento*. If they deem the value of work carried out to be higher than the amount declared when the licence was applied for, you will have to pay a proportionately higher licence fee than you expected.

Building materials on public roads or paths

If a skip holding building rubble will be on the road or pavement/path, or a metal fence round the building infringes on road or pathway and will be in place for some time, you pay a public-way occupation charge to the local *Ayuntamiento*. Where I live, this is 0.80 Euros per square metre per day.

Planning breaches

If you do not request a licence, or what was built does not correspond with what was applied for, you will have breached planning and will be subject to **a fine, and possibly a demolition order**.

In my town, the fine is between 1% and 5% of the budget of the work if it is possible to legalise the construction. The fine is 10% and 20% if it is impossible to legalise the work, in which case demolition proceedings are initiated. Aside from the fine, you still have to pay for the building licence for the completed works, whose value will be decided by technical personnel from the *Ayuntamiento*.

Before starting building

Before starting work, get a written quotation from the builder itemising what will be done, and the quality of the materials – i.e. the type and cost of tiles for walls and floors, doors, windows, etc. The budget should include:
- Details of the company that will do the works

- The owner's name
- The address of the property
- Description of projects with price of labour and materials
- Total price including taxes
- Completion date
- Date and signature of builder or professional
- Date and signature of applicant
- Guarantee
- The form of payment agreed

The builder should not charge for estimates. The constructor is responsible for any damage that he or his workers cause to the dwelling or to other persons or dwellings during work on-site.

Payment of local taxes

When? All receipts are annual. *Impuestos de Circulación* road tax is normally paid from March to May, and IBI, popularly known as '*Contribuciones*', from June to September. The time to pay may vary from year to year. From the date on the invoice, you have around three months to pay.

Where and how? A **Banker's Standing Order** is the most effective way; it avoids surcharges and having to find out when an invoice is due for payment.

Fill in an authorisation in the *Oficina de Recaudación Provincial* rates office, where they give you two copies. You give one to your bank and keep the other. You cannot make a standing order for annual rates if there are outstanding bills from previous years.

If the IBI is not paid direct from your bank, go to one of the banks listed on the notification that you will receive by post to your Spanish address (not your home country's address).

If you do not receive this notification, go to your local Recaudación Provincial rates office to get the bill, then pay it at one of the banks indicated.

Unpaid Road Tax or IBI

Invoices that go unpaid within the prescribed dates attract a 20% surcharge plus interest, and will also have the costs of legal action added if it is taken.

If payment is not made by a certain date, the Tax Collection Office will proceed to embargo bank accounts and then the property.

Register on the *Padrón* electoral census

The *Padrón* is the official record of inhabitants registered at the *Ayuntamiento*, Town Hall. It is also used to create the electoral census of persons aged more than 18, who can vote in elections. The census is of great importance as the registered number of inhabitants determines how much the local area gets from central and regional government towards the cost of: municipal services such as local police, refuse, water, sewerage, street lighting, local roads; and state services such as national police, doctors, hospitals, colleges, civil guard, highways, and courts.

If you are obliged to register, but do not, you will generally be viewed as someone who is cheating your city, town or village out of money it needs to pay for the services you are receiving.

Everyone who resides permanently in a Spanish municipality, and foreigners who have *Residencia* in Spain, **must register with the Town Hall**.

If a person resides in several localities in Spain, they must register where they live for the greatest length of time; they cannot be registered in two or more municipalities at the same time.

A person wishing to live in another municipality has to request from the Town Hall a document showing his or her removal from the census, and should present this to the Town Hall of the new municipality where he or she is going to live.

Registration on the *Padrón* is free, and can be done at any time of the year. Current advice from a *Gestoría* is that people who own a second home in Spain, but who are resident in another country, should not register on their local *Padrón*, as they could then be regarded as tax-resident in Spain.

Requirements for registration

As requirements may vary by province, you should check with your Town Hall regarding documentation. Where I live, you would present a copy of your *Residencia* at the *Oficina de Empadronamiento* census department at the *Ayuntamiento*. You would also show your passport and a copy of your *Escritura* title deeds, or a rental contract, to prove your permanent residence in Spain.

Advantages of being registered

Those registered may stand for **election or vote** in local and European Parliament elections. Currently though, foreigners cannot stand for or vote in Spanish Regional or National elections.

Being registered also allows you to request cohabitation, residence and registration certificates. These are needed for collecting unemployment and pension payments; requesting medical assistance in the outpatients department of the public hospital; various procedures with the administration; buying a car as a foreigner; and becoming a member of a Town Hall-provided *Hogar de Pensionistas*, pensioners' club, which has financial and social benefits.

National Census

This happens every five years when the government employs enumerators to call at homes with census forms that must be filled in for every member of the household. If they do not visit you, you must go to the Census Department of the Town Hall and provide the necessary information. If you were registered in the previous National Census and your information has not been taken when the new census is being checked, you will be excluded. Foreigners whose *Residencia* has expired and who within six months have not presented an up-to-date one to the Town Hall will also be excluded from this census.

To check that you are registered, go to the *Oficina de Empadronamiento* census department at the Town Hall. This is essential at election time: if you are not on the census, or there are mistakes in your data, you will not be able to vote. Changes of address must also be notified to this department.

Water

Once you buy property, transfer the water meter to your name. My water board charges for this are currently 125 Euros for a 15mm meter and 150 Euros for a 30mm one. It also takes a deposit of 95 Euros for the meter, a sum returned on sale of the property. Costs vary by area, so ask your lawyer or estate agent. When you buy new property from a developer, who should have installed a water meter, you need a document called a *Boletín* from him to prove that an approved plumber installed the plumbing. If you need to replace the existing water meter – maybe because it has developed a fault – the water board will charge around 400 Euros including IVA value-added tax. Any modifications needed to install a new water meter will add to costs. To have a water meter registered in your name for a new property, or to transfer an existing meter to your name, you need:

- For a new build property, the *Boletín* of installation and a photocopy of your *Escritura* title deeds
- For a resale property, photocopies of your *Escritura* and the water bill from the previous owners
- A photocopy of your NIE or *Residencia*
- Your bank account details to set up a standing order
- In some areas, a certificate from the Town Hall or *Recaudación Provincial* showing you owe nothing to local authorities.

Paying for water use

Water is not expensive despite lack of rainfall in many areas. The minimum charge if no water is used during the quarter and for either a 15mm or 30mm meter is eight Euros where I live, but can vary elsewhere. For me, the cost of water per cubic metre (m^3) consumed is:

- Up to 20 m³ - 0.23 Euros plus IVA
- 21 to 40 m³ - 0.48 Euros plus IVA
- 41 to 80 m³ -0.68 Euros plus IVA.

Disconnection of water because of non-payment

Payment is quarterly and due within a month of the invoice date, after which the water company sends a demand by registered letter. If payment is not made within 15 days of the demand, the water will be cut off.

The cost of reconnection is around 39 Euros for a 15mm meter and 118 Euros for a 30mm one, on top of the outstanding debt.

Electricity

Resale Property

To transfer the electricity contract to your name/s, present these documents to a power company's local offices:

- A photocopy of the *Escritura* title deeds
- A photocopy of your NIE certificate or *Residencia*
- Your bank account details for a standing order
- A certificate from your bank confirming that this is your bank account (*Certificado Titularidad de Cuenta Bancaria*)
- A copy of an electric bill from the previous owners
- The *Boletín* of the installation (see below).

Your lawyer or estate agent should contact the power company supplying the owners to see if you need two things done to allow supply to be transferred to your name. These are a new trip-switch system and/or replacement of wiring to the meter.

If so, you must use an approved electrician, who will give you a *Boletín de Instalación*. This certificate confirms that necessary changes have been made, and by an authorised professional. This can cost around **600 Euros** to **1,500 Euros** depending on the work, so ask your lawyer or estate agent to see if it is necessary.

When you, your lawyer, or estate agent visit the electricity company, it will ask for a contact telephone number for someone to let them in to the property so that a technician can check the system and install an ICP, a circuit breaker that will stop you drawing more power than you have contracted for.

This technician will normally call a few days after you have presented all the relevant documents at the electricity offices. There is a charge of approximately 32 Euros to transfer the electricity contract to your name.

New Property

To get a meter, present documents at the electricity company's local offices:

- A photocopy of the *Escritura* title deeds
- A photocopy of your NIE certificate or *Residencia*
- Your bank account details for a standing order
- A certificate from your bank confirming that this is your bank account (*Certificado Titularidad de Cuenta Bancaria*)
- The *Boletín* of the installation, given to you by the developer/builder
- A photocopy of the *Licencia de Primera Ocupación* from the planning department at the Town Hall, which should be given to you by the developer/builder

The charge for installing the electricity meter will be around 155 Euros for a meter rated at 4.06 kilowatts (kW) and 200 Euros for one of 5.75 kW. The power company will send the bill for installation to your bank for payment.

Tariff

When you apply for the electricity meter, you may contract up to the maximum kW approved on the *Boletín de Instalación*. The more kilowatts contracted, the higher the standing charge you pay whether the house is inhabited or empty. As a rough guide, a contract for 4.4 kW will mean a standing charge of 7.50 Euros every month plus the amount of power used.

Disconnection of electricity because of non-payment

Electricity bills are every two months, and need paying within 15 days, after which you receive a demand notice by registered letter. If payment is not made within 15 days of the demand notice, the supply will be cut off. The reconnection charge is around 38 Euros on top of the outstanding debt.

If you set up a standing order for electricity bills, there should be no danger of disconnection. However, Spanish banks cannot give you an overdraft if you are not resident in Spain. So if your bill is for 75 Euros and you have only 74 Euros in your account, they cannot legally pay, regardless of how good a client you may be. So you must **always ensure that you have sufficient funds in your Spanish account.**

Telephone

Applying for a telephone

There is intense competition to provide telephone services in Spain, but Telefónica, operating as Movistar, is the provider of lines and one of the more dependable suppliers of call packages. By all means shop around. Vodafone is another significant provider, and many companies allow you to sign up online too. But let us assume that you choose Movistar. Go to the nearest Movistar office or ring freephone number 1004 to apply for a line. You can also ask for someone who speaks English if you wish.

You may ring Movistar from a call box or a mobile. If you use a mobile, your call may go to the Madrid main offices, whereas you really need to speak to an operator in the province where you want the phone line.

When applying, you will need to provide your passport or NIE number, your full name and address in Spain, your bank details and name of your bank, and the twenty digits which are on the top right-hand corner of your Spanish chequebook.

If you apply for your telephone at a *Movistar* office in the town where you are buying property, you will need the following documents:

- A photocopy of your Passport or your *Residencia* or NIE certificate
- A photocopy of your *Escritura* title deeds or a rental contract for the property where you want the telephone
- Your bank details.

Tariffs

With regards to line installation with national provider Movistar, there are so many different offers of different packages, that it is impossible to cover all of them. My advice is check their web site to see the different offers.

Standing charges

Movistar applies a standing charge every month for the use of the line and regardless of how many calls were made. This charge was 19 Euros including IVA in 2015.

Reduced call charges

Calls within Spain are at a reduced tariff on: Monday to Friday from 22.00 hours to 08:00 hours; Saturdays from 14:00; and all day Sundays and holidays.

International telephone calls are at a reduced tariff overnight Monday to Saturday from 22.00 hours until 08.00 hours, all day Sunday, and on National Holidays.

Disconnection because of non-payment

The telephone is cut off 20 days after non-payment of the monthly invoice. Recently, the reconnection charge was roughly 15 Euros plus the outstanding bill. The line is normally reconnected within 48 hours of making payment.

Making telephone calls

To Spanish provinces: Dial the prefix for each province before the individual phone number.

International calls:

- 00 (to signify an international number)
- The number of the country (United Kingdom is 44; France 33; Germany 49; Norway 47; Sweden 46, etcetera)
- The prefix of the town or city but without the zero at the start of the area code. So 0207 for London becomes just 207
- The number of the subscriber

Doctors

Tariffs for private consultations: Where I live, charges for private medical consultations vary between 30 Euros and 60 Euros. A consultation with a basic blood analysis thrown in costs approximately 50 Euros.

Medical assistance at home ranges between 50 Euros and 120 Euros. Medical invoices should not include IVA value-added tax.

Banks

Hours of opening to the public are generally:

- Monday to Friday 08:30 to 14:00
- Local holidays: closed
- National holidays: closed.

There has recently been more variation in opening hours depending on the bank, the branch, and the type of location.

Some banks now extend opening hours at key points in the month when many people will be paying tax or IVA. Anyone aged 18 or older can open a bank account.

Just present your passports and a copy of your NIE certificates, giving your permanent address in your home country for correspondence if you are not living in Spain, and pay in a small amount to activate the account. If you wish, you may also open an account in foreign currencies. All except non-residents' accounts are subject to withholding tax of 25% on any interest that has been earned.

Schools

As more people choose to decide to live and work in Spain, I am constantly asked about the options regarding schools.

If you decide to place your child in a **Spanish state school**, the enrolment period is normally during April.

Go to the school of your choice, which would logically be nearest to where you are living, and ask for an application form. You will have to give a second- or third-choice school as there may be insufficient places available in your preferred school.

To register your child, you need to be able to prove that you are resident in Spain. Present a copy of your *Residencia* and *Empadronamiento* (certificate of registration on the electoral register) from the local Town Hall.

To obtain this certificate, go to your Town Hall to the *Oficina de Empadronamiento* census department, and register.

This will involve showing your passport or Residencia as well as a rental contract or a copy of your *Escritura* title deeds as proof that you are living permanently in the town or village.

If you arrive outside of the enrolment period, you need to check with local schools to see if it is possible to admit children at that time. You cannot take it for granted.

There are nursery schools for children from age three. Infant school normally starts at the age of 4 to 5 years, junior school at six through to 12, and secondary/senior school from 12 to 16.

The school year for infants and juniors normally starts around September 15, and a week later for Secondary/Senior school.

At the end of June, schools publish lists of books required, and which you have to buy, for the next year's courses. The list is posted on a notice board at the school.

If you prefer your children to have a **private education**, there are English-speaking international schools all around the coast of Spain and in some major inland cities including Madrid.

The cost of going private varies tremendously, so check in the area where you are buying to see what private schools are available and what they charge.

If your children are still quite young, one advantage of a **Spanish state school** is that, after an initial struggle, they will soon pick up Spanish and end up speaking it like a native, which helps them to fit in. Some parents put children into a state school until 12 years of age and then transfer them to a private school.

You should also be aware that private schools are not obliged to take your children. Some headmasters of these schools complain that parents who have not thought things through in advance sometimes resort to moral blackmail to force their children on schools even though class sizes may be at their limit and other pupils could suffer as a result.

Taking your Pets

It is now relatively simple to take your dog, cat, or any other pet into Spain provided you have the relevant documentation in advance. You need a European Union (EU) **pet passport** from your local vet.

To get this, your pet must have a **rabies injection** and have an individual **identification microchip** inserted. Organise the pet passport well in advance in case there are delays.

If you are moving from the United Kingdom and your local veterinarian cannot help – or if you have any questions – then ring the UK government's Department for Environment, Food & Rural Affairs (DEFRA) helpline at +44 (0) 8459 335577 or go to the website www.defra.gov.uk

Taking a **horse** to Spain is more complicated than for pets. Contact DEFRA or its equivalent in your own country for advice.

If you decide to sell up in Spain and **return with your pet to the UK**, as from January 1, 2012, DEFRA's regulations for taking a pet into the UK are as follows.

To avoid it being quarantined, get your pet **microchipped** before any other procedures for travel are carried out. After microchipping, your pet must be vaccinated against rabies.

There is no exemption to this requirement, even if it has a current rabies vaccination. Rabies boosters must be kept up-to-date.

The waiting period before entry to the UK is 21 days after the first vaccination date. A waiting period is not required for subsequent entries into the UK, provided rabies boosters are kept up-to-date.

If the vaccination is in two parts, the 21-day waiting period will be from the date of the second vaccination.

For animals being prepared in an EU country, you should get an EU pet passport. Please note that although Gibraltar is not an EU country, it can issue a pet passport for pets being returned to the UK.

Tapeworm treatment: DEFRA expects the European Commission to make proposals to allow the UK to still require pets to be treated against tapeworm.

Treatment must be 24 to 48 hours prior to travelling, and backed by an official certificate. There will be no mandatory requirements for **tick treatment**.

Regulations change. So do ring the DEFRA helpline or check the web site www.defra.gov.uk for the latest official rules. If you are selling your property and returning to a country other than the UK, you will need to check with your own authorities.

I know a company called **Airpets** that has specialised in shipping animals abroad from the UK for some 40 years. It is registered with IPATA, the International Pet & Animal Transportation Association.

Airpets books flights, handles veterinary documentation, collects pets, keeps them comfortably in kennels for as long as needed, and arranges for them to be collected at the airport and delivered to your new home. If you are planning to take your pets to Spain from the UK, check them out. Their contact details are:

Airpets
Spout Lane North
Heathrow
Middlesex
TW19 6BW
United Kingdom

Tel: +44 (0)1753 685571
Freephone in the UK: 0800-371554
Email: info@airpets.com   Website: www.airpets.com

National holidays

Local holidays will usually be listed on your Town Hall website or can be got from their offices. National holidays are:

January 1: New Year
January 6: Epiphany
March or April: Easter
May 1: May Day
August 15: The Feast of the Assumption
October 12: Spain Day
November 1: All Saints' Day
December 6: Constitution Day
December 8: The Feast of the Immaculate Conception
December 25: Christmas Day

Note: If a National holiday falls on a Sunday, the holiday will be celebrated on the following Monday. Sometimes, if a national holiday leaves only one working day before the next day off, maybe a Sunday or another holiday, post offices, some public offices, banks, shops and other businesses may also be closed on the intervening work day, a custom known as taking a '*puente*', a bridge.

For example, if May Day is on a Thursday, some businesses may also be closed on the 'bridge day', Friday, so that employees get a long weekend off. The government was talking of legislating to stop the practice of the *puente* by changing holidays that fall during the working week to a Friday or Monday. Meanwhile, just go with the flow and enjoy the party!

Appendix A: Property Transfer Taxes

Each region sets property transfer taxes (*Impuestos Sobre Transmisiones Patrimoniales*). In 2016, these were as follows (in Euros):

Andalucía: For an apartment, villa, townhouse, farmhouse, and including commercial premises:
- Up to 400,000: 8%
- 400,000.01 – 700,000: 9%
- 701,000.01 or more: 10%

A garage, or a parking space under an apartment block:
- Up to 30,000: 8%
- 30,000.01 – 50,000: 9%

Aragón
- Up to 400,000: 8%
- 400,000.01 – 450,000: 8.5%
- 450,000.01 – 500,000: 9%
- 500,000.01 – 750,000: 9.5%
- More than 750,000: 10%

Asturias
- Up to 300,000: 8%
- 300,000.01 – 500,000: 9%
- More than 500,000: 10%

Ávila
- One tax rate: 7%

Baleares (Balearic Islands)
- Up to 400,000: 8%
- 400,000.01 – 500,000: 9%
- 500,000.01 –1,000,000: 10%
- More than 1,000,000: 11%
- Garage up to 30,000: 8%
- Garage above 30,000: 9%

Canarias (Canary Islands)
- One tax rate: 6.5%

Cantabria

- Up to 300,000: 8%
- More than 300,000: 10%
- Garages up to 30,000: 8%
- Garages above 30,000: 10%

Castilla-La Mancha

- One tax rate: 8%

Castilla y León

- One tax rate: 8%

Cataluña/Catalunya

- One tax rate: 10%

Comunidad Valenciana

- One tax rate: 10%

Extremadura

- Up to 360,000: 8%
- 360,001.01 to 600,00: 10%
- More than 600,000: 11%

Galicia

- One tax rate: 10%

Guipúzcoa

- One tax rate: 7%

La Rioja

- One tax rate: 7%

Madrid

- One tax rate: 6%

Murcia

- One tax rate: 8%

Navarra

- One tax rate: 6%

Vizcaya

- One tax rate: 7%

Appendix B: Spanish Lawyers in UK

They can be useful for making a Power of Attorney should you need one unexpectedly, or could not arrange it when you were in Spain.

Scornik Gerstein
9-10, Staple Inn Buildings
2nd Floor
London WC1V 7QH
Tel: +44 (0)207 404 8400
Fax: +44 (0)207 404 8500
Email: london@scornik.com

J Dot. Polanco Abad & Asociados
Flat 208
Goulden House
Bullen Street
London SW11 3HQ
Tel: +44 (0)207 223 1116
Email: demigpol@aol.com

Maria Dolton (a specialist in Spanish Probate)
El Pinar
St Raphaels
Buxted
Uckfield
East Sussex TN22 4JS
Tel/fax: +44 (0)1825 733536

RDT Abogados
41, Lothbury
London EC2R 7HG
Tel: +44 (0)203 475 4041
Fax: +44 (0)203 475 4042
Email: info@rdtabogados.co.uk

Glossary of Terms

Abogado: Lawyer/Solicitor.

Administrador de Finca: Administrator of Land. An accountant who deals with paying taxes and keeping accounts for a Comunidad de Propietarios, Community of Owners. Usually known as simply 'The Administrator'.

Agente de Propiedad Inmobiliaria (API): An estate agent qualified in estate agency law and who has an official API registration number.

AGM: Annual General Meeting.

Ambulatorio: Local state-run health clinic.

Apostille: Apostille Certificate. An internationally recognised official seal legalising documents such as Power of Attorney.

Arrendamiento: Lease, leaseholders, sitting tenants.

Asesor Fiscal: Accountant.

Asociación Provincial de Instaladores: Association of Registered Electricians & Plumbers. Always use registered tradesmen by preference.

Ayuntamiento: Town Hall, local council, local authority. There is also a provincial authority (Diputación) for the county/state, and a regional authority (*Junta*). I live in Nerja in Málaga province in Andalucía region. So my tiers of 'local' government are Ayuntamiento de Nerja, Diputación Provincial de Málaga, and Junta de Andalucía. They affect planning, building, environment, taxes, business, health services, education, culture and transport.

Boletín de Instalación: A certificate issued by the electricity and water boards approving installation of electricity and water. Needed to obtain electric and water meters for new buildings.

Boletín Oficial del Estado: Official national, regional or provincial state bulletin publicising legal documents and issuing notices of public interest. For example, Málaga province's online version is at: **www.bopmalaga.es**

Cámara de la Propiedad: Register of rented property.

Cargas: Charges.

Valor Catastral: Rateable value as set by the town hall.

Certificado de Final de Obra: A certificate that the architect or developer must present to the local Town Hall stating that the building has been completed.

Certificado Descriptivo y Gráfico Con Linderos: A certificate from the Recaudación Provincial, provincial rates office, showing the official boundaries and registered square metres of a plot of land.

Certificado Negativo: 'Negative' Certificate.

Cesión: Rental contract for business premises.

CompraVenta: Purchase/Sale. Basically the Contract of sale for a property.

Comunidad de Propietarios: A Community of Owners with a President, Treasurer and Secretary dealing with day-to-day running of the estate, complex or apartment block. You belong to it by law.

Consejería de Agricultura y Pesca: Department of Agriculture & Fisheries at a *Junta*, the regional government.

IBI (Impuestos sobre Bienes Inmuebles): These are the annual taxes/contributions/rates paid by property owners to the local Recaudación Provincial (see below). Usually referred to simply as 'ibee' with the 'i' pronounced as in 'hit'.

Copia Simple: A copy of the original *Escritura* title deeds, but without signatures. It is sufficient to prove ownership and to arrange a bank loan.

Cortijo: A farmhouse. This is the house on a Finca.

Cuenta Ajena: Working as an employee.

Cuenta Propia o Autónomo: Self-employed status.

Declaración de Obra Nueva: Declaration of a new building. You go to the notary's office to make an *Escritura* declaring that you have built a dwelling on land that you own. If it is a new property but already built, this declaration can be done at the same time as the *Escritura* for the land.

Delegación de Industria: Delegation of Industry, the authority that issues the certificate for the installation of the electric and water meters.

Departamento de Extranjero: Foreigners' Department at the National Police station where NIE numbers and residence cards are applied for.

Departamento de Urbanismo: Planning Department of the Town Hall

Embargo: A charge registered at the Land Registry for unpaid debts. It can be actioned by a court order to auction off property to recover debt.

Empadronamiento: Registered on the Padrón electoral register.

Escritura: Title deeds for the property.

Expediente de Dominio: Document of proof of ownership, issued by the courts in the event that there are no *Escritura* title deeds for a property.

Finca or Finca Rústica: A farm. Often people refer to their *Finca*, meaning they have a house in the country, with land

Gestoría: A business run by a professional college-registered person dealing on other's behalf with official paperwork such as applications for *Residencia*, NIE, work permits, driving licences, transferring vehicle ownership, taxes etc. A person working here is a *Gestor*.

Gestoría Intermediario de Promociones y Edificaciones (GIPE): Registered Estate Agent.

Graduado Social: Specialist in social security and labour laws.

Grua: The tow-truck that takes your vehicle to the pound if you park wrongly, or which rescues you when your car breaks down on the road.

Hipoteca: Mortgage.

Hogar de Pensionistas: Pensioners' club or day centre.

Impuesto de Circulación: Road tax payable by vehicle owners.

Impuesto sobre Transmisiones Patrimoniales: The property transfer tax charged by the Land Registry.

INEM: The state-run unemployment and employment office/exchange.
Informe Urbanístico: A document from the Town Hall detailing what they will allow to be built on a given piece of land.

Inspección Técnica de Vehiculos (ITV): Official test of a vehicle's roadworthiness. Equivalent to the MOT in the United Kingdom.

Impuesto sobre el Valor Añadido (IVA): Value added tax (VAT)

Jefatura de Costas: Governmental department in charge of the coastal areas of Spain.

Junta: The regional government. Junta de Andalucía for example.

Ley de Costas: Coastal building laws.

Licencia de Apertura: Opening Licence for a business.

Licencia de Obra: A building licence which must be obtained from the Planning Department at the local Town Hall for all building work.

Licencia de Primera Ocupación: Licence of First Occupation, also known as the *Cédula de Habitabilidad.* Obtained from the local Town Hall, which must previously have seen the *Certificado de Final de Obra* (building completion certificate). Without this licence you cannot get an electric meter.

Licencia Fiscal: Fiscal Licence.

Memoria de Calidades: Building specifications.

NIE (Número de Identificación de Extranjero): An obligatory personal identification number for foreign residents in Spain. The same number is used as a person's Número de Identificación Fiscal (NIF), tax identification number.

NIF: Número de Identificación Fiscal (NIF), tax identification number. The same number as the NIE for foreign residents in Spain.

Notario: Public notary. A government-appointed lawyer who legalises documents including, among others, *Escritura* titles deeds and Powers of Attorney. Highly qualified and has the same status as a judge.

Nota Simple: A document issued by the Land Registry and showing registration details of a property. These include the present owner, and if there are any mortgages or other debts on the property.

Patrimonio: Wealth Tax.

Permiso de Circulación: A white card authorising a vehicle to be driven on the road.

Plusvalía: Local tax payable on sale of property. It is a percentage of the increase of the value of the land since it was purchased by the vendors.

Poder Notarial: Power of Attorney. This will be required if you are unable to attend the notary's office to sign the public *Escritura* title deeds. It is sometimes referred to simply as a *Poder*.

Precio de Compra: The purchase price of the property.

Recaudación Provincial: The provincial rates office which is sometimes physically located at the local Town Hall.

Rejas: Iron bars on windows.

Residencia: Having *Residencia*, residency status, means you have a document authorising you to live in Spain permanently with (most of) the same rights and (most) responsibilities as a Spanish citizen.

Segregación: Legal segregation - for example, the demarcation in law of the plot of land that you are buying from the rest of the land on a housing estate.

Seguridad Social: Social Security – both the governmental department and the social security payments that it takes and makes. Equivalent to the UK Department of Work & Pensions and national insurance contributions.

Seguro Decenal: A 10-year structural insurance for a property.

Tarjeta de Inspección Técnica: Equivalent to an official log-book for a vehicle.

Terreno de Regadío: Irrigated farmland.

Terreno de Secano: Dry land. i.e. not irrigated.

Testamento: Will & Testament.

Tráfico: Traffic Department where driving licences etcetera are issued.

Traspaso/Cesión: Leasehold property.

Usufructo: A legal term signifying a right to use a property. For example, you may buy a property for your children but have a legal right to use it while you remain alive.

Valor Castastral: Official rateable value of a property.

Lightning Source UK Ltd.
Milton Keynes UK
UKHW011059240319
339777UK00005B/13/P

Contents

Principal tables

Acknowledgements

We should like to express our thanks to all our friends and colleagues who have helped in the preparation of this book.

Mrs M. Alsford, Mrs D. Broadbent, Miss Carol Clarke, Mrs B. Collins, Mrs M. Fielden, Mrs Maureen Geddes, Mr D. Godden, Mrs E. Goss, Mr T. Hobbs, Miss C. Hodgson, Mrs D. Keeping, Miss E. Lloyd, Miss Diane Manning, Mr T. Newton Browne, Miss Myra Olsson, Miss Maureen Rees, Mr Asghar Siddiqui, Miss J. Spill, Miss L. Taconis, Mr Bob Turner, Mrs F. Watts, Mrs J. Watts, The West Midland Education Service for Travelling Children

and the staff and students at Bristol Nursery Nurses' College.

Lastly, we record our gratitude to our families for the tolerance and forbearance they have shown, and the support they have given.

Thanks are due to the following for allowing the use of copyright photographs: Mothercare, Wyeth Laboratories, The Daily Telegraph, The Mansell Collection and The Nursery World, and also to Topham Picture Library/Lynne Burley who supplied the cover photo.

CHILD CARE AND HEALTH

FOR NURSERY NURSES

Second Edition

Jean Brain Cert. Ed.
Molly D. Martin, S.R.N., H.V.Cert

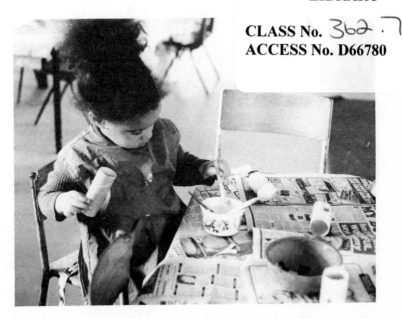

First published in Great Britain 1980
by Hulton Educational Publications Ltd
Raans Road, Amersham, Bucks HP6 6JJ

Revised and reprinted 1981
Reprinted 1982
Second edition 1983
Reprinted 1984, 1986

Text © Jean Brain and Molly D. Martin 1980, 1981, 1983
Illustrations © Hulton Educational Publications Ltd 1980, 1983

ISBN 0 7175 1196 0

Printed in Great Britain by
Richard Clay (The Chaucer Press) Ltd, Bungay, Suffolk

Foreword

Increasingly, responsibility for the care and education appropriate to the development and needs of young children is being shared between the parents and people trained in this specialised field. The nursery nurse is one of these people. Her skill is appreciated and applicable to many aspects of work with young children, and she can find employment in a wide variety of posts – in education, in day-care services, in residential social work, in the hospital services and in private families. Statutory and local authorities recognise her skill and training, as do voluntary agencies, and she can be found working both in this country and overseas.

To prepare for this skilled and rewarding work, training for the Certificate of The National Nursery Examination Board must be taken. During the lifetime of the N.N.E.B., a vast number of nursery nurses have benefited from this imaginative course, which has helped them to grow in confidence, as well as enlarging their knowledge, thus preparing them to work happily and successfully with young children, who have derived great benefit from contact with them.

It is appropriate, therefore, that Jean Brain and Molly Martin with, respectively, teaching and health-visiting backgrounds, who have tutored N.N.E.B. students over a long period, should find time to collect together their unified thoughts, knowledge and experience to make these available to students other than those they teach.

Bessie Wright
Past Chairman: National Nursery Examination Board

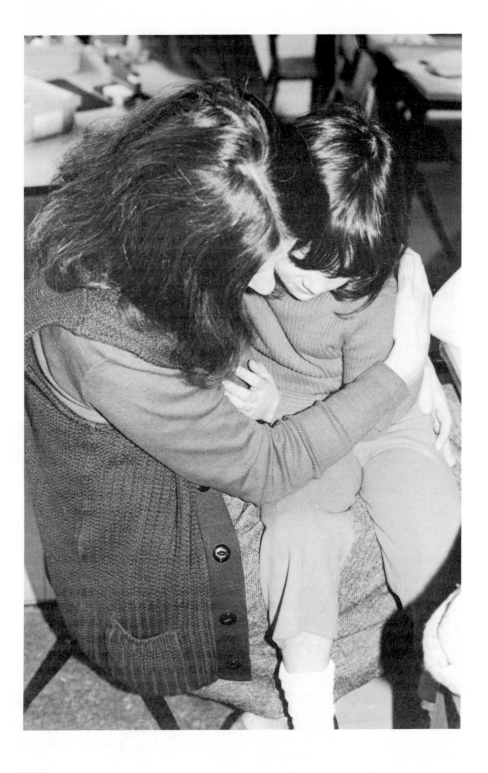

Introduction

So you want to care for children? Perhaps you have always cherished this ambition, or, perhaps it is an idea that has dawned recently, through your contacts with children in various situations.

It is sensible to find out what you are letting yourself in for. Caring for children is hard physical work which can also be mentally exhausting.

However, the rewards are infinite. To aid a helpless infant grow into a healthy well-adjusted child brings great joy. The value to society cannot be computed, but it must be very great.

Only comparatively recently has it been fully appreciated how vitally important are the years up to seven. Character, abilities, attitudes are all being formed during this period. Yet child-rearing is still under-valued. Anyone can become a parent, with no preparation or training. Although instinct will help a mother to do the right thing for her own child, instinct alone is certainly not sufficient when caring for other people's children.

Personal qualities in a nursery nurse

What qualities does an intending nursery nurse need? First, she needs to be a warm person who cares deeply about children in a way that is free from sentimentality or possessiveness. She must enjoy children's company and let this show through her dealings with them. She needs to be physically strong and healthy, and of wholesome and attractive appearance for the children. A sense of humour and a sense of proportion, patience and tolerance will be vital.

She must be able to get on with people, to accept them as they are without making hasty judgements. Resilience and self-control will be called for; so will ability to accept criticism, and a flexible outlook. Yet sensitivity, to adults as well as children, should underlie and characterise all she says and does.

The kind of person she is herself will determine the quality of the care she dispenses.

The National Nursery Examination Board

The Board was formed in 1945, conferring a nationally recognised qualification (N.N.E.B. Certificate) to fit women to work with young children up to the age of five. This was later extended to seven.

From the start, it was an imaginative and enlightened scheme, designed to continue the girls' education as well as train them for their chosen career.

Most courses are conducted within Colleges of Further Education, although one is housed separately. There are also a very few independent Colleges, the majority forming part of the state education system.

Students usually train for two years, at the end of which time they will take a national examination. Students must be sixteen or over when they embark on the course. The N.N.E.B. does not dictate academic entry qualifications, but competence in written English is an advantage and, for some courses, several O-Level equivalents will be required. In recent years, the emergence of boy students has made a valuable contribution to this predominantly female world.

Training varies with the centres, but the N.N.E.B. lays down a minimum number of days over a two-year period; 210 must be spent in college-based study, and similarly a minimum number of 140 must be spent in approved practical training establishments. Depending on areas and opportunities, practical training will take place in day nurseries, nursery centres, nursery schools, nursery classes, infant schools, hospitals, homes for handicapped children, or with private families.

Theoretical training in vocational subjects covers the development and care of the child from birth to seven. The first edition of our book aimed to cover the N.N.E.B. syllabus then in operation, as we interpreted it. In April 1982, however, an important new document was issued by the N.N.E.B., regulating the content of courses. While not intended to be a detailed syllabus, it outlines the skills and competences appropriate to a qualified nursery nurse, introducing changes of emphasis and fresh efforts to ensure that N.N.E.B. training meets present-day needs.

The present edition of this book reflects the new guidelines and responds to constructive comments from other tutors. Particular attention is paid to the one-parent family and children with special needs; road safety and the child in hospital are discussed in more detail; the charts on play now include progression, while child observations are brought into line with the new recommendations; professional responsibility and parent participation are the subject of a new section. Much of this new material, besides being an intrinsic part of the syllabus, also aims to develop the student's own outlook and professional attitudes.

Inevitably, any text-book which attempts to cover the content of a training course cannot deal fully with the knowledge required on every topic. Further reading, discussion and guidance are strongly recommended. We hope that besides outlining course content, our book also conveys the essential spirit of service to children and their families.

JB
MDM

Chapter 1
The family and the child

The family is the fundamental social unit in the western world. Members of a family are related by blood or marriage, and think of themselves as a separate group in society. From very early times people have lived in groups, partly for protection and partly for the mating relationship. Human offspring, unlike those of animals, needed quite a long period of protection and training in subsistence skills – hunting, self-defence, crop-growing, etc. With the development of lethal weapons, the men began acting co-operatively in hunting common enemies and getting food. Rivalry for mating partners became less important and so the man/woman relationship became more permanent and the family unit slowly evolved. It also took on the task of looking after the old and the weak.

The family unit has undergone immense change through the centuries. An illuminating and entertaining account of changes in family life, and in particular the place of children, can be found in *The History of Childhood*, edited by Lloyd de Mause, Souvenir Press. Unfortunately, we cannot here begin to do justice to this fascinating subject.

But, to appreciate the impact of more recent influences on the family and family life today, let us look at families a hundred years ago in Britain.

The nineteenth century saw the emergence of a new social phenomenon – the British middle class, a direct reflection of Britain's prosperity and influence in the world, built on industrialisation, trade and colonisation. The middle class imitated the ways of the rich and aristocratic, and this affected many aspects of family life.

Family life in the nineteenth century

1. The middle-class family of Victorian times. The Victorian middle-class family consisted of father, mother and usually five or more children; quite possibly, one or two further children would have died at birth or in infancy.

The father was often an autocratic, remote figure whose word was law. He was the provider, and the mother had no need to work. Mother would preside over several servants, including a governess who would be employed to care for and teach the children while young.

The girls probably did not go to school and their education at home would include accomplishments such as drawing, embroidery and playing musical instruments. They were expected to make a 'good' – meaning a financially satisfactory – marriage at an early age, to a suitable man of similar or higher social position. If still single at twenty-five, they were considered 'old maids', and had to find worthy occupations to fill their lives. Financial provision would probably be made by father or brothers.

Women were much the inferior of their husbands, with no property, legal,

voting or other rights. Even if divorce had not been scandalous and unthinkable it would have brought great economic problems to women.

Religion affected many aspects of family life. For example, church and Sunday school attendance were compulsory for family and servants. Sunday was a family day and any activities regarded as flippant or over-industrious would be forbidden.

The church taught that children were conceived and born in sin. Baptism began the process of redeeming them, and was urgently sought for delicate babies who might pass into the next world in their sinful state.

Children were expected to be 'seen and not heard' and to obey their 'elders and betters' implicitly. Spontaneity and individuality were not encouraged. Mother/baby and mother/child relationships, however, were characterised by much sentimentality, as can be seen in paintings and writings.

Displays of affection, or passion, between adults were taboo, and excessive modesty about dress and conduct was prevalent. In extreme cases, even the piano legs had to be covered! The sex act was held, by women at least, to be an unavoidable necessity in the procreation of children; prostitution records in large cities indicate that many Victorian men maintained an outward respectability, while indulging their sexual desires away from home.

Without easy travel and communication, people's lives tended to be narrow, both geographically and mentally. They would work near their homes, and not move far from their families when they married. Consequently grandparents, aunts, uncles and cousins – the extended family – were influential in family life.

2. The lower-class family. For the very poor family having relatives close at hand was vital for its old, ill, bereaved or unemployed members. Often the shared experience of a hard life, made slightly easier by family help and support, forged bonds of loyalty and affection between members. The husband was the chief breadwinner, but if money was short wives too would work, in light industry, domestic service, or laundrywork either in their own homes or outside. To 'take in washing' was often a humiliation for the respectable poor.

The working day, week and year were long and hard. A woman might be allowed a few *hours* off to have a baby when working at a cotton mill. In country districts a newborn baby might be carried to work in the fields, tied in its mother's shawl, while her many other children came along too. Bank holidays were great events, and a day out at the nearest seaside resort – probably Southend for Londoners, Blackpool for many northerners – would be looked forward to, saved for and talked about afterwards for the best part of the year by working people fortunate enough to afford it. Otherwise, families had little leisure time to spend together or apart; all their time and energy went on eking out a mere subsistence. For those undeterred by warnings about hellfire and damnation, there were the escapes of gin and ale.

Traditional remedies were used to treat the sick because doctors' fees were out of the question. Epidemics of typhoid fever and other diseases raged in towns from time to time, accelerated by insanitary housing conditions. Whole families might be crowded into one or two small rooms and beds; incest was commonplace.

After 1880 free education was compulsory and free for all. But the children of the poor left school at the earliest possible moment, by the age of thirteen, to begin work. In country districts, or areas with seasonal work, many children would be kept away from school to earn a few more coppers for the family budget at, for instance, potato harvesting or hop-picking. Apprenticeship in a trade was virtually the only further training available; college and university education was financially and socially out of reach for the children of the poor.

Family life in the twentieth century

In the second part of the last century, and the whole of this, far-reaching social and economic changes profoundly affected the family unit, and the quality of family life. Most were clearly of benefit, but others created problems and pressures.

A series of political reforms ended sweated labour of women and children and placed a greater economic responsibility on the male. In more recent times, working hours were steadily reduced, creating leisure for the masses.

The repeated raising of the school-leaving age reflected the enhanced status of the child in society, but also increased the dependency years. Life in a complex, technological age has made higher education and specialised training necessary for large numbers of young people, which has further lengthened the period of dependency.

Health and life expectancy improved dramatically and continuously with the development of medicine and science, drugs, preventive measures and knowledge of the factors that produce a healthy life-style. Infant mortality, although still not as low in Britain as we should like, is vastly reduced. Death is no longer an everyday occurrence and each individual life, from the ante-natal period onwards, is more precious, and the focus of high hopes and responsibilities for the parents. Paradoxically, now that death, suffering and acute illnesses, such as fevers which used to work up to a 'crisis', have almost passed out of our lives, with them has gone much drama. Some students of social behaviour believe that present-day problems such as depression or boredom leading to vandalism stem largely from this lack of real-life drama.

Because we live longer, marriages are undertaken for the best part of a life-time. As older people remain active, the popular image of white-haired granny knitting for and 'spoiling' her grandchildren may be replaced by a youthful fifty-plus-year-old who still does a full-time job.

Women were given the vote in 1928, mainly as a result of their contribution to the First World War effort in 1914-18. Subsequently, aided by legislation such as the recent Sex Discrimination Act, they have secured equal rights and oppor-tunities, although there is still room for improvement. Today's marriages are voluntary commitments of equal partners to one another.

On the subject of representation in government, we should remember that at the beginning of this century even adult male suffrage ('one *man* one vote') had not long applied in Britain. The twentieth century has seen a steady increase in direct participation in government by the people, and also an influence from the trade union movement and other bodies. Family considerations have been important in wooing the support of voters.

With a secure position in society, a good education and often career training too, many married women now choose to return to a former job, or take up a new career, after spending comparatively few years on child-rearing. In a later chapter, we shall look at how well society provides for the young children of such women. When the mother is working the father has to help with the household chores. Few modern families can afford servants. In any case, the idea of working as another person's servant is often distasteful, with its feudal echoes. Some marriages adopt a complete reversal of roles. The father stays at home to look after the house and children while the mother goes out to work. This makes sense if the mother can earn a higher salary, and both partners are happy with the arrangement. A woman can take maternity leave, knowing her job must be held open for six months. Many fathers are happy to be involved with the upbringing of their children, from birth onwards. There is no longer a taboo on male tenderness and in some countries fathers can claim paternity leave.

Women's equal rights to a social life have also been recognised, and whole families tend to enjoy leisure pursuits together, where once mother and children would have been left at home while father enjoyed his chosen hobby. We have to recognise also that marriage is no longer the one and only role for women. Many now *choose* to remain single. The term 'spinster' with its forbidding overtones has practically disappeared.

The general standard of living has improved greatly in the last fifty or so years. There is far less contrast between the lives of the so-called middle and working classes. Job and promotion opportunities have raised people's expectations of a comfortable, happy life. There is very little grinding poverty. But, when expectations are high, those who fail – for whatever reasons – stand out more painfully. Television programmes and many forms of advertising have encouraged a new materialism and acquisitiveness which can trivialise accepted values and are damaging to society.

Family planning methods and legalised abortion have enabled parents to limit their families to a chosen number – in recent years, one or two. Contraception has resulted in a sharp decline in the birth rate during the last decade, as economic pressures, inflation and the desire for a high standard of living have made married women plan for an eventual return to work. It remains to be seen whether economic or other factors will result in an upswing during the latter part of this century. Every child should and could be a wanted child. With such a power of choice, some parents find the responsibility too onerous. Newly-married wives may find the 'sensible' decision – to keep their job and defer motherhood for a while – hard to accept, when nature has designed their bodies for childbearing in the early twenties. Another power of choice, in this context, is the services of a fertility clinic for a couple who, two generations ago, would have remained childless.

Enlightened attitudes toward the study of man and the human body, and the development of psychology as a science, have freed sexual behaviour from the traditional sinful interpretation of the church. Sexual problems within marriage can be openly talked about and receive skilled and sympathetic help, so that sexual behaviour can be rightly and fully enjoyed by both partners.

Child psychology shows that positive promotion of all aspects of children's development is far better than repression. With the spread of such knowledge, through the press, radio and television, parents are now expected to keep abreast of the latest ideas on child-rearing and personal relationships, including careers guidance.

Easier divorce procedures are often blamed for the rising divorce rate and the resulting suffering of children. Undoubtedly, thousands of children do suffer every year through broken marriages; some are used as pawns in the preceding conflict; some are 'bought' and vied for with money and material possessions, some grow up with a distorted view of the absent parent, or his or her sex in general. Many have feelings of divided loyalty, loneliness, rejection, even guilt that somehow they were responsible for the break-up. But many others survive apparently unscathed. Large numbers also quickly adapt to a new parent and ready-made brothers and sisters. Most experienced people agree that for a child to live within a loveless marriage where partners stay together 'for the sake of the children' is infinitely worse.

However, the million or so children living in a one-parent family form a large part of the nation's statistics on poverty. Particularly vulnerable are unsupported young mothers, and children born illegitimately. (In children born outside marriage, there is still a distressingly high incidence of stillbirth, handicap and infant mortality.) Poverty, inadequate housing and social disadvantage commonly experienced by such families are more damaging than any trauma experienced during a breakdown, or the single-parent status. The fact that children of widows or widowers and, to a lesser extent, divorced parents, appear to suffer less in all respects, seems to indicate that even a short time living within a maturely-based family, with both marriage partners present, affords a child some safeguard against damage if a breakdown occurs.

Housing and sanitary conditions have become steadily better this century, thereby improving standards of health and mental well-being. Each new family *expects* to have its own home, and although local authorities cannot keep pace with demand, this is the goal towards which they strive. Unfortunately, after the Second World War, during a period of rising birth rate and diminishing availability of building land, many authorities built high-rise flats which have since been proved unsuitable and are frequently sources of discontent, depression, isolation and vandalism. They are particularly harmful to young mothers and children. In the private sector, there has been a great increase in the number of families who succeed in buying their own homes and achieve high standards of comfort and amenities. The high cost of labour for maintenance has meant that householders carry out most home improvements themselves. The sharing of labour by husband and wife increases their pride and joy in the home. Television has provided entertainment in the home, and is often a means of drawing family members together.

Geographic, occupational and social mobility has greatly increased. Two world wars extended the horizons of whole generations; improved education strengthened their desire for better jobs and housing, and governments strove to satisfy them. Motorised vehicles for a large section of the population made travel, for work and leisure, a practical possibility. This greater mobility and changing outlook also led to the growth of suburbs. As grown-up children moved away from their roots, however, family networks broke up, and the typical family today is a 'nuclear' family; that is, it consists of parents and child or children only. Contact between the nuclear family and other relatives now is often a matter of choice, and concern for relatives' well-being. Formerly, living in an extended family meant that contact was unavoidable. Today greater independence and more privacy in the personal lives and child-rearing patterns of the young mother and father are ensured. But children can be denied valuable contact with grandparents, peer cousins and other relatives who might enhance the sense of belonging to a distinctive, strong unit. For the parents, particularly young mothers, they can lead to a sense of isolation, lack of support and depression.

Economic independence – thanks to the welfare state – is welcomed by the older generation, but they, too, can feel lonely, abandoned, and deprived of the rejuvenating company of their grandchildren. The fact that people live to a greater age now also means that their years of retirement, which in many cases *can* mean years without a useful role, accentuate this sense of isolation. To offset this, improved health and freedom from poverty *can* make retirement a period of contented pursuit of interests and pleasures.

The welfare state has provided a 'safety net' for cases of hardship, unemployment, disability, child neglect, old age and so on. Critics claim that many of the traditional functions of the family have been taken over by the state, thus undermining the responsibility of the family.

Other less perceptible changes in society have had repercussions on family life. The historical influence of the church and the practice of church-going have diminished considerably. This fact is sometimes linked with a general 'moral decline' in family life and elsewhere. Yet however atheistic or secular a family appears to be, all our inheritance of ethics and moral code has descended from Christian teaching. Inner convictions and guiding principles in conduct are still passed on from one generation to the next.

Another subtle change has taken place in the status of the father in the family. Today, his job (probably industrial) is often simply a time-filling paid occupation, and affords him little satisfaction or self-respect. His position is very different from that of his craftsman or farming forebears. He plays only a minor part in a complex process. This lack of personal involvement may affect his personal and family life and even demean his standing in the family. Children educated to question past assumptions may not *automatically* revere him because he is their father. He is not necessarily the sole breadwinner, and must share the household tasks. Sources of dissatisfaction may multiply, and his view of his role in life may be hazy or tinged with disenchantment.

Let us take a closer look at the invisible forces at work *within* families, especially those which most affect the child. His position in relation to other family members is of great significance.

The small family and only child are common in society today. The traditional view that the only child must be a spoiled child may be partly true, for he will be the sole focus of the parents' love and attention, which may include material over-indulgence. On the other hand, many parents of only children, aware of this danger, may even be over-strict. They usually make special efforts to secure companionship for the child. He will probably develop social skills early in life, because he has no ready-made companions, he must win and keep them. He may become, of necessity, self-sufficient and prefer his own company to that of others. He may well be more than advanced in conversation, through adult company. His parents' expectations will probably be high, and they may over-protect or 'cling' to him, when he should be allowed increasing independence. He will miss the hurly burly of family life with brothers and sisters – teasing, rivalries, shared jokes, 'ganging-up' against parent or each other and the deep – often well-hidden – affection expressed at Christmas, birthdays and times of stress. Sharing, taking turns, waiting with other children are not quite the same if they only happen at school.

Large families are comparatively rare today. Traditionally they are happy loving groups in which to grow up, and indeed many undoubtedly are. Many others, however, are found in the poverty and 'problem' statistics. Sometimes the large number of children is the result of ignorance and carelessness rather than choice. If the parents are not reasonably well off and good 'copers', each new baby will increase their difficulties. Undoubtedly, such children learn to share, give and take, at an early age. Older children gain valuable experience in helping with younger ones. But the youngest may go short of adult attention and language stimulation. Material benefits have to be spread thinly. 'Hand-me-down' clothes and toys may be the lot of the youngest. There will be little privacy. Many people who have grown up in such a family feel that these disadvantages are, however, far outweighed by the experience of family solidarity, the development of resourcefulness, and the choice of particular closeness with one or more sibling, all of which may continue and afford great joy well into adult life.

The middle child out of three or five is often thought to be in an unenviable position; not for him the privileges and status of being the eldest, nor the babying and special treatment of the youngest. He may resent this, and resort to jealous or spiteful behaviour.

Twins often have to fight for their individuality to be recognised. Parents and teachers sometimes reinforce the image of 'the pair' by dressing them alike, referring to them as 'the twins' and so on. At times they may enjoy and even encourage this attention, but at others they long to make their mark as individuals. Often their early language development is slow, for they evolve their own private means of communication. Later, enforced closeness can accentuate differences in academic attainment, social success, etc. and lead to rivalry and resentment.

The child born to older (late thirties to fifties) parents is a common feature of family life today, now that wives' careers and second marriages are so prevalent. Such parents may be wiser and more patient, owing to greater maturity and life experience, but less physically energetic, and more aware of dangers and pitfalls, and therefore over-cautious and protective. They may not be familiar with contemporary child-rearing practices or, later, the fashions and freedom common to most teenagers today. This can be a particularly 'fraught' time for the child, who may be aware that his parents are different from those of his friends, and resent this.

The child born after an interval of years may experience some of the same effects, possibly coupled with those of being an only child. On the other hand, he may receive fond treatment from older brothers and sisters, and enjoy the company of contemporary nephews and nieces.

Readers can doubtless call to mind many other instances of how positions and relationships within families affect both their own functioning and the developing personality of the children.

The future of the family

There are pressures within and outside today's small family units. It is not easy to be a good mother, father, son, daughter – good in everyone else's eyes as well as one's own. In such a small and self-contained setting, each family member's role is constantly in the limelight. It is almost impossible to have an 'off' day, or disappear temporarily from the scene, without others noticing, and being materially and psychologically affected. This situation can lead to stress and discontent.

We have already seen how some of the traditional functions of the family – protecting the very young, or the old and weak members, for instance – have been, at least in part, taken over by the welfare state.

New attitudes to sexual freedom mean that we no longer *need* to get married in order to enjoy sex. Contraception has effectively separated marriage from the idea of having children. When a marriage contract can be so easily broken, does it have any validity in the first place?

Marriage in our society still has an aura of romance, however. But in other societies it does not. The Asians, for instance, appear to manage very well by tackling it as a practical, economic arrangement. Should we not then, in western countries, look seriously for alternative approaches to family life, or even change the whole concept of marriage, and the family as society's basic unit?

While young people and others search in communes and kibbutzim for an alternative, superior unit, marriage becomes more and more popular. Despite increased life expectancy, people marry earlier. Most divorced people remarry within a few years. Clearly then, the high divorce rate does not reflect a rejection of the institution of marriage. In the USSR, which has undergone revolution, civil war and a great sweeping away of traditional values, and where the state wields far more power over the individual than in Britain, marriage and family life still thrive, despite assumptions that they would fade out. We know from irrefutable evidence that the family is infinitely preferable as a setting for the child's development to the impersonal, multi-staffed institution.

Surely these facts strongly suggest that marriage and the family still fulfil the deep-felt needs of human beings.

In conclusion

As human beings, we need to care, and be cared for by others. To do this we need a few – comparatively speaking – close, lasting relationships, rather than many superficial ones.

We need to matter to others, and how much we matter largely depends on how much we contribute to their well-being. We need a degree of stability in our environment. We need to create surroundings of our choice, and unless there is some guarantee of the future of those surroundings, all our efforts are wasted. We want our lives to be more than a mere speck in the universe, a chance interval of time. We like to feel a sense of continuity – handing on the baton in life's relay race, rather than merely sprinting the hundred metres.

In a world where our daily work may be frustrating or uninspiring, we can derive deep satisfaction from life within a family. In a world of changing values, we feel we belong to one safe, steadfast unit. Helped by this inner security, most parents do their utmost to fulfil their family roles.

In many ways more, rather than less, is asked of parents today. They are expected to decide how many children to have, and at what intervals, depending on economic and other circumstances. They are expected to keep informed about all the institutions – clinics, schools, government agencies and so on – which will affect their children's development and education so as to derive as much benefit as possible from these. Catering for their children's physical, social, emotional and intellectual needs, parents must equip their children for a society which is itself constantly changing. A family which succeeds in this task contributes immensely to the community and is rewarded with status, prestige, reinforcement of its solidarity, and recognition of its identity.

We now have to consider in more specific terms how a good family life can benefit a child. In the first place, intimate knowledge of and interaction with loving parents who also love one another, gives the child a secure emotional base, where he *knows* he is loved and valued. He has no need to resort to attention-seeking behaviour, then or later. Building on shared experiences and memories, and emerging tastes, talents and characteristics, he gradually forms a clear picture of himself as an individual and feels at ease with that self. Text books call this 'self-image' or 'concept of self'. He will model his future conduct on that he sees in the home. He grows up with a clear idea of male and female roles in marriage, family and society. In moments of stress, he seeks refuge, comfort, reassurance from the family, and good moments are crowned by shared pleasure and pride.

As the years pass, he uses the family as a sounding board, punchbag, haven, anchor, cushion, and springboard. He learns to cope with failure and success, conflict, frustration, his own strengths and weaknesses and those of others. He learns loyalty to a group, and the safe feeling and confidence of belonging. He learns how to give as well as accept support. He contributes to the strength of the family and in doing so becomes stronger himself. Having received love, he can give it, wholeheartedly and wisely, without restraint, resentment or hopes of reward. In short, he can play his part in creating the next generation of good families.

Exercise 1

Multiple-choice questions

1. What is meant by a nuclear family?
(a) a family living in this, the nuclear age;
(b) a family consisting of mother, father and child or children;
(c) a family consisting of three generations and other relatives;
(d) a family with one child.

2. Which of the following innovations has most profoundly affected women's position in society today?
(a) easier divorce;
(b) opportunities for work outside the home;
(c) Women's Liberation Movement;
(d) the 'pill'.

Essay questions

3. How have parental roles within the family changed during the past fifty years?

4. What might be some of the difficulties facing a one-parent family today?

Project

6. Find out all you can about childhood in other cultures.

Suggestions for further reading

D. W. Winnicott, *The Child and the Family*, Tavistock Publications Ltd
David Kennedy, *Children*, B. T. Batsford Ltd
Edward Shorter, *The Making of the Modern Family*, Fontana
Eleanor Allen, *Victorian Children*, A. & C. Black Ltd
Russell Ash, *Talking about the Family*, Wayland Publishers Ltd
Eileen Bostock, *Talking about Women*, Wayland Publishers Ltd
Jean Collin, *Never had it so Good*, Victor Gollancz Ltd
Dulan Barber (Ed.), *One Parent Families*, Hodder & Stoughton Ltd
V. George and P. Wilding, *Motherless Families*, Routledge & Kegan Paul Ltd

Chapter 2
Marriage

Preparation for marriage

Western marriage today is a voluntary commitment to share one's life with a chosen partner. Young people are often 'prepared' for marriage in a semi-formal way in the upper half of secondary schools, in youth clubs, church classes for engaged couples, and elsewhere. The group leader may be a teacher, doctor, marriage guidance counsellor, family planning adviser, or health visitor. Precise information on sex and contraception may be given – as a responsible way of preventing unwanted births and abortions. However, this narrow interpretation of growing up has recently been broadened, and the whole subject is seen as education for personal relationships, of which marriage, naturally, is an important part. The group leader gives the young people a chance to air their views, and poses hypothetical situations, to stimulate deeper thought and discussion.

Is it possible to prepare people effectively for marriage? Probably not. Each marriage is a unique combination of two unique individuals. Therefore there can be no one formula for a happy marriage. We have all seen apparently ideal marriages flounder, and the most unlikely marriages flourish and last. Each evolves its own way of working to the satisfaction of the two partners within it. Those that do not either drift into sterile misery, or break up. Why then do we still provide education for marriage when success cannot be demonstrated?

The answer is partly that young people need to know that adults are trying to help and guide them, and are concerned for their well-being. Besides, this exchanging of opinions helps young people broaden their understanding and tolerance of others and helps them to examine their own attitudes towards the sex roles, the function of marriage and what may be expected of them in marriage. It is a modifying (perhaps only very slightly) influence in the heat of a moment's emotions.

Whether or not young people attend such classes, they all have preconceived ideas about marriage. They derive these:

1. most importantly from their own families;
2. from the marriages and homes of others;
3. from the television, films, advertising, the press, radio.

1. One's own experience of family life, and the marriage at the centre of it implant such deep feelings and attitudes that they are difficult to analyse – even recognise. Sometimes, in our own marriage we seek something as far removed as possible from what we know. In other cases we seek something similar.

2. Seeing other kinds of marriage – for instance where a wife is the chief breadwinner, or where there is a large, loving family – can be enormously broadening and beneficial.

3. Popular ideas on marriage are often unrealistic and glamorised. Young people should understand that a gleaming kitchen, with every latest appliance and refinement is not essential to a good marriage. Nor are the sex and family roles in real life stereotyped, as they often appear in the media. It is not unmanly to change nappies or take a turn with the saucepans, and it is not unwomanly to find home-making not wholly fulfilling. And the stereotype mother-in-law, fierce and formidable, is often far from the truth.

Inside or outside formal sessions, young people can be helped to see the many reasons why people marry, and why they choose the partners they do. Physical attraction is an overwhelming, yet superficial, part of it. Practicalities like loneliness, unhappiness at home, proximity and availability can all play a part, as can social pressures and a wish to conform. Complex emotional factors are also involved. Many people seek in their partners a quality they feel themselves to be lacking. This may work – if both partners are not seeking the same quality, or if the quality was not perceived from too slight an acquaintance. A good marriage can transform the personal development and emotional well-being of both partners. Gaps and wounds remaining from former less happy relationships can be filled in, or healed. But as personalities grow, needs and expectations change. The good marriage, allowing for this, grows and changes accordingly.

Such a close relationship, must produce ambivalent feelings and conflict. It is often only with the person with whom we feel most safe that we are confident enough to be aggressive and reveal our innermost selves, not all of which is lovable. The value of communication cannot be overstressed. If this breaks down, the marriage is doomed. Where there is genuine affection and – very important – a sense of commitment, communication resolves most difficulties and problems of adjustment.

These are a few of the deeper implications of marriage. But marriage should not be presented in too sober or depressing a light. Although it involves surrendering a certain amount of personal freedom, the partners should ideally exchange this narrow freedom for a deeper one within which each can grow.

Preparation for parenthood

Many schools offer instruction and discussion in parentcraft. Opinions vary about how and when this should be done. Sadly, often only the less academic pupils are given this opportunity, and sometimes only the girls. Statistics shows that young parents are most likely to come from this group but *all* prospective parents could undoubtedly benefit from learning how to handle a baby. The utter dependency of the newborn can thus be understood. The parents' role in ministering to his needs can be shown, with practical demonstrations in bathing, nappy changing, making up feeds, etc. Most young people respond well to such sessions, and on this physical level education in parentcraft is probably most effective at this stage.

Later, when baby is on the way, ante-natal classes can offer a more detailed preparation. Besides instruction on reproduction and the birth process, advice on how the mother can prepare her body by exercises and correct breathing can be given to *both* parents. Handling routines can be learned or re-learned.

At this stage, committed to parenthood, the young couple are usually receptive to advice on a deeper level. They can be made aware how, by performing these tasks for the baby, they will also fulfil other needs – for close contact and emotional security. Foundations will be laid for relationships and the means of communication. The need for mental stimulus can also be stressed, and again, both partners shown the importance of suitable equipment, play materials, making an environment safe and introducing stories and books at an early stage. Such topics will provide the themes for meetings of Mother and Toddler Clubs later on in the child's development. In recent years there have been several excellent television series about this stage in a family's life.

Preparation for parenthood is not, of course, confined to formal sessions. An awareness of all the many reasons *why* people have babies is important; it is not always to crown a happy marriage – a joint adventure in 'person making'. Some girls deliberately get pregnant to escape from an unhappy home life, lack of success at school or socially. Some 'trap' a man reluctantly into marriage. Some single women choose to be unmarried mothers for personal fulfilment. Sometimes pregnancy is a desperate bid to save an ailing marriage. Sometimes, even with contraception widely available and accepted, it is a half-deliberate 'mistake' because a couple, or more probably a wife, feels that planning babies is too cold-blooded. Contraception, after all, is not a natural phenomenon. Biologically, women are designed to produce babies in their early twenties.

In matters of timing, the head must often rule the heart. Most people believe that a baby is entitled to a start in life of economic and financial security – otherwise he will be affected physically. Emotionally too, he will suffer if, for instance, parents are harassed by money worries, or his arrival has curtailed either parent's training or career, or ended hopes of paying off a mortgage. Timing also involves awareness of the couple's adjustment to each other, and their emotional stability. It often takes a little while for a couple's sexual relationship to settle down satisfactorily, or gradually change from being their main preoccupation. Parenthood is bound to cause a little disruption here, so it is important that a mutually satisfactory and balanced approach has been achieved.

The fact must be faced that a baby will bring some restrictions. Money will almost certainly be shorter and have to stretch further. This will affect social life, hobbies, holidays, and many of the small pleasures of our too-materialistic society. Sleep and privacy may be affected. Many demands will be made on parents, but especially on the mother. Although today there is a much more relaxed approach than formerly about babies happily fitting into parents' lives, it is still true to say that expectations of a pink, cuddly bundle who will bring only light, joy and love into his parents' lives may be quickly followed by disillusionment and resentment. An expectant mother may not immediately experience a great surge of maternal feelings towards her baby. Apparent 'failure' here can bring reactions of guilt and anxiety. The attitudes of her mother and mother-in-law and the advice they give her during this waiting period may be critically influential – for good or bad – as she will be extra sensitive, and very anxious to do the right thing. As parents, the husband and wife will be the targets of much conflicting advice; even the 'experts' differ. Skill at picking one's way through such advice takes time, tact and maturity.

Parentcraft is not something that is learned once and for all. Parents go on learning all their lives, until the role merges into that of grandparent.

In the early days, many different individuals and agencies will play a part – the midwife, doctor, health visitor, baby clinic and above all, the young parents' own families. Besides information, advice and expertise, all these people should give reassurance and support, dispel alarm, discourage comparison with other babies, and help the parents to enjoy the whole procedure, grow in self-confidence and reap the maximum rewards.

Reproduction

All animals and plants reproduce in order to continue their species, and pass on characteristics to the next generation. Human beings are mammals and their reproduction is sexual; one male and one female together can produce offspring by each contributing one cell – a spermatozoon from the male and an ovum from the female.

Although the reproductive system is complete at birth, it is not mature, and boys and girls only become capable of producing babies at puberty which takes place some time between the ages of nine and eighteen years. The changes from girl to woman and boy to man are very gradual processes; the time taken varies with each individual. The physical changes needed to mature the reproductive system are determined by the pituitary gland which lies at the base of the brain in both sexes. At puberty the pituitary produces secretions known as hormones which travel through the bloodstream to all parts of the body, causing the production of sperm in boys and ova or eggs in girls, and changes known as secondary sexual characteristics in both sexes. These physical changes are usually completed before a person becomes mentally or emotionally mature. This can lead to problems. For example, a baby can be produced by juvenile parents who lack the maturity to devote the necessary amount of time and energy to his upbringing.

The male reproductive system

Secondary sexual characteristics which develop at puberty
(a) broadening of shoulders and development of muscles;
(b) growth of hair in the pubic region, on the chest and under the arms;
(c) change of voice from a high pitch to a low pitch due to growth and development of vocal chords;
(d) production of sweat which has a characteristic odour (intended to attract the opposite sex) by the opocrine glands in the skin;
(e) increase in size of penis;
(f) production of semen (fluid containing spermatozoa) which may be emitted.

(A) *Scrotum* – a loose bag or sac of skin outside the body containing the testes. The sac is retracted towards the body when cold and away from the body when hot to enable the sperm to stay at the optimum temperature, which is slightly below normal body temperature.

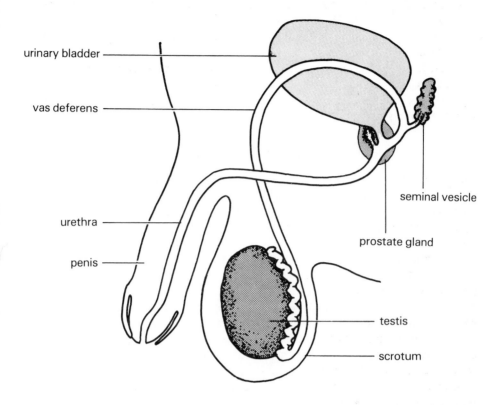

urinary bladder

vas deferens

urethra

penis

seminal vesicle

prostate gland

testis

scrotum

(B) *Two testes* – produce spermatozoa.

(C) *Vas deferens* – a duct or tube, leading from each teste upwards to loop under the bladder and join up with the urethra, which carry spermatozoa.

(D) *The urethra* – a tube leading from the bladder through the penis to the outside of the body.

(E) *The seminal vesicles* – these produce fluid which joins the spermatozoa in the vas deferens.

(F) *The prostate gland* – also produces fluid which joins the spermatozoa in the urethra.

The fluid containing spermatozoa is known as semen and it collects in the top part of the urethra and vas deferens ready to be released during sexual intercourse or masturbation. The penis is made of erectile tissue which means that during sexual stimulation the tissue is suffused with blood which enables it to become firm and erect and therefore capable of entering the female vagina. During the climax of the act semen containing millions of spermatozoa is ejected and deposited in the vagina. The spermatozoa are shaped like minute tadpoles, with a head and a long flexible tail which enables them to move rapidly into the female uterus and up into the fallopian tube to meet the ova.

The female reproductive system

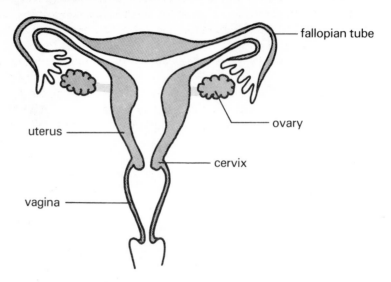

fallopian tube

ovary

uterus

cervix

vagina

Unlike that of the male, the female reproductive system is inside the body and is completely separate from the urinary system. The organs lie between the bowel and the bladder and urethra, and consist of:

(A) *The vagina* – a narrow corrugated passage which leads from the exterior of the body to the uterus.

(B) *The uterus* (or womb) – a hollow pear-shaped organ, size 7.5 cm × 5 cm × 2.5 cm (3 in × 2 in × 1 in) and which protrudes into the vagina at the lower end, forming a cervix or neck.

(C) *The fallopian tubes* – two narrow tubes which lead from the upper two corners of the uterus.

(D) *The ovaries* – two small almond-sized glands which contain ova, or eggs. Approximately every twenty-eight days during a woman's reproductive life, one of the ova 'ripens' and is released into the fallopian tube.

Secondary sexual characteristics which develop at puberty
(a) rounding of hips;
(b) enlargement of breasts;
(c) growth of hair in the pubic region and under the arms;
(d) production of sweat, which has a characteristic odour, by the opocrine glands in the skin;
(e) beginning of menstruation.

The menstrual cycle is the name used to describe the regular preparation of the uterus to receive a fertilised egg (ovum), and the subsequent discarding of the uterine lining if the egg is not fertilised. For most women this occurs during a period of twenty-eight days but it may vary between twenty-five to thirty days.

The cycle is controlled by hormones produced by the pituitary gland, which, in turn, stimulate the ovary to produce further hormones called oestrogen and progesterone. At the beginning of the cycle oestrogen produced by the ovary causes the lining of the uterus to thicken. This continues for about ten days until the ovum is released from the ovary and is wafted into the fallopian tube. With the liberation of the ovum the ovary begins to produce progesterone as well, which causes the uterine lining to become even thicker and more ready to receive the fertilised ovum. This continues for another fourteen days but then, if the ovum is not fertilised, progesterone ceases to be produced. This 'cut-off' of progesterone causes the lining of the uterus to deteriorate and to be shed for three to five days. This is known as the menstrual period, and is facetiously referred to by obstetricians as 'the weeping of a disappointed uterus'.

Two days after the period is completed, the entire cycle begins again. However, if the ovum is fertilised, about six days after its release it becomes implanted in the uterine lining. The fertilised ovum produces another hormone which causes the ovary to continue producing progesterone. This prevents the uterine lining from being shed, therefore there is no menstrual period.

Incidentally, the hormone produced by a fertilised ovum is called chorionic gonadotrophin and this hormone is excreted in the urine, where it can be detected and used as confirmation of pregnancy a week after fertilisation has taken place.

Contraception

For thousands of years people have sought ways of controlling their own fertility, but it is only in the past twenty years that this has been universally possible with any degree of certainty.

Several methods of contraception are now available and many general practitioners give advice on family planning. Family planning clinics exist in the majority of health centres and most of the contraceptive devices can be obtained on prescription. The following are used in Great Britain:

1. The sperm can be killed by the use of *spermicides* in the form of foams, creams, pessaries or jellies. These are inserted into the vagina just before intercourse. Although fairly efficient, it is recommended that this method is used with a mechanical barrier as well.

2. A temporary or permanent *barrier* can be placed between the egg and the sperm to prevent them meeting:
(a) a rubber diaphragm cap which is inserted into the vagina and prevents sperm entering the cervix. When used with spermicidal cream this is very effective;
(b) a condom; this is a rubber sheath which encloses the penis, after erection, but before penetration, so preventing sperm entering the vagina. When used with spermicidal cream it is very effective;
(c) *female sterilisation* (this is permanent). The fallopian tubes are cut and the cut ends are tied so that the egg cannot travel to the uterus;
(d) *male sterilisation* (this is permanent). Both vas deferens are cut and the cut

ends are tied so that sperm cannot travel through the tubes. This is called a vasectomy.

3. The egg can be prevented from being released. If a woman is given 'the pill', which is usually a mixture of the female hormones oestrogen and progesterone, or progesterone alone, ovulation does not occur. This is the most effective method at present.

4. The conditions inside the uterus can be made unsuitable for implantation of a fertilised egg. This is caused by inserting an intra-uterine device consisting of a loop or coil of plastic wire into the uterus.

5. Use of the safe period. Since ovulation occurs only at monthly intervals, then it is possible for a woman to work out when this happens and avoid intercourse within two to three days of this date. If a woman has a regular cycle of menstruation, it is a simple matter, because ovulation occurs fourteen days before the next menstrual cycle. To be certain of the date of ovulation, the temperature can be taken daily, because at ovulation time there is a slight drop of about half a degree (F) followed by a rise of about one degree (F). This method takes time and self-control but many parents manage to plan their families this way and it is the only method allowed to Catholics.

Pregnancy

Conception takes place when a spermatozoon reaches the ovum in the fallopian tube and penetrates it. This is when pregnancy begins and it continues until the birth of the baby. Immediately after the sperm and the ovum unite, they begin dividing, first into two, then into four, then into eight cells, and so on. These cells will eventually become the baby and the placenta (or afterbirth).

At the same time as this cell division is taking place the fertilised egg (or morula, as it is called at this stage) is being wafted down the fallopian tube into the uterine cavity. Then, at about the sixth day after conception, the morula will embed itself into the lining of the uterus (or womb).

The development of the fertilised egg is very rapid. Soon the morula will separate into two halves that will become the foetus and the placenta and, by about the twelfth week, the foetus will be recognisable as a baby.

The foetus obtains nourishment and oxygen from its mother via the placenta, which is attached to the wall of the uterus. Between the placenta and the foetus is the umbilical cord which acts as a lifeline carrying food and oxygen to the foetus and removing waste products. Food, oxygen and the waste products are exchanged through the walls of the placenta and uterus and the mother's bloodstream.

The foetus is surrounded by a bag of membranes which contain fluid in which the baby floats. The fluid acts as a cushion, protecting the baby from any blow. It also enables the baby to have free movement and exercise which aids its physical development. Most of the baby's development occurs during the first three months of pregnancy; during the remaining six months the baby will grow and mature until he is ready to cope with the outside world. Because of the rapid development, the foetus is very vulnerable to any damage in the early weeks of pregnancy. At one time it was thought that the placenta acted as an impenetrable barrier to anything which could harm the developing foetus but we now know that certain viruses can get through to the baby, and some drugs too. Smoking can also be harmful to the baby's development. The degree of damage suffered by the foetus will largely depend on what stage it has reached. For example, if the mother has German measles (rubella) at the time the baby's ears are developing, then the baby will probably be born deaf. On the other hand, if the damage occurs very early in pregnancy, there may be such a distortion of development that the foetus is unable to survive and the pregnancy will end in abortion.

Heredity

The hereditary factors passed to a baby by its parents are contained in the twenty-three chromosomes present in both the ovum and the spermatozoon. When the ovum and the spermatozoon combine to form a single cell, each of the twenty-three chromosomes from the ovum unites with a matching chromosome from the spermatozoon and twenty-three distinctly different pairs are produced. These forty-six chromosomes form the blueprint for the new individual and, as the cell divides and sub-divides, each new cell will contain an identical set of chromosomes.

At the moment of conception the sex of the baby is decided in the following way. One particular pair of chromosomes are known as the 'sex chromosomes', and the sex chromosome from the ovum is always an 'X' one. But the spermatozoon may contain either an 'X' or a 'Y' chromosome. If the sperm contains an 'X' chromosome then the baby will have 'XX' chromosomes, and will be female. If the sperm contains a 'Y' chromosome then the baby will have 'XY' chromosomes, and will be male. This means that the sex of a baby is always determined by the father's sperm. It is probably a matter of random chance whether a sperm containing an 'X' chromosome or one containing a 'Y' chromosome reaches the ovum first. But, nevertheless, more boys are conceived than girls. The ratio is fairly constant at 106 boys to every 100 girls. However, boys are more vulnerable to injury and disease and this causes the ratio eventually to even out.

Each chromosome carries thousands of genes and each gene contributes to the general make-up of the child. For example, a gene from one chromosome determines eye-colour, another will determine the shape of the eye, and so on.

Because the chromosomes are in matched pairs, it follows that every individual has two genes for each characteristic, one from each parent. Although genes look alike, they can carry different instructions. For instance, a person could have a gene from his mother containing instructions for a round chin, and a corresponding gene from his father containing instructions for a pointed chin. He may be born with the round chin but, because he also carried the gene for a pointed chin, he could pass the pointed chin characteristic on to his future children.

In many cases it is not known why one gene of a pair is used in preference to the other; indeed it may be accidental. But in some cases a gene can be 'dominant' or 'recessive'. Dominant genes always take precedence over other genes so that if one parent contributes this type of gene then the child will always inherit that particular characteristic. Recessive genes, on the other hand, always allow other genes to take precedence. A good example of this is with genes that determine eye-colour, because the genes controlling dark colours are dominant. If a child has a blue-eyed mother who has passed on her blue-eyed characteristic, and a brown-eyed father who has passed on his brown-eyed characteristic, then the child will have brown eyes. However, the child will also carry the gene for blue eyes inherited from his mother, so that when he becomes a father he could pass either the blue gene or the brown one. In some families it is possible to see certain characteristics carried down through each generation in this way, for example, a cleft chin.

As each chromosome carries about 15 000 genes, it can readily be seen that the possible combinations of genes are endless, even when children have the same parents – hence every child is a different individual, apart from identical twins, which are formed when the fertilised ovum divides into two, and so have the same chromosomes and genes. But differences in people can also occur because of environmental effects, so that even identical twins may show some variation in characteristic and development if they are brought up separately.

B = gene for BROWN EYES

b = gene for blue eyes

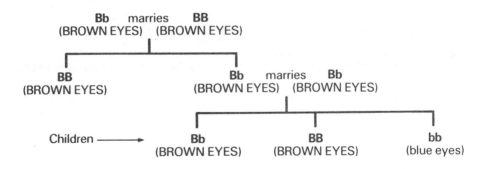

Exercise 2

Multiple-choice questions
1. If two brown-eyed parents produce a blue-eyed child, then:
(a) both parents must have had a blue-eyed parent;
(b) both parents must carry a blue-eyed gene;
(c) both parents must have had two blue-eyed parents;
(d) one parent must carry a blue-eyed gene.

2. The purpose of the placenta is to
(a) protect the baby from any foreign body;
(b) act as a cushion;
(c) digest food for the baby;
(d) enable the exchange of food, oxygen and waste products between mother and baby.

3. The most effective method of family-planning is:
(a) the 'pill';
(b) the rhythm method;
(c) the inter-uterine device;
(d) withdrawal.

Essay questions
4. 'Every baby should be a wanted baby.' Elaborate this statement, and explain how this is possible in today's world.

5. Explain what factors a couple should bear in mind when planning a family.

Discussion topic
6. Is marriage really necessary? What are the advantages and disadvantages?

Suggestions for further reading

Geraldine Lux Flanagan, *The First Nine Months of Life*, Heinemann Ltd
Eric Trimmer, *Having a Baby*, Heinemann Ltd
Dennis Fox, *Facts for Life*, Macdonald Educational Ltd Granada Television
Kenneth Rudge, *Relationships*, Macmillan Education Ltd
Jacky Gillott, *Connexions – For Better for Worse*, Penguin Books Ltd
Joy Groombridge, *Connexions – His and Hers*, Penguin Books Ltd
Ellen Peck, *The Baby Trap*, Heinrich Hanam Publications
Diagram Group, *Mothers (One hundred mothers of the famous and infamous)*, Paddington Press Ltd

Chapter 3
Preparation for baby

Signs and symptoms of pregnancy

1. menstruation ceases – there is no period;

2. early morning sickness – may vary between slight nausea and actual vomiting;

3. lassitude and tiredness;

4. frequency in passing urine and/or constipation – this is due to alterations in muscle tone caused by the hormonal changes;

5. chemical test of urine for pregnancy is positive by about the fifth day after conception.

Ante-natal care and advice

Most women wait until they have missed their second period before consulting a doctor for confirmation of a pregnancy and the beginning of ante-natal care. However, some authorities feel that the mother should be examined earlier than this, perhaps even before pregnancy begins. This is because a healthy mother will have fewer problems during her pregnancy and has the best prospect of producing a healthy baby. Also, as the foetus is at its most vulnerable during the first twelve weeks of pregnancy, the mother, if seen early, could be warned of the possible dangers to the baby of smoking, drug-taking or exposure to any infectious disease.

Ante-natal care is mainly preventive medicine – detecting potential problems and either stopping them developing, or minimising their effects on the mother or baby. The aim of good ante-natal care is a fit mother and a fit baby at the end of pregnancy. It is of little use to deliver a healthy baby if the mother is not in a fit state to take proper care of him.

Usually the mother-to-be will first visit her own family doctor (general practitioner). Some doctors do not undertake ante-natal care, and if this is the case they will refer the mother to another doctor in the same health centre or to a maternity hospital.

On the first visit, a full examination is made of the mother's general health, as well as confirming that she is pregnant. The date of delivery is calculated by adding nine calendar months and seven days to the date on which the last menstrual period began. This last date is used because it is the one which is easily remembered. It is not usually possible to ascertain when conception actually took place, as there are no visible signs. Taking an average of thousands of pregnancies, it was found that the commonest length of pregnancy varied between thirty-eight and forty-two weeks, so that the average was forty weeks from the first day of the last menstrual period. The date of birth given to the mother is referred to as the estimated date of delivery, or EDD. The doctor will ask the mother for details of any family illness or past personal illness which may affect her pregnancy. A full examination is carried out to determine the present state of her health. This will include the following:

1. The mother's heart function is tested, because pregnancy can be a burden to a woman with a defective heart.

2. The blood pressure is measured because an abnormal blood pressure is an indication that disease is present; investigations and treatment at this stage may prevent future problems. Also the blood pressure may rise during pregnancy because of 'toxaemia of pregnancy', so it is necessary to know the mother's normal blood pressure for purposes of comparison.

3. The urine is tested for the presence of abnormalities:
(a) sugar – which may mean the mother is a diabetic needing treatment;
(b) albumen – which usually means that the kidneys are not working as efficiently as they should;
(c) pus – which indicates an infection is present in the urinary tract.

4. The blood is also tested:
(a) to determine the blood group, which is recorded so that if the mother should need a blood transfusion the correct blood can be given quickly;
(b) to determine the rhesus factor, because if the mother is rhesus negative she could produce antibodies which could affect her baby's blood, causing him to need an exchange blood-transfusion at birth. This condition more commonly affects second or subsequent babies but, if a mother is found to be rhesus negative early in her first pregnacy, it is possible to protect her future babies by giving her an injection within forty-eight hours of the birth, which will prevent her forming any antibodies;
(c) for anaemia – this can affect both mother and baby if not treated early in pregnancy;
(d) to check whether the mother is suffering from syphilis, because the baby will be affected unless treatment is started early in pregnancy.

5. A check is made for varicose veins, as these tend to become worse during pregnancy.

6. Teeth are examined and the mother is advised to go to the dentist for a check-up.

7. The size of the pelvis is checked and any abnormalities noted.

8. The mother is weighed and measured.

Arrangements for the confinement are discussed at this early visit. At present about 99 per cent of births take place in hospital although, if all is normal and her doctor agrees, the mother can choose to have her baby at home with a community midwife in attendance. Some mothers may choose to go into hospital for the delivery only and come home within forty-eight hours of the birth, provided the doctor agrees and all is well with the mother and baby. In this case, in many areas, the community midwife and doctor will go into the hospital to attend to the delivery and then the same midwife will visit the mother daily at home until the baby is fourteen days old. The choice of home delivery or a shortened hospital stay will obviously depend on there being adequate domestic help in the house, as the mother should not be doing housework.

Other mothers will go into hospital when labour begins and will stay for about six to ten days after the birth. The decision about the place of birth depends not only on the mother's choice, but also on various medical factors, because certain groups of mothers have a slightly higher risk of complications at the delivery. These mothers should be in hospital where there are facilities to deal with any problem promptly. Examples of women 'at risk' include women over thirty years of age having their first baby and diabetic mothers. In other cases, warning signs of complications such as a raised blood pressure, may occur during pregnancy, indicating that this mother would be best to have her baby in hospital.

The mother-to-be usually attends the ante-natal clinic monthly until the sixth month of her pregnancy and then more frequently for the last three months. At each visit checks are made on the mother's health. She is weighed, her blood pressure is taken and her urine is tested. Any abnormality in one or more of these tests can indicate problems needing further investigation. One of the hazards of pregnancy is the development of pre-eclamptic toxaemia which, if left untreated, can lead to fits in the mother and death of the foetus. Although a lot of research has been and still is being carried out on this condition, little is known of the cause. However, if a mother shows any of the signs of the disease – raised blood pressure, albumen in the urine and excess weight gain due to water retention – rest in bed and the use of sedatives can prevent her condition deteriorating.

During the course of pregnancy tests can be carried out to check for specific abnormalities in the baby. A maternal blood test at sixteen to seventeen weeks may reveal an excessive amount of a substance called alphafeta protein (A.F.P.). This could mean that the baby has spina bifida or another neural tube defect. If a second blood test also shows a high result, then an amniocentesis is performed. This involves taking a sample of the fluid surrounding the baby and gives a more definite diagnosis. Amniocentesis is also performed if there is a higher chance than normal of the baby's having a genetic disease such as Down's Syndrome. A positive diagnosis will give the parents a chance to decide whether or not to have the pregnancy terminated.

As the baby grows in the uterus the doctor or midwife can, by palpating the mother's abdomen, determine the position of the baby and listen to his heart with a foetal stethoscope. His size and rate of growth can also be monitored. If there is any cause for concern, an ultrasonic scanning machine can be used to check the position of the baby in the uterus and gauge its size and maturity. It will also show the position of the placenta and whether there is more than one baby. Another test used to show whether the baby is growing is an estimation of the amount of oestriol in the mother's urine over twenty-four hours. A low result can indicate that the placenta is failing and treatment is necessary.

Nearer to the estimated delivery date the midwife will check that the baby is in a good head-down position ready for birth and the head is 'engaged'. This means that the head has passed through the bony pelvis. If this is so, then the baby can be born normally, as the head is the largest part of the body at this stage in life.

All expectant parents may attend and participate in parentcraft classes held in health centres and maternity hospitals. These classes explain the process of pregnancy and birth, advise parents on the care needed during pregnancy and how to look after the baby. They usually take the form of weekly discussion groups over periods of ten to twelve weeks. Each week a different subject is discussed and this is followed by a demonstration and practice of various exercises and methods of relaxation which will help the mother to co-operate in the birth of her baby. The birth is described in detail and films are shown, so that both parents know what to expect. This is very important, and helps lessen the fear of the unknown which can cause tension, leading to increased pain in labour and birth.

During classes and at ante-natal examinations, the mother is advised about the care of her health. Some topics discussed during the ante-natal period are:

1. Diet (see Chapter 6 on food). The mother must eat a good mixed diet containing protein, calcium iron and vitamins. She should not increase her consumption of carbohydrates, because this is unnecessary for the baby and will make the mother put on weight. During pregnancy the mother should not put on more than 20 lbs (9 kilos) in weight, otherwise there may be problems at the birth and the mother may have difficulty in regaining her figure afterwards. On the whole the baby will take the nutrients he needs at the expense of his mother, so if her diet is poor her health will be affected first. Iron is especially important, because in the last two months of pregnancy the baby stores enough iron to last him until he is about six months old. Consequently if the mother is already anaemic, she will become more so at this time. If, on top of this, she loses more blood than usual at the birth, she will be in a poor state of health to care for her baby. Because of this, iron tablets are usually prescribed to boost the mother's diet. Vitamin A, D and C tablets are also advised as a supplement to her diet.

2. Clothing. Clothing should be loose and comfortable, preferably hanging from the shoulders rather than the waist, which usually disappears early in pregnancy. Breasts should be supported by a well-fitting brassière, which should be checked for size at intervals because the breasts enlarge as pregnancy advances. Shoes should have medium heels and be comfortable so that the mother stands up straight.

3. Exercise and rest. Exercise is necessary and will not harm the baby, provided it is regular and the mother does not get over-tired. Cycling, horse-riding and walking are all beneficial in moderation. Rest is also important – a rest during the day with the feet up and a regular reasonable bedtime all help to keep the mother-to-be healthy and happy.

4. Care of teeth. Dental care is free for all pregnant women and they should make full use of this facility. During pregnancy the baby takes calcium for his bones and teeth. This may leave the mother short, so affecting her dental health.

5. Smoking. This should be avoided if possible because strong evidence suggests that smoking affects the baby's rate of growth. Babies born to mothers who smoke are often smaller than the average. If the mother is a chain-smoker and finds it very difficult to give up, she is persuaded to try to reduce the number of cigarettes she smokes to under ten daily.

6. Drugs. No drugs of any description should be taken by a pregnant woman, unless they are prescribed for her by a doctor who is aware of the pregnancy.

7. Maternity benefits and services are available to all pregnant women. They are as follows:

(a) free ante-natal care;
(b) free hospital care;
(c) free services of doctor, midwife, obstetrician, paediatrician and health visitor;
(d) free prescriptions until the baby is one year old;
(e) free dental care until the baby is one year old;
(f) home help services for a small charge;
(g) free milk and vitamin tablets if the family is on a low income;
(h) Maternity Grant – this is a lump sum paid to the mother to help with the expenses of the birth. If twins are born, the grant is doubled;
(i) Maternity Allowance – this is a weekly sum payable for approximately eighteen weeks to expectant mothers who have been in full employment until they are twenty-six weeks pregnant. It is paid from twenty-eight weeks pregnancy until six weeks after the birth of the baby;
(j) Working women who become pregnant have a right – on certain conditions – to six weeks' paid maternity leave at 90 per cent of their basic wage and reinstatement in their job up to twenty-nine weeks after the baby's birth.
(k) They can also have paid time off work for attending ante-natal clinics.

8. The layette and equipment. Planning and preparing the baby's room and buying clothing and equipment can be an enjoyable part of pregnancy which both parents can share. Shopping is best carried out during the middle months of pregnancy before it becomes too tiring for the mother. Many shops catering for babies' needs will send catalogues on request and these can be a great help. Books on baby care usually list suggested clothing and equipment. Generally it is best to buy only the minimum and then add more when the size of the baby is known. New babies are often given presents of clothing, which may duplicate clothes already bought. Babies grow very rapidly in their first few months, so that most clothing is usually outgrown rather than outworn.

There are several points to remember when buying clothing for a baby. Firstly, the materials used for the clothing should have the following qualities for comfort and safety:

(a) warmth;
(b) softness;
(c) lightness of weight;
(d) absorbency;
(e) ease of washing;
(f) non-irritating to baby's sensitive skin;
(g) non-flammable.

Natural fibres such as cotton and wool are usually found to be the most comfortable fabrics to wear because of their absorbent qualities, but cotton is not very warm and wool needs very careful washing. Some babies' skins may be sensitive to wool and find it irritating. A wool/cotton mixture, such as Viyella or Clydella, combines the good qualities of both fibres and is ideal for comfort. Man-made (synthetic) fabrics, such as nylon, terylene, acrilan, courtelle and orlon, have become very popular in recent years because of their cheapness compared with natural fibres. They have many advantages, being hard-wearing, warm, soft and light. They are also easily washed, and quickly dried, and need little or no ironing. However, their big disadvantage is that they do not absorb moisture and this makes the clothing uncomfortable, especially in hot weather. They should not be worn next to the skin because of the discomfort and also because some children develop an allergic rash from contact with synthetic fibres. But fabrics which contain a mixture of synthetic and natural fibres, such as wool and cotton, overcome many of these disadvantages. The material is absorbent and easily washed and dried, requiring little or no ironing.

Clothing for a baby should have the following qualities:

(a) It should be of simple design, so that it is easy to put on and take off.
(b) It should have easy fastenings – no fiddly ties.
(c) It should be easy to wash and iron.
(d) It should allow free movement.
(e) Seams should be flat, so there are no uncomfortable ridges.
(f) It should be suitable to the climate.

A basic list of clothing and equipment

24–36 nappies
3 pairs plastic pants
4 nappy pins (safety type)
3 vests
3 day dresses, rompers
   or all-over suits
3 nightdresses or all-over suits
3 cardigans or jumpers
3 bonnets
3 pairs mittens
3 pairs bootees
2 pram suits or sleeping bags
3 bibs or feeders
tray, bag, basket or box for toilet
   requirements
cotton-wool balls in plastic container
   with lid
soap
talcum powder
baby shampoo

2 flannels (if used)
brush and comb
nail scissors
simple baby cream, such as Vaseline
   or zinc and castor oil
3 towels
apron for mother, plastic/towelling
pail with lid for soiled nappies
bath and stand
low chair without arms
6 cot sheets
4 cot blankets
1 cot spread
pram
pram mattress with waterproof cover
4 sheets (but the same sheets and
   blankets could be used for cot and
   pram)
3 blankets
1 pram cover

crib and mattress, sheets and blankets   sun shade (canopy)
    (if wanted)   cat net
cot   safety harness
cot mattress with waterproof cover

Nappies

100 per cent cotton terry towelling. These consist of a large square which can be folded into a triangular or kite shape and pinned on the baby like a pair of pants. An alternative version now on sale is the padded triangular shape, which fits better but is more difficult to wash and takes longer to dry than a flat square. Cotton terry towelling is ideal for nappies because it absorbs a large quantity of fluid. It also washes easily and can be sterilised by boiling. Recently it has been possible to buy terry towelling nappies made of terylene, or of 50 per cent cotton and 50 per cent viscose. These are not suitable because of their poor absorbent qualities, although they wash and dry easily. When the baby passes urine, it is not absorbed into the fabric, but remains on the skin causing the nappy to rub, and results in a sore bottom.

The baby will need at least six clean nappies every day, so if they can be washed daily then twenty-four will be enough. However, if the mother's washing and drying facilities are poor, more will be required.

Muslin nappies. These are made of squares of muslin which can be folded in the same way as terry towelling nappies. They are very soft and light and can be washed and dried easily and quickly. Muslin nappies are useful for the very tiny baby, the baby with a very sensitive skin and the baby who lives in a hot climate. But they are not very absorbent because they are so thin, so they are mostly used as nappy liners for terry towelling nappies.

Disposable nappies. Nowadays these are mostly made of a pad of absorbent material with a plastic outer covering which does away with the need for pants. Instead of safety pins, small sticky tapes hold the nappy in position. These nappies are available in various sizes to ensure a snug fit. Disposable nappies are satisfactory in use, provided the manufacturers' instructions for disposal are carefully followed. They are invaluable when travelling or on holiday because of the time saved by not having to wash, dry and fold nappies. They are also hygienic because there is no need to carry soiled nappies home to wash. Disposables seem expensive, but if the cost is compared with the cost of conventional nappies, washing powder and electricity for washing machine and dryer, it will be found that there is very little difference. Moreover, if the time saved is spent with the baby, then the baby will derive considerable benefit.

Nappy liners. There are several types of liner available:
(a) Disposable tissues may be put inside the terry towelling nappy, to prevent it being badly soiled. The tissue and excreta can be shaken down the lavatory and flushed away, leaving only a wet nappy to wash.
(b) One-way liners may be washable or disposable. They allow urine to soak through to the outer nappy, whilst remaining dry themselves, so that the baby has a dry surface next to his skin. They are very useful at night because when

the baby stops his night feed, he will sleep through and not be disturbed by a wet nappy. They are also useful if the baby has a sore bottom owing to his concentrated urine affecting his skin.

Plastic pants
If conventional nappies are used, plastic pants will be needed, otherwise clothing and bedding become saturated every time the nappy is wet. They should be chosen with care, making sure that the leg holes are loose enough to allow some ventilation. The more expensive ones with adjustable side fastenings are best, not only for comfort, but also because the better-quality plastics are softer and can be washed many times without deteriorating.

Vests
As vests are worn next to the skin, they should be made of cotton or a wool/cotton mixture for comfort. The easiest ones to put on are those with an envelope-shaped neck which goes over the head.

Dresses, rompers, nightdresses
These can be obtained in various fabrics, and choice depends on time of the year and climate. Cotton, wool/cotton mixture or cotton/synthetic mixture are all suitable. The clothes should be easy to put on and do up. Sleeves should be wide-fitting, preferably raglan, and seams should be flat to avoid rubbing the skin.

All-over suits
These are very popular with mothers and have the advantage of being all in one. However if they are used there are three important points to consider:
(a) They must be big enough. The 'stretch' should only be used to allow a reasonable fit, because the baby will not be able to stretch the fabric himself – instead he will be restricted by the elasticity in the suit. If he cannot move freely he will lack exercise and can become very cold. He will also feel very frustrated. A baby's bones are very soft and a too-tight garment could cause deformed feet in the same way as badly fitting shoes or socks.
(b) They should be made from cotton or a cotton/nylon mixture for warmth and absorbency. All-nylon suits are not at all comfortable.
(c) They should not be used day and night, as the skin needs ventilation. So if they are worn during the night then a dress should be worn during the day, or vice versa.

Cardigans or jumpers
These may be hand-knitted or bought. Again, a wool/nylon mixture is better than an all-synthetic material. They should be knitted into a firm, close fabric rather than too much openwork, as the baby's fingers can get caught in the wool. Raglan style sleeves are easier to put on.

Sleeping bag/dressing gown
These are very useful garments, as they can be put on like a coat and closed like a

bag at the bottom. They can be used in the pram and at night so that it does not matter if blankets are kicked off – the baby will remain covered and warm. They are usually made of a brushed synthetic material and are satisfactory when worn over natural fabrics.

Bonnets, mittens and bootees
These can be hand-knitted or bought and should be made from wool or wool/nylon mixture.

Bibs and feeders
These are best made from cotton terry towelling. Plastic is not suitable because a plastic bib can easily flap up over the face and form a seal, causing suffocation.

Toiletries
These should be as plain as possible. There are many bath-time products on the market and mothers and nurses may find all the advertising claims confusing. As a general rule, a baby needs nothing other than a good baby soap for his skin, and this should be used sparingly and always well rinsed off. Baby shampoo is useful for hair washing, but again should be very well rinsed. Baby powder may be used for a light dusting after the bath. If the baby develops a dry skin, sore bottom or any other skin problem, medical advice should be sought before buying any of the preparations in the chemist's shop. A baby has very sensitive skin and can easily develop an allergy to an ingredient in a new product. Once an allergy develops, it may cause problems for the rest of his life. Some lotions, oils and creams even though promoted as being good for baby's skin, may contain complicated ingredients about which little is known of their effect on the human skin.

Cribs and cots
A crib is a small cot which may be used for the first two months of a baby's life. It is not essential and nowadays many babies go straight into a big cot. Some mothers use a carrycot placed inside the big cot for the first few weeks to make the baby feel secure.

Cots are covered by the British Standards Institution BS 1753 and there are several points which must be observed if the cot is to carry the 'kite' mark of the Institution.

(a) Spacing of bars – these should be not less than 7 cm (2¾ in) and not more than 7.6 cm (3 in) apart to prevent a child jamming his head between them.
(b) Cot sides should be 50 cm (20 in) high measured from the top of the mattress.
(c) Dropside fastening should be safe, so that the child cannot undo it.
(d) Paintwork should be lead-free.
(e) Mattress should be firm, so that the baby cannot bury his head.

A mattress with a waterproof covering is a good buy, as it saves having to use waterproof sheets. The sheets can be of cotton/polyester in summer and cotton flannelette in winter. Fitted cot sheets which fit over the mattress are very convenient and easy to use, so worth the extra cost.

Blankets can be of wool or a wool/synthetic mixture. Cellular blankets are good because they are light in weight and warm. The warmth is due to the fact that the tiny holes trap air which acts as an insulator. Many shops sell baby duvets, but these are not suitable as they are lightweight and not tucked in, so could easily slip over the baby's face and cause suffocation. Similarly, 'baby nests' are not suitable for use in a cot or pram where the baby is left alone to sleep.

The pram
The pram chosen depends on the use made of it. There are many types on the market from very large to very small. If the pram is to be used for long shopping expeditions and walking out, then a large one, which is well sprung, would be the best choice. On the other hand, if the mother drives and wants to take the baby in the car, the type of pram which divides into a carrycot and folding wheels would be the better choice.

Again the British Standards Institution has various regulations about prams:

(a) Material used should be physically and chemically free from substances harmful to the child.
(b) Materials used should be resistant to normal weather conditions and use.
(c) Materials should be reasonably non-flammable.
(d) Brakes should be on at least two wheels and should be out of reach of the child.
(e) Wheels should be strong and well attached.
(f) Provision should be made for fitting a safety harness.
(g) Padding should be firm to prevent suffocation.
(h) Hood should be positioned to deflect rain.
(i) Inside depth should be at least 19 cm ($7\frac{1}{2}$ in) above the mattress.
(j) Design of the pram should ensure maximum stability.
(k) Soft-body prams should have fittings which are safe and will not become detached from the chassis or allow the body to fold up during use.

In addition, a shopping tray which fits under the pram, across the axles, is safer than one fixed to the handlebars, as the weight is distributed more evenly. A cat net is necessary to prevent a cat getting into the pram to sleep and so smother the baby. In summer a fitted canopy will protect the baby from direct sunshine.

The pram mattress should be firm and waterproof. Sheets and blankets are necessary, the same as those needed for the cot. As a general rule three covers are needed over the baby, as well as a sheet, so that two pram blankets and a coverlet are sufficient. In the early days a baby does not need a pillow at all, but from about four months will like to be propped up when awake to see what is going on in the world. A special 'safety' pillow can be used for this. He will need a safety harness from about eight weeks of age, because of his increasing mobility.

The baby's room
When planning the room, allowance should be made for the baby's growing interests and future activity. If possible, it should be a bright, sunny room with adequate space for play.

Walls – bright and colourful; washable; area for pictures, including child's own paintings later; area at child level can be painted with blackboard paint when baby is old enough to use chalk.

Ceiling – white will reflect light; a hanging mobile within child's field of vision.

Floor – cork tiles, plastic or linoleum are all easy to clean and provide a good surface when child is learning to walk; colourful, washable rug.

Windows – large, providing adequate ventilation; guarded by bars for safety; curtains in light, washable materials, lined to keep out light when baby sleeps.

Heating – if possible a steady background heat is best. Safety factors are important here. In order of choice
(a) central heating radiators;
(b) oil-filled electric radiators;
(c) fan heater;
(d) open coal fire with an adequate safety guard.

Lighting – a central light; a bedside lamp for reading.

Furniture – this should be both sturdy and washable, as the child will pull himself to his feet by holding on to it. In addition to the cot, bath on stand and low chair: a chest of drawers for baby's clothes; a hanging cupboard; a low cupboard for the baby's toys; a low table and chairs will be useful later; a screen can protect the baby from draughts – this can be improvised by covering a two-winged clothes airer with material.

Exercise 3

Multiple-choice questions
1. The most reliable indication of pregnancy is:
(a) morning sickness;   (c) missed period;
(b) fainting;   (d) frequency of passing urine.

2. A routine blood-test is carried out in early pregnancy to:
(a) check blood-pressure;   (c) discover the baby's blood group;
(b) see if there is any infection;   (d) check whether mother is anaemic.

3. When a woman is pregnant she is advised to:
(a) rest as much as possible;   (c) refrain from intercourse;
(b) carry on normal life,   (d) eat for two.
    taking care not to get too tired;

4. It is best to use a fabric containing natural fibres for a baby's clothes because:
(a) it washes easily;   (c) it looks pretty;
(b) it is absorbent;   (d) it comes in a variety of colours.

5. Two thin layers of clothing are better than one thick layer because:

(a) they look nicer;
(b) they are warmer;
(c) thin clothes are cheaper;
(d) they are more absorbent;
(e) they are easier to wash and dry.

Essay questions
6. What is the aim of ante-natal care, and how is this achieved? List the statutory services available to pregnant women in Britain.

7. Plan a room suitable as a nursery for a new-born baby. How could it 'grow' with the baby?

Project
8. Visit the local shops and choose a suitable layette. Give reasons for your choice of each item, including the material it is made from and the cost. Compare the cost of using conventional nappies and laundering with the estimated cost of disposable nappies.

Suggestions for further reading

D.H.S.S. Leaflet, *Maternity Benefits*
Anna Coote and Tess Gill, *Women's Rights*, Penguin Books Ltd

Chapter 4
Parenthood

The birth of a baby

By the time an unborn baby has reached the thirty-eighth week he is usually in the head-down position ready for birth and the mother will have already experienced minor contractions and relaxations of the muscles of the uterus. Like all muscle fibres, the uterine ones shorten (contract) and lengthen (relax) in use, but in labour these fibres gradually shorten altogether because when they relax they do not lengthen as much as before. The process of birth consists of the gradual shortening of the muscle fibres which cause the cervix to 'thin' out and slowly open to enable the baby to pass through. At the same time the baby's head is being pushed down into the vagina by the pressure of the contractions and later in labour by active pushing by the mother. The birth of a baby is a long, slow process, and may be painful for the mother, although the amount of pain varies. The birth of a first baby takes on average fourteen hours and for a second and subsequent child it could take about eight hours.

Labour is described as being in three stages:

1. first stage – this is the longest part and lasts until the cervix is open;

2. second stage – the baby is pushed out;

3. third stage – the placenta or afterbirth is expelled.

1. First stage. There are three possible ways in which labour begins and a mother is advised to contact her doctor/midwife or hospital when any of these things happens:

(a) the onset of contractions occurring at regular intervals and gradually becoming more frequent;
(b) a 'show' – a small plug or blood-stained mucus which blocks the cervix comes away as the cervix opens (this is not always noticed);
(c) the membranes rupture ('breaking of the waters') and some of the fluid surrounding the baby gushes out of the vagina.

During this stage the mother will experience some discomfort as the contractions become more frequent. At first it helps if the mother moves around, but towards the end of this stage she will probably place herself in the most comfortable position. Discomfort varies from mild cramp to real pain. Relaxation exercises may relieve this; otherwise various drugs can be given, including gas and air administered by the mother herself. Sometimes a local anaesthetic is injected into the space around the spinal cord to block off the pain messages. This is known as an epidural.

2. Second stage. At the end of the first stage when the cervix is fully-dilated (open) the mother usually experiences a great urge to push down with her abdominal muscles when each contraction occurs. The vagina gradually stretches as the baby's head is pushed down the canal and outside the mother's body. After the head is born, there is a pause and then with another contraction and push from the mother the rest of the baby is born. This second stage may take about twenty minutes. The baby usually cries immediately. The midwife will clean his eyes and mouth with swabs and separate him from the placenta by tying the umbilical cord in two places with catgut (or synthetic material) and cutting between the ties, or she may use a clip. He is very quickly examined, wrapped in a wrapper and given to his mother to hold.

3. Third stage. There is a slightly longer pause and then the mother feels another contraction and the placenta is pushed out of the vagina. Sometimes the midwife or doctor will help this by pulling gently on the umbilical cord. There may be some bleeding at this stage from the raw area in the wall of the uterus left by the placenta. The uterus rapidly contracts, which prevents further bleeding. Sometimes a drug is administered to the mother to accelerate this contraction.

After the birth is completed the baby's condition is assessed at one minute, five minutes and ten minutes, using the APGAR score (see page 51). Then he is weighed and measured and examined for any defects. He is labelled with a bracelet which gives his name, sex, date and time of birth. A label is also prepared for his cot which will be ready and waiting for him. His mother is encouraged to cuddle him and check for herself that the label is correct and that he is a normal, healthy baby. This is very important for 'bonding' to begin. Not only does a baby need to 'know' his mother, but she needs to get to know her baby. Father is usually present at this time even if he chose not to be there at the birth.

Other methods of birth

1. Induction. Birth can be induced by rupturing the membranes around baby, or by giving the mother an artificial hormone which stimulates contractions of the uterus. This is done mainly for one of three reasons:
(a) The baby is overdue – about a week after the EDD.
(b) The mother has toxaemia so the birth is induced early (from 3–8 weeks) to avoid complications.
(c) The placenta is beginning to fail.

2. Episiotomy. A small cut, called an episiotomy, may be made in the mother's vagina to ease the birth and prevent tearing. It has to be stitched under local anaesthetic after the birth.

3. Forceps delivery. If progress is slow in the second stage of labour, or if either baby or mother is showing signs of distress, the doctor may decide to use forceps, a pair of large blades which can be put around the baby's head. The doctor can then guide the head and ease it out of the vagina. This is usually performed under a local anaesthetic and an episiotomy is needed before inserting the forceps.

4. Caesarean section. If, for some reason, the baby cannot be born through the vagina, then under an anaesthetic an incision is made through the mother's abdomen and the wall of her uterus and the baby is extracted. The placenta is also removed and then the incision is stitched up. The mother is usually in hospital some days longer and the baby may need special care for a short time, but usually both recover reasonably rapidly. Reasons for caesarean births vary, but the most common reason is that the mother's bony pelvis is too small for the baby's head to pass through. Another reason is that the placenta may be positioned in the lower part of the uterus, preventing the baby's head from advancing.

5. Breech birth. Sometimes a baby does not settle in the head-down position, but instead 'sits upright' in the uterus so that his bottom is ready to be born first. Usually this can be diagnosed in the middle months of pregnancy and the baby can be turned by pushing him through the mother's abdomen. If the mother goes into labour with a breech baby, there may be complications because when the body is born the baby may take a breath before his head is out of the vagina. Other complications, such as early separation of the placenta or compression of the umbilical cord, may cause brain damage by starving the baby of his oxygen supply.

The post-natal period

Although most mothers appear exhausted at the time of birth, because it is a period of hard work, the majority recover almost immediately. They see their baby – and it has all been worth while! However, a period of rest is necessary and usually the baby is placed in a warm cot whilst his mother is given a blanket bath and then a cup of tea. She is left then to rest and if she is too excited to sleep a sedative may be given.

The following day she can begin to care for her baby, whilst she herself is being cared for by the midwife. During the next six to ten days the mother and baby get to know one another. The mother's uterus gradually contracts to its original size and the raw area of the placental site heals up. There is a small vaginal loss which gradually ceases. A watch is kept for any fresh bleeding which indicates that the healing process is not taking place. A check is also kept on the mother's temperature, as a rise could indicate infection entering the raw area in the uterus. Strict hygiene measures are practised to prevent such infection which can have serious consequences for a mother.

The mother is encouraged to practise post-natal exercises to 'tone up' her muscles and help her regain her figure. Breast-feeding begins with the help and supervision of the midwife. The baby is weighed at regular intervals and, after a small initial loss, should begin to gain about 28 g (1 oz) a day if feeding is adequate.

Also during this period, mothers are shown how to care for their babies. Bathing, changing and topping and tailing, sterilising bottles and making up feeds are all demonstrated. As soon as the mother is able and confident, she is encouraged to change her baby and look after him. The baby's umbilical cord gradually shrivels up and usually falls off between the fifth and seventh day. In the meantime it must be kept dry to prevent infection so a special powder is used, and, in some hospitals, the baby is not bathed until the cord is off.

Before being discharged from hospital or care of the midwife, the baby is given a complete examination to ensure that there are no defects, because many of these can be put right at this early stage. The mother is also examined and given an appointment for a post-natal examination six weeks after the birth.

Any creative process is hard work. Not only has the mother created a new baby who has brought awesome responsibilities, but her body has undergone a tremendous change.

Following the long period of expectation, it is understandable if she should now experience a sense of anti-climax. The hormonal changes, as her body goes back to normal, cause mood swings which may make her suffer from depression. Both she and her husband may fail to understand the physical origin of these feelings, especially as the common belief is that her prevailing mood should be one of elation. Relatives and visitors tend to concentrate on the lovely baby and seldom ask the mother how she is.

Few married couples realise what is in store for them. The physical demands of the baby can be exhausting. He will need four-hourly feeds round the clock at first, and as each feed takes at least half an hour, this is a large proportion of the day. There are the additional household duties – washing, ironing, etc. – besides the usual cleaning and meal preparation. Some mothers feel overwhelmed at first by the amount of work involved. There is little energy left for the mother to treat her husband as she did before. It requires a mature man to accept this and realise that it is a temporary state of affairs. Satisfactory sexual relationships may not be resumed as soon as the husband would like, which could cause rifts. Again, the man needs to exercise tolerance and understanding.

He may have to overcome jealousy and resentment at this small creature taking over the home. Some men are unable to adapt, and react by abdicating their responsibility as a parent and resuming their former social pastimes. The mother, at this stage, is wary of baby-sitting arrangements, and in any case, lacks the energy to join her husband. This can lead to further tensions.

Fortunately most parents do adapt. The pleasure from having created a family more than counteracts the problems. If the marriage was good to begin with, the child will cement the relationship.

In the past twenty years there has been a blurring of mother and father roles, and therefore a revolution in the position of the father. Now it is accepted that he should be involved in all aspects of the ante-natal preparation, birth and ensuing care of the baby. Fathers involved in this way are found to have a much closer bond with both wife and child, leading to a close family relationship. It is important that the mother does not become so wrapped up in the baby that she excludes the father from these activities. The mother of the family is the pivot around which the family revolves, and from now on her attitudes will chart the family's future.

Her physical health is of prime importance. If at all possible, help should be provided for her during the first weeks of the baby's life. Often there is a relative able and willing to help at this time. Failing this, the social services department of the local authority can provide a home help on a doctor's recommendation.

Payment is according to family income. This help relieves the mother of some of the household duties so that she can concentrate on the baby, and both she and her husband can enjoy him to the full.

The health visitor will visit after the tenth day to give advice on the care and health of mother and baby. She is a trained nurse with midwifery experience and special training in the care and development of children and the promotion of good health. She is usually attached to the practice of the mother's family doctor and visits all babies and children on his list. By law all births must be notified to the local authority which informs the health visitor responsible, so that she can visit the mother as soon as possible after her return from hospital. In many cases she will already be known to the mother because she has paid ante-natal visits or been involved in parentcraft classes. When she calls the health visitor will invite the mother to attend the local child health clinic to have the baby's development assessed. During the next five years she can, if needed, be a great source of support to the family.

Six weeks after the birth, the mother should attend a post-natal clinic where she is given a physical examination to ensure that her body has returned to its pre-pregnant state. Her doctor may check for anaemia, which is often the cause of tiredness after childbirth. This is an ideal time for the mother to be given family planning advice so that she can space her family.

Most doctors recommend a two-year gap between babies, but of course this is largely a matter of personal preference, and the mother's ability to cope. Other factors affecting parents' decisions here include the economic circumstances of the family, whether the mother is planning to return to her former career, the ages of the parents, and the ultimate size of the family they hope to have.

The growing family

Another period of adaptation for the family occurs when the second baby is born. Wisely and sensitively handled, this can be a happy and rewarding time for all concerned. It must be remembered, however, that for the first child it could be traumatic. From being the focus of all the parents' love and attention, he has to adjust to being one of a pair.

With the young child (under five) lengthy explanations about the coming baby are unnecessary. Once the pregnancy has been established at about three months, casual references to babies can be brought into conversation with both parents. There are many children's books dealing with the subject, but they should be carefully chosen to suit the child's age and understanding. Opportunities to admire babies seen on shopping expeditions, outings to the park, etc., can be used. The wise mother will not mention the new baby as though he will be a ready-made playmate. This can lead to deep disappointment. The child can be involved in practical preparations for the baby. If any equipment used for the child is to be passed on, the transfer should be done well in advance – for example, the change from cot to bed. Any other major changes in the child's future life – for instance, starting playgroup or nursery school – should also be planned in advance so as not to coincide with the actual birth. Arrangements for the care of the child during the mother's confinement should be carefully considered, especially if the child is to leave his home. The inevitable separation from mother can be made easier by accustoming him to short periods in other homes without her.

The ideal arrangement for the birth is that the baby is born at home and the older child can remain in his own home with a familiar adult. However, most doctors prefer the baby to be born in hospital, even if the mother comes home within forty-eight hours. In any case, for the child it is best to stay in his own home. If this is not possible, then the home he goes to should be one he knows.

As soon as possible after the birth of the baby, he should see his mother. Nowadays hospitals are aware of the bond between mother and child and allow unrestricted visiting. The reunion of mother and child is most important to establish the relationship; time together is needed before the introduction of the baby. Some parents like to present the child with a special gift at this time. A doll can be particularly useful in preparing the child for sharing later in the care of the real baby.

Many children find it hard to cope with their jealous feelings on seeing the closeness between mother and baby, particularly during breast-feeding and bathing. This may lead to difficult behaviour and is commonly seen in children under stress. A reversion to baby ways, such as wetting, soiling, refusing food and bedtime mutiny, may occur. This is known as regressive behaviour and can be exceedingly trying, both to the harassed mother and staff at the nursery, who frequently see children undergoing this stress in the family. The child strives by any means to gain extra love and attention. Understanding adults will realise that this is a normal and transitory stage. The child should be helped to overcome his feelings, not by punishment or projecting guilt feelings on to him, but by making time to give him complete individual attention. In the home, the father can help a great deal by showing the child the delights of being the older one. With care and forethought, the baby can to a large extent be fitted into the existing routine of the family, thus minimising disturbance to the older child. Visitors to the family can assist by showing attention to the child before going to the baby and by refraining from comments and criticisms of the child's behaviour. Great toler-ance, self-control and understanding are required of all concerned adults at this time. When the child makes himself most unlovable that is when he most needs love. Physical contact, cuddles and spoken assurances of love will go a long way to counter his temporary insecurity. So will a retained 'special' bedtime routine with stories, etc., difficult though it may be to keep going. Play materials which lend themselves to expressed aggression and anger, such as dough, woodwork, sand, earth, hammer toys and so forth are also beneficial as they healthily channel the hate and resentment away from baby. Even so, it is not wise to trust the child alone with the baby. Mothers often deceive themselves that *their* child feels only love towards the new baby; even if this is so, the young child has no idea of how to express that love safely. Violent rocking, and embracing which is more akin to throttling are common; so is the 'sharing' of wildly unsuitable play materials. Fortunately babies are tough creatures and, happily, survive much rough handling, but it is sensible to avoid situations which could give rise to anxiety and tension on the mother's part, and guilt and feelings of rejection on the child's.

A nursery nurse seeking a position as nanny will often be taken on by a family at this very time. She would do well to remember that the child is being expected to accept another new face at this critical stage, and moreover will be 'forced' into her company for long periods, when he would probably much rather be with Mummy or Daddy. She may also have to cope with expectations of grandparents, and possible tension between adults in the family. She must remember the need for consistent handling of the child and must realise how badly he needs frequent contact with his mother, and assurances of what a valued member of the family he is. The baby will not suffer from a little 'neglect' at this stage; her prime concern should be the well-being of the older child. Extra trouble taken and understanding shown now will pay dividends in terms of adjustment and happiness of the whole family in the months to come.

Exercise 4

Multiple-choice questions
1. How long after the birth should the mother undergo a post-natal examination?
(a) two weeks;
(b) two months;
(c) six weeks;
(d) not at all, as long as she feels fit.

2. A two-year-old exhibits regressive behaviour after the birth of his sister. To deal with him you, as mother or nanny should:
(a) explain carefully to him why such behaviour is not acceptable;
(b) tell him he is a big boy now;
(c) ensure individual time and attention for him when the baby is asleep;
(d) find a relative or friend to take him out of the way as much as possible.

3. Who is the most appropriate person from whom to seek advice about a two-week-old baby with feeding problems?
(a) midwife;
(b) hospital;
(c) grandmother;
(d) health visitor.

Essay questions
4. What factors would influence parents planning the timing of their second baby?

5. How should a mother prepare a child of two for the birth of a brother or sister?

Project
6. Follow the developments, in a family you know well, during and after the arrival of a second child. Note especially the domestic arrangements at the time of the birth and the older child's reaction. Study the parts played by all adults in contact with the family to help them at this period.

The APGAR Score: an assessment of the condition of the newborn baby based on normal expectations

APGAR Score	Score 0	Score 1	Score 2	1 min.	Score at 5 min.	10 min.
1. Heart rate	absent	below 100	over 100			
2. Respiratory effort	absent	irregular, slow or weak	lusty cry, good chest movement			
3. Muscle tone (in all four limbs)	limp	poor tone, some movement	active resistance, strong movement			
4. Reflex irritability (response to flicking soles of feet)	no response	slight withdrawal	vigorous withdrawal of leg, strong cry			
5. Colour	blue or pale	body pink, extremities blue	completely pink			
			Total scores			

The maximum score is 10 and if the score is less than 7 at 1 minute, less than 8 at 5 minutes, or less than 10 at 10 minutes, it will indicate the need for special care and a close follow-up during the baby's early years.

Suggestions for further reading

Claire Rayner, *Family Feelings*, Arrow Books Ltd
Sylvia Close, *Toddler and the New Baby*, Routledge & Kegan Paul Ltd

Chapter 5
Care of the young baby

Attending to a baby's needs

A newborn baby's needs are simple, but urgent and of vital importance. They appear to be mainly physical but, in keeping him clean, fed and comfortable, we are fulfilling other basic needs as well.

To achieve and maintain physical and mental health, all human beings, whatever their ages, have certain basic needs:

Physical	*Mental and emotional*
1. food	9. security
2. cleanliness	10. affection
3. rest	11. stimulation
4. exercise	12. social contacts
5. fresh air	13. independence
6. warmth	
7. medical care	
8. protection from infection and injury	

Obviously, these will sometimes overlap, and during babyhood and childhood the emphasis may move from one aspect to another, but the basic needs will remain the same throughout life. So, when we plan the daily care of a baby, we must ensure that all his needs are covered. This planning is especially important in busy nurseries where a 'good' baby could easily be overlooked.

In practice it is difficult to separate the physical care from the mental and emotional needs but, for the sake of clarity, each will be dealt with separately, remembering that they all contribute to the proper care of the baby.

1. Food (See Chapter 6 for greater detail). Most normal babies will want to be fed approximately every four hours, and any routine planned would have to be arranged around the feeding schedule. Usually babies are settled into a routine before leaving hospital or the care of the midwife. Commonly this means that feeds are given at 6.00 a.m., 10.00 a.m., 2.00 p.m., 6.00 p.m. and 10.00 p.m. (and 2.00 a.m. also, if necessary). There is no need to be rigid about these times, but obviously the baby must fit in with the mother's (nursery nurse's) routine and she has other duties as well as the care of her baby.

As a general rule, if the baby wakes and cries more than three hours since his last feed, it is better to feed him early rather than let him cry until feed-time. If it is less than three hours since the last feed, then he is probably thirsty, or may need attention. He should be offered cool, boiled water, and be picked up and comforted. Should early waking and crying occur often, then it would be wise to add an extra 25 mls (1 oz) of milk to his bottle if he is bottle-fed. The breast-fed baby may need some extra milk, too. On the other hand, if the baby sleeps for more than five hours after a feed (except in the middle of the night) then he should be woken and offered his feed, because sleeping for such a long period may be an indication that he is ill.

As the baby grows older, he will establish his own pattern of feeding and sleeping, and his mother (nursery nurse) should adapt to this and become more flexible. Breast-feeding enables a mother to be more flexible over the feeding routine, but she still needs a framework so that she has time for her other duties.

2. Cleanliness. Cleanliness is very important to the health of a small baby because he is vulnerable to infection. He has not had time to build up his own resistance to infection, and the resistance inherited from his mother is by no means complete. Therefore, he needs to be protected from as many germs as possible. Germs live on our skin and all around us, especially in dirt, so cleanliness of the baby and his surroundings will help to reduce the risk of infection. The skin also needs to be kept clean to enable it to carry out its function to excrete waste products.

A high standard of personal hygiene is necessary in a person caring for a young baby, as germs can easily be passed on by dirty hands and dirty habits. It is even more important when babies are in nurseries, because infection can also be spread from one baby to another by the hands of the nurse. Handwashing by mother (nursery nurse) before handling the baby, before preparing his feed, and after changing his nappy is essential and should become an automatic action.

The baby's surroundings should be kept clean:

(a) His room should be cleaned daily and well ventilated because sunlight kills germs and fresh air will dilute their numbers.
(b) His cot and pram should be cleaned regularly, and the bedding changed frequently.
(c) Clothes need to be changed morning and evening.
(d) His nappy should be changed whenever necessary, and at least every four hours.
(e) Clothing and nappies should be washed daily and rinsed well and, if possible, dried in the open air.
(f) Nappies need to be boiled or treated with a sanitising preparation to kill germs.
(g) Special care is needed with feeding equipment which must be cleaned and sterilised after each use.
(h) Cleanliness for the baby should be incorporated in his daily routine.

Bathing baby
He will need a bath or all-over wash at one end of the day, and a 'top and tail' at the other end. This can be fitted in with the mother's (nursery nurse's) preference. Some mothers prefer to bath their babies in the morning before the 10.00 a.m. feed. Other mothers prefer the evening because Dad wants to be involved and he is often only available at this time of day. If the baby is restless

and miserable in the evening, a bath may soothe him and can be a good preliminary to bedtime. When the baby gets older and begins to crawl, the evening is probably the best time for his bath, because he can get so dirty playing on the floor that this is the best way to clean him. Whenever the bath is given it is best to choose a time just before a feed, rather than after, because he needs peace and sleep following the feed to enable digestion to take place.

Bath time has other values as well as cleanliness. It is a time of contact between mother and baby when affection is shown and there is much shared enjoyment. It is also an opportunity for exercise as the baby is able to kick and splash the water with great enjoyment.

There are many variations in methods of bathing a baby, and most young mothers are shown at least one way. Some adults prefer to stand up to bath a baby, so the bath is placed on a table and a changing-pad is used beside the bath to undress the baby. Another method is for the mother (nursery nurse) to sit in a low chair with the bath on a stand in front of her. The baby is undressed on his mother's lap. This latter method gives the close contact that the baby needs and is more natural. However, many new mothers feel very unsure of their ability to hold the baby on their knees and, if this is the case, they may feel safer in using the table method.

Sitting method:
   (1) Ensure room is warm – close windows and check the temperature. It should be about 21°C (70°F).
   (2) Collect all the equipment needed:

low chair	soap
bath on stand	cotton-wool swabs in
bucket with lid for soiled nappy	covered container
container for other washing	paper bag for used swabs
set of clean clothes, including	shampoo
nappy	talcum powder (if wanted)
mother's apron	brush and comb
towel	nail scissors.

   (3) Have baby's feed ready, if bottle-fed.
   (4) Wash hands.
   (5) Put some cold water in the bath.
   (6) Add hot water to make the bath water the correct temperature. Either use a thermometer 38°–40°C (100°–105°F), or test with bare elbow when water should feel pleasantly warm.
   (7) Put on apron.
   (8) Pick up baby and undress to nappy.
   (9) Wrap baby in towel, keeping his arms inside.
  (10) Using first a swab dampened with bath water, then a dry one, wipe each eye separately from the nose outwards. Discard each swab after one wipe.
  (11) Wash face with a damp swab. Wipe around nose and ears but do not probe into them.
  (12) Dry face with corner of towel.
  (13) Hold the baby under the neck and shoulders with one hand, and tuck his

legs under your arms so that you can hold his head over the bath. Using your other hand, scoop up bath water to wet his hair. Add a small amount of shampoo, then wash head thoroughly by rubbing this in. Then rinse well.

(14) Move baby back on to your lap and dry his hair with the corner of the towel. NB: The shampoo should only be used once or twice a week because it tends to dry the scalp.

(15) Unwrap towel around baby and remove nappy.

(16) Place nappy in bucket with lid.

(17) If nappy is soiled, clean baby's bottom with swabs.

(18) Soap both hands and massage all over the baby's body, making sure the lather reaches all the creases – neck, under-arms, groin and between fingers and toes.

(19) Grasping the baby securely by putting one wrist and hand under his neck and shoulders and holding the arm furthest away, use the other hand to hold his legs. Lift him into the bath, releasing his legs when he is fully in the bath so that he is in a half-sitting position.

(20) The free hand can then be used to splash and rinse off all the soapy lather.

(21) If the baby is happy in the bath, let him kick and splash for a few minutes – this time should be increased as he gets older.

(22) Lift him out on to your lap and wrap loosely in the towel.

(23) Pat, rather than rub, him dry, making sure that he is dry in the creases.

(24) Discard damp towel.

(25) Smooth on a little talcum powder.

(26) Put nappy on first.

(27) Dress him and give him his bottle.

Method of 'top and tail':

(1) Collect equipment:
    bowl of warm water
    cotton-wool swabs
    paper bag for discarded swabs
    soap
    talcum
    towel
    clean clothes
    low chair and table
    nappy bucket with lid
    container for soiled clothes.

(2) Wash hands.

(3) Spread towel on lap and undress baby to nappy.

(4) Clean face with damp cotton-wool swabs, and dry.

(5) Clean hands of baby with swabs.

(6) Put on clean vest.

(7) Remove nappy and place in bucket with lid.

(8) If soiled, clean bottom with cotton-wool swabs.

(9) Rub soap on one hand and use this to wash nappy area thoroughly.

(10) Rinse with swabs, or a flannel may be used.

(11) Dry with towel.

(12) Smooth on a little talcum.

(13) Put on clean nappy.

(14) Complete dressing.

3. Rest – sleep. Many 'experts' claim that a young baby will sleep twenty hours a day. However, close observation of babies reveals that they vary considerably in the amount of sleep needed. A newborn baby invariably falls asleep after a feed, and should be allowed to sleep in reasonably quiet surroundings as long as he will. Many babies 'cat-nap' during the day, and when awake are content to lie watching any movement or activity around them and then fall asleep again. Crying is usually because of boredom. Therefore it is important to provide visual stimulus in the baby's surroundings to interest him when awake. His room should be colourful, with hanging mobiles moving in the air. When he is outside in his pram, put it where he can see something interesting, such as branches of a tree.

As he gets older, his periods of wakefulness become longer, and he is best put to sleep near mother or nurse during the day so that she can talk to him when he is awake. Normal household noises should not disturb him and this is better than leaving him isolated in his room. If he has enough stimulation and contact with others during the day, he should sleep well at night. It is wise to begin a regular bedtime routine because this establishes the habit of sleep. A bath or 'top and tail' can be followed by feeding and winding, and then he can be put into his cot in his own room, with a cuddle and perhaps a lullaby from nurse/mother. This will all suggest to him that it is time to go to sleep. He should then be left alone, someone should be within hearing distance. If nurse/mother hovers over him to see if he will sleep, he soon begins to realise that it is easy to get attention. Many babies have a 'sleep' cry, so if he does not settle at once it is worth waiting five minutes before going to him. Of course, he should not be allowed to get too distressed and if he is still crying after five minutes, check that he is not uncomfortable. Staying with him for a while may be necessary but he should not be taken to wherever he spends his daytime hours, or he will come to want this every night.

In the early weeks the baby may wake at four-hourly intervals for a feed but, surprisingly quickly, will adapt to night-time sleeping as soon as he is able to take enough food during the day.

4. Exercise. All babies need exercise because this encourages good circulation which, in turn, improves muscle-tone, and aids development of muscles.

All movement, including crying, is exercise, and opportunity must be given for this. The baby's clothes should be loose enough to allow free movement, especially of arms and legs. Bed clothes should not be tucked in so tightly that movement is hampered.

In the past, babies were 'swaddled' most of the day and night. They were wrapped up very tightly in a shawl, or even sewn into their clothes. It was thought that this would make a baby feel more secure. Certainly, some babies will sleep better when wrapped up, but it is no coincidence that since the practice of swaddling was abandoned, babies have shown earlier motor development. When a baby is learning to move and control his body, he needs plenty of opportunity to practise. Therefore, at some time during the day, he should be placed on a rug on the floor, without his nappy, so that he can kick and move freely. In summertime this can be done outdoors. When the baby is in his bath, time should be allowed for him to kick and splash.

As the baby gets older, and stays awake for longer periods, more of his time should be spent on the floor. A play-pen can be used for short periods, but it is better to remove valuable or dangerous objects from the room and give the child freedom to explore, roll over and pull himself up on the furniture rather than imprison him in a small area.

5. Fresh air. We all need fresh air to provide oxygen. When air is trapped in a house it becomes stale. After it has been breathed out it contains more water vapour, more carbon-dioxide and it is much warmer. There is still a good proportion of oxygen, so the effects of poor ventilation are mainly due to increased warmth and moisture which cause an unpleasant humidity. As humidity increases, human beings become distressed and, if left in these conditions for long, can become ill and eventually die. The humidity supplies micro-organisms with ideal conditions to multiply rapidly. This is why infection can spread so easily in poorly-ventilated rooms. It is especially important for the nursery nurse to be aware of this in a nursery where several babies are together in the same room.

Babies' rooms should be aired thoroughly at least once during the day by opening windows and doors to create a strong draught. There should always be a window or ventilator open, except in very cold weather. The baby should be protected from draughts by a screen.

The baby should be taken out into the fresh air every day except in extremely cold or foggy weather. In the summer he can sleep in his pram in the garden during the day.

Sunlight is very beneficial to all human beings, but care should be taken when exposing a baby to the sun. His skin must become accustomed to sunlight gradually, to avoid sunburn, so he should be protected from very hot sunshine by a sun-shade on his pram, and a hat. Starting with five minutes exposure one can increase the length of time by five minutes every day as appropriate.

6. Warmth. The new baby, emerging from the constantly controlled warmth of the uterus, has little ability to maintain that temperature for himself. His temperature-regulating mechanism is very immature and will not become fully effective for many months. In addition, he has a relatively large skin area in proportion to his weight and so can rapidly lose body heat by evaporation from the skin when exposed to cold air. As small babies do not move a lot, they will not generate much heat from exercise, either. It is important to realise that a baby who is cold can rapidly become colder. Unfortunately, the cold baby does not look cold and does not usually protest. In fact, he appears to be contented and has a healthy pink colour. It is possible for his condition to be overlooked so that he develops hypothermia, which can lead to death if undetected.

The baby should, therefore, be kept in warm surroundings, especially in the early weeks. His room should be at a temperature of 21°C (70°F) for the first two weeks of life, then it can be reduced to 18°C (65°F). A check should be kept on the temperature, especially during the night, to ensure that it does not drop below 16°C (60°F). The ideal form of warmth is central heating, but a guarded nursery fire or fan-heater would be suitable. With constant heating the room must not be allowed to become too dry – a bowl of water placed near the heat source will prevent this.

The baby's pram should be sturdy and weatherproof, and his clothing should be loose and thin to prevent restriction of movement. Natural fibres such as wool and cotton are warmer than man-made fibres such as nylon, courtelle, polyester and acrilan. Two thin layers are better than one thick one, because air trapped between the layers acts as insulation. The baby should be warm when his clothes are put on, or the clothes will only serve to keep him cold. The cot or pram can be pre-warmed in cold weather by a hot water bottle which is removed before the baby is put in. When bathing or exercising a baby, make sure the room is warm and after the bath dry him and dress him quickly. The clothes can be warmed before use on a radiator or in front of the fire. The baby should wear a bonnet when outdoors in cooler weather, as he can lose a lot of heat from his bare head. A sleeping-bag/dressing gown is useful at night, so that if the baby kicks off his blankets, he is still covered. He should not be put outdoors in very cold or foggy weather because breathing cold air will chill him rapidly, even if warmly clad.

To test whether a baby is warm enough, it is best to put a hand under the covers and feel his abdomen and chest which should be pleasantly warm to touch. Babies' hands and feet often feel cold, so are not a good indication of internal temperatures. If the baby is very cold, the best way to warm him up is to cuddle him, meanwhile raising the temperature in the room. Do not wrap him in more blankets, as these will only keep him cold. If he is very cold and unresponsive, then medical aid should be summoned as fast as possible.

7. Medical supervision. A baby is usually given a thorough examination after birth to ensure, as far as possible, that he is healthy and has no defects. Specific tests can be carried out for phenylketonuma, hypothyroidism, and dislocatable hips, all of which can be corrected at this early stage. Although it is rare to find anything wrong, it is worth examining all babies for the sake of the few who may have a defect which can probably be put right at this early stage. Even if the defect cannot be put right, it may be possible to prevent it getting worse, or to lessen the effects.

Most doctors like to examine a baby at intervals throughout the first five years, to ensure that he is developing in the normal way. Usually such examinations take place at these stages: six weeks, nine months, two years and three and a half years. In some areas some of the tests are carried out by health visitors in the home, otherwise a clinical medical officer will do the tests in the Child Health Clinic. Some general practitioners have extra training so that they can test children registered with them.

Various tests can be given at different stages. For example, between six and eight months a hearing test can be carried out to ascertain whether the child has any defect of hearing. If there is such a defect, then he can be fitted with a hearing-aid, and, even if the aid does not wholly overcome the baby's deafness, it will still be immensely valuable if it lets him hear some sounds. A baby who has never heard any sounds at all will have great difficulty with language development.

Soon after birth the health visitor will call to see the mother and baby. At the first visit she will check that the mother and baby are well, and advise on the care of the baby, if the mother needs any help. Her aim is to be a friend of the family and, by giving the mother help and advice, make sure that the baby grows and develops into a healthy individual.

A health visitor is a state registered nurse who has had extra training and experience in child development and family welfare. Besides visiting the mothers at intervals, she also runs the local Well Baby Clinics and invites mothers to attend there with their babies. At the clinic the babies can be weighed and progress is checked, while mothers can meet and compare notes. This can give reassurance to a mother and help to make friends for herself and her child.

Signs of good health

clear firm skin	taking feeds well	interested
good colour	sleeping well	contented
bright eyes	a slow, steady weight	normal development for
shiny hair	gain	age
firm muscles	alert	

Illness is rare, but there can be minor problems which may worry the inexperienced mother or nursery nurse. If there are doubts, then a health visitor or doctor should be consulted.

Hiccups
These are common in young babies and can be safely ignored.

Excessive crying
Babies vary considerably in temperament – some are placid and contented, others are active and some will cry and demand attention. If a baby is crying, go to him and pick him up and comfort him. Try to discover and correct the cause, which may be any of the following: hunger, thirst, coldness, over-heating, wet nappy, pain due to teething or colic, boredom, or it may be just that he wants his mother. This last reason may be difficult to deal with, and there are times when the only solution is to carry the baby around with you for part of the day. It is worth asking the doctor to check that the baby is well and that there is no other reason for the crying.

Colic (three-month colic)
This usually occurs in the first three months of life (hence the name) and can be very distressing. A typical case is a healthy normal baby who is contented most of the time except after the 6 p.m. feed, when he appears to be in extreme pain. He screams and draws up his knees. Picking him up and cuddling him may soothe him for a short while, as will rubbing his tummy or back or giving him a drink of cool boiled water. But, whatever you do, the screaming continues on and off all the evening. Then at 10 p.m. he takes his feed and settles down and sleeps all night. There is little anyone can do in the way of treatment, apart from nursing the baby, but the doctor can prescribe medicine which *may* help. Whatever treatment is given, this evening colic will usually last for about eight weeks, so that often by three months the problem disappears. The condition is not yet fully understood, but babies do not seem to suffer any harmful effects from it.

Teething
Teething should not cause illness but it may cause a lot of discomfort which can

lower a baby's resistance to infection. Teething usually begins at about six months, and this is the stage when the antibodies the baby obtained from his mother are diminishing and he has not produced enough of his own to give him protection from all infections. Therefore it is important not to assume that any illness is 'only teething', because a serious infection could possibly be overlooked until it is too late.

Signs and symptoms of teething:
(a) dribbling (salivation);
(b) red patches on cheeks;
(c) sore chin and chest from dribbling;
(d) child bites on anything available – his fist, mother's chin and jaw, edge of cot, etc.;
(e) reluctance to suck because of pain (but not sufficient to stop him eating);
(f) sore bottom – this is due to loss of fluid by dribbling which leads to concentrated urine causing soreness;
(g) fretfulness and misery.

Treatment:
(a) Give extra fluids to drink – cool boiled water.
(b) Give him something to bite, e.g. hard rusk, bone ring or teething rattle.
(c) Comfort him.
(d) Try one of the proprietary brands of teething jelly.

Consult the doctor if:
(a) He pulls his ears.
(b) He has diarrhoea and/or vomiting.
(c) He becomes chesty.
(d) He becomes very distressed.

8. Protection. There are two important areas of risk where a baby is especially vulnerable and will need protection:
(a) *Infection* (see Chapter 8 on Germs and disease). The newborn baby has little resistance to the germs he will meet, so he needs to be protected as far as possible until he has developed some defences.
   (i) The best protection a baby can be given is to be breast-fed, because breast milk is uncontaminated and contains antibodies which help fight infection.
   (ii) The need for cleanliness has already been mentioned, especially the sterilisation of bottles.
   (iii) All water and milk should be boiled.
   (iv) If the baby has all his needs fulfilled, he should have good general health which will help him resist infection.
   (v) He can be immunised against specific infectious diseases, such as tuberculosis, whooping cough, diphtheria, poliomyelitis, tetanus and measles.
(b) *Accidents* (see Chapter 18 on Accidents and First Aid). Accidents are one of the chief causes of death for children under five. This is because children have little sense of danger and are often in the charge of careless adults.

As baby grows up and becomes more mobile, his natural instinct is to explore and experiment, so a safe environment must be provided to enable him to do this. Adults caring for a child must always be aware of potential dangers and should guard against them, without being too negative or frightening the child.

9. Security. A newborn human baby is among the most vulnerable and helpless of all animals, and to survive he must be cared for and protected. He is probably aware of this in a limited way, because he has an innate fear of falling, and if held insecurely will cry. This makes it difficult for the inexperienced mother or nursery nurse because the crying can make the adult even more nervous. The baby senses this and reacts by more crying. Therefore he needs to be handled in a firm, confident way to make him feel secure.

The establishment of a regular routine helps the mother/nursery nurse to be confident and sure, and as the baby learns to expect certain actions to follow others he begins to develop a trust that his needs will be satisfied. He learns to anticipate, and to recognise various signs. For example, the sound of water running and bath preparations tell him that it is nearly bathtime. Anticipation and regular fulfilment of his needs build up his feeling of security. This is especially true of feeding. Sucking milk gives a baby intense satisfaction because his hunger is satisfied and sucking is a comfort to him.

Having a stable, loving mother and frequent physical contact with her is very important to a child's inner security. His mother's pleasure in him will convey itself at a very early age and make him feel a worthwhile and important person in the home.

10. Affection. A small baby needs one person's consistent care so that he develops a deep relationship. Once this relationship is formed, he can branch out and make others and gradually widen his contacts. The quality of that first relationship is very important, because it can colour all future expectations and feelings about whether people are 'good' or 'bad'. If he is treated with love and tenderness, and all his needs are met by this person, then he will grow up with friendly feelings towards others and confidently expect that people will be kind to him.

It does not seem to make a difference to the child's well-being and development whether this first relationship is with his own mother or a substitute – such as a nursery nurse – provided this one person cares for him consistently for the first few months of his life.

From about four weeks, the baby recognises his 'mother' and will smile and begin to make noises when she leans over him. This brings a response from his mother and leads to a two-way communication. This is part of the process known as 'bonding', and we know from recent research that this is just as important for the mother as for the baby. It is seen also in the animal kingdom where, if the baby is separated from its mother for a period of time, the mother may completely reject it.

Among humans lack of bonding can sometimes be seen in cases of concealed parental violence (baby battering). Investigations shows that the children who suffer in this way were often born prematurely and received special medical care which caused an unnatural separation from their mothers in the early weeks of life when bonding should take place.

Fortunately, most parents find it easy to love and show their love to their baby. But if there should be a feeding problem, excessive wakefulness or constant crying, then it is important to seek help and advice. If not dealt with, these problems can lead to feelings of failure and fatigue which may end in the mother's rejecting her child.

The growth of love between mother and child is encouraged by close physical contact, which happens naturally as she looks after the child's physical needs. But there should be time, too, for face-to-face contact, talking and singing to the baby, and the enjoyment of playing together. It is not a question of 'spoiling', but of giving the baby the emotional necessities of life. Of course, he should be fed and allowed to sleep, but when awake he needs the company of his mother and family so that he knows where he belongs. He should not be left alone to cry for hours 'so that he will learn to amuse himself'.

Finally, lack of affection and stimulation can affect growth and development. Children in institutions, who are looked after by a variety of people, are often small for their age and backward in many aspects of development, especially walking and speech. Some of these babies, who have never been mothered, later develop severe personality disorders. But, now that the effects of lack of affection are understood, people are realising that institutions should be smaller and more like a normal home. The children are placed into 'family groups', and each group has a 'mother' to look after them. Students in day and residential nurseries will be conversant with family grouping and realise the importance of the 'mother figure'. By caring for her children over a period of time, she can create an invaluable mother/child relationship and this makes all the difference between looking after their physical needs and really 'caring' for them.

11. Stimulation (play). All human beings need stimulation in order to learn about the world around them, and young babies are no exception. In the very early days of his life, a baby will appear just to sleep and feed, and not need stimulation, apart from that caused by hunger. However, even a newborn baby is awake for short periods so from the beginning ways should be found to make his environment stimulating and interesting.

Stimulation of a baby's senses should start as early as possible. By seeing, hearing, touching, tasting and smelling he experiences many objects, events and sensations. At first they make little sense, but gradually he is able to sort them out and use the information to form ideas about the world.

Sight

A baby can tell the difference between light and dark at birth and can see, but barely follow, a moving object. From about two weeks, the baby will gaze at his mother's face when she talks or attends to him. By six weeks he recognises her and smiles at her.

At birth a baby's eyes tend to work separately but, from six weeks, he is gradually able to use them efficiently together. By the time he is three months old, he can focus on an object and follow its movements quite well. So, from early days, as we have mentioned, the baby should have some visual stimulation – colours to look at, a hanging mobile, which will move gently in any current of air, and toys such as strings of beads strung across the pram. When his pram is out of doors it should be placed so that he can see something interesting, such as trees and people, when he awakes.

His mother, or nursery nurse, should spend time talking to him, allowing him to gaze at her face. Later, as he becomes more active, brightly coloured, well-designed toys should be provided for play on the floor.

Hearing

Hearing sounds, and responding to them with his own noises, are the beginnings of a baby's speech.

At birth he can only hear high-pitched sounds but, by ten days, he can hear all sounds audible to the human ear. From about three months he begins to turn his head, trying to see where sounds come from; he can also make all the sounds necessary for speech. By six to seven months he can locate sounds fairly accurately.

To stimulate speech development, babies should be talked to and placed where they can hear voices around them. A baby enjoys the sounds of family activity and will respond when someone talks to him, by making his own noises in reply. As he grows older, he begins to experiment and 'play' with his own voice. There is no need for absolute quiet when a baby is asleep; he can sleep undisturbed through all normal domestic noises in the same way that people living near a railway line are able to sleep with trains thundering past.

One of a baby's first playthings is a rattle, and he will react to the sound of it by first stiffening, 'quieting' and, later, by kicking and using his voice. Musical boxes and bells also stimulate a baby with their familiar, enjoyable sounds. Attractive musical sounds appeal to babies and, from early days, they can be soothed or settled to sleep by mother or the nursery nurse singing a lullaby.

Touch

A baby's skin is sensitive to touch, and very early in life he responds with pleasure to stroking and patting and the feel of bath water. Later, he enjoys being tickled and curls up in anticipation. His lips are especially sensitive, and this, combined with *taste*, makes him enjoy sucking, especially at the breast.

Sucking is necessary to a baby, not only for satisfaction and comfort, but also for finding out more about things than his senses of sight and hearing can tell him. A baby uses his sense of touch to find out more about himself by sucking his hands and, when he can manage it, his feet. As soon as he can hold an object he attempts to get it to his mouth and feel it with his lips and tongue. Touch teaches the baby the difference between a soft, woolly blanket and a smooth, cold rattle. Therefore toys with different textures should be provided for him to explore in this way.

Smell

A baby's sense of smell reinforces his visual and aural impressions. He learns to

associate people, and things, with their particular odours. The smell of his
mother's body becomes as familiar to him as the sight of her face or the sound of
her voice.

The stimulus that adults give stirs up curiosity and enthusiasm in a baby and
helps him become mentally alert. A baby should be given the chance to use all his
senses. He needs freedom of movement and space to move around in, a familiar
adult to talk to, and a selection of toys suitable for his age and ability.

Playthings for a baby should be chosen carefully, bearing in mind the
following:
(a) colour – bright, primary colours attract the eye;
(b) safety – no sharp edges or loose pieces, no dangerous wires, eyes securely
    attached in cuddly toys, lead-free and colour-fast paint, shatterproof;
(c) hygiene – washable or easily cleaned;
(d) size and weight – not too large or too heavy for a baby to handle, not too tiny
    or it may be swallowed;
(e) shape – interesting and varied, suitable for a baby to hold;
(f) texture – interesting varieties;
(g) quantity – not too many toys should be provided at the same time, as this can
    be confusing.

Suggestions for play materials
(a) *0–3 months:* mother's voice, own voice, mobiles and lightweight rattles (to be
    hung where they can be seen), strings of beads across the pram, musical box,
    music;
(b) *3–6 months* (during this period the baby learns to grip and relax, and can hold
    toys): bath becomes enjoyable – kicking and splashing, bath toys, plastic
    cups, rattles – manufactured or home-made, bell-on-a-stick, coloured beads
    on a string, teething rings, teddy bear;
(c) *6–9 months* (during this period the baby can sit up and may crawl):
    finger-plays and games – e.g. 'This little pig went to market', saucepans with
    lids, wooden spoons, bricks and blocks, ball, drums, cotton-reels, musical
    toys, more bath toys including colander, measuring jug, sponges and flannel;
(d) *9–12 months* (during this period the baby becomes mobile – crawls, creeps or
    even walks): baskets of oddments of different textures, push-and-pull toys,
    push-along baby walker, strong books, small toy cars, rag doll, old handbag.

12. Social contacts. At first, the newborn baby needs only his mother or
mother substitute. But as he grows older his interests widen to include his father,
and then his brothers and sisters. Later, familiar adults such as grandparents,
aunts and neighbours are greeted with smiles and gurgles. His mother remains his
anchor and, during his first year, he always turns to her for reassurance and
approval. He should be given opportunities to meet other people, and watch
children playing – for example, in shops and supermarkets and parks, and in
other people's houses.

13. Independence. A young baby is wholly dependent on his mother or
mother-substitute, but gradually he becomes less helpless and, over the years of
childhood, steadily develops the ability to take care of himself.

Part of the skill of being a parent is to let a child develop naturally as an independent being, whilst protecting him from any adverse consequences. Letting the child learn new skills when he is ready to do so, taking over when he is tired or 'just not in the mood', takes skilful observation, understanding and knowledge of a child's character. But it is of great importance, because we now know that if a child is not allowed to practise a skill when he is ready, it will take him far longer to learn.

Exploration is an important biological drive and begins very early in life, so that the baby should be allowed the freedom of the floor to kick and roll over, crawl and walk. Practice is necessary for normal physical development, and freedom to experience things first-hand is essential for emotional and intellectual development.

Planning a routine

All these various needs have to be considered when planning a baby's routine. We must also remember that mothers and nursery nurses have their own needs and should have time to pursue them. A mother is a wife as well, and will need time for her husband. She also has housework, cleaning, washing, shopping and cooking, all to be done during the day.

Most babies are settled into a feeding routine by the time they leave hospital, so that it is a question of fitting the other needs into a daily programme.

Suggested daily routine for a baby of under six months

6 a.m. (or when baby wakes): change nappy; feed; sleep.
9.30 a.m.: top and tail, to be followed by:
10.00 a.m.: feed; sleep – outside in pram if possible.
11.00 a.m.: baby can be taken out shopping, or to the park in his pram.
2.00 p.m.: change nappy; feed; sleep; when he wakes, place him on the floor and allow him to kick. Talk to him.
5.15 p.m.: prepare bath and bath baby, allowing time for playing in the bath.
6.00 p.m.: feed; sleep.
10.00 p.m.: change; feed; sleep.

Exercise 5

Multiple-choice questions
1. A baby is teething when suffering from the following signs and symptoms:
(a) dribbling and rubbing his gums;
(b) crying most of the night and pulling his ears;
(c) diarrhoea and vomiting;
(d) a 'chesty' cold.

2. Young babies sleep:
(a) twenty out of the twenty-four hours;
(b) twelve hours at night;
(c) according to their individual needs;
(d) best in very quiet surroundings.

3. Which of the following statements is correct?
(a) A baby should be put outside every day, regardless of the weather.
(b) A baby should be put outside every day, except in very cold or foggy weather.
(c) A baby should never be put outside in winter.
(d) A baby should be taken out for a walk every day.

4. A baby of under three months would be attracted to a plaything because:
(a) it is safe;
(b) it is improvised;
(c) it is colourful;
(d) it is washable.

5. A mother should talk to her baby:
(a) when he can understand language;
(b) when he begins to respond to her;
(c) from birth;
(d) not for at least six months – it's a waste of time.

Essay questions
6. What are the basic needs of a young baby of under six months? How can these be met in the day nursery?

7. How does a mother show affection to her baby? What could be the effects of lack of care?

Suggestions for further reading

Ronald and Cynthia Illingworth, *Babies & Young Children*, Churchill Livingstone
Mary and Richard Gordon, *A Baby in the House*, William Heinemann Ltd
Hugh Jolly, *Commonsense about Babies*, Times Newspapers Ltd
Penelope Leach, *Baby and Child Care*, Michael Joseph Ltd
James and Joyce Robertson, *A Baby in the Family*, Penguin Books Ltd

Chapter 6
Food

To understand the principles of planning the feeding of babies and young children, the student must know the component parts of foods and how they are digested and used in the body.

Food is found in many forms and must be broken down so that the body can absorb it and then reform it into a state that it can use. For example, carbohydrate is converted into simple sugars, which can easily be absorbed and then used for energy.

We need food for various reasons:

1. to form new body cells for general growth;
2. to repair any damaged body cells;
3. to provide us with energy:
(a) to maintain body temperature;
(b) for all muscle movements.

Digestion

Food enters the body and travels through the alimentary tract (digestive system), a long hollow tube stretching from the mouth to the anus. Different parts of the tube perform different functions and may differ in shape. Food travels along the tube by peristalsis, a muscular churning action which pushes the food onward.

There are two types of digestion.

1. Mechanical. The breaking down of food by teeth and peristaltic action which grinds it into a soup-like consistency.

2. Chemical. At various stages in the alimentary tract fluids called enzymes mix with the food and cause chemical reactions which split complex food into simple forms (see diagram).

Once food is broken down it can be absorbed through the walls of the small intestine and blood vessels into the bloodstream. From there it is taken to the liver where it is re-formed into substances which the body can use and distributed by means of the bloodstream to wherever it is needed. The parts of food which cannot be digested, for example, roughage, collect in the lower part of the large intestine (rectum) and when sufficient in amount are excreted through the anus as faeces. This usually occurs every twenty-four to forty-eight hours. All the time that the residue of food remains in the large intestine water is being absorbed from it, so if there is a delay in emptying the rectum the waste products become firmer and harder and, when eventually evacuated, painful. This is known as constipation.

Digestion takes place all the time and the whole process is delicately balanced and synchronised. We feel hunger when the stomach is empty – usually about

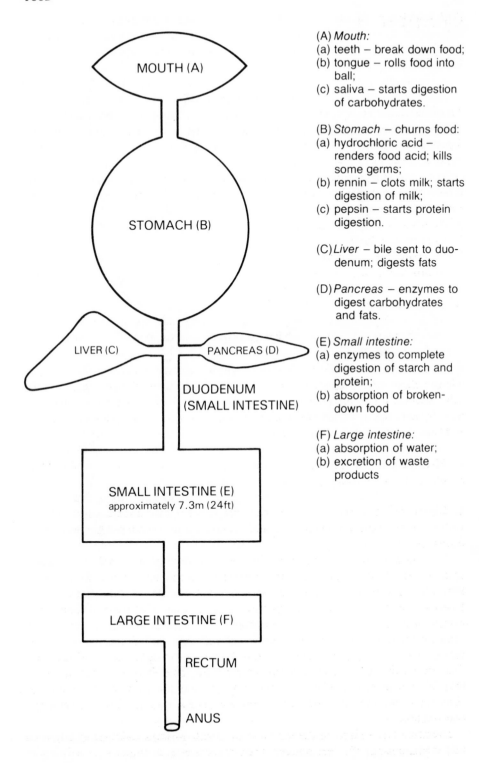

(A) *Mouth:*
(a) teeth – break down food;
(b) tongue – rolls food into ball;
(c) saliva – starts digestion of carbohydrates.

(B) *Stomach* – churns food:
(a) hydrochloric acid – renders food acid; kills some germs;
(b) rennin – clots milk; starts digestion of milk;
(c) pepsin – starts protein digestion.

(C) *Liver* – bile sent to duodenum; digests fats

(D) *Pancreas* – enzymes to digest carbohydrates and fats.

(E) *Small intestine:*
(a) enzymes to complete digestion of starch and protein;
(b) absorption of broken-down food

(F) *Large intestine:*
(a) absorption of water;
(b) excretion of waste products

MOUTH (A)

STOMACH (B)

LIVER (C)

PANCREAS (D)

DUODENUM
(SMALL INTESTINE)

SMALL INTESTINE (E)
approximately 7.3m (24ft)

LARGE INTESTINE (F)

RECTUM

ANUS

four hours after a meal. This gives us an appetite for food. When food is anticipated by the sound of preparations, the smell of cooking and the sight of a meal, saliva is produced in the mouth, ready to start the digestive process, and the stomach, too, produces its enzymes. An increased blood supply is needed by the stomach to give it the extra energy to cope with the meal. If the body is involved in other strenuous activities when digestion in the stomach is taking place, the extra blood supply is not available and indigestion may follow. For example, if a child is jigging up and down in his chair, or if he is seriously worried about his ability to eat his 'nice' dinner, any extra energy will be used up in these activities instead.

It is, therefore, best to eat at regular intervals, approximately four to six hourly. A quiet period before a meal to relax and anticipate, and a calm, unhurried atmosphere during the meal aid good digestion. Meals should be attractive and well presented, with a contrast of colour and texture, and meal times should be enjoyable, social occasions.

Types of food

There are many different types of food or nutrients and the student must know the classification of foods and what each type does in the body. The charts on the following pages provide a summary.

This may look a formidable list, but a study of the main sources of the nutrients will show that most people eat most of the foods mentioned. There are many fads and customs about diet, but nutritionists and dietitians generally agree that mixed diets are best. When religion forbids the eating of certain foods then alternative sources of the nutrient are usually found, so that the diet is balanced. If children are offered a wide variety of foods, they will instinctively choose a diet which is best for them, provided they have not been given an excess of sugar early in life and so developed a craving for sweetness.

It is possible to measure the *energy content* of food and this is expressed in kilojoules or the more familiar calories. We can estimate the amount of energy needed by a person, taking age, sex and occupation into account. Again, this can be expressed in kilojoules. To balance the diet the two figures must match.

You will see from the charts that the main energy-giving foods are fats and carbohydrates. It is possible to use protein as an energy source as well, but this is very wasteful of an expensive resource. We know from research that a certain amount of protein is necessary, varying according to a person's age. For example, a young baby will need a high proportion of protein in his diet because he is growing rapidly and needs material for new body cells. On the other hand a person in middle age will need only enough protein for repair of wear and tear.

So diets are planned by first calculating a person's protein requirements in kilojoules, and then making up the rest of kilojoules by adding fruit and vegetables, fats and carbohydrates, making sure that enough roughage, vitamins and minerals are included.

However, if a person eats enough food to feel satisfied, and remains healthy with a static weight, then he must be having a satisfactory diet.

Name	Some main sources	Function	Effect of too little	Notes
Proteins			if early in life when brain is developing rapidly, may prevent child reaching his intellectual potential.	Made up of any combination of 22 amino-acids, 8 of which are essential to man. Excess protein is used as energy source or excreted in urine.
(a) Animal proteins	meat fish eggs cheese milk	1. to build new body cells for growth; 2. to repair wear and tear in body cells.	1. poor growth and development; 2. poor healing powers. *Extreme* kwashiorkor – death	Contain all 8 essential amino-acids.
(b) Vegetable proteins	soya bean peas beans lentils nuts			Contain only some of the 8 essential amino-acids so good variety must be eaten.
Carbohydrates	sugar flour	to provide energy and heat.	1. lack of energy; 2. thinness; 3. feel cold.	Excess is stored as body fat.
Fat	lard olive oil butter cheese nuts meat fat	1. to provide energy and heat; 2. to carry fat-soluble vitamins; 3. to form padding in body, for example around kidney; 4. to make food more palatable.	1. lack of energy; 2. feel cold; 3. thinness; 4. vitamin A and D deficiency.	

Minerals	Sources	Function	Deficiency	Notes
Iron	liver eggs chocolate meat	forms haemoglobin in red blood cells which carry oxygen around body.	anaemia: pallor; breathlessness; lack of energy.	
Calcium	milk cheese butter bread flour	1. to build strong bones and teeth; 2. aids clotting of blood when injured; 3. to aid normal working of muscles.	1. rickets (bones fail to harden); 2. dental caries; 3. delayed blood clotting; 4. cramp in muscles.	Works together with vitamin D and phosphorus.
Phosphorus	milk cheese fish oatmeal	1. to helps build strong bones and teeth; 2. needed for the formation of body enzymes and all body tissue.		Deficiency rarely occurs alone because calcium will also be deficient.
Iodine	sea foods water supply vegetables may be added to salt	working of the thyroid gland which regulates use of food in body.	*Adult* goitre – enlarged thyroid gland. *Baby* – cretin.	
Sodium chloride (salt)	added to food kippers bacon	to maintain concentration of blood.	cramp in muscles.	too much: thirst; dehydration.
Potassium	cereals	needed for growth.		

Name	Some main sources	Function	Effect of too little	Notes
Fluorine	water supply may be present naturally or added artificially	to combine with calcium in teeth so making enamel more resistant to decay.	dental caries.	
Vitamins				
A fat soluble	milk butter cheese cod liver oil margarine	1. to promote growth; 2. aid to healthy skin; 3. prevention of poor night vision.	1. retarded growth; 2. poor resistance to infection especially skin infections; 3. poor night vision.	Animals can make vitamin A from carotene.
Carotene (red and yellow vegetables and fruit)	carrots tomatoes apricots			
B (group) water soluble	yeast marmite wheatgerm milk meat green vegetables	1. to aid healthy working of muscles and nerves; 2. to aid conversion of carbohydrate to energy and iron to haemoglobin.	1. wasting of muscles; 2. loss of appetite; 3. digestive disturbances; 4. anaemia etc.	There are at least 9 'B' vitamins.

C water soluble	oranges lemons blackcurrants green vegetables	1. to act as 'cement' for bone, skin and blood; 2. to aid resistance to infection.	1. scurvy (bleeding under skin, gums); 2. poor resistance to infection.	Easily destroyed by heat.
D fat soluble	milk butter cream egg yolk margarine cod liver oil sunlight	to combine with calcium for bone and teeth formulation.	1. rickets – bones fail to harden; 2. dental decay.	vitamin D can be made in skin by the action of sunlight on substance in skin
Roughage	cell walls of vegetables (cellulose) apples celery bran	help digestion by adding bulk to food which stimulates peristalsis.	constipation; diverticulitis; ? bowel cancer.	
Water	present in all foods	makes up 70 per cent body tissue. necessary for all the workings of the body and to help eliminate waste products.	thirst; constipation; dehydration; death.	

Nursery nurses are not expected to be experts but they do need to know how to plan a suitable diet. The following is a useful guide to the daily needs of adults and children. We begin with a basic amount of protein for the average adult, add fruit and vegetables and then make up the energy requirements, as needed, with carbohydrate and fats. Obviously a manual-worker will need more energy-giving foods than a female clerk but both will have the same basic protein requirements. Pregnant women, adolescent children and children under seven need extra protein because of their growth requirements. A child under seven in fact needs more protein than his father.

DAILY FOOD NEEDS OF NORMAL ADULT

Protein
285 ml (½ pint) milk
1 egg
28 g (1 oz) cheese
56–84 g (2–3 oz) fish
serving of nuts
peas, beans or lentils
50–100g (2–4 oz) meat
570 ml (1 pint) water

any 3 items of protein (3 of one kind or one each of 3); any 3 servings of fruit and vegetables

Fruit and vegetables
orange
grapefruit
apple
potato
swede, carrot, cabbage

Sugar and preserves – enough to make food palatable. Other carbohydrates (flour, bread, cake, etc.) – variable according to energy needs and appetite.
Fats – enough to make food palatable.

1. Pregnant women. They will need extra protein, calcium, iron and vitamins. Therefore add to normal adult diet: 570 ml (1 pint) milk, 1 egg, 1 orange, vitamin A and D tablets, iron tablets (if prescribed by a doctor).

2. Lactating women. They will need extra fluids, protein, calcium and vitamins.
Therefore add to normal adult diet: 570 ml (1 pint) milk, vitamin A and D tablets.

3. Children one to five years. They will need extra protein for growth, extra calcium for bones and teeth.
Therefore add to adult diet: 285 ml (½ pint) milk, vitamins A, D and C in the form of drops.

4. Infants from birth to one year. The very rapid rate of growth during the first year of life means that small babies need a large amount of protein in their diet. They also need some carbohydrate and fat for energy, some calcium and all the vitamins.

Breast-feeding
All a baby's nutritional requirements can most easily be provided during the first four to six months by breast milk with the addition of vitamin A, D and C drops.

From four months onwards the baby also needs iron, which can be provided by the addition of other foods such as egg yolk, liver and meat during the weaning period.

Breast milk is ideal for babies; not only does it contain almost all the nutrients they need, but the protein contains all the essential amino-acids in the correct proportion for the human body. Breast milk is therefore easily absorbed, needing very little digestion. There are many other advantages to breast-feeding, which can be listed as follows:

(a) The carbohydrate in breast milk is in the form of lactose, which is not sweet to taste, so avoids the danger of the baby developing a craving for sugar.
(b) The milk is unlikely to be contaminated, as it comes straight from mother to baby.
(c) Breast milk is at the correct temperature.
(d) It is economical.
(e) Very little preparation is required.
(f) Breast milk contains protective antibodies and vitamins which help protect the baby from infection.
(g) There is evidence to suggest that a breast-fed baby is protected from developing an allergy.
(h) Breast feeding gives the ideal mother and baby contact which aids 'bonding' and therefore the baby's emotional development.
(i) The baby must suck vigorously in order to obtain milk and this helps good jaw development.
(j) Breast-feeding helps the mother's figure to return to normal by causing the uterus to contract more rapidly.
(k) Breast-fed babies very rarely develop obesity.

The majority of mothers could breast-feed their babies if they wished. However there may be problems in the beginning and the mother will need encouragement and help to establish good breast-feeding. During the ante-natal period it is important for the positive aspects of breast-feeding to be emphasised, so that the mother has an optimistic approach to the subject. Most normal babies will turn instinctively to the breast and suck and, if the mother is relaxed all she need do is guide her baby to her nipple. Problems arise if the mother becomes tense and anxious, because this will be communicated to her baby.

Occasionally the baby may be sleepy and uninterested during the first few days. Problems may then arise because the flow of milk is stimulated by vigorous sucking. Other problems which can occur include poor nipple formation, sore nipples and a temporary excess or shortage of milk. Although the baby is put to the breast soon after birth, the milk does not appear immediately. At first a fluid called colostrum is produced. This is very valuable to the baby as it contains many antibodies. About the second or third day the mother may experience discomfort as the milk 'comes in'. Expert help is usually given in maternity units and most problems can be overcome.

By the time the mother and baby leave the care of the midwife, breast-feeding should be well established. The baby is usually being fed every four hours and is sucking for ten minutes on each breast at every feed-time, although a small baby may be fed three-hourly at first and others may be fed 'on demand'. The baby is fed during the night as well as the day, but this is usually discontinued by the baby himself at about four to six weeks of age when he can take enough milk during the day to last all night.

Requirements for breast-feeding
(a) low, comfortable chair;
(b) a drink for mother;
(c) a clock in sight;
(d) a tray containing bowl of water, swabs in jar with lid, container for soiled swabs, soft towel.

Method
(1) Baby should be changed and made comfortable.
(2) Mother should wash her hands and then clean her nipples with swabs and water, drying them carefully.
(3) She should sit comfortably with baby on her knee, leaning slightly forward and guiding the baby to her breast – a pillow on her knee under the baby may help to get baby in the right position.
(4) The baby will 'fix' by opening his mouth wide and taking the nipple far back into his mouth. Sucking is a 'munching' action with the lips behind the nipple.
(5) The baby's nose should be kept free to enable him to breathe.
(6) The baby should be offered alternate breasts at each feed. Ten minutes sucking at each breast will be sufficient. A pause is needed after the first ten minutes, and when feeding is complete, in order to bring up any air (wind) swallowed with the food. To bring up baby's wind:
　　(i) Support him sitting on your knee by placing one hand on his tummy. Use the other hand to rub his back gently until he 'burps'; OR
　　(ii) Put the baby over your shoulder and gently rub his back.

Signs of adequate feeding. Most mothers worry about whether the baby is getting enough milk, but there are several pointers which indicate that he is satisfied:
(a) He will be contented and will sleep most of the time between feeds.
(b) He will gain weight steadily at the rate of 115 to 225 g (4 to 8 oz) a week.
(c) His stools (faeces) will be soft, yellow and inoffensive, and may be infrequent. (This is because there is very little residue from breast milk.)

Signs of underfeeding
(a) Misery – the baby may cry a lot and will probably wake one to two hours after a feed.
(b) The baby will look anxious and worried.
(c) The weight gain will be small – under 56 g (2 oz) a week.
(d) His stools will be small and dry and may be green.
(e) He may become too lethargic to cry.

Test weighing. If there is any doubt about the adequacy of the feeds then the amount of each feed can be measured by test weighing. The baby is weighed just before his feed and then immediately after, without changing clothes or nappy.

Subtract the first weight from the second and this will give you the amount of milk taken. To be accurate this should be recorded over twenty-four hours and averaged out.

Average requirements. For estimating a baby's food requirements, we use the following formula:

$2\frac{1}{2}$ fl oz milk per pound body weight over 24 hours;
or 150 ml milk per kilogram body weight over 24 hours.

For example:
A 4.5 kg baby needs: A 10 lb baby needs:
700 ml per 24 hours   25 fluid oz per 24 hours
= 5 feeds of 140 ml   = 5 feeds of 5 oz

Some babies will require up to 25 ml (1 fl oz) more in each feed to satisfy them.

Insufficient milk. If the baby is not getting enough breast milk, then the first thing to do is to reassure the mother that this often happens for a temporary period and that it is possible to increase the milk supply by various measures:

(a) Ensure that the mother is getting plenty of rest and not too many visitors. Provide household help.
(b) Encourage mother to drink more: Milk, milky drinks, 'Complan', beer, etc.
(c) The baby should be offered extra milk (of the proprietary kind sold for bottle feeding) to make up the correct amount after each feed. He should still be put to the breast to suck for ten minutes each side, as sucking stimulates the breast to produce more milk. Extra milk should be given immediately afterwards, either by spoon or in a bottle. This is known as complementary feeding and can be continued for one to two weeks. In most cases it will be enough to encourage extra milk production, so that the baby will in time refuse the complementary feed.

However, if these measures do not succeed then it may be necessary to change to bottle-feeding. If a change from breast-feeding to bottle-feeding is decided upon, then it should be achieved gradually by substituting one bottle for one breast-feed each day until the baby is having all feeds by bottle. The mother's breast milk will then dry up naturally as the baby ceases sucking.

Artificial or bottle feeding

Some mothers are unable to produce enough milk for their babies, especially in the case of twins; other mothers do not wish to breast-feed at all, so that a substitute has to be found. The word 'substitute' is used deliberately, because even in this modern age, we cannot make a perfect copy of breast milk.

Most artificial feeds are based on cow's milk because this is readily available. If we compare the composition of cow's milk with breast milk we notice several differences. The percentages are approximate.

		Breast milk %	Cow's milk %
Protein	Casein	1	3.4
	Lactalbumin	1	0.5
Sugar		7	4.0
Fat		3.5	3.5
Mineral salts		0.2	0.7
Water		87.3	87.9

The main differences are in the protein, sugar and mineral salt content. The protein is not only increased in amount in cow's milk but there is a change in proportions. Instead of equal small amounts of casein and lactalbumin there is three times the amount of casein and the lactalbumin is reduced by half. As casein is a difficult protein to digest, this amount may cause problems to a baby.

For many years babies were fed on cow's milk modified in the following way:

Water was added to dilute the protein, the milk mixture was boiled to make the casein more digestible and sterilise the milk, and finally cane sugar was added to make the sugar content similar to that of breast milk. The mineral salt content was ignored, as it was thought that the baby could excrete any excess. When dried milk was introduced, the milk was modified in a similar way before being dried – the drying process helped to break up the casein and rendered it germ-free so that it could be kept for a much longer period. Some dried milk had some of the fat content removed and was known as 'half cream' milk, which was suitable for very small babies. Evaporated milk was also used, with similar modifications.

The next development in baby feeding was the introduction of 'humanised' milks, which were spray-dried instead of roller-dried as in the past. The result was more like breast milk, with a finer curd and therefore more easily digested. Being spray dried, the milk powder was much easier to mix with water. These milks had vitamins and iron added as well, but the natural mineral content remained the same as straight cow's milk.

However, the majority of babies thrived on ordinary dried milks, which for many years were thought to be satisfactory substitues for breast milk. But in the early 1970s research began to suggest that young babies' kidneys have only a limited ability to get rid of excess mineral salts. Furthermore, some have even less ability than others. If the kidneys cannot excrete excess mineral salts, the body gradually becomes overloaded and this imbalance can cause illness. In fact there was evidence to suggest a link with sudden 'cot deaths' which occasionally occur in bottle-fed babies under three months of age.

In older children and adults, excess mineral salts (which include common salt) can be excreted in the urine by the kidney, using water already present in the body cells and bloodstream. This leads to thirst, which can easily be satisfied by drinking water, so that the important water balance of the body is maintained.

If a young baby becomes thirsty he cannot ask for water. He can only cry. Most mothers assume the baby is crying because he is hungry and respond by giving more milk which he takes eagerly because of his thirst. But the milk only serves to increase the burden, because it contains more mineral salts. This situation can be exacerbated if the baby is losing fluids for any reason – for example diarrhoea or a runny nose due to a head cold. Inaccurate measuring or adding extra milk powder when making up milk feeds is another danger, for it will make the milk too concentrated.

To avoid these problems it was recommended in a government report in 1976 that all babies under six weeks of age should be fed on breast milk or milk with a low mineral salt content. Humanised milks were rapidly adapted so that the mineral salt content was the same as in breast milk. These milks include SMA (Gold Top), Osterfeed and Premium Cow and Gate and, in practice, most babies stay on these milks until they are fully weaned. However, a few babies seem dissatisfied with these milks because they are so rapidly digested, in which case Cow and Gate Baby Milk Plus or SMA (white cap) may be better alternatives, because they are designed to stay in the stomach longer. A baby's feed can be made by the method below. But it is always most important to follow the manufacturers' instructions.

Requirements
(a) milk powder and scoop;
(b) a container of sterilising fluid in which is immersed:
   (i) wide-necked feeding bottle; (ii) screw collar and cap; (iii) 2 teats; (iv) 1 plastic spatula.

For cleaning bottle after use:
(c) a bottle brush;
(d) detergent;
(e) salt.
   NB: Milk is an ideal medium for the growth of germs so cleanliness is essential to prevent infection. Dried milk should be kept in a covered container in a cool place. All equipment must be cleaned and sterilised to kill germs, and hands must be washed before making up the feed.

Preparation
(1) Fill kettle and boil.
(2) Read instructions on packet (for amounts see page 78).
(3) Remove bottle from sterilising unit.
(4) Pour correct amount of boiled water into the bottle.
(5) Cover with lid and screw top.
(6) Cool to body temperature by holding under running cold water.
(7) Measure and add correct number of scoops of powder to bottle – make sure all measures are levelled off with the spatula. The powder should not be packed down in the scoop.
(8) Replace lid and screw top on bottle.
(9) Shake gently until powder and water are mixed.

The milk made in this way should be at the correct temperature for the baby. Put the teat on the bottle, then check temperature by allowing a few drops of milk to fall on your wrist. It should feel pleasantly warm. If cold, the feed can be warmed up by standing the bottle in a bowl of hot water; if too hot, then cooled in a bowl of cold water. If need be, enough bottles can be made up to last twenty-four hours. They should be stored in a refrigerator and can be warmed up when required, as described above.

Immediately after the feed is given, the bottle and other utensil should be cleaned and sterilised by the following method:

(a) *Cleaning*
(1) Pour away any remaining milk.
(2) Rinse bottle and teat, outside and inside, under cold-water tap.
(3) Wash all utensils in hot detergent solution using a bottle brush for the bottle.
(4) Clean teat by turning inside-out and rubbing with salt (removes milk film).
(5) Rinse all utensils again in cold water.

(b) *Sterilising*
(6) Immerse all utensils in a solution of one part sodium hypochlorite to eighty parts of water.
(7) Make sure all equipment, including teats, is immersed in the fluid.
(8) Cover and leave for at least one and a half hours or until needed.
(9) The solution needs to be changed every twenty-four hours or it will lose its effectiveness.

(*NB:* Metal should not be sterilised in this way or it will rust.)

There are many brands of sterilising fluid containing sodium hypochlorite on the market and it may be obtained in liquid, crystal or tablet form. Follow the directions given on the packet for making up the correct solution. In an emergency, when a sterilised bottle is needed urgently, utensils can be sterilised by boiling. All utensils except the teat should be immersed in a saucepan of cold water, brought to the boil, and boiled for ten minutes. The teats should be added for the last minute of boiling. A lid should be used on the saucepan and the pan should remain covered until its contents are needed.

Method of giving a bottle feed. A spare sterile teat should be available in a covered container in case the one in use becomes blocked.
(1) Baby should be changed and made comfortable.
(2) Mother/nurse should wash hands.
(3) Mother/nurse should sit comfortably and cuddle the baby as if she were breast-feeding.
(4) Check temperature of milk and flow from teat.
(5) Introduce the teat into baby's mouth, holding the bottle up to ensure that the teat remains full of milk.
(6) If baby sucks the teat flat, then remove teat and allow air into bottle.
(7) Halfway through feed remove bottle and 'wind' baby as for breast-feeding and again at end of feed.
    The feed should take ten to fifteen minutes and it is usually given four-hourly, as in breast-feeding.

Problems which may occur
(a) Baby takes too long to feed or refuses to feed:
    (i) Teat hole may be too small – enlarge by using a sterilised darning needle.
    (ii) Baby's nose may be blocked – medical aid.
    (iii) Baby may be ill – medical aid.

(b) Baby wakes and cries after one or two hours:
    (i) Baby may be thirsty – offer boiled water.
    (ii) Baby may be hungry – offer boiled water and at next feed time increase milk by 25 ml (1 oz).

Vitamin supplement
All babies need extra vitamin A, D and C, usually given in the form of drops. Dosage depends on whether the baby is breast- or bottle-fed, and if bottle-fed, which brand of milk powder. Read instructions which come with drops.

Water
Extra cool boiled water should be offered between feeds, especially during hot weather.

Weaning
This means the gradual change over from milk to mixed diet, as in family meals. Fashions change and in the past have gone from one extreme to the other. Babies have been suddenly weaned at nine months, and gradually from two weeks. However, most babies are found to be ready for extra food around three to four months and they thrive best if there is a gradual transition from milk to mixed feeding. Between three and four months the baby will be waking early for feeds and if he is given extra milk it will not satisfy him. He should not, in any case, be given more than 230 ml (8 fl oz) – a bottleful – at each feed.

It is necessary to start weaning a breast-fed baby by four months because the baby's stock of iron, obtained from his mother before birth, is being used up and breast milk does not contain enough iron to make up for this. Bottle-fed babies do have the advantage of iron being added to humanised dried milk. By about five to six months the baby is beginning to chew, whether he has teeth or not, so, at that age, he should be given food to chew on.

Methods of weaning vary, but there are several important points to remember: (see also chart opposite)
(a) Start gradually by offering just one teaspoon of sieved food before one of the baby's feeds – 10 a.m., 2 p.m. or 6 p.m.
(b) If he refuses, try giving some of his milk first and then the 'taste'.
(c) Use a plastic spoon as this is softer to his gums.
(d) Preferably give savoury foods, rather than sweet, to encourage a liking for savoury flavours.
(e) Food containing iron should be introduced early, e.g. bone broth, egg yolk, chocolate, liver.
(f) Once he has accepted the 'taste' at one feed time, introduce another 'taste' at another feed time, and then a third taste, so that he is having solids at 10 a.m., 2 p.m. and 6 p.m.
(g) Then gradually increase and vary the solid food.
(h) If baby refuses, leave for three to four days and then start again.
(i) Do not introduce more than one new food at a time, so that if baby is upset, the cause will be obvious and the offending food can be avoided for a couple of weeks.
(j) As soon as baby begins making chewing movements (between five and six months) whether he has teeth or not, introduce more solid food to his diet –

that is, mashed instead of sieved, and hard rusks to chew.

NB: Do not leave him alone with a rusk, as he may break off a piece and choke on it.

(k) As soon as he is willing and keen, give him a spoon and let him try to feed himself. Food should be in small pieces rather than mashed, so that he can use his fingers and/or spoon easily. He should also be introduced to a cup when ready.

Stages in weaning

Milk = milk from breast or bottle. Each stage may take from 3 days to 2 weeks.

Stage	6 a.m.	8 a.m.	10 a.m.	12 midday	2 p.m.	4 p.m.	6 p.m.	10 p.m.
	milk		milk vitamin drops		milk		milk	milk
1 (4 mth)	milk		milk vitamin drops		milk		1 teasp. dinner milk	milk
2	milk		1 teasp. breakfast milk vitamin drops		milk		1 teasp. dinner milk	milk
3	milk		1 teasp. breakfast milk vitamins		1 teasp dinner milk		1 tablesp. 'tea' milk	milk
4 (5 mth)	milk		1 tablesp. breakfast milk vitamins		dinner + fruit juice in cup		1 tablesp. 'tea' milk	milk
5 (6–7 mth)	fruit juice or water in cup	breakfast milk		dinner + fruit juice in cup		'tea' milk	milk at bedtime	
6 (9 mth)	fruit juice or water	breakfast milk in cup	fruit	dinner + juice in cup		'tea' milk in cup	milk at bedtime	

Suitable food for weaning

Note: In the menus listed below a CHOICE of suitable foods is given.

(a) *3–5½ months:* All home-cooked food should be put through a 'baby-mouli' or liquidiser to make it a smooth semi-liquid mixture. No extra salt should be added, as babies need very little salt and too much can cause problems. Tins or jars of strained baby food, or packets of freeze-dried foods for weaning, are useful at this stage because of the small amounts needed. But they are expensive, and eventually the baby must get used to home cooking, so the sooner he does so the better.

Breakfast (10 a.m. feed): baby cereal – milk (no added sugar), egg yolk (lightly boiled), mashed banana, fruit puree (apple/apricot/prune), tin or jar strained baby food;

Dinner (2 p.m. feed): bone and vegetable broth, scrapings of roast joint – potato – gravy, steamed kidney, liver, white fish, braised steak, tin or jar strained 'dinner';

'Tea' (6 p.m. feed): egg custard, milk pudding, cauliflower cheese, grated cheese on cereal, fruit puree or egg yolk (not the same as breakfast).

(b) *5½–8 months* (from the time baby begins to chew): Stop making food into puree – mash instead.

Breakfast: as above, or: scrambled egg, Weetabix, porridge, crisp bacon, crisply fried bread, mashed sardines;

Dinner: as family: minced or chopped meat, chicken or bacon + vegetables, steamed white fish + vegetables, 'junior' tin or jar dinner, followed by fruit puree;

Tea: rusks, sandwiches – Marmite, egg, flesh of tomato, grated cheese, plain sponge cake, jelly, bread, jelly jam, honey, any tin or jar 'junior' supper;

(c) *8 months onwards* – 'finger' food. Change to cow's milk.

Breakfast: as above; may need two courses, i.e. cereal + egg, whole boiled egg with toast fingers;

Dinner: as above, + salad vegetables cut small;

Tea: as above, cheese on toast, wholemeal bread.

Under 1 year: Avoid food which is very salty, i.e. salt bacon, kippers. Avoid highly-seasoned food such as curry. Avoid food containing pips.

From one year: The child's diet should be the same as the rest of the family. Sample menus for the one year old are as follows:

Early morning	fresh orange juice	tomato juice	fresh orange juice
Breakfast	Weetabix + milk boiled egg toast fingers milk	porridge toast + jam milk	crisply grilled bacon fried bread toast milk
Mid-morning (if wanted)	milk	milk	milk
Dinner	minced beef and gravy mashed potato carrot apple water to drink	liver and bacon casserole potato chopped cabbage fruit jelly water to drink	chopped chicken roast potato cauliflower pineapple dessert water to drink
Tea	cauliflower cheese pieces of orange sponge cake milk or milky tea	sandwiches wholemeal bread grated cheese Madeira cake banana milk	salad with grated cheese carrot, chopped lettuce + tomato wholemeal bread and butter
Bedtime (if wanted)	milk or hot chocolate	milk	milk

Special diets

From time to time a nursery nurse will have in her care a child on a special diet. Sometimes the child will be unable to eat certain foods because of the family's beliefs, which must be respected. In other cases the child may be suffering from a disease which can be controlled by a special diet or by avoiding certain foods. Whatever the reason, it is important for the nursery nurse to know from his mother exactly what the child can or cannot eat. *All* staff at the nursery or school must be aware of this diet so that no mistakes are made.

A vegetarian diet. The term 'vegetarian' has various meanings so it is essential to find out what is meant when the parents of a child say they are vegetarian. In some cases, the family simply does not eat meat, but others are true 'vegans' and do not eat any animal products at all. In between are the Hindus, whose vegetarian diet is based on the doctrine of *Ahimsa* which says that it is wrong to kill any living animal or fish for food, but permits the eating of animal products which do not involve killing, for example eggs, milk, butter and cheese.

If a child must not eat meat, then meals provide few problems because meat protein can be replaced by using eggs, cheese and milk or a mixture of vegetable proteins. But, in the case of the true vegan with his restricted diet the biggest problem is to ensure that there is enough protein for growth and sufficient iron for the maintenance of good health. Children need more of these nutrients than adults because of the large amount of growth which takes place. In normal diets the easiest way to provide protein and iron is by including a mixture of meat and animal products in a child's meals. This is because proteins are made up from a selection of about twenty-two amino-acids, of which eight cannot be manufactured by the human body. These *eight essential* amino-acids are all found in meat, eggs, fish, milk and cheese. Iron is also present in meat and eggs.

Only human milk and eggs supply the essential amino-acids in the correct proportions for humans but, by giving a mixed diet containing meat and animal products, we can ensure a child gets sufficient protein for his needs. The protein which is present in vegetables, such as nuts, peas, beans and lentils is known as an incomplete protein because it only contains a selection of some of the essential amino-acids. This means that a child must eat a large amount and variety of vegetables to ensure that all the essential amino-acids are available. Iron is present in green vegetables, but it is in the form of iron oxide which is not readily absorbed by the human body. Fortunately iron is also present in bread, curry powder, cocoa, chocolate, baked beans and lentils. Most vegetarian diets provide adequate amounts of the vitamins and calcium.

By co-operating with his mother, it is possible to ensure that the vegetarian child has a balanced and varied diet every day.

Some religious beliefs specifically forbid the eating of certain foods and these must be respected. Examples of these are:

Jewish diet. Observant Jews do not eat pork in any form and this includes food cooked in pork fat, pork sausages and bacon. An orthodox Jew will only buy his meat from a 'kosher' butcher because he knows that the animal has been killed and the meat prepared in the accepted way, according to the 'Talmudic' ritual.

Hindu diet. Hindu people consider the cow to be a sacred animal and will not eat beef. They consider the pig to be unclean and uneatable. Some Hindus are also vegetarians.

West Indian Rastafarians. This small group of people eats a diet which excludes all animal products including eggs, milk, cheese and butter. If the baby is not breast-fed, then he will have to be fed on a 'milk' made from soya bean. It is essential that all these children have vitamin D supplements because of the very real danger of rickets on this diet. In addition, iron may be short, so these children and their mothers should be checked regularly to ensure that they are not becoming anaemic.

Diet for the overweight child. A child who is overweight should be examined by a doctor who will prescribe a diet for him, usually a low carbohydrate one, so that his meals will consist mainly of protein and vegetables. He will not be allowed in-between snacks of sweets, biscuits, crisps or sweet drinks and the sugar, bread and cake content of his diet will be reduced. Chips are usually forbidden. This can cause him a great deal of misery at first, and a child on this sort of diet needs a good deal of support and encouragement. Meals should be colourful and interesting with plenty of varied vegetables to fill up his plate. Sometimes it helps to use a smaller plate – the meal looks bigger! He can have carrots, apples and celery in between meals and this may help to console him.

A child with an allergy. There are children who are found to be allergic to specific foods, for example, cow's milk or eggs. Usually the child has a reaction such as vomiting, an eczema-like rash, or 'wheezing', after he has eaten the offending food, or allergen. In these cases these particular foods must be avoided at all costs. If the allergen is cow's milk then a substitute such as goat's milk or a fluid made from soya bean can be used.

   Eggs are more difficult to avoid because many cakes, biscuits and puddings are made with eggs and these must also be withheld.

A gluten-free diet. A child suffering from coeliac disease is invariably on this diet, because his bowel is unable to digest gluten, which is the protein in flour and many other cereals. Whenever he eats gluten he suffers from diarrhoea, sickness and loss of weight, so all foods containing gluten must be excluded from his diet. Cakes, bread and biscuits, etc., should be made from gluten-free flour. Manufactured foods which are gluten-free are now specially labelled with a symbol representing a crossed-out ear of wheat, so that they are easy to identify.

A diabetic diet. A child suffering from diabetes has difficulty in converting carbohydrate into energy because he does not produce enough insulin. To correct this deficiency, insulin is usually given daily by injection and the amount of carbohydrate in the diet is carefully balanced to the amount of insulin. The diet *must* be adhered to – both the timing of meals and the amount of food are important. The child must eat his meals at the time prescribed following his injection of insulin, and all food must be measured and weighed out exactly.

Diet for phenylketonuria. A child suffering from this defect is unable to make use of the amino-acid phenylalanine, which builds up in the brain, causing damage leading to mental retardation. If this condition is discovered early enough, and the child put on a diet low in phenylalanine whilst his brain is developing, then the damage is avoided. Unfortunately, most proteins contain phenylalanine, so that much of the child's food must be specially manufactured and is obtainable only on a doctor's prescription from a chemist.

Diet for galactosaemia. This is a similar condition to phenylketonuria, but in this case the affected child cannot use galactose, which is a type of sugar. Again specially manufactured foods, with a low galactose content, are necessary.

Diet for cystic fibrosis. This disease affects the chest and pancreas. Excessively sticky mucus is produced and causes problems in the lungs. Mucus also blocks the tube carrying enzymes from the pancreas, and this means that some digestion, especially that of fats, cannot take place. The child is usually given a low-fat diet and, in addition, may be prescribed pancreatin – an extract of pancreatic enzymes – to be given daily before meals.

Exercise 6

Multiple-choice questions
1. Which of the following foods is the best source of vitamin 'C'?
(a) steamed-sponge pudding;
(b) cooked cabbage;
(c) an orange;
(d) milk.

2. Lack of vitamin 'D' will cause which one of the following diseases?
(a) scurvy;
(b) rickets;
(c) anaemia;
(d) pellagra.

3. How is protein used in the body?
(a) to strengthen nerves;
(b) to make fat;
(c) to harden bone;
(d) to repair wear and tear.

4. A child suffering from coeliac disease:
(a) must be given a special diet, from birth;
(b) must avoid eating meat;
(c) must avoid gluten in his diet;
(d) must have his meals at regular intervals.

5. Which of the following is the best source of iron?
(a) chocolate;
(b) milk;
(c) biscuit;
(d) apple.

Essay questions

6. How would you prepare a bottle-feed for a normal baby of three months of age? Describe how you would give the feed to the baby.

7. Describe when and how you would wean a baby from milk to a mixed diet. How can you ensure that this child has a balanced diet and enjoys his meals?

Project

8. Plan all the meals for three days for the following family, making sure that each member has a diet suitable for his or her needs:
(a) mother, three months pregnant;
(b) father, manual worker;
(c) son, aged five years;
(d) daughter, aged one and a half years.

Suggestions for further reading

Sylvia Close, *The Know-How of Breast-Feeding*, John Wright & Sons
Patty Fisher and Arnold Bender, *The Value of Food*, Oxford University Press
Elizabeth Norton, *Feeding Your Family*, Mills & Boon Ltd
Present Day Practice in Infant Feeding, HMSO

Chapter 7
Care of the child

Basic needs

1. food;
2. cleanliness
3. rest and sleep;
4. exercise;
5. fresh air and sunlight;
6. warmth;
7. good health;
8. protection from injury and infection;
9. security;
10. affection;
11. stimulation;
12. social contacts;
13. independence.

The needs of a child remain the same at any age, but changes in emphasis and in the pattern of his daily routine will occur naturally as he grows from a passive baby to an active child. As he becomes more mature and more able, more will be expected of him, so that he gradually moves towards ultimate independence. The small baby's routine is based on his four-hourly feeds, but once weaning begins his mealtimes gradually change to come into line with those of the rest of the family. He can then become an active participant in family life. All his needs will overlap, but in the following pages they will be dealt with separately, before planning a routine to encompass them all.

1. Food (see Chapter 6 on Food). A child needs a mixed diet containing a wide variety of nutrients at regular intervals during the day. He should have one pint of milk and extra vitamin A, D and C drops until he is five years old. He needs protein for growth and repair, calcium for bones and teeth, iron for his blood and some fats and carbohydrates for energy. However, he should not be given too much sugar, as this will affect his health adversely. If he is given snacks such as sweets or biscuits, or drinks such as lemonade or cola, between mealtimes, they can spoil his appetite for protein meals, cause his teeth to decay and make him grow too fat. If he should need something to chew between meals, then an apple or a carrot should be enough and if he is thirsty, water is the best thirst-quencher. Sweets are best given as a special treat after a meal.

From the time a baby is able to sit comfortably and steadily in a chair, he should be allowed to sit up to the table with the rest of the family. When he shows willingness, he should be given a spoon and allowed to try and feed himself. Help should be given, of course, and his food should be chopped into small pieces, rather than mashed, so that he can easily pick it up, either with his fingers or his spoon. He will make a mess at first, but gradually with practice becomes more proficient. Sitting with the rest of the family at the table will enable him to watch and to copy. A child learns by imitation and it is important to let him practise new skills when he is ready and willing, because that will be the right time for him to do so.

A baby of ten months will probably still be having a bottle-feed or a breast-feed last thing at night, and it is important that he continues this practice until he is ready to give it up. Not only is it a source of food but sucking brings comfort and satisfaction to a child. Most babies spontaneously give up this last feed some time between one year and eighteen months because they find other sources of comfort.

Until he is about a year old, a baby will eat almost all the food he is offered because he needs it for growth. But, from this age, his appetite will taper off for two reasons. First, he will no longer need as much for growth and secondly his interests wi.i have widened, so that meals will not be as important to him as they once were. This reduction in appetite can cause much anguish in mothers, and nurses too, if they do not realise it is a normal occurrence. A child is quick to sense anxiety and may take advantage of this and refuse to eat in order to draw more attention to himself. Provided he is offered a good balanced diet at mealtimes and is not given sweets and other snacks in between, he will eat what he needs. It is unnecessary to entice a child to eat, or to force food into him. It does a child a disservice to make him eat food he does not need, bearing in mind that one of the biggest problems of malnutrition in Britain at the present time is obesity. Fat children are not fit children and fat children often become fat adults. Once the habit of over-eating is established, it can be very difficult to break.

Small, attractive helpings should be offered at family mealtimes. Food should look inviting with a contrast of colour and texture. The child should sit with the family and no comment should be made on his eating. After a certain length of time his plate should be removed, whether the child has eaten or not. The atmosphere at mealtimes should be that of an enjoyable social get-together which is conducive to good digestion. A period of outdoor play before a meal will often stimulate an appetite, but there should be a quiet ten minutes just before a meal with a regular routine of handwashing and general preparation.

If a child has an actual dislike of a particular foodstuff, then it is best to present it in a different way, or provide a substitute without comment. For instance, milk can be given in the form of milk puddings, milk shakes or hot chocolate. If soft boiled eggs are disliked, try hard-boiling them, or a raw egg can be added when mashing potato. Some children prefer to eat vegetables raw rather than cooked and there is no reason at all why they should not have them that way. Nothing is gained by forcing a child to eat a hated food; the child usually wins anyway. He may vomit it, or store it in his cheeks like a hamster. One of the authors' children resorted to filling his pockets with mashed potato because otherwise he would have been made to eat it by his nursery school teacher.

Children can become very conservative in their tastes and mostly prefer familiar foods, so it is important in the early days, when they will accept it, to give a wide variety of different foods. If they are presented at three or four years of age with an unknown food, many children will automatically say they dislike it. Sometimes the problem can be overcome by suggesting that the child helps himself to a very small sample to taste.

As the child becomes more mature he can be encouraged to join in the conversation at the table. Later he will want to be involved in preparations, such as laying the table and cooking the meal. This will all add to his enjoyment of mealtimes.

When a child starts nursery school or begins having school meals, there may be difficulties at first, such as refusal to eat because it is all so strange to him. He may never have seen a properly set table before, or used a knife and fork. Some children are still being spoon-fed at three years of age because their mothers dislike mess; others may be fed separately from their family, and some children sit watching television while they eat and are not used to sitting at a table. Therefore it is important for a nursery nurse to ensure that a new child is made familiar with the arrangements and the routine of mealtime in the nursery. If this is done in a kindly way, the other children will follow her example and will assist the newcomer to settle down. Most children eagerly conform if they are shown the way.

2. Cleanliness. From about eight months of age, a baby should be on the floor most of his waking time, which means that he will need his daily bath more than before. Once a baby has achieved a sitting position, he makes great efforts to become mobile. He progresses from 'swimming' on the floor, to rolling over and over, crawling and creeping and later on standing and walking. By the end of the day his knees and elbows will have become very grimy and a bath in the evening is a good idea, as it not only cleans the child but also acts as a good prelude to bedtime.

Somewhere between six and ten months of age he will have graduated to the 'big bath' and this will give him more space in which to play. After a wash all over he should be allowed time to enjoy this and be able to splash around for pleasure. Toys which float, and those which sink, plastic cups and containers for scooping up water and sponges for squeezing all add to the fun of bathtime. After the bath it is important to ensure that the child is dried thoroughly, especially in all the creases, such as those between his toes.

A child should have his own towels, flannel, toothbrush, hairbrush and comb. They can be marked with a symbol which he can begin to recognise as his own, or in a family each child could have his own colour.

On waking in the morning the baby will need a 'top and tail', but when he has finished using nappies, washing his face and hands only will be sufficient. He should have clean underclothes and socks daily. During the day, hands should be washed after using the lavatory or potty, and before meals. Nails should be kept clean and trimmed weekly. His hair should be brushed and combed daily and washed once a week, when a check should be made for the presence of nits and lice. His comb and brush should be washed at the same time as his hair.

Children often hate having their hair washed because they dislike water being splashed on their faces. The easiest way is probably to wash the hair while the child is having a bath. The head should be tipped back when rinsing, to avoid water on the face. A spray attachment is very useful for this. Use a baby shampoo because the solution will not sting if it should come in contact with the eyes.

Teeth cleaning, after meals and last thing at night, should begin as soon as a tooth appears. There is no need for toothpaste at this stage – a soft brush and tap water are sufficient.

All this starts to teach good habits, and as soon as a child is willing he should be encouraged to help with washing and dressing himself and cleaning his teeth. With practice he will gradually become more proficient, so that by about five years of age he should only need reminders and supervision.

Care of the teeth
Although the first teeth are only temporary, it is important to prevent them from decaying. There are several reasons for this:
(a) Care of the teeth forms a good habit which will continue throughout life.
(b) Decayed teeth cause pain.
(c) Painful teeth may prevent a child from eating properly.
(d) Painful teeth prevent a child chewing, which could adversely affect his jaw development.
(e) These first teeth act as 'spacers' for the permanent teeth; if a tooth has to be removed because of decay then the other teeth can close together, causing overcrowding when the second teeth come through.

Tooth decay (dental caries) is caused by plaque. Plaque is a jelly-like coating of carbohydrate debris which clings to the teeth. This coating forms an ideal medium for bacteria, because it provides food, warmth and moisure. Bacteria plus plaque produce acid, and it is the acid which attacks the tooth enamel. It gradually dissolves the hard enamel, eventually penetrating to the pulp or inner core of the tooth where the nerve endings are. There is no pain until the nerve endings are exposed. Once there is a hole, then bacteria can get into the pulp of the tooth and may cause an abscess. Usually the tooth has to be removed when it reaches this stage.

Prevention of dental caries can be tackled in several ways:
(a) by making the enamel of the tooth harder and so more resistant to decay by giving fluoride by mouth;
(b) by cutting down the amount of carbohydrate (especially sugar) consumed – don't let children chew sweets all day. If they must have sweets, then they should be given over a short period and the teeth cleaned afterwards;
(c) by cleaning off plaque as frequently as possible – clean teeth after meals, and especially before bedtime, with a good toothbrush, making sure that all surfaces are brushed;
(d) by giving hard foods such as carrot and apple to encourage chewing and to scour teeth;
(e) by visiting the dentist regularly so that any early cavities can be detected and filled before they become big and painful.

Toilet training
This usually begins at about ten months of age. The choice of this age is logical because the child:
(a) is capable of understanding what is wanted of him because he understands language;
(b) is physically able to sit steadily on a pot;
(c) is capable of some bowel control;
(d) may at this stage be showing definite signs when he is about to have his

bowels open, for example, red fáce and a quiet, concentrated manner;
(e) he may at this stage be having his bowels open at a regular time each day
    (perhaps after breakfast).

A baby is very anxious to please his mother or nursery nurse and will try to
co-operate with her, so it is possible to capitalise on this. Praising the child for
effort will help to increase his co-operation. A calm, matter-of-fact attitude is
best. Talk to him about what you want. Sit him on the pot for about five minutes
after breakfast or at a time he usually has his bowels open. If he does perform,
then praise him; if not, just dress him again. If he doesn't object, the child can be
placed on the pot for about five minutes after every meal and this will then
become part of his routine. Eventually he will get the message, but it does take
time and patience. He will have some difficulty in 'letting go' at first, so that
sometimes he will sit on the pot and do nothing and then when he stands up and
relaxes, his bowels will open. This is not a deliberate action – he cannot help it.
Gradually this problem is overcome as he becomes more mature.

Helpful hints
(a) Putting the child into pants may help because
    (i) it makes him feel grown up;
    (ii) it is difficult for him to accept that it is now wrong to wet his nappy,
         when it was all right before;
    (iii) when he does wet, he is well aware of it, as there is no nappy to soak up
          the urine.
(b) If he rebels against the pot, it is best to leave it alone for a week or two and
    then start again.
(c) It is important to have the right size pot or lavatory for the child. He should
    be able to sit comfortably with his feet squarely on the floor.
    NB: If an adult-sized lavatory is used, then a small stool or box should be put
    in a position so that the child can rest his feet on it.
(d) Some children are frightened of the lavatory and the flush and these fears
    should be respected. Others prefer to sit on the lavatory, possibly with a
    special seat to make the hole smaller. Boys may prefer to stand up to pass
    urine.
(e) Clothes such as pants and trousers should be easily removed as the need to
    use the pot is often urgent.

Bowel control is usually attained before bladder control. By about eighteen
months the child will indicate or give a vocal warning of a bowel action,
sometimes after the event, but mostly before. By about two years he should have
control and be able to indicate in time. In fact, he often has such control that he
can refuse to have his bowels open if he thinks it will annoy his mother, or if he
wants to demonstrate his own power to control his actions.

Bladder control comes a little later. By one year nine months a child will
usually report when he wants to pass urine, but may be too late. By about two
years he should have control during the day, but accidents may still occur.
Between two and a half and three years of age, night control is possible, but this
varies with different children. Girls usually attain control before boys. Once

control is achieved then the next step is teaching the child to cope with his own toilet needs. Again, clothes should be easy for him to remove and he will need reminders and supervision. Regular visits to the lavatory should become part of his daily routine, especially after breakfast and before going to bed. Time must be allowed for this, so the morning and evening routines should not be rushed.

Toilet training should be straightforward, but problems can arise if too much is expected of a child too soon, or if the whole business is taken too seriously. A child cannot attain bowel and bladder control until his central nervous system has matured enough to let him control the muscles in his pelvic area. Just as there is a large variation in the age at which a baby can walk (nine months to two years) so there is also a variation of age at which a child controls his bowels and bladder. It is important for those in charge of children to be aware of these variations, so that they do not compare one child unfavourably with another, or expect too much from individual children.

Even after a child has control, there may be accidents or setbacks. For instance, losing control of his bowels or bladder is one way in which a toddler can get back his mother's attention from the new baby. It can also be a way of annoying his mother, or asserting himself. It should also be remembered that if a person is frightened, he tends to pass urine more frequently and may get diarrhoea (this is a side effect to the production of adrenalin which is produced when a person is frightened, to enable him to fight or run away), so this may explain why children 'in care' are often incontinent.

Most children gain complete control of their bowels and day control of their bladder fairly easily, but night time control of the bladder often take much longer. In fact about twenty to twenty-five per cent of children still wet their beds at five years of age. However, by ten years of age, the figure is about 0.05 per cent. As so many children do still wet their beds at five it should not be considered abnormal. Unfortunately many people regard bed-wetting at three years of age, as abnormal and can create problems by conveying to the child that this is 'dirty' and wrong. Children cannot make a distinction between what they do and what they are. So these children may begin to feel they are dirty and unworthy of love. The tension and worry created by these feelings can increase bed-wetting. Threats used to induce the child to be dry only increase his fear.

In the authors' experience 'treatment' for bed-wetting before the age of seven years often increases the problem. If a child is still wetting the bed at the age of five he should be seen by a doctor, so that his urine can be tested in case there is a physical reason for wetting, such as a urinary infection (this is very rare). Apart from this, the best attitude to the child with this problem is one of optimism. Protect the mattress by continuing to use a plastic sheet on the bed. From the age of four years stop using a nappy at night. Make sure there is a light on at night so that he can see his way to the toilet – or give him his own torch to keep under his pillow. Train him to pass urine just before bedtime. Some people find it helpful to 'lift' the child and take him to the lavatory in the late evening. If this is done, then the child must be woken up completely, otherwise he is being trained to pass urine in his sleep. This may cause sleeping problems, and if it does the practice should be stopped.

An optimistic attitude from the whole family, praise for a dry bed and very little comment when it is wet will help a child gain control. However, if bed-wetting continues after six years of age then the doctor should be consulted again. The medical name for bed-wetting is enuresis and it is one of the common problems which concern parents and nursery nurses in the early years.

Other problems include sucking – thumbs, fingers or blankets, nail-biting or picking, masturbation, etc., and they will be discussed in Chapter 14.

Soiling

It can be distressing and irritating to find that after a child has mastered bowel control he begins soiling his pants every day. It may be that he is unable to clean himself properly after having his bowels open, so this child needs some help. More commonly this problem arises because he delays having his bowels open and consequently becomes constipated. The faeces becomes dry and hard and create a blockage around which liquid faeces tend to seep, thus soiling his pants.

The reason why a child delays having his bowels open could be one of the following:

(a) He has much more interesting things to do, so he ignores the 'call'. After a while his rectum will stop signalling that it needs to be emptied.

(b) His morning routine may be so rushed that he may not have the time or opportunity to try to have his bowels open.

(c) He may have been constipated on a previous occasion and found it extremely painful when he did eventually pass the stool, so he tries to avoid this pain. *NB:* In some cases there may be a split in the anus caused by the passage of a very hard stool and this is extremely painful.

(d) He may be rebelling against his mother trying to show her that he is in control and will have his bowels open in his own good time.

(e) Extreme deprivation and other emotional reasons may result in soiling.

The best treatment for this problem is to give him a diet which contains extra fluids, and roughage (bran, porridge, prunes, vegetables and fruit) and to encourage the child to try and have his bowels open at the same time each day – usually after breakfast when the meal has caused peristalsis to increase. This can re-establish the habit of emptying his bowels at regular intervals.

If this does not work within two to three weeks or if the child appears to be in pain, then the family doctor should be consulted.

Another cause of soiling (and also smearing of faeces) may be threadworms in the child's intestine. These worms come out of the anus to lay their eggs around it and cause intense irritation. The child scratches in and around his anus and his fingers become contaminated with faeces which are wiped on his pants or anywhere else. Diagnosis is easy, as the worms can be seen in his faeces. They look like threads of cotton and when freshly passed will move around. Treatment is simple – a medicine prescribed by a doctor will kill the worms. The life cycle of these worms can be broken by ensuring that the child's hands and nails are scrubbed frequently to prevent him transferring the eggs to his mouth (see Chapter 9 on diseases).

3. Rest and sleep. As a baby grows he will need less sleep. By about a year he should be sleeping about thirteen hours a day, at least eleven of these hours being night time. His day-time naps will gradually become shorter but he should still be given the opportunity for rest periods, one during the morning and another after his midday meal. If he does not want to sleep, then a quiet period in his cot with some toys will serve as a restful time for the child and for his mother or nursery nurse. From about two years the child will enjoy a story read to him or a quiet sitting period watching a suitable programme on television.

Children vary a lot in the amount and character of sleep needed. Some children catnap for short periods at intervals during the day, others need one to two hours of unbroken sleep at one time during the day. The child's routine should be adapted to allow for his particular needs.

A regular routine at bedtime is essential if the good sleeping habits established during babyhood are to continue. It also helps to give a child a feeling of continuity and security. The child should be warned in good time that bedtime is approaching and should be given ten minutes to finish his game. He can then be encouraged to help tidy up his toys and get undressed. A bath at bedtime should be a 'winding down' period which is soothing and conducive to sleep. If a final bedtime drink is part of the routine, then the child's teeth should be cleaned afterwards. Then he should be tucked into bed affectionately. A story should be read to him and his bedtime 'ritual' with favourite toy or 'cuddly', light on or off, curtains pulled back or not, etc., should be observed. He should then be left to sleep.

If he has had an interesting day, with his needs satisfied and adequate physical and mental stimulation, he should sleep well. A good test of whether he has had enough sleep is to note whether he wakes naturally in the morning. If he does not, and has to be woken, then he needs more sleep.

Unhappiness should be avoided at bedtime – if a child has been in trouble during the day, all should be forgiven before he goes to bed. Meals, especially the last one of the day, should be adequate and easily digested. A child's room and bed should be comfortable and welcoming. Never use bed as a punishment because it can cause sleep problems if a child comes to associate bed with misery.

Crying when put to bed. This may be just a 'testing' time in which he tries to get his mother back, so wait at least five minutes before returning. Then comfort him, tuck him in and leave him to sleep.

Screaming when left in bed. This is very difficult to deal with. Probably the best cure is to sit with him until he goes to sleep. Do this in a matter-of-fact way. Tell him you will stay and read a book or do your knitting and do just that. It is unwise to pick him up and take him downstairs, for he will come to expect that every night.

Try to find out the cause of his problems and remedy it. Sleep problems can be caused by:

(a) a feeling of banishment from the rest of the family. This may be remedied by not rushing his bedtime preparations and by sitting with him for a while;

(b) jealousy – there may be a new baby, or an older child who is allowed to stay up later. Extra attention during the day may help to overcome this;

(c) insecurity – the worst kind of insecurity stems from having parents who are always in conflict with one another. The stability of the child's home is shattered each time they argue and he may be too frightened to go to bed in case one or other of his parents should leave while he is asleep. It is important for parents to avoid arguments in front of children. Small children respond more to the tones of voices raised in argument. What is only a small dispute to an adult can sound very frightening to a child, and keep him awake worrying. Similarly, other worries about events during the day can cause sleeping problems. Look over the child's routine and see if he needs more attention or more demonstrated affection;

(d) fear of the dark – provide him with a light;

(e) other fears – try to find out what they are and help overcome them. For example, if he is frightened of a large dark cupboard then take him in with you during the day and explore it together.

Bad dreams; screaming in the night. This is fairly common and the child does not usually wake up. If he does, he cannot tell you what is wrong, so don't ask him. Just go to the child and cuddle and comfort him until he is calm and settled.

Falling out of cot. Once a toddler starts climbing and trying to get out of his cot he is likely to have a fall. The best remedy is to put him into a bed where, if he falls out, it will only be a small drop.

Waking in the night. If a child wakes at night and comes into his parents' room, the best thing is for one parent to take him quietly and firmly back to his own bed and stay with him until he settles down to sleep again. This can be a wearisome task in the middle of the night and the temptation to take the child into his parents' bed is very great. But the alternative to taking the child back is to have him expecting to come into his parents' bed every night.

Early waking. Place some toys at the bottom of his cot or bed so that when he wakes up there will be something for him to do.

4. Exercise. Exercise is essential for good growth and development. Muscles which are used become 'toned' up, which enables them to perform more tasks and to become more efficient. Active muscles need food and oxygen which is carried by the bloodstream. They also produce wastes (carbon dioxide and water) which are removed by the blood. Therefore active muscles increase and stimulate the circulation of blood. The presence of extra carbon dioxide in the blood stimulates respiration so that breathing deepens in order to expel it. Therefore, more oxygen is taken into the lungs and all the body benefits because increased oxygen supply leads to:

(a) increased activity, especially in sweat glands, liver and kidneys;

(b) improvement in appetite and digestion;

(c) stimulation of nervous system resulting in clearer mental processes.

Children are naturally active creatures but they do need space, opportunity and stimulation for exercise. If a child is kept strapped in his pram all day he will at first make strenuous efforts to move, but after a time will give up his efforts and become passive. A baby should be placed on the floor for increasingly long periods of time, so that his natural curiosity will give him the impetus to become mobile. Furniture should be stable so that he can safely pull himself to his feet. Push-along trolleys, push-and-pull toys and balls will all help to increase his mobility. Later, as he becomes more skilful, tricycles and go-carts, a climbing frame, paddling pool and sand-pit will all provide stimulation for different activities which will aid his growth and development. The day should consist of alternating periods of quiet, restful play and active, noisy play, especially outdoors so that the child can let off steam.

5. Fresh air and sunlight. Activity in the fresh air has a stimulating effect on the whole body and if possible all children should play outdoors for part of every day. Good ventilation in buildings is important, because it circulates fresh air and so replenishes oxygen. Well-ventilated rooms in nurseries and schools help to reduce the spread of infection between children, because germs prefer the conditions found in unventilated rooms – warmth and humidity.

Sunlight is necessary to all life. It warms the earth and gives us light. We all feel better when the sun shines. Sunlight on the skin enables the body to produce vitamin D. It also kills many germs. However, care should be taken when exposing young children to the sun, because of the danger of burning. Sun-hats should be worn and a suntan lotion used on the skin to prevent burning. This is especially important at the seaside because a fair skin can burn very quickly when sunlight is reflected off the sea. Exposure should be for gradually increasing periods each day.

6. Warmth. As a child matures, his body becomes better able to control its temperature. He will still need warm surroundings for comfort, but because he is more active will be able to keep warm more easily.

Clothing
Materials used for clothing should be as follows:
(a) capable of being easily washed;
(b) hard-wearing;
(c) absorbent;
(d) warm;
(e) safe – flameproof.

As already discussed in the section dealing with the layette, the most suitable materials are fabrics made from natural fibres or a mixture of natural and synthetic fibres. Synthetic fibres are uncomfortable next to the skin because they do not absorb moisture.

Clothes should have the following qualities:
(a) They should be easy to put on and take off and fastenings should be simple, so that a child can easily learn to become independent, for his toilet needs and for dressing and undressing himself.
(b) They should not restrict. Restrictive clothing can be unsafe and will frustrate an active child.
(c) They should be safe in design. For example, there should be no loose ends, as with wide flared trousers which could catch on projections.
(d) They should be suitable for the occasion – for example, not too dressy for nursery school or the child will worry about keeping them clean.
(e) The child should have some choice in colour and design. When buying

clothes take the child with you and select two or three suitable articles and let him choose between them.

A suitable outfit for children

(a) underwear: cotton pants, cotton vest, cotton/nylon socks (summer), woollen socks (winter);

(b) boys: dungarees, or long or short trousers, shirt, jumper or cardigan and anorak or other jacket (for colder weather);

girls: pinafore skirt or trousers and blouse (or dress), jumper and anorak (for colder weather).

In addition children need pyjamas or nightdresses and a dressing gown. In very cold weather children also need a hat and gloves. In wet weather, wellington boots are useful to keep their feet dry. A child needs at least three sets of clothing, so that one can be worn whilst one is being washed, and the other is in the drawer ready for use.

Shoes. A baby will not need shoes until he has learned to walk properly. His bare feet will give him a better grip on the floor, and shoes at this stage would only hinder him. As the bones in children's feet are not fully calcified, they are soft and can easily be deformed by shoes or socks that are too tight. In China, girl babies' feet used, at one time, to be bound tightly so that the toes were doubled back, and this meant that the feet grew that way and the forming bones set in that position. This is an extreme example of deformity, but it does serve to illustrate how a child's feet can easily be pushed out of shape. Tight all-over suits, socks, shoes, bootees and even tightly tucked-in bedclothes can damage the feet. It is not painful to the child because at this stage his bones are flexible, and the effects are not usually seen until he is much older – perhaps in middle or old age when corns, bunions, hammer toes and other allied problems give rise to pain and lack of mobility.

Children's feet grow fairly rapidly, so socks and shoes should be carefully fitted and checked every three months for size. A stretch sock should be big enough to fit the foot, not to be stretched by it. When shoes are bought, both feet should be measured for length and width and the shoes fitted by a trained fitter. Some manufacturers of children's shoes have special courses where shoe-shop assistants are trained in the correct fitting of children's shoes. It is well worth seeking out a shop with trained assistants.

Slippers should also be carefully fitted. Where possible, children should be encouraged to run around without shoes and socks in the house, as the feet benefit from this freedom.

7. Good health. As already mentioned, children should be seen at regular intervals by a doctor to ensure their development is progressing at a normal rate and that there are no defects. They are usually examined between three and four years as a pre-school check to anticipate any problems which might occur when they start school. For instance, if speech remains immature, then a mother can be shown how she can help her child overcome it, and professional help can be brought in if necessary.

In most areas, once a child is at school he will be seen by the school nurse annually for a 'health survey', when cleanliness and general state of health are assessed. He is also weighed and measured and his eyesight is tested. Hearing is tested once, on entry to school, by an audiometrician. Any problems arising can be referred to the appropriate authority after parents have been informed. Many education authorities have stopped doing routine medical inspections, because it is rare to find any undiagnosed physical defect at this time. Instead, parents are sent a questionnaire on their child's health. When this is returned, the school doctor (clinical medical officer), head teacher and health visitor get together to discuss each child and assess whether he needs to be examined. The records from the health visitor and Child Health Clinic are consulted, together with the questionnaire. If the parent reports problems, or the child is not progressing as he should at school, a medical inspection is arranged, to which parents are invited. Children who present no problems are not examined at all.

Early visits to the dentist are important, too, so that the children will get used to him before any treatment is actually needed, and also to ensure that only minor future treatment will be necessary to prevent loss of teeth. Most dentists will begin regular inspections from about two and a half years of age. This is a good time to begin, because the twenty temporary teeth are usually complete by this age and a child is capable of co-operating. First visits are often just a 'ride' in the chair and a brief glimpse of the teeth but, gradually, as the surgery and dentist become more familiar, the child will allow a more thorough inspection. His mother or nursery nurse should accompany the child into the dental surgery.

Signs of good health	*Signs of subnormal health*
clear firm skin – good colour	pallor – skin looks doughy
bright eyes	dull eyes
firm, well-developed muscles	flabby muscles
breathing through nose – mouth closed	mouth breathing
eating well with good appetite	constantly runny nose
sleeping well	poor appetite
bowels normal	poor sleep
normal progress and development	constipation
weight and height within normal limits	poor progress and development
alertness	apathy
interest	miserable, whining disposition
contentment	dullness
ability to accept frustration of wishes	

If a child presents any signs of subnormal health one must check his daily routine and see if any changes can be made to improve his health. In any case, the family doctor should be consulted about the child's general health. (Signs of acute illness are dealt with in Chapter 9 on care of the sick child.)

8. Protection. A child over one year of age still needs some protection from infection but has developed a certain amount of immunity to his family's germs. His drinking water or cow's milk (in Great Britain) need not be boiled after he is a year old. Provided his feeding bottle and teat are cleaned thoroughly with very hot water, they no longer need be sterilised. However, care should still be taken with handwashing, disposal of nappies, use of potty, etc. This is especially important in the day nursery and nursery school because a child takes longer to build up a resistance to the many different germs he will meet there.

The course of immunisation against whooping cough, diphtheria, tetanus and poliomyelitis is usually completed by the end of the first year, but this may vary from area to area. Usually an injection of triple vaccine (diphtheria, pertussis and tetanus) and a dose of polio vaccine by mouth is given at six, eight and twelve months. Measles vaccine is given by injection about fourteen months. Then the child should have a booster of triple vaccine at four and a half years of age so that he has protection when he starts school. In some areas a baby is also immunised against tuberculosis at one to two weeks of age.

Protection from accidents is especially necessary for the one to seven year old as they are a major cause of death. (See Chapter 18, page 263.)

9. Security. A child's security is founded on his close relationship with his mother and, later, with all the other members of his family. He needs to be aware that he is part of a united family group. A regular and consistent routine will give structure to his life by forming a pattern so that he knows what to expect and what is expected of him. He needs a few simple rules which will maintain a simple standard of behaviour within his capability. Discipline is really a matter of control which will gradually become self-control, but until that happens we must help him, both by giving him rules to follow and showing him by example. He should be allowed to pursue his own interests provided there is reasonable consideration for others. If he is not given any rules at all and is allowed to do as he wishes, he will get the impression that nobody cares what he does.

A child likes to please his mother and this fact can be used to advantage. Praise for 'good' behaviour or efforts to help will enable a child to learn in a positive way what is acceptable. A child usually knows the meaning of the word 'No' from about nine months of age – he also responds to his mother's tone of voice. But 'No' should be used in moderation, or it ceases to have any meaning. A child under two and a half years is not amenable to logic, so it is better to be positive and direct his activities towards what you want than to keep using the negative. Constant criticism can destroy a child's security, but distraction from an activity you do not like is a useful alternative.

From about three years of age children love rules and regulations and will soon tell newcomers to the nursery that they are 'not allowed to do that', etc. Children enjoy belonging to an ordered society where things remain much the same, apart from certain events which are predictable – for example, birthday parties. They also like to feel that the adults in their life have similar attitudes and standards. This can be difficult in a nursery or school because standards do vary. It is very important for a nursery nurse to avoid innocently causing conflict in a child's mind by voicing criticisms or remarks which could apply to his mother. It is better to try to find out what is done at home and then resolve any differences in a tactful way. Mothers should be free to visit the nursery or nursery school at any time and see for themselves how activities are carried out and how well their child is settling down. It is to be hoped that both mother and nursery nurse can learn from one another for the ultimate good of the child's security and development.

A child's security also involves having his own possessions and a place to keep them – even if it is only a cardboard box. Ideally he needs a cot or a bed of his own, a cupboard and drawers for his own toys and clothes. This is especially important for the child in residential care or hospital, as keeping his own possessions and wearing his own clothes will continue to provide a link with home.

If a child during his first seven years grows up with a feeling of belonging and being a valued member of a family group, it gives him an inner security which should last all his life and which nothing is likely to destroy.

10. Affection. A child needs someone to love him unconditionally, despite his faults. This unconditional love is closely linked with security.

Love can, and should, be demonstrated by cuddles and hugs and other physical contact, but these are only the outward signs. To pick up a child and kiss him is an easy way to demonstrate love, and it can be done even when affection is absent. But to deal with a young child's dirty nappy cheerfully and wipe up his vomit needs a basis of real affection. The quality of care and concern brought to bear on all the duties and chores – especially the tiresome ones – of rearing a child show him just how deeply he is loved and wanted.

Mothers and nursery nurses should show their affection by talking and listening to a child and praising his efforts. They should let him see the pleasure they get from his company. A child needs to be reassured that he is 'a good boy' and given approval so that he feels a valued person. The worst thing that can happen to him is to lose his mother's or nursery nurse's approval, so it is necessary to let him know, when he is naughty, that it is the deed you dislike and not him. To threaten to withdraw love is a terrible punishment and should *never* be used.

The deepest kind of love must normally come from a child's natural mother. Other people can only do their honest best. Nursery nurses must possess an affectionate nature, because a child can detect differences between impersonal concern and truly affectionate care.

11. Stimulation (see Chapter 15 on play). Much of a child's stimulation arises out of his natural curiosity which impels him to explore and discover. But curiosity needs satisfaction so that it can continue to help a child's development. Opportunity and space, as well as playthings suitable to his age and ability, must be provided to stimulate his five senses. Once he is mobile and on the floor, all kinds of things will interest him and many playthings can be improvised – saucepans and lids, wooden spoons, plastic beakers and cups and spoons, old handbags, paper bags, clothes pegs, etc. A child also needs to play with natural materials such as water, sand, clay and mud so that he can explore their qualities. Through play he learns about the world around him.

Stimulation also comes from his mother's pleasure in his efforts and achievements. She will share with him the triumph of being able to stand upright and walk and make sounds which gradually take on meaning. Talking, singing and reading to him, listening and responding to his noises, and interpreting those noises, will all help to encourage his all-round development as well as speech and language.

A child's surroundings should be bright and gay and his own attempts at drawing and painting should be displayed on the walls for all to see.

12. Social contacts. Until about two years of age a baby is very dependent upon his mother and the rest of the family and they, together with family friends and neighbours, provide all the social contacts a child needs. Between one and two years many children become shy of strangers and an enforced separation during this time (such as a hospital stay) can be harmful.

From about two years of age a child should gradually become more confident and ready for more contact with the outside world. The two-year-old child will like to play alongside other children and, towards the end of the year, the beginnings of co-operative play will be seen.

By three years of age most children are ready to join in group play, and this is the usual age for starting nursery school or play group. Provided a child has a secure background, he should settle into a group and enjoy the companionship of others, eventually being able to dispense with his mother's continual presence. Within a group he widens his outlook and learns the 'give and take' necessary in social life. From three years of age a child should be able to relate to other adults as he does to his mother and respond to a friendly approach. By the time he begins 'real' school, at five, he should be friendly, confident, able to make friends and play in harmony with others.

13. Independence. Gradually, a child must become less dependent on others, although his mother will remain his anchor. Until two years of age, he will want to be near her all the time. From about the age of two he begins to move away from this dependence on his mother, and this change should be encouraged. The first two years should be regarded as a preparation towards a child's independence. He must learn, gradually, the skills needed to care for himself so that he can eventually take over from his mother. Learning to feed himself, dress and undress himself, attend to his toilet needs, etc. cannot be achieved without opportunity to practise. When he shows he is ready to learn he must be encouraged to try and be praised for his efforts. Gradually from about two years of age he should take over these personal tasks so that by the time he is seven only reminders are needed.

Exercise 7

Multiple-choice questions
1. If a child of twenty months consistently refuses to eat boiled eggs, what would you do?
(a) force him to eat them;
(b) play games, e.g., 'aeroplanes', to coax him to eat some;
(c) serve egg in other forms, with no comment;
(d) remove eggs altogether from his diet.

2. A child of eighteen months refuses to sit on the pot. How would you deal with this problem?
(a) leave toilet-training for two weeks, then start again;
(b) force him to sit on the pot;

(c) punish him each time he soils himself;
(d) tell him you don't love him if he does not use the pot.

3. What preparation is most likely to lead to a good night's sleep for a young child?
(a) a good romp with his father;
(b) a discussion of the day's events, including misdemeanours;
(c) a bath, a story and a cuddle;
(d) letting him stay up until he is really tired.

4. For which of the following diseases is there no immunisation to protect the child?
(a) measles;
(b) whooping cough;
(c) gastro-enteritis;
(d) poliomyelitis.

5. Which of the following would be the most suitable play material for a child of between one and two?
(a) a book of pictures for colouring;
(b) a rattle;
(c) a clockwork toy;
(d) small blocks in a pull-along truck.

Essay questions
6. Describe a satisfying day in the life of *either*
(a) a one-to-two year old *or*
(b) a four-to-five year old
fulfilling all their essential needs?

7. What might lead you to suspect that a young child in your care was less than completely happy and healthy, and how would you deal with it?

8. How does a mother, or a mother-substitute, show affection to her child, and why is this so important?

Project
9. Improvise a toy suitable for a one-to-two year old, and explain its value and relevance.

Observation
10. Observe a baby or a young child at bathtime.
Notice his anticipation, initial reaction to water, reaction to being washed, reaction to having his hair washed, removal from the water.
How does he play? How does he show his enjoyment of the water? Does the bathtime ritual affect his mood afterwards? How did the adult interact with the child to make it an enjoyable experience?

Suggestions for further reading

Gwendolene E. Chesters, *The Mothering of Young Children*, Faber & Faber Ltd
Lee Salk, *What Every Young Child Would Like His Mother to Know*, Fontana/Collins
M. L. Kelmer Pringle, *Caring for Children*, Longman Group Ltd

Chapter 8
Germs and disease

Infection

People who choose to work with babies and children must always be alert to the dangers of infection which can make a child seriously ill, and even cause death. A baby is born with little defence against germs and, as they are all around us, on our skin, in our noses and throats and in the air we breathe, the child is at risk all the time. Fortunately, as children grow older and encounter the many different germs, they gradually develop an ability to fight them.

We cannot keep a baby in a germ-free atmosphere, and it would not be a good idea if we could, because he would never develop any resistance to infection. But until he has developed resistance, we must protect him by ensuring that his environment does not contain an overwhelming number of disease-causing germs.

Germs are a category of micro-organism, so-called because they are so small that they can only be seen under a microscope; in fact you could fit about 80 000 on the head of a pin. They are mostly organisms consisting of only one cell, so they have a very simple make-up. Many of these micro-organisms are harmless; some are even essential to maintain life on earth, but others cause various diseases in man.

The many thousands of types of micro-organisms are divided, and subdivided, into groups. The two main groups are:

1. Non-pathogenic (harmless to man)
These include:
(a) the organisms which turn milk into cheese;
(b) The organisms which convert organic matter (leaves, faeces, urine, etc.) into fertiliser.

2. Pathogenic (causing disease in man)
There are many subdivisions but the most important ones include the following:
(a) *bacteria* divided into groups according to shape:
     (i) cocci (round shape); *examples:* streptococci, staphylococci;
     (ii) bacilli (rod shape); *examples:* tubercle bacilli, tetanus bacilli;
     (iii) vibrios (curved shape); *examples:* cholera.
(b) *viruses* – these are so small that they cannot be seen under an ordinary microscope; *examples:* measles virus, influenza virus.

In addition to bacteria and viruses there are some other more complicated living organisms which can cause disease in man. These are:
(a) *protozoa* – simple one-celled animals; *example:* amoebae which cause amoebic dysentry;

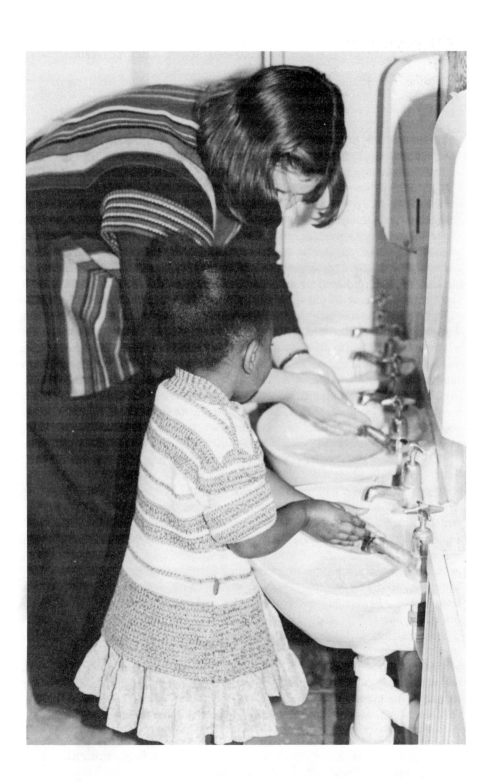

(b) *fungi* – *examples:* thrush, athlete's foot, ringworm;

(c) *animal parasites* – *examples:* lice, intestinal worm, itch mite (scabies).

Most of the micro-organisms are able to reproduce by simply splitting into two and, when conditions are favourable, will do this every twenty minutes. Consequently, one or two germs can become millions in a few days providing that their essential needs are supplied. These are:

(a) moisture;

(b) warmth – average human body temperature;

(c) food;

(d) time.

Some of the organisms need oxygen, but others do not. Some are tougher than others, and can survive longer in an inhospitable environment. For instance, some of the bacilli are able to form a tough outer covering and survive without food or moisture for a considerable time. This is known as a spore formation and spores can be found in dust and dirt. When conditions become favourable to spore, it will resume its old life-style.

So although micro-organisms surround us, they are more likely to be found in warm, moist places favourable to their survival. The areas on the human body providing ideal conditions for micro-organisms are warm parts where there is moisture and food (from perspiration or other body fluids). So, although we have the micro-organisms all over our skins, they are concentrated in the armpits and groin and any breaks in the skin surface. They also occur in large numbers in the body openings – mouth, throat and nose and anus and therefore will be found in used tissues, handkerchiefs, sheets and used dressings from wounds and on potties, lavatory seats and lavatories.

In the home and nursery most organisms are found in warm, moist places with poor ventilation – in the bathroom on damp, used face-flannels, sponges, toothbrushes, towels, bathmats and carpets; in the kitchen on damp tea-towels, dishcloths, floorcloths and mops, and on exposed food, utensils and crockery which has traces of left-over food. Micro-organisms also thrive in overcrowded, under-ventilated rooms, where the air breathed out is warmer and contains more water vapour.

Infection occurs when pathogenic organisms enter the body and develop and multiply, producing toxins (poisons) which cause symptoms such as raised temperature, headaches, loss of appetite and various aches and pains. An organism may also produce a specific reaction, such as a skin rash.

Some germs can cause only one particular disease. Diphtheria bacillus, for instance, only produce diphtheria in man. Others cause different diseases according to where they are in the body. For example streptococci will cause tonsillitis if lodged in the tonsils, but will cause nephritis (kidney infection) if lodged in the kidney.

Micro-organisms can enter the body in three different ways:

(a) *inhalation* – breathed in through nose and throat;

(b) *ingestion* – swallowed through the mouth (usually in food or drink);

(c) *inoculation* – penetrating through the skin, usually through a break.

A disease is said to be *infectious* when the organism causing it can easily be transmitted from one person to another, or to a live or inanimate host on which it lives until it infects another person. These are known as direct and indirect infections respectively.

A disease is said to be *contagious* when the organism causing it can only be transmitted by actual bodily contact.

Direct infection

Actual contact is not always necessary for direct infection but the person being infected must be within the range of the infecting organism.

1. Droplet infection. When we speak we constantly spray out mostly invisible droplets of moisture from our mouths and noses. These droplets contain any of the organisms present in a nose, mouth and throat and can be passed on to any person within the range of the droplets. If a person coughs or sneezes without covering his nose and mouth, the droplets will be propelled several yards and could be inhaled by all the occupants of the same room.

In a similar way droplets from urine and faeces can be sprayed around the lavatory area. These droplets can easily contaminate hands, with the result that the organisms may later be transferred to food and eaten.

2. Kissing. Organisms will be transferred directly from mouth to mouth.

3. Sexual contact. Again a direct transfer of organisms.

4. Touch. Touching an infected skin will result in a transfer of organisms.

Indirect infection

Objects which carry infective organisms must supply some of their needs as well, or the organisms would not be able to survive for long. So, although cups, plates, pens, books and so on are often blamed for the spread of infection, they are not such a likely cause as hands, which are warm and moist with sweat. The exceptions to this are the bacilli organisms, some of which can turn into spores and survive for long periods without food, moisture and warmth. However, the commonest diseases caused by spore-forming organisms are tuberculosis, tetanus and diphtheria and we can be protected from these by immunisation.

The commonest causes of indirect spread of infection are as follows:

1. Hands. As already stated, hands can become contaminated with pathogenic organisms, especially by airborne droplets. People can infect themselves by licking their fingers or eating food with contaminated hands. They can also infect other people if they prepare food and drink for them.

2. Flies. The common house-fly prefers to feed on excreta and garbage, which are ideal breeding sites for infective organisms. Flies carry these germs in their bodies and stomachs and distribute them wherever they land. As flies feed by regurgitating some of their stomach contents on to food before sucking it up, it is easy to see how the organisms can be transferred to exposed foodstuffs prepared for human consumption. Typhoid fever and food poisoning are two examples of diseases spread this way.

3. Mice, rats and cockroaches. These can all carry pathogenic organisms on their bodies and contaminate man's food supply.

4. Food and water. Both can be contaminated at source and so infect people.

5. Certain types of dust. Those which contain animal dung and street rubbish may contain pathogenic organisms which can contaminate uncovered food.

6. Carriers. Some people are carriers of pathogenic organisms, although they are not ill at all. They may have in the past suffered from the disease but are now fit. The organisms may be carried in large numbers in the nose and throat or bowel. The commonest organisms carried in this way are the streptococci in the throat and the food poisoning germ in the bowel.

Such people can be a menace if they are not careful of personal hygiene, especially if their work is the care of young children or the preparation of food for others. They can infect large numbers of people before being detected.

These people can be identified by taking throat swabs or specimens of faeces for bacteriological examination, as the pathogenic organisms can be detected. This is often done in maternity hospitals, nurseries and food factories when an epidemic occurs. It can also be performed before a person is engaged for an occupation where employing a carrier would be hazardous to other people, for example a cook or midwife.

Fortunately we do have certain natural defences against pathogenic organisms and sufficient knowledge to protect ourselves and those most vulnerable to infection.

Natural defences

1. Good general health. This will help a person fight infection.

2. Natural specific protections – examples of these are:
(a) Acid produced by the stomach will destroy some organisms.
(b) Tears contain an antiseptic which prevents organisms multiplying.
(c) An intact skin acts as a barrier to most organisms.

3. The white blood cells. These will devour pathogenic organisms. When infection begins, the white blood cells increase and, travelling via the lymphatic system, go to the site of the invasion and fight the organisms either on the site or in the nearest lymphatic glands.

4. Immunity. Antibodies present in the blood stream are able to neutralise specific pathogenic organisms. There are several types of immunity:

Natural immunity
Antibodies are passed on from mother to child before birth and after birth in breast milk. This will protect a baby to a certain extent, until he is able to produce his own antibodies.

Actively acquired immunity
(a) If a person has an attack of an infectious disease, the presence of the organism and its toxins stimulates his body to produce antibodies to neutralise them. Afterwards the body retains the ability to produce these antibodies should the organism be met again.
(b) A similar reaction will occur if the person is given a modified (weakened) organism or its toxins. The disease itself does not appear but the stimulus is sufficient to induce the body to produce antibodies. This is known as vaccination or immunisation.

Passively acquired immunity
Antibodies can be given to a child who has been in contact with a serious infectious disease. Serum (liquid part of blood) is taken from a person who is convalescent from the disease as it will contain antibodies. This protection does not last long, but protects the child long enough for him to make his own antibodies.

Other defences

We can also protect against infection in several other ways:
1. by building up resistance;
2. by reducing the number of pathogenic organisms;
3. by preventing the spread of the organisms.

1. Build up resistance
(a) Ensure that people are as fit as possible by supplying their physical and mental needs.
(b) Ensure that the skin is kept intact and thus prevent organisms entering the body in this way:
  (i) Avoid cuts and breaks.
  (ii) Use hand cream to prevent 'chapping'.
  (iii) Good nutrition aids good skin.
(c) Breast-feed babies so that they receive the maximum amount of antibodies from their mothers. Also breast-fed babies usually have good general health so can resist infection.

(d) Protect babies from specific infections with immunisation. Diseases which can be prevented by immunisation include measles, diphtheria, poliomyelitis, whooping cough, tetanus, rubella and tuberculosis. A doctor will advise on when immunisation should take place.

Although there are slight risks attached to immunisation procedures, they are statistically very small compared with the risk of catching these diseases and developing complications leading to permanent disability or death.

2. Reduce the number of pathogenic organisms. There are several methods of doing this:

(a) Kill the organisms. It is impossible to kill all pathogenic organisms because any effective method would kill *all living organisms* indiscriminately. However, sometimes one has to kill organisms. Those which cause gastro-enteritis, for example, may be present in a baby's feeding bottle, and they can be destroyed by sterilisation. Pathogenic organisms can be killed by several methods:
   (i) application of a chemical solution such as sodium hypochlorite solution;
   (ii) exposure to heat by boiling and cooking;
   (iii) exposure to heat and pressure, as in pressure cooking;
   (iv) exposure to radiation;
   (v) exposure to sunlight.
(b) Prevent reproduction of the organisms. This can be achieved by depriving the organism of one or more of its conditions for survival. For example:
   (i) moisture – therefore we should dry articles; hang up towels and face flannels to dry;
   (ii) warmth – most pathogenic organisms need the same temperature as human beings, so we can either raise or reduce the temperature to prevent reproduction (as in pasteurisation of milk or the refrigeration or freezing of food);
   (iii) food – we should wash skin to remove perspiration;
   (iv) time – we should eat meals as soon as they are ready.
(c) Dilute the organisms. Good ventilation ensures circulation of air which dilutes the organisms. Washing the skin with soap dilutes the number of organisms on our skin.

3. Prevent the spread of pathogenic organisms by:
   (i) good personal hygiene;
   (ii) good hygiene in the home and nursery;
   (iii) public health measures.

Good personal hygiene
This is essential for anyone caring for children, because not only does it help to prevent the spread of infection but it teaches the child good habits. Children learn by imitation, and much of the teaching of good hygiene they absorb unconsciously. It is far easier to be clean if one has been trained since childhood, as it becomes automatic.

Good personal hygiene should include the following:

(a) a daily all-over wash or bath;

(b) handwashing and nail-scrubbing: before meals, before preparing food, before touching baby, after using a lavatory, after changing a napkin, after touching a pet, after using a handkerchief;

(c) use of handcream to prevent cracks in the skin;

(d) regular nail-trimming and filing;

(e) cleaning of teeth after meals and before going to bed;

(f) daily brushing and combing of hair and weekly washing; it should be trimmed regularly;

(g) covering of nose and mouth when coughing or sneezing;

(h) careful disposal of tissues and handkerchiefs – used handkerchiefs and tissues should be put in a covered container (a paper bag will do) until they can be dealt with – handkerchiefs must be washed and boiled; tissues should be burned or flushed down the lavatory;

(i) frequent changing and washing of clothing – underclothes and tights should be washed daily, and other clothing as necessary;

(j) isolation of sick adults and children – if an adult in contact with children develops a cold, sore throat, diarrhoea or a skin infection, she should report sick and remain isolated from children until she is better.

Hygiene in the home and nursery

Home: General cleanliness and neatness in the home are necessary, to reduce the numbers of pathogenic organisms present and to help prevent accidents. It is better to rely on a good standard of cleanliness and good ventilation to prevent the spread of infection, rather than lavish use of disinfectant, which tends to give a false sense of security. In any case, if a disinfectant is powerful enough to kill all germs, it will also destroy our body cells, so is a very dangerous thing to have in the house. Most domestic disinfectants sold in the shops are really antiseptics, which means that in the correct solution they prevent germs multiplying. This can also be achieved by reducing the temperature or depriving the germs of food or moisture.

There should be a daily routine of tidying and cleaning. Floors should be cleaned regularly and furniture and ledges dusted with a clean, damp duster. Carpets, rugs and upholstery should be cleaned regularly with a vacuum cleaner to remove dust. Rooms should be well ventilated so that they get a change of air. Beds and bedding should be aired daily by turning the bedclothes back and opening the windows wide for about twenty minutes. Sheets, pillowcases and towels need to be changed weekly. In addition to these daily chores, regular washing and cleaning of walls, paintwork and windows is needed. The kitchen and the bathroom need extra care because both can provide ideal conditions in which germs can multiply.

Kitchen: Modern fittings and surfaces have made kitchens much easier to clean. All working surfaces and the floor should be washed daily with hot, soapy water and scrubbed once a week. However, repeated scrubbing may in some cases be rather drastic and not necessary for modern laminates and composition flooring, and here manufacturers' instructions should be followed. Cupboards should be kept tidy. The food cupboard or store-room should be well-ventilated. This cupboard and the refrigerator should be cleaned weekly. Perishable foods should be kept in a refrigerator. Cooked food should never be left exposed because of the danger of contamination, especially from flies. Flies can be kept out by fitting fly-screens over the windows and a plastic strip curtain over the doorway. If they do find their way into the kitchen, they can be killed by the careful use of fly-spray. However, if the kitchen is kept clean and all food is covered, they will not be tempted in. Food scraps, dirty plates, milk bottles and open rubbish bins all invite the presence of flies. So food scraps should be disposed of quickly, and the rubbish-bin should have a lid on at all times and should be emptied at least once a day. A waste-disposal unit under the sink is very useful and hygienic because it minces up all organic rubbish, which is then flushed down the drain.

Washing up should be done immediately after meals, and the sink and draining board wiped down after use. Sink cleaning with a suitable proprietary cleaner should be carried out after washing up the utensils from the main meal of the day. Mops, dishcloths and floorcloths should be well rinsed after use and hung out to dry. Once a week they should be sterilised by soaking in household bleach or boiling in water.

Washing up is best carried out by the following method, using a double sink:
(1) Remove food scraps.
(2) Rinse all food debris by holding the plates under a running water tap and using a mop or brush.
(3) Use very hot water and detergent to wash crockery and utensils – start with the cleanest glasses and crockery, leaving the dirtiest items and saucepans until last.
(4) Rinse in very hot water in the second sink.
(5) Place in a rack and allow to dry – if the rinsing water was hot enough, this will only take a few minutes.

Hand washing facilities should always be available in the kitchen so that hands can be washed before preparing food.

Bathroom: All members of the family should have their own flannel, towel, toothbrush, etc. There should be enough hooks, racks and rails for these items to be hung up to dry after use. Family members should be trained to rinse the washbasin and clean the bath after use and to hang up towels and flannels and the bath mat to dry. If this procedure is followed, then the bath and basin will only need a thorough cleaning once a week, using an appropriate cleanser.

The lavatory should be checked daily, the seat should be kept dry, and bleach or some other cleanser put down last thing at night. Once a week the seat and lavatory basin should be scrubbed with hot soapy water and rinsed and dried. The lavatory brush should be hung up to dry after use. The floor of the bathroom and lavatory should be washed weekly. Ventilation is important, so windows should be left open when practicable.

The nursery or nursery school: As in the normal home, a regular routine of tidying and cleaning must be carried out daily. In addition, extra care must be taken to prevent the spread of infection from child to child. Children can fairly easily build up a resistance to the germs present in their own homes, but take far longer to do so for the many and varied germs of all the other children. The younger the child, the longer it will take for him to build up such a resistance. It follows that in the day nursery where there are very young children a high standard of cleanliness is absolutely necessary. Many children are admitted to day nursery because of poor social conditions, which means they are often in a poor state of health because they live in substandard housing and eat an inadequate diet. Consequently they have even less resistance than the normal child. Another reason why infection can spread rapidly and easily in a nursery is that children have habits which encourage the spread of germs. For example, they pick their noses, lick their fingers and cough over other people unless they are watched every moment of the day.

Nurseries and schools usually have their own routines to ensure cleanliness and these will vary. Student nursery nurses will learn in their practical situations how to clean and care for the nursery as well as for the children. Although actual practices vary, the principles remain the same – cleanliness and good ventilation both help to reduce the number of pathogenic organisms.

In the children's rooms floors are usually cleaned daily by cleaners, but nursery nurses often carry out the damp dusting and general tidying necessary. Waste paper bins and bins containing used tissues must be emptied daily. Tables will need to be wiped down before and after use. All rooms should be thoroughly aired by opening all the windows for a while before the children arrive in the morning and again at mealtimes. A window should be left open during the day.

In the bathroom every child should have his own flannel, towel, toothbrush, brush and comb. These are usually marked with a symbol for each child so that he can recognise his own. There should be provision to hang these articles up separately so that they dry between uses. They should be washed weekly in hot, soapy water, and rinsed and dried in the open air.

Each child who needs one should have his own potty, which should be emptied and washed thoroughly in hot, soapy water after use.

Lavatories should be kept dry. Once a day the seats, lavatory pans and surrounds should be scrubbed with hot, soapy water and rinsed and dried. Household bleach can be left in the lavatory-pan overnight and flushed away in the morning before the children arrive. Children should be supervised at all times in the lavatory and bathroom so that puddles and spills can be wiped up immediately they occur. The children should be taught to pull the flush and to wash their hands after using the lavatory. The handbasins should be rinsed after use and cleaned thoroughly once a day with a cleaning powder.

Nappies – any excreta can be brushed off into a lavatory pan or sluice (this task is made easy by the use of disposable nappy liners). The nappy should then be rinsed thoroughly in cold water, wrung out and placed in a covered container. Methods of washing nappies depend on the facilities available. They can be soaked in a nappy cleansing solution (according to directions on the packet) or they can be washed in hot, soapy water and boiled. Whatever method is used, they must be rinsed thoroughly in plenty of water and dried in the open air if possible.

In the nursery kitchen, as in the home, all surfaces must be kept clean and flies and other pests must be kept out. Washing-up is often carried out in a washing-up machine which, because of the heat produced, will sterilise crockery and utensils. If there are babies under one year of age in a nursery, there should be a separate milk kitchen where feeds can be prepared and feeding equipment cleaned and sterilised. All babies should have their own feeding utensils marked with their name and kept separate from one another. The room should be cleaned daily – all surfaces should be washed and dried.

Cots for babies and beds for the older children should each be marked with the child's name and kept separate, not only from the point of view of hygiene but also so that the child has a place of his own. Bedding should be changed frequently and the cot or bed should be cleaned thoroughly after a child leaves the nursery, before using it for another child.

Any child suffering from a cold, sore throat, diarrhoea, vomiting or a skin infection should be isolated from other children until he has recovered. Similarly, any nurse suffering in this way should stay away from work until cured.

Public health measures. It was not until the early 1800s that it was recognised that the public authorities could take various sanitary measures which would help to prevent the spread of infection and improve health standards. The first Public Health Act was passed in 1848 and was followed by another in 1878 which laid the foundations for modern public health. These are based on the environmental needs of any community which are:

(a) a supply of pure water;
(b) the prevention of water and air pollution;
(c) the provision of adequate drainage;
(d) the removal and treatment of sewerage and refuse;
(e) a supply of clean, wholesome food;
(f) healthy dwelling houses;
(g) regulation of disease by notification and prevention of the spread of infectious diseases;
(h) provision for burial of the dead;
(i) registration of births and deaths.

The Public Health Acts are administered by Environmental Health Officers who work in the Public Health Departments of the Local Health Authority.

Exercise 8

Multiple-choice questions

1. Infectious diseases are mostly passed from person to person by means of:
(a) articles handled by an infected person;   (c) droplets;
(b) lavatory seats;   (d) personal contact.

2. Which house is the most hygienic?
(a) one where the floors are scrubbed with disinfectant;

(b) one whose drains are cleaned daily with disinfectant;
(c) one which is aired daily by opening all its windows;
(d) one in which all the occupants have a daily bath.

3. Which of the following articles is most likely to harbour a large number of pathogenic organisms?
(a) an old book;
(b) a dish of warm rice-pudding left in the kitchen for some time;
(c) an unopened bottle of milk;
(d) a lavatory seat.

4. Which of these micro-organisms can turn into a spore when survival conditions are unfavourable?
(a) tetanus bacilli;   (c) streptococci;
(b) influenza virus;   (d) fungus.

5. Which of the following diseases can be prevented by immunisation?
(a) chicken-pox;   (c) mumps;
(b) measles;   (d) impetigo.

Essay questions
6. What do you understand by the term 'immunity'? Describe the different types of immunity, briefly. How do we use our knowledge of immunity to protect young children from various diseases?

7. What precautions should be taken in the 'baby-room' in a day nursery to prevent the spread of infection?

Suggestion for further reading

A. B. Christie, *Infectious Diseases*, Faber & Faber Ltd

Chapter 9
Common infectious diseases and the sick child

Infectious diseases which affect young children are becoming much less common since the advent of mass immunisation campaigns and public health measures to prevent the spread of infection. We are able to protect children from many diseases by means of immunisation. Unfortunately, as a generation grows up never having seen just how serious and damaging are these diseases, the number of children being immunised drops. This leads to another epidemic.

There are risks attached to being immunised, just as there are to any medical procedure, but many people fail to realise that the risk of an adverse reaction from immunisation is far lower than the risk of damage from the actual disease. In the past, thousands of children died from complications following diseases such as measles, whooping cough and diphtheria.

Most infectious diseases follow a similar pattern, although the organisms causing the disease and their manifestations are different. First the organism enters the body. Then follows a period of incubation during which the organism multiplies rapidly. This is when the child will be most infectious, but there will be no outward signs of the disease, although the child may be miserable and 'off colour' towards the end of this stage. The next stage is when the disease manifests itself and causes the child to become obviously ill. His temperature will be raised, causing him to shiver and be generally miserable with aches and pains, and a rash or some other specific sign will appear. After a period of illness, the signs and symptoms will subside and the child will either recover or will become more ill with complications.

Although the nursery nurse is not expected to diagnose a child's illness, she should be aware of the signs and symptoms and the progress of the common infectious diseases. It is important for her to know when medical aid is needed and to know what to expect if a child in her care has been in contact with an infection. In all cases of suspected infectious disease a doctor should be called and his instructions should be followed if the child is subsequently nursed at home. The following charts summarise the causes, symptoms and treatment of the commonest infectious diseases.

Caring for sick children at home

Many parents and nursery nurses are hesitant to call a doctor to a sick child because they fear it may prove to be something trivial which does not warrant a doctor's attention. However, it is better to be safe than sorry and as a child's condition can change from hour to hour he can become seriously ill very rapidly. If you are in doubt, telephone the child's doctor and ask advice, rather than wait until late at night and have to call him out. The following list of conditions indicate an urgent need for a doctor's advice:

1. severe pain;
2. suspected ear infection – pulling ears, banging head, etc.;
3. vomiting – for twenty-four hours if a baby under one year;
4. diarrhoea – for twenty-four hours if a baby under one year;
5. abnormal urine;
6. hoarseness or noisy breathing;
7. loss of interest in what is going on around him by baby under one year;
8. rash which causes irritation or is accompanied by illness;
9. convulsions or fits;
10. raised temperature:
    – a temperature of 38.3°C (101°F) or higher;
    – a temperature above 37.3°C (100°F) over a period of four hours.

Every nursery nurse should be able to take a child's temperature and read a thermometer. The normal temperature range for a child is 36.1°C to 37.2°C (97° to 99°F) and temperatures are usually slightly higher in the evening. Young children do not have an efficient temperature regulating mechanism, so their temperatures rise easily when they are excited or playing. Therefore a raised temperature must not be used as the only indication of illness.

1. To take a temperature. Always shake mercury column down to below 35° (95°F). For children under fourteen years of age temperatures should be taken in the axilla (armpit) or groin.
(1) Explain to the child what you are doing and show him the thermometer.
(2) Sit child on your lap.
(3) Dry axilla (or groin) with a towel.
(4) Place thermometer between two folds of skin.
(5) Hold limb and keep thermometer in position for *three minutes*.
(6) Remove thermometer, put child in cot.
(7) Read thermometer and record temperature.

Temperatures may also be taken in the rectum but only by a trained and experienced person. When quoting a temperature to a doctor, always say where temperature was obtained, as there is a slight difference in reading.

Care of thermometer
Wash well in luke-warm water after use. Shake mercury column down to below 35° (95°F).

Casual use: Dry and replace in case.

Daily use: Place in a small jar of antiseptic solution. Cotton wool in base of jar will prevent damage. The thermometer will not need to be washed again before use.

2. To check the pulse. It is useful to be able to count a child's pulse rate as well as take his temperature, because the pulse can give information regarding the rate and force with which the heart is beating. It may be felt on the thumb side of the wrist where an artery passes over a bone. The first three fingers should be placed over the artery and the rate counted for a full minute. A child's pulse is usually about 120 beats a minute.

120

Infectious diseases

Disease	Cause	Spread	Incubation period	Signs and symptoms	Rash or specific sign	Treatment	Complications
Diphtheria	diphtheria bacillus	direct contact	1–6 days	sore throat, slight temperature, prostration, pallor	grey membrane in throat	rest, fluids diphtheria antitoxin, antibiotics, diphtheria toxoid	paralysis of muscles, throat obstruction, heart involvement
Scarlet fever	haemolytic streptococcus	direct contact: droplets; indirect contact	2–5 days	sudden onset of fever, sore throat, vomiting, 'strawberry' tongue, flushed cheeks, pallor around mouth	*1st or 2nd day:* bright red rash with raised pinpoint spots behind ears, spreading to trunk, arms and legs; skin peels after 7 days	rest, fluids, observation for complications, antibiotics	middle ear infection, kidney infection, heart involvement
Tonsillitis	streptococcus or staphylococci	direct infection droplets		very sore throat, white patches (pus) on tonsils, swollen glands in neck, aches and pains in back and limbs	no rash	rest, fluids, medical aid – antibiotics	middle ear infection
Measles	virus	direct contact: especially droplets	10–15 days	misery, high temperature, heavy cold with discharging nose and eyes, *later* harsh cough, conjunctivitis	*2nd day:* Koplik's spots; white spots inside cheek *4th day:* dusky red, patchy rash; starts behind ears and along hairline, spreads to face, trunk and limbs	rest, fluids, sponging to reduce temperature, dark room if photophobia	eye infection, chest infection, middle ear infection, encephalitis

Disease	Cause	Spread	Incubation period	Signs and symptoms	Rash or specific sign	Treatment	Complications
Rubella (German measles)	virus	direct contact droplets	14–21 days	slight cold, sore throat, slight fever, enlarged glands behind ears, pains in small joints	1st day: rash-like sweat rash, bright pink; starts at roots of hair; may last 2–24 hours	rest if necessary (mild disease)	none unless patient pregnant woman; virus can seriously affect foetus in first 12 weeks of pregnancy
Chicken pox	virus	direct contact droplets	7–21 days 14–21 days	slight fever, irritating rash	1st day: red spots with white raised centre on trunk and limbs, mostly very irritating	rest, fluids, lactocalamine or solution of bicarb. of soda on spots	impetigo
Pertussis (whooping cough)	Haemophilus pertussis	direct contact droplets	10–14 days	heavy cold with fever followed by cough	2 weeks: spasmodic cough followed by characteristic cough and vomiting	rest, supporting during and coughing, feed after bout of coughing	bronchitis, broncho-pneumonia, haemorrhage, due to strain of coughing, prolapse of rectum, mouth ulcers, debility, encephalitis
Mumps	virus	direct contact	7–28 days	fever, headache, swelling of jaw in front of ears, difficulty opening mouth	no rash	rest, bland fluids through straw	orchitis (inflammation of testicles), meningitis encephalitis (rare)
Infective hepatitis ('jaundice')	virus	direct contact: especially droplet; indirect contact: food or water	23–35 days	gradual onset of headache, loss of appetite, nausea, urine dark, faeces pale putty colour	5th–7th day yellow skin, itching, also yellow conjunctiva	fluids with glucose, fat-free diet, isolation	liver damage, meningitis

Disease	Cause	Spread	Incubation period	Signs and symptoms	Rash or specific sign	Treatment	Complications
Poliomyelitis	virus	direct contact: especially droplets; indirect contact: food or water	5–14 days	sudden onset of headache, stiffness of neck and back followed by paralysis	no rash	rest, medical supervision	permanent paralysis
Gastro-enteritis	may be bacillus or virus	direct contact; indirect – infected food and drink	7–14 days; ½ hour–36 hours	vomiting, diarrhoea, dehydration	no rash	fluids – water only, urgent medical aid	weight loss, debility, death
Dysentery	(1) bacilli (2) amoebic	flies	1–2 days; 1–2–7 days	vomiting, diarrhoea – blood and mucus, abdominal pain	no rash	fluids and medical aid	dehydration
Food poisoning	Salmonella or Clostridium welchi	indirect: infected food or drink	½ hour – 36 hours	vomiting, diarrhoea, abdominal pain	no rash	fluids only 24 hours	dehydration
Typhoid and paratyphoid fever	Salmonella typhi	direct contact; indirect contact: especially food and drink	12–14 days	headache, malaise, diarrhoea/constipation, fever	7th day: red papules on abdomen	rest, hospital (medical aid)	intestinal haemorrhage, intestinal perforation

3. Routine for the sick child. When a child is ill he tends to regress and act as though younger than his true age. He may become very frightened so he needs a familiar person to care for him and to stay close to him. It is a good idea to keep as much as possible to his normal routine, whilst making adjustments for his illness, because this makes him feel secure. He still has the same needs for cleanliness, rest and food, etc. but the provision of these needs will have to be adapted to his condition.

The sick room should be warm, cheerful and uncluttered. It will need to be well-ventilated and easily cleaned without causing too much disturbance to the child. If possible there should be a water supply and washing facilities in the same room. A potty should be available for the child so that he doesn't have to be taken to the lavatory. The mattress should be protected by a mackintosh because even if he has achieved bladder control, he may regress during his illness. Whilst he is very ill a child will want to stay in bed, but once he is on the mend he should be allowed to get up and dress. He can lie on the top of the bed or a settee for rest periods. When he is in bed let him lie in the most comfortable position for him. For example, if he has a cough he will want to be propped in a sitting position. This can be done with pillows for the child over a year, but if it is a young baby then the head of his cot can be raised by propping the legs securely on blocks. In this case make sure the baby is lying on his side.

A child will still need his daily bath, but, if necessary, this can be in the form of an all-over wash in bed. His hair should be brushed and combed daily and his teeth should be cleaned after every meal to keep his mouth fresh. He will need to be encouraged to use the potty before and after meals, and his hands should be washed after the toilet and before he eats. His bed should be made night and morning, and sheets and pillowcases changed frequently.

A sick child will not feel like eating, so meals must be light and appetising and in small helpings. Suitable foods include egg custard, steamed fish, chicken, milk pudding and ice cream. If he does not wish to eat, offer plenty of fluids and make sure that he drinks them.

If you have to carry out any nursing procedure explain what you are going to do first, and then proceed. Medicines are best measured into a small glass or cup rather than a spoon, and the child can be offered a sweet afterwards. Tablets can be crushed and mixed with jam. Do not put medicines in baby's bottle or a child's food because unless all the milk or food is eaten the correct dose will not be taken. Medicine must be taken and most children will accept the fact if you are firm and honest with them.

4. Hygiene during sickness. A sick child becomes very vulnerable to any infection because his resistance is lowered by his illness. Therefore the nurse should be scrupulous in her personal hygiene to protect him from further illness (see page 112).

5. Prevention of infection. If a child is suffering from an infectious disease it may be necessary to isolate him from people who have not already had the disease. Some doctors believe that, as the most infectious time is during the incubation period, it could be too late to prevent infection spreading when the disease becomes obvious. However, the dangers of infection remain until the main signs and symptoms, such as a rash, have subsided; so if you do not want other children to be infected they should be kept away from the sufferer until this period is over. A child attending day nursery or nursery school will usually be excluded until his doctor says he is clear of infection.

6. Very high temperature and dehydration. These are two of the most dangerous conditions for a child and they often occur together, causing serious problems needing hospital treatment. As a child is unable to regulate his temperature as finely as an adult, it can rise rapidly, causing a convulsion or fit. This can be very frightening to the child and to the adult in charge and may even lead to brain damage. The best treatment is prevention. Even without a thermometer it is possible to tell that a child's temperature is rising. He looks limp and miserable. He shivers because the air feels cold to his hot skin and when you touch him his body feels very hot. The easiest way to bring down a child's temperature is to put him in a bath of tepid water for about ten to fifteen minutes. This can be repeated at intervals. In bed he should be lightly clad and be covered with only a sheet. Resist the temptation to wrap him up because he is shivering – this will only make his temperature go higher. If a bath is not practicable, then strip off his clothes, place a towel under him and sponge him down with very tepid water. Pat him dry with another towel. Like the bath, this can be repeated whilst waiting for the doctor to arrive.

Dehydration occurs with fever or if the illness causes a loss of fluid, such as vomiting, diarrhoea or a head cold. The mouth and tongue become dry and parched and cracks appear on the lips. The child's urine is sparse and very concentrated, which gives it a dark colour. Dehydration means that the body fluids are not balanced and as this balance is necessary for health the child can become very ill. The treatment is prevention, by giving a sick child frequent drinks of water or any other fluid. If it is a baby under a year, then the fluid should be cool, boiled water and if he is too weak to suck from a bottle, then he must be spoon-fed at frequent intervals. The older child can have a variety of fluids – freshly squeezed orange juice or ice lolly, tomato juice, lemon barley water, glucose drink, clear soup, beef broth, or beef extract. These must be offered at frequent intervals because he will not ask for them or help himself. A straw (especially a 'bendy' one) may be useful to persuade him to drink, or a special glass or a doll's cup and saucer.

7. Convalescence. Fortunately, because a child's condition can change so rapidly, he usually recovers very quickly. He will need a period of convalescence so that he can recover his strength and adjust back to normal life again. He will also need a nourishing diet high in protein to repair his damaged body cells and he should not be allowed to get over-tired.

Amusing a sick or convalescent child means planning ahead and good organisation. As the child will regress, activities suitable for a younger-aged child should be provided, remembering that a child has a very short attention span. If he is confined to bed, a large tray or bed table is useful for his games. He can have a variety of materials and toys and most of the activities carried on in nurseries can be adapted to play in bed. If he must rest, reading stories, letting him listen to records and singing to him will all help him to relax. See Chapter 15 on play.

Hospital

When a child has to be admitted to hospital, if at all possible time should be given to prepare him for this, so that he knows what to expect. Explain as simply and truthfully as you can what will happen to him and emphasise that he will be coming home again. Most hospitals have arrangements for mothers (or nannies) to stay with their child all day and in some cases sleep in. It is very important for the child to have his mother (or mother substitute) with him to maintain his emotional security. Before admission, find out the policy of the hospital concerned so that you can be realistic. Many hospitals send out a booklet explaining procedures. You can also obtain information from The National Association for the Welfare of Children in Hospital (NAWCH) which publishes several helpful leaflets for parents and books for young children. Of course, if the hospital admission is an emergency, there will be little time for preparation, but despite the haste and probable panic, try to make some truthful explanation, such as, 'The doctor in hospital will try to make your pain better.'

When packing, make sure you take the child's favourite toy as a link with home. If he usually has a piece of blanket to suck, or a 'cuddly', or a dummy, let him take it with him. Tell the staff his nickname and any special word he may use for the potty, etc.

If the child is to have an operation then explain to him in simple language what will happen. Children are much better than adults at accepting the truth and can cope with pain provided they are not scared of the unknown.

When you have to leave the child be calm, tell him when you will be back, say goodbye and go quickly – don't try to slip away unnoticed because this will make him lose faith in you. It may help to leave your scarf or glove for him 'to look after', as this will reassure him you will be back.

Children's wards are mostly informal, homely places with specially trained staff who are aware of children's needs. Parents are usually welcomed and help with much of the nursing care. The children are allowed to be up and dressed in their own clothes as soon as they are fit enough. Play is encouraged by 'the play lady' who is probably a trained nursery nurse. School-aged children attend the hospital school during school hours. The majority of children enjoy their time in hospital and settle well. Occasionally there are problems when the child comes home. He may regress in behaviour and be difficult for a while. So long as sympathy and understanding are given, he will soon regain his sense of security.

Further charts on children's ailments

The following charts set out a further list of ailments, including skin diseases, which may occur in the early years of childhood, with notes on symptoms and when to seek a doctor's advice. Some of these ailments are contagious, and are therefore transmitted by close physical contact. In a day nursery or nursery school it is usual to exclude the child until he is said by a doctor to be free from infection. In the home, isolation is not necessary, provided treatment is being given and the normal rules of hygiene are adhered to (see page 112).

Disease	Cause	Contagious or not	Signs and symptoms	Treatment
Skin diseases Ringworm	fungus	yes (may be caught from family pet)	circular red, raised area with white scaly centre; itching; if on scalp – hair breaks off	doctor – usually antibiotic cream
Impetigo	staphylococci	yes	yellow, oozing sores with scab on top; itching; usually around nose and mouth	doctor – usually antibiotic cream
Scabies	'itch' mite (*Acarus scabius*); female mite burrows under skin and lays 20–30 eggs; eggs hatch out in 3–4 weeks and repeat cycle	yes	burrows visible as red raised spots especially between fingers; intense irritation; sleeplessness	doctor – Lorexane or benzyl benzoate lotion; all family members should be treated as instructed; sheets, pillowcases, blankets, clothing should all be washed thoroughly before re-use after treatment
Nettle rash	allergy to food, dogs or drugs, etc.	no	pink raised weals or blotches; may be swelling; itching	find allergen and avoid it; calamine lotion; doctor if associated with sneezing, raised temperature or runny nose
Sweat rash	heat too many clothes	no	pinpoint red spots; fretful baby	cool bath, calamine lotion; less clothing;

Disease	Cause	Contagious or not	Signs and symptoms	Treatment
Eczema	not always known, may be allergy	no	red angry rash, especially at backs of knees and in front of elbows; may be dry and scaly or moist; very irritating	doctor – special creams; stop child scratching; avoid use of wool in clothing
Intertrigo (sores in creases, e.g. neck)	insufficient drying after bath	no	sore red areas in neck creases or under arms or groin	zinc and castor oil cream; prevent, by drying child thoroughly after bath
Nappy rash	variety of causes: (1) faulty washing of nappies (2) dirty nappy left on too long (3) diarrhoea (4) insufficient fluids, leading to concentrated urine (5) infection, such as thrush (6) allergy to nappy liner/cream/softener in nappy, etc.	no	red area over buttocks and groin; may be scaly; may be blisters or raw patches	find cause and eliminate (1) wash nappies – boil or use sanitising powder; rinse very well; dry in fresh air (2) change nappy frequently (3) treatment for diarrhoea (doctor) (4) give extra boiled water to drink (5) treatment for thrush (doctor) (6) change nappy liner brand; stop using creams/lotions or washing softener in nappy; expose buttocks to air – leave off nappy as much as possible; Drapoline cream (medical advice)

Disease	Cause	Contagious or not	Signs and symptoms	Treatment
Verruca	?virus	?yes	wart on sole of foot – looks like a black speck – hurts when pressed	doctor or chiropodist for removal
Cradle-cap (scurf on head)	(a) inefficient washing of hair, especially rinsing (b) too much washing of hair	no	(a) brown greasy patches on scalp (b) flaky white patches	once a week: apply liquid paraffin or olive oil overnight; wash thoroughly next day; prevent by washing hair once a week – rinse very well
Eye conditions Blepharitis	not known	no	crusts (like scurf) on eyelashes; may be redness	bathe with cool boiled water and sterile swabs 5 times a day; doctor if no improvement
Conjunctivitis ('pink eye')	?virus ?bacteria	yes	itching and pain in eyes; red inflamed eyes; may be discharge	doctor isolation separate towel, flannel, etc.
Stye (abscess on root of eyelash)	staphylococci (poor health pre-disposes)	no	painful swelling at root of eyelash; pus collects (as boil)	doctor
Other conditions Thrush	fungus, via unsterile dummy or bottle teat	yes	white patches inside mouth; sore mouth; diarrhoea, vomiting may be present	doctor strict hygiene measures to prevent spread via dirty hands

Disease	Cause	Contagious or not	Signs and symptoms	Treatment
Threadworms	threadworms (1) egg swallowed (2) develop into worms in intestine (3) worms come outside anus at night to lay eggs (4) this causes itching (5) child scratches – eggs are deposited under nails (6) child licks fingers or sucks thumb – swallow eggs	yes	presence of threadworms in stool (white cotton-like pieces); sore anus; itchy bottom; sleeplessness; lack of appetite	doctor Pripsen all children in family should be treated; hygienic measures to prevent infestation: prevent scratching – tight pyjamas; nails cut short; scrub hands and nails before eating
Pediculi capiti (lice)	head lice	yes	head scratching; presence of nits (eggs) – white specks which are stuck to hair; presence of lice – small insects which move along hair	Prioderm lotion – follow directions; 'Derbac' comb – a metal comb used on hair to remove nits; all family should be treated
Constipation	various: poor diet – lack of fluid; lack of roughage; lack of vitamin B faulty habit training poor muscle tone emotional blackmail	no	hard stool painful evacuation headache listlessness abdominal pain	give extra fluids, extra roughage, extra vitamin B; encourage more exercise; encourage daily attempt to have bowels open

Disease	Cause	Contagious or not	Signs and symptoms	Treatment
Colic ('3 months colic')	air (wind) in bowels baby takes in air when feeding	no	screaming baby draws up legs in obvious pain often 6 p.m. to 10 p.m.	warm boiled water to drink; massage 'tummy'; comfort him; put baby on abdomen to sleep; 'Gripe' water may help; usually improves after 3 months of age; doctor, if severe
Hernia	weakness in muscle wall	no	(1) umbilical: bulge around umbilicus (2) inguinal: bulge in groin (3) hiatus: constant vomiting	(1) doctor – may correct itself – usually left until baby 1 year, then possibly surgery (2) doctor – usually surgery necessary (3) doctor; sit child up, especially after meals
Diarrhoea	various infection diet	yes no	loose, frequent stools abdominal pain	doctor within 24 hours if under 1 year old, 2 days for older child; boiled water only to drink for 24 hours
Vomiting	various may be infection may be feed wrong may be defect, e.g. pyloric stenosis may be regurgitation	yes no no	evacuation of stomach contents	doctor within 24 hours if under 1 year old; doctor if continuous in older child; boiled water only to drink

Disease	Cause	Contagious or not	Signs and symptoms	Treatment
Hypothermia	extreme cold	no	quiet 'good' baby; pink hands and face; body feels icy; later: unconsciousness	doctor; meanwhile: remove covers, raise temperature in room, cuddle baby; (try to prevent – warm room)
Infantile convulsions	high temperature	no	pale bluish colour; eyes turn up; twitching of muscles; unconsciousness; may stop breathing	doctor; meanwhile: cool bath or sponge down to bring temperature down; (try to prevent – see Nursing Sick Child)

Exercise 9

Multiple-choice questions
1. Which of the following is a description of impetigo?
(a) a wart on the sole of the foot;
(b) an eye infection;
(c) infected spots around nose and mouth;
(d) a fungus infection.

2. Which of the following diseases does not cause a rash?
(a) measles;
(b) chicken-pox;
(c) rubella;
(d) whooping-cough.

3. If a child has a temperature of 39.5°C (103°F), which of the following actions should you take?
(a) no action, just watch him;
(b) give him an aspirin;
(c) wrap him up to keep him warm;
(d) put him in a tepid bath, and call the doctor.

4. Thrush is caused by which of the following organisms?
(a) fungus;
(b) streptococci;
(c) bacillus;
(d) staphylococci.

5. Which of the following diseases cannot be prevented by immunisation?
(a) measles;
(b) mumps;
(c) diphtheria;
(d) tuberculosis.

Essay questions
6. Why is diarrhoea such a serious disease in a young baby? What could be the cause of it and how can it be prevented?

7. Describe how you would care for a child aged five years, who is suffering from a feverish cold and cough.

Suggestions for further reading

Gerard Vaughan, *A Pictorial Guide to Common Childhood Illness*, Arcade Publishing Magazine Ltd
Eva Noble, *Play and the Sick Child*, Faber & Faber Ltd
James Robertson, ed., *Hospitals and Children*, Victor Gollancz Ltd

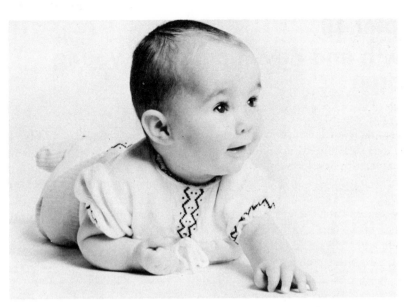

Stages in mobility: two to three months

Stages in mobility: four months

Chapter 10
Growth and development of young children

Whilst growth is an increase in size, development is an increase in ability. In practice, it is difficult to separate the two. The process of growth and all the different aspects of development interact with and are dependent on one another. For example, a baby will not start responding to his mother until he is capable of identifying her as a distinct person. However, for the purposes of study, it is necessary to separate these aspects but, at the same time, to note how the interactions take place. All babies follow the same pattern but, as they are all individuals with different environments and experiences, there are bound to be variations within this pattern, especially in the timing of the various stages. It is useful to know this pattern and its variation because it gives us a means of measuring progress.

For many years babies and children have been regularly weighed and measured and these results compared with a table of average weights and heights for various ages. But although this was a useful pointer to normal development, it was by no means a thorough guide.

Tests. The concept of developmental tests in conjunction with measuring was much slower to materialise. Hundreds of children were examined to determine the average ages for the various stages of development. Tests were devised to make use of this research. Now it is common for children to be examined at intervals from birth onwards for developmental assessment – that is to make sure that the child is growing and developing at an average rate. This has led to an earlier diagnosis of 'backwardness' or 'failure to progress' and enabled help to be given much earlier. A good example of this is the story of Michael. Michael was nine months old when brought for his first check-up, his very young mother not having thought it necessary before this time. He was found to be about three months behind in his development. His mother described him as a 'good' baby who never gave any trouble. Investigations revealed no physical reason for delay in development, but on talking to his mother it became obvious that Michael lacked stimulation. His mother expected him to lie in his cot all day. She seldom spoke to him because she herself was desperately unhappy and depressed. An attempt was made to explain to her Michael's need for attention and she was referred to her own doctor for treatment of her depression. Because there was very little improvement in the situation, Michael was admitted to a day nursery where he rapidly responded to the stimulating environment. Fortunately his mother formed a good relationship with his nursery nurse and began to take pride in Michael's achievements. At two years of age Michael was well within the normal range of development. But if the deprivation had continued, he could have remained backward all his life.

Hearing and sight. Impairment of hearing and sight are developmental defects

134

which can be easily recognised by deviations from normal and by specific tests. The earlier this sort of defect can be detected, the sooner help can be given which can minimise the effect of the disability on the child's future life. For example, if a child is found to have poor hearing, he can be fitted with a hearing aid from about six months of age. This means that he may hear normal speech and therefore have a chance to learn to speak normally.

It is essential for the nursery nurse to know how a child grows and develops. She is often the closest person to a child and, by her knowledge and observation, she could be the first to notice that the child is not progressing as well as he should. So, as well as learning in theory what to expect at various ages, the student nursery nurse should also develop her powers of observation by watching children wherever she goes. There are always babies and children in shops, buses and parks, etc. as well as in the nursery or school. An interesting and useful exercise is to watch normal children playing and try to estimate their ages. This helps you to know what is normal, and is essential if you are to be able to detect what is abnormal. Your written observations, which are part of the NNEB course, are meant to help you develop these powers of observation.

Growth of children

If you compare a newborn baby with an adult, you will see that not only is the baby obviously a lot smaller, but he is a different shape as well, because his proportions are all very different. His head appears to be very large compared with his body; in fact it is just over half the size of an adult head. Although the baby's body is small, it is his arms and legs that are extremely short. Therefore it is obvious that most of his growth must take place in the long bones of his legs and arms. Indeed, by four months of age his limbs will already be beginning to lengthen and his proportions will have changed.

Long bones form early in foetal life as cartilage, a thick, rubbery substance which bends easily. During later pregnancy and childhood, calcium, phosphorus and vitamin D are gradually deposited on to the cartilage to form hard bone. The process is known as ossification and it continues until all growth ceases, which is usually some time between twenty and twenty-four years. Most of the ossification takes place during foetal life and early childhood – hence the need to ensure a good supply of calcium, phosphorus and vitamin D in the diet during the first five years of life.

The ossification of the long bones starts at both the extreme ends and the centre of the cartilage, and the patches gradually spread towards each other, eventually leaving a 'neck' of cartilage at each end which enables growth to continue (see diagram).

By studying X-rays of children's long bones, it is possible to estimate a child's age by the degree of ossification. This is known as the 'bone age'. It is a useful guide for estimating future growth. For example, if a teenager is very small, X-rays may reveal that there is still a fair amount of cartilage present so that the child can be reassured that he will continue to grow. But once the long bones of the legs and arms are fully ossified, then no more growth can take place. In most people this occurs at about twenty-one years of age.

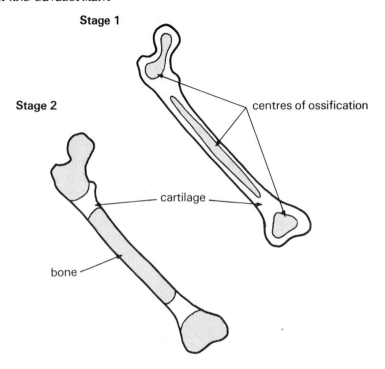

Development of bone

Teeth develop in a similar way. Here the process of ossification is called calcification, and the outer surface of the teeth (the enamel) becomes much harder than bone. The first 'teeth buds' form in the gums by about four months of pregnancy and the buds of the second, or permanent, teeth form just before birth. The buds are small pieces of cartilage and, by birth, the process of calcification of the first teeth has begun. Some babies are born with one or two teeth, but more commonly they begin to erupt between six and ten months of age when they are fully calcified. The second teeth have already begun calcifying and they will begin to erupt from about five years of age.

The first teeth are usually complete by about two and a half years of age. There are twenty in all and they consist of eight incisors which are chisel-shaped for biting and are in the front of the mouth, four canines and eight molars which are flatter in shape to enable chewing and mastication to take place. They usually erupt in a definite order:

(1) two lower central incisors;
(2) two upper central incisors;
(3) two upper lateral incisors;
(4) two lower lateral incisors;
(5) four first molars;
(6) four canines;
(7) four second molars.

They are known as deciduous teeth because, like the leaves of deciduous trees, they are shed. Around five years of age the roots of the first teeth are gradually absorbed by the body so that they become loose because of lack of anchorage. At the same time the second teeth are pushing upwards. Eventually, one by one, the first teeth fall out and the new ones erupt. In most children these processes occur at the same time, but sometimes a child will have a gap for a while before the new tooth appears. There are thirty-two permanent teeth, consisting of four incisors, two canines, four premolars in each jaw, and they gradually erupt during the next ten years or so, during which time the jaw must grow forward to accommodate the thirty-two larger teeth which will replace the twenty small 'baby' teeth. This growth of the jaw is a gradual process from about six months of age but there is a spurt of growth between five and seven years of age and this accounts for the change from a 'baby face' to one with more adult characteristics.

Since the teeth calcify early in life, it follows that calcium, phosphorus and vitamin D are extremely important in the diet for the first five years of life. If fluoride is also given by mouth in the first five years, it will combine with calcium and phosphorus to make the enamel surface of the tooth harder and more resistant to attack from bacteria which leads to decay. Applications of fluoride after the teeth have erupted are not so effective because the fluoride must be absorbed through the surface of the teeth, which limits the amount available. However, this treatment will help to reduce the rate of decay.

Although most growth continues at a steady rate throughout the body, there are exceptions, the most striking being the brain, the skull and the reproductive organs.

Brain and skull. The growth and development of the brain, spinal cord, eyes and ears are very rapid until about two years of age, when sixty per cent of their development is complete. By the time the child is seven years of age, they are almost adult size. The skull also grows rapidly to accommodate the enlarging brain. At birth it is 33–35 cm (13–14 in) in circumference, while at one year of age it is approximately 45 cm (18 in) and by seven years it is about 50 cm (20 in). The average circumference of an adult head is 55.8 cm (22 in).

The skull is made up of flat plates of bone which join together to form a box-like structure. There are two gaps (called fontanelles) created by the spaces at the joints of the skull bones.

The fontanelles are covered with membrane which protects the brain. They gradually close as the bones of the skull grow together. The posterior (back) fontanelle is usually closed by six to seven weeks, the anterior (front) one by about eighteen months. If the fontanelles are slow in closing it is an indication of poor bone growth, possibly owing to lack of calcium and vitamin D.

Sexual organs. In contrast to the rapid early growth and development of the brain and skull, the sexual organs grow very slowly until about the age of ten, and then, with the onset of puberty, there is a period of rapid growth and development, which begins earlier in girls than boys.

Weight. Weighing and measuring a child at regular intervals is a useful guide to

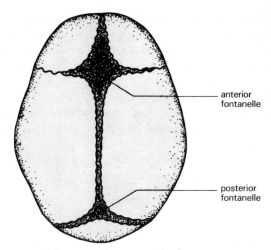

Top of head of young baby

his state of health, especially during the first year of life. If a baby is gaining weight steadily then we know that he must be getting enough food and making use of it for growth. If, in addition, he is happy, lively and active we can be sure that all is well. On the other hand, if a small baby does not gain any weight for two to three weeks it is an indication that something is wrong. It may simply be that he is not getting enough food or it could be that because of vomiting or some other reason he is unable to absorb the food. (If too much weight is gained, then it is an indication for the child's diet to be regulated to prevent obesity.)

However, weighing and measuring need to be carried out over a period of time at regular intervals so that the pattern of growth can be seen. The average new-born baby weighs about 3.400 kg (7 lb 8 oz) but his weight could be anything between 2.50 and 6 kg (5½ lb–14 lb), so when studying a baby's weight gain it is necessary to know his birth weight. Variations in the lengths of babies are not so big, the average length being 50 cm (20½ in) within a range of 45.5 cm–55.8 cm (18–22 in). Boys are usually slightly heavier than girls, although boys and girls tend to grow at much the same rate in the first seven to ten years.

Age	Height (cm)	Weight (kilos)	Height (in)	Weight (lb)
Birth	52	3.400	20½	7½
5 months	63.5	6.800 Double birth weight	25	15
1 year	71	10.000 Treble birth weight	28	22
1½ years	76	11.700	30	26
2 years	83.5	13.600 Four times birth weight	33	30
3 years	94	16.000	37	34
4 years	101.5	18.000	40	39
5 years	106.5	20.400 Six times birth weight	42	45
6 years	111.5	22.000	44	48
7 years	119.5	23.800 Seven times birth weight	47	52

These figures show that a baby grows very rapidly indeed during the first year of life. After this, growth slows down to a steady rate. This fact is important because it demonstrates how unreasonable it is to expect the one to five year old to eat as enormously as he did in his first year. He does not need such large meals because his growth has slowed down.

The child's eventual height will depend mostly on hereditary factors, bearing in mind that most children are slightly taller than their parents. A useful prediction of a child's eventual height is obtained by doubling his height at two years of age.

Factors which affect growth adversely are as follows:

1. poor diet, especially lack of protein;
2. poor general health, often associated with poor diet;
3. serious illness;
4. lack of exercise;
5. lack of sufficient rest and sleep;
6. lack of affection, security and stimulation;
7. lack of growth hormone which is produced by the pituitary gland (very rare).

1. It is no accident that the teenagers of today are larger than their grandparents. Increasing knowledge of diet, and the lessening of dire poverty, have meant that most modern children have the right foods for growth and good health. Before the Second World War it was possible to guess the social class of a person by his height and his health. People from the upper classes always had adequate food so their children tended to grow tall and strong. They also appeared to be, on average, brighter and more active. This has led to the belief that a poor protein diet in the first two years of life (when the brain is growing and developing rapidly) will prevent a person reaching his full intellectual potential. Such a theory is difficult to prove because poor diet is often linked with so many other socio-economic problems in a child's life. But logically this may be the reason why many people in the newly-developing countries are unable to use their resources to their full advantage.

2. and 3. If a child has a series of minor illnesses or one serious illness, growth is often held back for a while, although most children catch up rapidly when they are fit again.

4. Lack of exercise will lead to poor muscle 'tone' which slows down growth.

5. Lack of rest and sleep tends to slow down growth.

6. Evidence suggests that emotional problems in a child caused by lack of affection, security and stimulation can result in a slowing down of growth.

The development of children

The process of development is continuous from conception to maturity. So the first observable signs are when the baby begins to kick in his mother's womb.

Although man is an animal, there are some differences that make him superior in some respects to all other animals. These differences can be summarised as follows:

1. the ability to stand upright and walk, thus leaving his hands free for food gathering, defence and other activities;

2. the ability to use his index-finger in opposition to his thumb. This enables him to perform fine movements and to use implements;

3. the ability to use a spoken language and to think abstractly – this allows him to communicate and reason;

4. the complexity of his emotions and social relationships.

The study of a child's development, therefore, is really observations of these aspects.

The human baby is one of the most helpless of creatures at birth, yet, by the time he is a year old, he has a rudimentary mastery of many of the skills necessary for his future life. By his first birthday he is mobile, in some way or other – either by rolling over, 'swimming' on the floor or by crawling, creeping or even walking. He has an understanding of speech and will be communicating his needs by pointing and/or using his voice. His manipulative powers are developing, so that he can pick up objects, examine them and discard them if not wanted.

Physical and motor development

The newborn baby has very little control of his body but he does have reflex movements which are essential to his survival. A reflex movement is an automatic response to certain stimulus – there is no conscious control. A good example of a reflex movement is seen when a person treads on an upturned drawing pin. The foot is removed very rapidly without the need to think 'I must move my foot'.

The baby's reflexes include the following:

1. 'rooting' reflex – when his cheek is touched he will turn his head and 'search' with his mouth for the nipple;

2. sucking reflex – when a nipple or teat or any other object enters his mouth he will suck strongly;

3. palmar and plantar reflexes – when an object is placed in the palm of the hand, the fingers will grip the object firmly. Similarly, if an object is placed on the sole of the foot, the toes will curl around it. This reflex was essential when the baby had to cling to his mother's hair. It is a throw-back to our prehistoric ancestry;

4. 'startle' reflex – in response to any sudden movement or noise, the baby will visibly 'jump' and spread his arms and legs wide whilst screaming;

5. stepping reflex – if you hold a newborn baby upright on a flat surface, he will make stepping movements with his feet.

In addition to these reflex movements, the newborn baby communicates by crying; he can wave his arms and legs and turn his head from side to side. When placed on his tummy, he can lift his head from the floor momentarily, but when he is held upright his head will fall back unless it is supported.

Gradually the reflexes vanish and are taken over by conscious controlled movements. His crying becomes more concentrated and more a demand for services.

Motor development. Motor development and control of movement follows a set pattern, the earliest development being the control of the eyes and lips. From then on development follows two principles:

1. The control of the head and back is followed by the gradual control of the rest of the body from the head downwards.

2. The control of the larger muscles and big movements must come before control of the smaller muscles and finer movements.

In addition there are various periods in a baby's life during which he is 'ready' to master a certain skill, such as sitting up or walking, because his body has become capable of doing so. And if the right stimulus is given at this time then he will achieve this skill easily. On the other hand, if stimulus is lacking then his development will be impaired. This means that a child cannot be 'taught' a motor skill until his muscles are capable of performing it. Therefore it is essential to supply the correct stimulus at the right moment for him.

Motor development follows a pattern, although the age at which a child reaches each stage varies quite considerably. Some stages of this development may be apparent for only a day or two, others may last for many weeks.

A baby starts to 'learn' to walk even before he is born. By kicking and other movements in the uterus, he is exercising his muscles and helping in their development. After birth the first stage towards becoming upright is the raising of his head, followed by the lifting of his head and shoulders. He must gain control of his back, trunk and arm muscles, so that he can sit up, before he gains control of the leg muscles so that he can walk. This is why it is important to give a baby plenty of opportunity to move from early days. Equally important is to let him walk in his own time and not try to force this development by putting him in a baby walker contraption.

Factors that will help him are:

1. good diet and good health;

2. opportunity to exercise – because this increases muscle tone which helps development;

3. plenty of freedom to move around and explore from early days;

4. bare feet – avoiding any restriction of shoes; better grip on floor;

5. stimulation – fun and encouragement from mother/nursery nurse;

6. push and pull-along toys.

A chart to show the progression towards walking and dexterity follows:

Approximate Age			
2–6 weeks	lips ↓	sucks	
		smiles	waves arms and legs
	eyes ⋮	focus eyes	
	neck ↓	lifts head	can hold rattle in hand for few minutes if it is placed there
3 months	shoulders ↓	lifts head and shoulders	
	arms	rolls over ↓	'swipes' at objects with hands
6 months	⋮ ↓	sits with support ↓	can grasp small toys with both hands. Holds rattle and looks at it.
7 months	trunk	sits alone	uses whole hand to hold;
9 months	↓	crawls ↓ creeps ↓	stretches hand to reach out; pokes at small sweet; can grasp between finger and thumb; cannot drop voluntarily; holds, bites and chews biscuit; grabs spoon when being fed
1 year	legs ↓	stands with support ↓ walks with support ↓	picks up with precise pincer grip; can drop toys; can point to things; can use both hands freely; holds spoon but cannot use it effectively; waves bye-bye
1 year 2 months	feet	walks alone	can feed himself with spoon

Walking may be accomplished at any time between about seven months and two years. The average age is about thirteen months for a girl and fourteen months for a boy. The baby also learns to control his hands and use them purposefully, so that by the time he is eighteen months old he is usually walking well and is able to feed himself with cup and spoon.

From this age both developments proceed rapidly. From mastery of walking, he progresses to crawling upstairs to walking upstairs and climbing on furniture. By two and a half years he is running and jumping and kicking a large ball with some degree of accuracy. By the time he is approaching seven years old he will be able to run on his toes and will be active and skilful in sliding, climbing, swinging and hopping. He will also be able to dance to music.

The hands become more and more efficient, especially for finer movements, so that by two years he can unwrap a small sweet and pick up pins and needles. By two and a half he can pull down his own pants at the toilet, although he cannot always get them up, and can eat skilfully with spoon and may use a fork.

By the time he is approaching seven years of age he can use a knife and fork, print accurately and draw recognisable pictures.

Exercise 10

Multiple-choice questions
1. Where does the most rapid growth take place in a child during his first year of life?
(a) in the long bones;   (c) in the liver;
(b) in the brain and skull;   (d) in the genital organs.

2. By what age should a baby have doubled his birth-weight?
(a) six weeks;   (c) one year;
(b) eight months;   (d) five months.

3. Fluoride aids good health because:
(a) it helps growth;
(b) it makes strong muscles;
(c) it combines with calcium to form strong teeth;
(d) it helps convert iron to haemoglobin.

Essay questions
4. How does a baby learn to walk? What stages must he go through? How can a mother or nursery nurse best help a child acquire this skill?

5. Describe how a child acquires manipulative skills during his first two years of life. What part is played by the mother, or the nursery nurse, in helping a child develop these skills?

Observations
6. Observe a child of between three and six months lying on the floor. Describe his movements and attempts to become mobile. How does he respond when you talk to him, and when you offer him a toy?

7. In the same way, observe a child of between nine months and twelve months. Compare and contrast the two children's activities. Say how they differ.

Suggestions for further reading

Arnold Gesell, *How a Baby Grows*, Hamish Hamilton Ltd
Arnold Gesell, *The First Five Years*, Methuen & Co., Ltd
Mary D. Sheridan, *The Developmental Progression in Young Children*, HMSO
Mary D. Sheridan, *Spontaneous Play in Early Childhood*, NFER Publishing Co
Mary D. Sheridan, *Children's Developmental Progress*, NFER Publishing Co

Chapter 11
Intellectual growth and development

The human brain and nervous system

The way we employ our brains is commonly thought to be what chiefly distinguishes man from the animal kingdom. The adult brain weighs about 1.3 kg (3 lb), and consists of a pinkish-grey mass protected by the shell. It is cushioned against bumps and blows by shock-absorbing fluid, and is wrapped in three membranes. It is the headquarters of a most complicated communications network, and is fed messages via the millions of nerve fibres supplied to all parts of the body. Information received (for instance, seeing a potential accident and taking appropriate action to prevent it) is triggered by messages or impulses from the appropriate brain centre.

There are three main message centres in the brain; the medulla oblongata takes care of automatic functions like the pumping of the heart and breathing, the cerebellum controls the voluntary action of the muscles, while the cerebrum is the seat of consciousness, memory, reason – in fact learning and personality.

Relatively speaking, at birth the baby's brain is nearer physical maturity than most other organs of the body. In fact it is fully functioning before birth. Its growth will virtually be complete by the age of seven. Scientists are only just beginning to learn more about the relationship of the size and structure of the human brain to an individual's functioning, or intelligence. It is not a simple matter of 'the larger the brain, the more brainy the owner'. We do know that oversized or undersized brains do not work as well as they should. We also know that the brain can be damaged at birth, thereafter impairing the functions of mind and/or body. We now also believe that the development of the brain can be stunted by a diet deficient in protein, in the child up to the age of about two. It is a subject on which current and future research may furnish us with keys to improving every child's optimum brain development.

Learning and intelligence

The newborn baby is helpless and incapable. All he can do is cry and suck. All other skills and responses have to be learned, and the way he learns is first through the thousands of sense impressions his nerve cells receive and transmit to the brain, hands and eyes playing a particularly important part here. Very gradually he will learn to organise all this stored information and make some sense of both his environment and his own body, and the way the one reacts with the other. For instance, he discovers through repetition that the sight and sound of mother's presence means that he is going to be picked up and probably fed.

He is almost ceaselessly active, while awake. He appears curious and interested in his surroundings. He can attend to things he wants to investigate further.

Having discovered a new accomplishment, such as crowing, hand-clapping or raising his head, he proceeds to repeat and repeat it, and obviously enjoys doing so. Quite early on, he also imitates spontaneously. Thus he seems to possess inbuilt aids to learning, both motivation and means. The *enjoyment* will later develop into a sense of achievement and pride, the *repetition* into perseverance and persistence. *Curiosity* will remain an impelling urge to find answers, and *imitation* will bring him the benefit of adult and other models.

Thus equipped, the child begins to develop what we know as intelligence. A reasonable degree of intelligence is really proof of the effective functioning of the brain and nervous system, and the way this helps the individual to deal successfully with all the events and situations that arise in his life.

Intelligence covers a whole range of quite different abilities – for instance to perceive and recognise accurately, to retain and recall experiences, to solve problems with only one correct solution, to solve problems with a variety of possible solutions by applying recalled and relevant facts, to evaluate and criticise one's own solutions and seek to adjust them. Such abilities can undoubtedly be improved with guidance and help. Approximately one-third of these intellectual skills will have been mastered by the time the child is six. Nearly fifty per cent of the child's mental capacity will have developed between birth and the age of four, a further thirty per cent between four and eight, and the remaining twenty per cent between eight and seventeen.

Levels of thought

Intellectual development, however, is not a straightforward progression – the child acquiring more and more adult intellectual skills, from infancy and throughout childhood. In order to understand the child's intellectual development more fully we need to realise that the young child perceives the world in a very different way from adults or even older children. Jean Piaget, the Swiss psychologist, spent many years studying his own and other children's modes of perceiving and thinking, and his findings have greatly influenced teaching methods in recent years. Very briefly, he found that there appear to be four stages through which children pass in the development of their mental capacities. The age ranges for each period are the *average* ages at which children demonstrate the characteristics of thought of each period.

The stages are:
1. The sensory-motor stage from birth to two;
2. The pre-operational stage from two to seven;
3. The concrete operational stage from seven to eleven;
4. The formal operations stage from eleven to fifteen.

During the first stage, the baby and infant perceives and learns directly and entirely through his five senses, and his own actions – in fact he does not so much think as act. In the next stage, the child can think (helped by his growing acquisition of language) but he thinks intuitively. He does not reason, nor can he think in any abstract way. A child at the next stage can think logically about situations and events he knows about, and a child at the ultimate stage can think and reason abstractly – the prerequisite of formal intellectual study.

We need to look more closely at the pre-operational stage, and we must understand that the small child is an egocentric being, seeing the world only from his own point of view, and in relation to his own limited experience. We can see it in his total lack of understanding of 'long ago' and 'far away': how many of us have been asked if we were alive at the time of the dinosaurs, or have been asked to 'fix' the timing of a promised future treat by stating whether it is 'before my birthday'? Some of us still retain a mental picture of a setting we imagined for some far-off story we heard as infants; almost always it approximates – quite incongruously – to a place we knew in childhood. This story was obviously so far removed in time and distance from anything we could understand that in our mind's eye and memory we had to turn it into something we *did* know. We can see the child's egocentric thinking in the way he will hit out at a chair he has bumped into, or talk to a statue or shop dummy. Everything, it seems to him, must be possessed of life, as he is.

Because he cherishes ideas of things he would like to own, or roles he would like to play, he sometimes talks and acts as though they are real. He may even take the prized possessions of someone else because he has little concept of ownership. He cannot tell the difference between fantasy and reality, and may believe that things dreamed or daydreamed really happened. He believes that the adults who direct his life also direct the universe, and may cry angrily if mother 'lets it rain' on the day of a proposed picnic.

He attributes his own tastes and preferences to other people, as we can see in his choice of presents to those he loves. He will be confused about relationships, because he can think in one dimension only. Nursery nurses often have to answer the question 'Is that your Daddy?' when husband or boyfriend visits the nursery. It is also difficult for young children to realise that one person can play two roles – for instance mother and teacher. It is essentially a here-and-now world that the child at this stage inhabits. All his thinking branches outwards from himself and his own experience.

Yet, during this stage, if he is offered sufficient real-life experience, he begins to move towards the next stage of logical thought and reason. He makes discoveries about, for instance, the way materials behave, and he sees there is a consistency and pattern in what happens. Thus he can form ideas (concepts) about, for instance, objects that float and sink. He 'knows' in a very real sense, because he has learned (not been taught) certain facts to be true; he comes to expect other things to follow. He can group objects together by some common characteristic. Such mental ability will later be very important in the more formal and advanced studies in his primary and secondary education.

Implication and application

Here, then, are the guidelines for all who are concerned with the healthy development of young children.

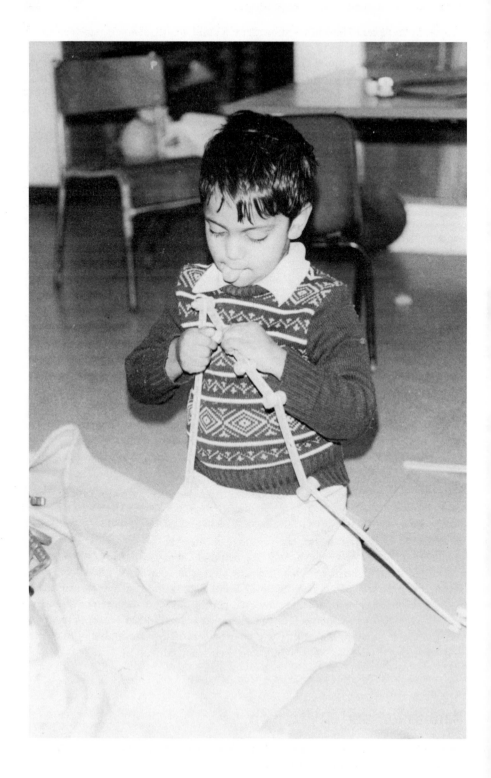

1. The nursery years are clearly a crucial stage in the child's intellectual development.

2. We should approach any testing of intelligence with caution.

3. We should avoid labelling children intelligent or unintelligent; a child who at this age may appear to be either may simply be at a different stage of intellectual development from his peers.

4. We should keep our expectations of children's intelligent behaviour very flexible.

5. We should accept that we cannot artificially hurry children from one stage to another; the physical maturation of the brain may be involved. Undoubtedly the amount of stimulation and first-hand experience in a child's life so far has a great bearing on the stage he has reached.

6. We can see that active first-hand experience (often in the form of play) is not a 'frill' or pill-sweetener to intelligent thought and development. It is an integral part and stage of learning.

7. We should be aware all the time of the contributions we can make, depending on the stage the child is at, in stimulating mental processes and growth.

Play and language

Through play we stimulate interest and curiosity which result in learning. Enjoyment and activity are the keynotes of play, and they work with the child's inbuilt drive to learn. Novelty, variety and spontaneity are other aspects of play which accord with the child's mercurial moods and limited powers of concentration; they will also aid memory.

It is not enough, however, to set the scene for play and then just leave the child to get on with it. Play must be structured to exercise his developing intelligence and mental processes. (We shall deal with this aspect more fully in the chapter on play.) We need to watch and listen to each child's action and reactions so that we can offer material which all the time is challenging him and preparing him for the next step.

Most importantly, he needs help in developing the tool of language so that he can make his thoughts clear, put them in order and express himself. Language is a way of expressing happenings. Without it the child will never be able to deal with an abstract world (or even a concrete world) and so will be greatly handicapped in all later learning.

The three Rs

We cannot leave this subject without a brief word on a matter which troubles many parents of pre-school children.

If the nursery years are such a vital stage in the child's intellectual development, why is not more time spent on giving children a head start in their formal education? Surely this is one of the prime tasks of nursery education?

The answer is really both yes and no. Of course we are concerned at nursery with building a sound foundation for later literacy and numeracy skill. But our preparation for these is frequently not recognised as such by parents, who look only for superficial evidence such as counting out loud and writing names. Our preparation goes much wider and deeper. Educationists over the years have been able to analyse the skills required for mastery of the three Rs – and there are a great many of them. Visual and auditory perception and discrimination are two obvious examples. Spotting small differences and similarities between items or symbols is another. Matching, sorting, grouping, ordering, grading, cultivating a left-to-right eye movement across a page, are still more.

None of these skills will be attainable unless the child has developed reasonable co-ordination between hand and eye, control of the working of his body, and accurate small manipulative movements.

Furthermore, as we have already seen, children learn by doing. Before about five they cannot deal successfully – or for any sustained period of time – with abstract ideas or symbols. First-hand experience, in all its richness, must come first. Parents do not always realise the importance of language as a foundation for later learning. They are apt to say 'He talks all the time at home – there's nothing new about that!' What they perhaps do not realise is that the skill and expertise of the trained adults at nursery who, unlike busy mothers at home, have nothing to do other than concentrate on the children, can develop the art of communication to a far higher degree than is possible in most homes. This will happen through questions and discussions, books and stories, rhymes, finger plays and songs. Without a working vocabulary of some 2000 words, the child at five will be at a disadvantage, educationally speaking, when he begins 3R work at the infant school. Lastly, many parents do not fully appreciate that a good nursery environment can give the child such self-confidence, grounding in learning skills, and such a positive and enthusiastic approach to school generally that he will indeed be off to a head start when he begins the next stage of his education.

Link with all-round development

We cannot separate a child's intellectual development from his physical, social and emotional state. To learn effectively, the child must be sufficiently well-fed, healthy, comfortable and wide awake. He cannot function mentally in a stuffy, dark, cold or overheated atmosphere.

Some less tangible obstacles to learning are insecurity, conflict and tensions, fear of making mistakes, hostile attitude to authority, discrimination, non-involvement with the other children, discouragement.

The child needs to feel relaxed, happy and secure in order to feel self-confident, and to welcome intellectual challenge. He needs to trust and feel at ease with the adults, and be accepted by his peers.

Children with learning difficulties

All kinds of factors affect children's ability to learn effectively. They must be well and comfortable, physically. They must feel secure, confident and relaxed. They need to trust adults and be at ease both with adults and their peer group. But some children are disadvantaged in their learning tasks for specific and serious reasons.

(a) Some have limited inherited intellectual endowment.
(b) Some are brain-damaged before, during or after birth. This may affect the development of perceiving, moving, talking. They may be easily distracted and hyperactive (not to be confused with a normal lively child).
(c) Some develop inadequately functioning sensory organs (for example, hearing, sight) which, to some extent, will cut them off from stimulation in their environment and the normal feedback. This tends to be self-reinforcing.
(d) Some children are not stimulated by adults; early learning opportunities, and critical learning times are missed.

All these children will exhibit restricted cognitive (learning) development.

Factors such as physical handicap, communication problems and disturbed or bizarre behaviour will also naturally affect children's learning ability. In the last case, it is often unclear whether the behaviour is a cause or result of children failing to make progress; attention-seeking behaviour is a common alternative means of self-assertion. Many children will exhibit more than one of the characteristics listed above. Thus it can be seen that 'slow learner' is an umbrella term.

Most slow learners are only mildly handicapped and about 8 per cent to 10 per cent of the total are catered for in normal facilities. A good day nursery, which offers nurture, individual attention and stimulation by adults and other children, can do much to compensate a child with reduced intellectual capacity. The ratio of such children to 'normal' children should not be high, otherwise this measure will be self-defeating.

Nursery schools are particularly well equipped to help such children and prevent real retardation. Much attention is paid to the development of perceptual, motor and language skills and also emotional maturity. There must, however, be suffi- cient adjustment to the need, speed, interest and capacity of each child.

Modern infants schools, too, with their emphasis on active experience, group work, non-streaming and individual attention, can offer compensatory and preven- tative help. Such children will, though, take longer and need more help, and carefully graded steps, in order to develop concepts, see relationships, understand explanations and instructions, and be able to apply specific concepts learned to general situations.

Specialised help. This is available, from nursery school level upwards. It is difficult to assess accurately the intellectual ability of small children. Formal testing will be influenced by the mood of the child, his intimacy with the tester and his general health. A variety of tests can be performed from the age of about seven upwards, however. The most traditional of these test memory, spatial relations, perception of similarities, problem-solving and verbal reasoning. Attempts in recent years have been made to produce tests that are non-verbal and 'culture fair', so that no child shall be disadvantaged because of background.

Intelligence quotient is arrived at by first building up a profile of the child's mental age:

$$\text{I.Q.} = \frac{\text{Mental age}}{\text{Chronological age}} \times 100 \text{ (expressed as a percentage)}$$

It is a measure of *performance*, not competence. It is a fairly accurate predictor of performance in school, but not of the long-term future. Nor does it measure all aspects of cognitive development – for instance, the stage of logical thinking that the child is at.

Other, newer tests measure locomotor skills, personal/social skills, eye/hand co-ordination, and give a wide profile of special abilities. They can be used on children from two to sixteen.

A head teacher, or possibly a doctor, health visitor, or social worker who is concerned about a child's progress can, with the consent of the parents, request a visit from a Child and Family Guidance team. The team, consisting of an educational psychologist, a psychiatrist and a social worker, will come to the school. The psychologist will test the child to see what he is capable of and find out what the problem is. He will give advice and recommend a programme for the child which the teachers will follow through. Alternatively, he may recommend that the child goes to a diagnostic unit for a period of careful assessment and monitoring. A special school for educationally subnormal children (E.S.N.) has in the past been one eventual answer.

If the problem is primarily one of behaviour, the child and his family may need regular sessions at the Child and Family Guidance Clinic, where a programme of behaviour modification and therapy will be carried out. In serious cases, the child may need to leave home and attend a boarding school. The social worker on the team will give support to the family, and liaise between them, the school and the clinic.

Sometimes parents themselves ask for testing to be carried out if, for example, they believe their child to be under-achieving at school. Where, as is usual, the first move is made by the head teacher, great tact is needed to gain the parents' co-operation. If the *educational* aspect of the problem, and personnel involved, is stressed, the parents are less likely to feel threatened, or that their child's mental health is in question.

The child with difficulties in speech or communication can be helped by specialists who visit the nursery or school. The child of infant age and above who has a specific problem in one of the three Rs may receive help from a L.E.A. advisory teacher who will test him and set a programme for his teachers to follow through. Reading, as the most easily identifiable area, seems to come in for most attention.

Dyslexia. A dyslexic child is a child of normal intelligence who is unable to translate sounds into letter symbols and to understand written material. Sometimes letters are confused or reversed, or words are 'telescoped'. Some dyslexic children have no clearly defined left or right handedness (laterality), or eye/hand co-ordination. Memory, too, may be affected.

In pre-school children, dyslexia will appear as marked immaturity in reading-readiness skills such as matching, sequencing, left-to-right eye movement. Older children will be slow to master the 3R's, which leads to an increasing sense of failure.

Specialist teachers, having first diagnosed specific problems, design a programme to be conducted at the child's own rate of learning, which will enable him to benefit from normal education. This may include breaking words up into syllables, multi-sensory and pictorial materials, and much repetition.

Exercise 11

Multiple-choice questions
1. An intelligent child is one who:
(a) has proved himself on IQ tests over a period of time;
(b) has clever parents and grandparents;
(c) comes from a middle-class background and expresses himself well;
(d) one whose brain and nervous system function effectively, enabling him to interact successfully with his environment.

2. Only one of the following statements is true. Which is it?
(a) Intelligence is a fixed entity and cannot be improved upon.
(b) Environment has no influence on a child's eventual intellectual ability.
(c) The growth of the brain will be virtually complete by the age of seven.
(d) There is no connection between diet and brain development.

3. A small child's thinking is egocentric. This means:
(a) he is conceited;
(b) he has no feelings for other people;
(c) he sees the world from his own standpoint, in the context of his life experience so far;
(d) he is selfish and greedy.

Essay questions
4. Parents of a child in your nursery school group confide to you that they are worried because their son is not learning to read or write. How would you answer them?

5. Give examples, from your own experience if possible, of how learning can be hampered by physical, emotional, social or environmental factors.

Suggestions for further reading

Alice Yardley, *Young Children Thinking*, Evans Brothers Ltd
Jean Marzello and Janice Lloyd, *Learning Through Play*, Penguin Books Ltd
Vorna Hildebrand, *Introduction to Early Childhood Education*, Macmillan Publishers Ltd
David Fontana, *The Education of the Young Child*, Open Books Publishing Ltd
R. Gulliford, *Special Education Needs*, Routledge & Kegan Paul Ltd
Margaret Donaldson, *Children's Minds*, Fontana Books
Jean Augur, *This book doesn't make seńs ceńs sceńs sense*, 56 Richmond Road, Staines, Middlesex TW18 2AB
Peter Congdon, *Dyslexia: Towards a better understanding*, GCIC publication

Chapter 12
Language and communication

Development of speech and language

Scientists have discovered that some animals have their own systems of communication; different noises can convey such messages as 'Keep off! That's my territory!' or 'Come here – I fancy you'. We all know that parrots and myna birds can be taught to utter certain sounds at a given signal, and some domestic pets can be taught to respond vigorously to commands or 'trigger' words. One corgi dog becomes quite ferocious if he hears his most hated sounds uttered, even as syllables of words with quite different meanings, such as 'catalyst' or 'octopus'.

But free, spontaneous speech and complete understanding – in other words communication – is the prerogative of man. Communication is concerned with both the physical production of speech – pronunciation, inflection, range, auditory discrimination and so on – as well as knowledge and awareness of language itself – using symbols, labelling, meanings, memory, sensing moods.

The baby's earliest sounds and communication

The newborn baby has what might seem a daunting task – to master all the complexities of a communication system, particularly in the English language which is unusually rich in vocabulary, and complicated in grammatical structure.

The baby's first sound is breathing, closely followed by crying. We might say this in itself is a message which tells us he has been born active and healthy. When he cries, his face will be contorted, the lips stretched wide, and a rather nasal 'a' sound emerges. This might be called an *urgent cry*, and will be heard repeatedly over the next few weeks when the baby wants something – food, relief from pain, relief from discomfort, or from boredom or loneliness.

At the age of a few weeks he will begin to make other, less urgent noises, sometimes called *comfort sounds*. These often occur after a feed, when baby is replete, relaxed. There is still saliva present in the mouth, and the sound may resemble a wet 'goo-goo', as the baby relives, perhaps, the pleasurable sucking sensation.

By about two or three months, the baby's lip muscles have gained strength from practised sucking, and we hear the *first definite sound* – M. A little later comes a hard G sound, bringing the palate into play now, then possibly a nasal N. About the sixth month, with the eruption of the first tooth or teeth, the baby happens upon the first *dental* sound – D. Soon after this, he begins to elongate these first sounds, so that we hear 'Ma', 'Ba', 'Na', 'Da'. These are the *root sounds* of babies all over the world, and from them, depending on how their parents, or those looking after them, select certain sounds to reinforce and shape to their liking, encouraged by smiles, hugs and repetition, the child's future language will grow.

These are the sounds, plus other blurred and indefinite noises that the baby will play with on his own. They form a sort of experimental play which we call *babbling*, and which is clearly enjoyable to the baby. Sometimes certain sounds seem to represent a call for attention, or delight on seeing mother. The pleasure of parents and their response sets up a two-way communication. Within a warm relationship, early attempts at communicating flourish. Baby says 'Da . . . Da' and mother hugs him, smiles, and says in an affectionate, proud tone 'Yes, Dada. It's Dada, isn't it? Dada's coming. Here's Dada!' and so on. Thus the baby learns to make certain sounds in certain situations.

Sometimes a slightly older baby, left alone, will imitate the general buzz of adult conversation in his babbling. This is good practice for him in using different inflections, and also helps to develop vocal cords and the mechanisms of speech.

Another game he plays which helps him to acquire speech is to put his fingers or a hand over or in the mouth of a loved adult who is holding him and talking to him. Through such investigation, he is learning, in a literally first-hand way, about movements of tongue, lips, teeth, reverberations through the lips from the voice box.

At this stage, between approximately five and nine months, his *understanding of and response to language* is just as important as his utterances. He hears 'bye-bye' and comes to associate it with all sorts of things happening – someone waving a hand, a hug, a kiss. The smell of perfume or aftershave, the feel of a soft cheek or bristly beard, a retreating figure, the sound of a door closing, a car starting up. Soon he has only to hear the word and he automatically waves himself. Thus we see that association and imitation are both going to play an important part in his powers of communication.

Other forms of communication in infancy

Of course, it is not only through crying and early vocalisations (utterances) that babies communicate. They have no difficulty in letting us know what they do not like – for instance, puréed spinach or minced liver. Joy at being picked up or played with will be expressed in laughs and smiles and bouncing up and down. Resentment at being held by a stranger, or held when he wants to be left alone, will be expressed by pushing, kicking and rejecting with arms and legs. From about nine months he will also point at objects he wishes to make contact with. By about nine months, the baby often has about *four or six recognisable words*. Parents will have fashioned whatever, in their own language, are acceptable baby versions of 'mother', 'father', 'baby', 'good-bye', 'grandmother', perhaps 'dog' or 'cat'. They will have identified themselves with one of these early words, and will attach meaning, for the baby, to the others. Parents are thrilled when the baby progresses as far as this; he seems to be on the threshold of real speech.

At about this time, however, there often comes a period of apparently little progress. This is because baby is concentrating on the absorbing business of crawling, standing, walking. All his energy and efforts are going into these skills, and his concentration engaged in the fascinating world he now finds he can investigate. Like any other human being, he cannot devote himself wholeheartedly to several different things at once.

Progress with speech and understanding

Between one year and eighteen months his vocabulary begins to expand noticeably. He copies from adults, especially mother, labels for things (nouns) in his world, the things that are of most importance to him – dinner, bath, sweets, biscuits, potty, ball, garden, pushchair. He will use one word, helped out with gesture and facial expression, to mean a variety of different things. For instance 'ball' (which will probably sound like 'baw') may mean 'I've got a ball,' or 'There is a ball,' or 'Bring me that ball,' or 'Play ball with me,' or 'Look at my ball and admire it,' or 'There is something resembling a ball,' (pointing to an orange, for example). Now, as throughout the whole period of language acquisition, the child understands far more than he can express.

Between about eighteen months and two years, a few simple verbs appear – 'go', 'come', 'eat', etc. Then when we hear him put together some of his nouns and verbs, for instance 'Daddy come' or 'doggy eat' and then later 'doggy eat dinner', we say he is talking in sentences, in fact he is *really talking*. Of course, he often gets the word order wrong, and does not yet attempt pronouns, prepositions, adjectives or adverbs. Nor can he cope with tenses or noun/verb agreement. This stage of talking is often called *'telegraphese'*, because it is rather like the brief, simple style of telegraph messages; but, whereas adults deliberately leave out the small linking words, the infant has not yet learned them.

The negative appears very early on, always before the positive, and pads out meaning very effectively – for instance: (sadly) 'No Daddy come', (looking out of the window) or (defiantly) 'no go play toys'.

Often these early sentences express commands or requirements. Another interesting development at about this time is that the child begins to substitute words for actions or things, whereas before he always used them together. Now, if you ask him, 'Where is the ball?' when none is in sight, he will look round for it, showing us that he has truly grasped the word and its meaning, and can visualise the real object from the heard symbol alone.

Individual children vary greatly at this stage in the size of their vocabulary. Gesell found the extremes to be as low as five, and as high as 1200 or more words. Much depends on encouragement to talk, and how much adults reinforce and expand the child's utterances. When a cat enters the room and Timothy says 'Look! Kitty!', one mother may say 'Yes' or 'Mm' abstractedly, or ignore him completely, but another may say 'Yes, here's Kitty. She wants us to stroke her; oh isn't she soft and smooth?'. Of course, the child will not understand every word, but grasps the gist and can guess at meanings of new words, because he hears them in context; he also hears intonation used appropriately, and senses interest, and is given the impetus to go on.

The child's third year sees a tremendous expansion of vocabulary and progress also in sentence length, and general confidence. Questions will arise, often the favourite being 'What's that?'. Word order will be strange, and grammar comes only with difficulty, but intonation will help to suggest the meaning.

By the age of three, he may have a vocabulary of 800 or more words. He will now know many more verbs, which will widen his use of language. He will be able to converse very simply with other children, without adult help. His memory comes into play about this age, indicating that we need language in order to store information and experiences. If we look back to our earliest remembered experiences, we usually find they occurred about three. The three-year old asks many questions; 'What's that?' is still a common one, though it may refer to objects already known to him. He is talking for the sake of talking, and of staying in verbal contact with loved adults. He has now grasped pronouns – 'I', 'Me', 'you', which are confusing – some prepositions – 'in', 'on', 'at', 'to', etc. – and plurals. He can name many of the parts of his body, and knows some colours. He has grasped the idea of changing the present tense into the past where necessary. The appealing (to adults) and indiscriminate way in which he usually adds 'ed' to form the past tense of verbs, shows that he is absorbing some rules of grammar, and applying them in a logical manner. He will say 'Daddy digged the sand', 'I runned all the way'. His acquisition of language is clearly not a simple matter of imitation alone.

By about four, his vocabulary may be about 1500 words. His sentences noticeably lengthen, with more adjectives, and also adverbs. This is the classic age of asking questions, but now they will be 'why?' and 'how?' questions, showing us that he is probing for more complicated information – for reasons and explanations. A four-year-old can ask some disconcerting questions, 'Who made the clouds?', 'Where does the sun go at night?', etc, in this way constantly adding to his knowledge of the universe. He enjoys nonsense language, too, repeating a word several times with alterations to make it sound sillier and sillier, and chuckling heartily at the joke. He revels in exaggerations and tall stories. He is apt to fall over himself (verbally) in his haste to convey something; he may even appear to stutter. He leaves off beginnings of words, saying 'cause' for 'because' and may repeat such a word several times while he gathers his thoughts in order to deliver the next part of the speech with sufficient impact. He mispronounces many words and still uses some baby forms of words. He will often keep up a private and totally unselfconscious commentary on what he is doing; this could be said to be thinking aloud, and it will soon develop into silent worded thoughts.

The five-year-old's vocabulary is usually about 2000 words strong. His speech is clear and distinct, and he can make himself understood by strangers. He may still confuse R and W, S and TH, as foreigners do. But his word order, tenses, subject and verb agreement, plurals, etc. are usually correct. To all intents and purposes, he has mastered his mother tongue.

The uses of language

As adults, we know that it is very largely through the tool of language that we organise and arrange our lives. Through language we come to understand more and more of the world about us. With it we initiate and sustain relationships. We select and manage events and people to our advantage (as in pay negotiations), convenience (as in domestic arrangements), pleasure (as in social invitations). Language allows us to discuss and resolve problems, effect compromises, and gives us the key to the delights of literature and intellectual challenge. We therefore use language in a variety of ways – ways so different that the style of the language itself changes enormously. Compare, for instance, the language employed by barristers in a court of law, and that used by teenagers chatting on the telephone. Yet all are using their mother tongue, and using it appropriately to the particular need. Without the power to talk and make ourselves understood, we should probably be ineffectual, passive, ignorant, friendless, exploited, boring and bored individuals. We might even be pugnacious, because clashes of will must be resolved somehow.

It is interesting to watch the young child develop his use of language, so that eventually for him, too, it becomes this invaluable tool.

If we listen to any short snatches, or longer sustained conversations at nursery, we are soon aware that from the third year onwards all children seem to use language for:

1. protecting their own rights and property ('Get off! I had it first!') and ensuring their own comfort and pleasure ('I like this swing. I'm going to stay here all day.');

2. initiating and maintaining relationships with other children and adults ('Will you be my friend?');

3. reporting on present experience ('I'm painting a big, big lorry.');

4. directing their own and others' actions ('You're the baby and I'm the mummy.');

5. asserting their own superiority ('My one's better than yours.').

The following, more adult, uses of language, however, are noticeable only in children who are cared for by adults who actively encourage the child to communicate:

1. reporting on past experiences ('When I went to Longleat');

2. co-operating with others towards agreed ends ('I know! Let's be spacemen!');

3. anticipating and predicting the future ('It might fall down if we do it like that.');

4. comparing possible alternatives ('Glue's better than sticky tape.');

5. seeing cause and effect, and connections between events ('Now it's raining, so we can't go outside.');

6. explaining how and why things happen ('He pressed it too hard – that's why the wheel fell off.');

7. attending to abstract problems (for instance, of a character in a book) and suggesting possible solutions ('*I* would have chopped the dragon's head off!');

8. referring to symbolic uses of materials in imaginary games (while placing grass on small plastic plates): 'This is our supper. It's spaghetti. Umm, lovely!';

9. justifying behaviour ('Anyway, *he* pushed *me* first!');

10. reflecting upon his own and other people's feelings ('When our Gran died, my mum cried all day, she was so sad.').

It is not difficult to see how these latter uses of language give the child a much more powerful grasp of events, and much greater depth as a thinking, self-regulating individual, bound up as they are with thought, learning, understanding, reason, choices, emotion, and empathy with others.

How, then, can we fulfil our role during the nursery years in enriching children's language skills?

The role of the adult

1. First of all, we must be approachable in ourselves, and our attitudes. We can help to create a relaxed friendly atmosphere in which the child will feel free to talk.

2. We can cultivate our own listening skills – *really* listening to what each child is saying, and showing our attentiveness by concentrating on him alone, staying still, looking at his face – preferably on the same level – refraining from interruptions, letting him finish, giving the response he is looking for, whether it be amusement, mock horror or admiration. Only in this way will he grow in self-confidence as a talker – and a person.

We can encourage listening skills in the children, by *telling* stories, introducing *listening games* with instruments, domestic sounds, the sounds in nature, etc.

3. We can provide stimulating surroundings which will give children plenty to *talk about*. A bare, drab, or unchanging room or play materials will not inspire conversation.

4. We can particularly encourage all forms of dramatic play which involve much talking. Puppets, dolls, masks, two telephones, a well-equipped home corner and dressing-up clothes are good starting points.

5. We should show our own interest in and enthusiasm for the content, the beauty and fun of language. Books, stories, finger plays, poetry, word games, songs all have an important part to play.

6. We should always give a good example in use of language, with correct grammar and pronunciation, word endings, etc. We should modulate our tone pleasantly, avoiding shouting, whining, snapping or hectoring. We should employ different sentence forms, and introduce new, lively and relevant vocabulary wherever possible.

7. We should direct children's attention to potential talking points whenever they occur, in pictures, on displays, the birds on the bird table outside. We

should always be ready to carry on a short discussion that has arisen spontaneously – for instance, about some cakes that a group of children have just made.

8. We should be alert to fresh ideas from outside the nursery as a stimulus to conversation. These may be suggested by interesting items the children bring in, visitors to nursery, or visits out which can be organised. Even the shyest child will respond well to such fresh impact.

9. We should make our questioning thought-provoking, and requiring a properly formulated sentence as reply, rather than a straight 'yes' or 'no' or one-word factual answer like 'red'. We should ask 'how?' and 'why?' questions. Some children not used to being talked to much may need some help here – for instance, 'How does our hamster eat his food? He takes it in his front paws . . . etc. That's how he eats, isn't it?'. We can frame our questions thus: 'I wonder what will happen if . . .', 'How would you feel if . . .' and then show we value what the children offer in reply.

10. We should be quick to spot specific speech defects, difficulties, or lack of progress, talk about these to our superiors, note what steps are taken, then do all we can to help to overcome these problems.

11. We should accept the children's verbal contributions, including mistakes, but where necessary, rephrase and give him back the correct version in an uncritical, oblique way, so that he does hear the correct version. For instance:
Martin: We wen over my Nan's Sundy and dun fruit pickin'.
N.N.: You went to your Nan's on Sunday, did you Martin? And you did fruit picking? That was exciting!
We should also encourage children to talk descriptively and precisely. For instance, 'You know, it was a thingummy' does not adequately describe a small black beetle.

12. We should answer children's questions simply and honestly, even when they concern something we find embarrassing. For instance 'Are you going to die soon, now you're quite old, Mummy?'. We must bring up the child to trust words spoken by trusted adults.

13. We can use the media whenever appropriate to extend and stimulate language. Some children's television programmes (properly used and shared by adults, never as a *substitute* for talking), and the use of tape recorders can offer much lively and original material.

14. In our semi-formal talking times we should constantly be aware of bringing in *all* members of the group, and leading them into the more advanced uses of language. Some talking times can be rather unprofitable if one or two confident and forthcoming children monopolise the conversation. They probably already enjoy plenty of opportunity and encouragement to talk at home, whereas others, who would have benefited from such a nursery session, will in consequence hang back and be reduced to silence.

15. We can make the best use of mealtimes, so that they are truly social occasions.

16. We should avoid talking *down to*, or *at* children, and, most important, should avoid *talking all the time*. Pauses are a most effective part of speech, as any public speaker or actor knows, and quiet periods throw into sharper focus the periods when we have much to share verbally. Children quickly learn to 'switch off' a constant verbal barrage.

17. We should aim at spending about ten minutes a day, on a one-to-one basis, with children experiencing difficulties.

18. We should use singing, music, rhythm and other forms of expression to encourage communication and confidence. It is no coincidence that often the only remnants of a foreign language we once half-learned when young, which we later either remember or would dare to utter, are the words of a song.

Difficulties in language development

There is an important difference between the child who has poor speech, and the child who has poor language, although the two conditions are sometimes found together.

If it is purely a problem of articulation, probably stemming from defects in the speech mechanisms, the child will require expert professional advice and help, probably regular sessions with a speech therapist.

A failure to develop communicable language, however, is a much more complex and common problem. The reasons will probably involve physical, environmental and emotional factors. When seeking reasons, it is often possible to eliminate or identify certain *physical factors*, which will go some way towards helping the situation. It is thus very important that every young child should have a physical examination by a doctor, including a hearing test, before adults assume that language difficulties must be due to environmental reasons. The sort of conditions which may be present include:

1. hearing loss due to a permanent condition;

2. periods of hearing loss due to past or present catarrhal conditions affecting the ears, or enlarged adenoids, etc.;

3. autism;

4. mental subnormality;

5. malformation of palate or teeth;

6. cerebral palsy.

Environmental and emotional factors which may explain language retardation, as it is called, include:

1. history of battering, accident or illness;

2. immaturity;

3. shyness;

4. deaf parents who do not talk to child;

5. parents of low intelligence;

6. background lacking in stimulation (the child may have been kept for hours in pram or cot, or may have very young mother (or a mother suffering from depression) who does not realise the importance of talking to baby;

7. mixed-language home, or home/nursery situation;

8. over-indulgent home where all child's needs are met by others without need for him to talk (perhaps a child of elderly parents, or last in a big family);

9. twins;

10. history of unhappiness and instability in home background;

11. lack of maternal affection (may be from home of care or unsatisfactory fostering or child minding);

12. temporarily unsettled state (caused by starting nursery, moving house, etc.).

Any or all these reasons may be compounded by emotional difficulties when the child feels different, inadequate, or excluded from peer contact. Unhappiness may reveal itself in withdrawal, aggressive behaviour, finding unacceptable outlets for frustration.

How the adult can help

For the child with communication difficulties, more so than with the 'normal' child, we must begin at the point the child is at. For instance, it is useless to fire 'open-ended' questions at a Chinese child who can barely speak any English, or to expect a desperately shy child to enter instantly into jolly finger play groups. Relationships come first, as with all things. Quiet, casual looking at pictures or books together for a few minutes at a time may well be the beginning stage. We should never underline a child's difficulties by drawing attention to him in a group or forcing him to talk. On the other hand, occasionally we may have to 'act dumb' if a child who can talk but has not experienced the need at home continues to try and make himself understood at nursery by merely tugging at our skirts and pointing.

We can introduce simple tongue-twisters and other articulation games to a group which includes a child with difficulties of this kind. We can select stories which involve participation by the children in repeated phrases etc. Bubble blowing is helpful to children who are tense and communicating poorly because it relaxes the throat muscles. Rhymes involving actions of any sort are effective in reinforcing meanings and aiding memory. Music, movement and other forms of expression, such as painting, offer alternative avenues of communication; success and enjoyment in these often spills over into greater success in verbal communication, and breaks down self-consciousness and reserve.

In summary, we might say that for children with communication difficulties, we need to abide by all the guidelines set out on page 160, but we must do so more consciously and intensively, without, of course, letting the child know that he is the focus of concern. Nursery nurses, because they frequently deal with the individual child in a personal way more than teachers, are in a better position to help him communicate. They should take every opportunity during the day that lends itself to establishing communication, suiting it to the individual child's needs and abilities.

Our aim, working through warm relationships, stimulating surroundings, activities and approaches, is to produce children who are eager, self-confident, competent, interested and interesting communicators. As a foundation for the whole of their future education and future life, we can do them no greater service.

Books and stories

Books and stories play such a vital part in a child's language development that we need to give them separate consideration. They are at the same time a means to growing competence in language, and a source of pleasure in themselves.

We who probably derive great pleasure from books might be surprised to learn that a survey (Plowden Report, 1967) showed that nearly thirty per cent of homes in Britain possessed five books or fewer. We should, therefore, not assume that all our children will come to nursery with a ready-made interest in books, or knowledge of how to care for and respect them. Unless we can encourage such an approach, however, and sustain the interest already present in our more privileged children, we shall be doing our charges a disservice.

Despite the extensive use of audio-visual aids in teaching at all levels today, books are still indispensable, and an essential component of learning throughout life. They can be sources of practical information, aids to our powers of expression, and a window on other worlds we might never otherwise know. They offer emotional release and comfort, escape from dreary reality, insight into human relationships, companionship, entertainment, beauty, humour and uplift. We should try to share with others – rather like the evangelists of old – this precious world we possess.

Choosing books

1. **About one year.** From the age of about one year or even earlier, the infant's perception will have developed enough for him to take pleasure in sharing of a short, simple picture book, with his mother or the person who looks after him. The book itself should be tough, wipeable, light and easy to handle on a lap, with rounded corners. It should feature familiar (to the infant) objects, drawn with clear outlines, bright colours (red is the first colour children take notice of), uncluttered by background detail, shadows etc. Print is not necessary at this stage. The objects must mean something to him – for instance, the mug or plate he drinks and eats from, the teddy bear he plays with, and so on. Thus each

picture is a talking point. Mother says, for instance 'Car. Yes, a car. It's like Daddy's car isn't it? How does Daddy's car go? It goes brrm, brrmm, doesn't it?' In this way, the child learns to identify the picture symbols he sees with a real object in his life, and the spoken and heard word. He also learns to set each object in its context, knowing what it is like and what it does. As well as gaining in language, he is coming to associate books with pleasure and the pleasurable close contact with those he loves. This close contact, 'special' time devoted solely to him and books, will continue, probably at bedtime, for many years.

2. During the second year. He will now like to spend a little longer on a book than the few minutes his first picture book took, and now that he is independently mobile and upright, his knowledge of his surroundings has become wide enough for the subject matter of the book to be slightly less domestic.

3. By about two. He will now be able to follow a simple unfolding of events he knows about – *Timmy's day* or *Jennifer's Birthday* etc. These will not contain a plot as such, but there will be a little action, and maybe a kind of climax – for instance when Jennifer blows out the candles on her cake. Such a book will have a few words with each picture, but mother will probably still expand content and meaning ('Let us blow the candles out, shall we?' and so on). A slightly more advanced version of this kind of book might be *Shopping with Mother* or *Andrew Goes to the Zoo*. Now there is more action, and it takes place outside the home, but it is all very much based still on a character and events the child can identify with, and, of course, there must always be a satisfactory ending. Pictures will continue to play an important part in the book, and they will be bold, clear, bright, easily recognisable, and free from sentimentality.

4. At about three. The child should now be ready for a simple plot, and the central character may now be an animal or animated vehicle (train, truck, etc.). Children of this age happily accept the idea of this talking, thinking, feeling 'hero'; this is because they do not yet differentiate between reality and fantasy. But they cannot yet cope with pure fantasy, such as goblins and witches. The idea of such creatures as these will be alarming and may even give them night terrors, because they do not *know* that, for instance, goblins will not visit them in the night. Events and characters should still be familiar and wholesome, and should reinforce the child's sense of security and his place in the world. Hence tales of rejecting stepmothers, etc. should be avoided. Now that the child is more competent in expressing himself, he will love a story that invites participation in a repeated phrase, and an element of predictability, since his imagination and memory are both developing. There can be more print per page, but it is important that illustrations reflect directly the main sequence of action, so that the child can 'read' the story on his own, or to his friends, away from the adult.

5. Between three and five. For children between three and five, books can begin to feature characters and events slightly outside the child's first-hand experience, thus broadening his horizons. The setting of a simple tale may now be on a boat, or on a farm, for instance. There will be more than one central character now, and these characters will be more three-dimensional, thus feeding the child's capacity for greater self-awareness and awareness of others. They may even do 'naughty things', or undergo some disconcerting experiences, but all will be well in the end. They may be involved in emotionally charged real-life situations, and, through an enlightened exposition of, for instance, going into hospital, moving house, accepting a new baby in the family, the child listening is helped to come to terms with them himself; he is a little better prepared for such an eventuality; he is comforted to be assured that other children have experienced disquieting occurrences, but have come through unscathed.

Humorous books now come into their own. The humour may be of a slapstick kind, or it may be based on a topsy-turvy situation, the discomfiture of an unlikeable adult, or a triumph of small creature over large and powerful one. Taste for such humour shows us that children of this age now possess a good grasp of what is and is not likely or possible in the real world, and also how satisfying it must be to them when small and defenceless wins the day.

6. After the age of about five or six. The child is beginning to differentiate between fact and fantasy. He is also beginning to reach out more, in mind and imagination, to the world of long ago and far away. This, therefore, is the stage when we can introduce some of the rich inheritance we possess of fables, fairy stories and traditional tales. Such stories embody many age-old values and themes we still try to uphold today: goodness brings its rightful reward; appearances can be deceptive; crime does not pay; perseverance brings results; money does not necessarily bring happiness; life is full of 'alarums and excursions', but things usually work out all right in the end. Set down thus, they read like a string of truisms, but children respond well to such themes, wrapped up as they are in colourful characters and flamboyant settings. Stories which labour a moral point – so popular with the Victorians and after – are generally not appreciated today. 'Lessons for life' should come through naturally in the characters and events themselves. Traditional tales also possess a pleasing symmetry, and well-balanced elements of predictability and surprise; there is usually a climax, and a happy ending.

Children of this age can also begin to appreciate tales of some historical and Biblical characters, and tales of children from other lands.

Five- to seven-year-olds will be able to cope with more adventures in a story, several twists and turns of the plot, numerous characters, 'baddies'. They like the titillation of a scare, as long as it is of manageable proportion, and is either resolved happily in the end, or is presented in a humorous way. For instance, there are some delightful books on themes like burglars and ghosts, in which elements of fear and thrill are finely balanced by rational explanation and humour. This is not true of some of the more horrific fairy tales, however, which, we should remember, began in an age when death was much more a fact of everyday life than it is today, and also when the virtue of courage (we might call it brutality) was prized much more highly than that of humanitarianism.

7. Factors governing choice. In selecting books for children of all ages, we need to consider above all whether *we* like them. If we do, our enthusiasm will be evident and the story will be a success. We should guard against the understand-able temptation to introduce automatically stories we ourselves liked as children; memory can play tricks on us; we were probably older than we realise when we enjoyed a certain book so much. Our own background, too, may have been very different from that of the children we care for today, thus influencing taste. For instance, does the idea of a 'nanny' insisting that a six-year-old puts on smart gloves to walk into town mean much to multi-culture working class children living on a council estate?

We should naturally consider the age, understanding level, backgrounds, tastes and interests of the children for whom each book is intended. We need to consider the language content – imaginative? enriching? or oversimplified, sentimental or boring? – the length, the illustrations, the lay-out, the cover and general appeal of the book's appearance, the durability, and the price in relation to all these other factors.

Reading and telling stories

We should try both to read and tell stories to our young children. Each approach has its merits, the first directly introducing the charms of a book, complete with relevant illustrations, the second enabling the adult to enter into a direct, dramatic situation with her listeners, using facial expressions, gestures and voices, unhampered and to best effect. Both approaches need preparation, beginning with selection.

About ten minutes is a long enough story session for the under-fives; the over-fives can concentrate a little longer. The children should ideally be in a small group for intimacy, and should all be seated comfortably where they can see and hear clearly. Potential disruptors should be separated and placed strategically at the outset. The whole group should be contained (not squashed) into an area like a book or home corner. If the children are not in a quiet receptive mood, they should be calmed down with a few finger plays or similar activity at the beginning of the session. Visual aids can be used if the story is told, and can add greatly to the interest, provided they are introduced at an appropriate point and all the children can see or touch them without breaking into the flow. Different and interesting voices should be used for different characters, and volume, tone, pace and pitch all varied, to avoid monotony and make the story truly come to life. If this is happening, there will be few interruptions. Questions and comments should be woven in – and answered fully at an appropriate time if possible – but not allowed to spoil the continuity. When the story has ended, if it has been a success there will probably be a few seconds' pause while children come out from the spell. Then there may be the sound of a thumb coming out of a mouth, and a request 'Can we have it again?'. The story teller should avoid the mistake of putting the children through a comprehension test on the story. If she feels questions and discussion are called for, she should make her questions open-ended. 'I wonder what *you* would buy your Mummy if you wanted to give her a special treat?', etc. The acting out of stories heard, or the suggestion that all 'draw me a picture' of it, are not appropriate follow-ups for nursery age children, and may even dampen enthusiasm for future story sessions. If the story has been a success, it has been an immensely worthwhile experience in its own right, and will live on in the children's imagination where it took root.

1. A love of literature. This is probably caught rather than taught, and a great responsibility lies with us as the adults who are in a position to influence children's developing attitudes.

2. The adult's enthusiasm. Our own enthusiasm or lack of it, will come through all our dealings. We can show interest and enthusiasm in such matters as books brought in from home by children. (These are frequently not to our taste, which calls for tact.) The arrival of new books for the nursery can be happy occasions, with the pleasure of anticipation. We can let the children see us refer frequently to books for information, for instance in cookery. We can make story times intensely enjoyable occasions for all.

Using and caring for books

We can demonstrate and teach *care and respect in the handling of books* (hand cleanliness, method of page turning etc.) and involve the children in setting aside and repairing damaged books, so that they remain attractive and appealing for a long time.

We can include books in *displays*, and in *follow-up* work to visits, themes or projects going on in the room.

We can teach the children the use of simple *reference books*, and for older children who can read, the mastery of an index.

We can suggest *making class or group books* about, for instance, autumn, our bodies, or whatever is the current interest.

We can provide and maintain an attractive, well-sited and laid out *book corner* where the children can enjoy books individually or in small groups, sitting in comfort, quiet and a good light. For young children at home, books should be kept on proper shelves, not thrown in boxes with toys.

We can frequently *change the selection of books* available to the children, inside and outside the book corner, and display them in new and eye-catching ways.

We can keep ourselves informed of *newly-published children's books* and constantly be appraising them, with the next book allocation allowance in mind, or as ideas for forthcoming Christmas and birthday presents for nephews and nieces, godchildren and so on. About three thousand new children's books come on to the market every year. This is why we have not attempted here to give examples of different points made. Some authors and fictional characters go on for ever, but many date quickly and are superseded by new trends. It is dangerously easy to get in a rut, so we must keep an open mind.

We can be enthusiastic and helpful both in the children's use of the *local public library*, if visited, or school lending library, and encourage interest in book fairs or similar exhibitions held for parents' benefit.

We should always be ready to *talk to parents about books* if they want advice or suggestions for children's books at home.

We can select, collect and introduce the children to *poetry*. We can share with them the beauty of ideas and language, the humour, the fun of play with words, the stimulus of seeing something familiar through the eyes and mind of another individual, who is observant, sensitive and has the gift of expression. In this way, poetry will not seem something apart from everyday life, but another vivid means of communication, intense and living.

Exercise 12

Multiple-choice questions
1. A three-month-old baby communicates:
(a) by crying only;
(b) by crying and gurgling;
(c) by gestures, facial expressions, actions, cries and some verbal utterances;
(d) by vocalisation only.

2. Children in their second year, hearing language around them, understand:
(a) more than they can express themselves;
(b) almost everything;
(c) only sentences spoken to them directly;
(d) only sentences used in conjunction with objects or actions.

3. If a child of nearly five has far fewer than 2000 words at his command, it means:
(a) he must have special attention if he is not to be at a disadvantage, socially and intellectually, when he begins infant school;

(b) he must be mentally subnormal;
(c) he must see a speech therapist;
(d) he must have a hearing loss.

Essay questions
4. A child of four in your nursery group has articulation difficulties. He is receiving treatment through speech therapy. How might you be able to support this treatment and help him generally?

5. How might language retardation in a five-year-old give rise to difficulties?

Observation
6. Over a period of time, at three different intervals, observe the same child's ability to communicate (0–6 months, 6–12 months, 12–18 months are suggested ages).

Notice:
(a) early vocalisation and jargon;
(b) use of gesture, facial expression, tone of voice;
(c) clearly articulated words;
(d) length of phrases and sentences;
(e) word order;
(f) new and interesting vocabulary;
(g) confidence and spontaneity when talking to adults or other children.

7. Record on tape or paper a conversation between children of infant age. Analyse how the participants were using language.

Questions on books and stories

Multiple-choice questions
8. The most suitable content for a book for two-year-olds would be:
(a) pictures of familiar, single objects, named;
(b) fairies, elves and pixies;
(c) cautionary tale of a 'bad' boy;
(d) simple tale, based on familiar domestic happenings with a happy ending.

9. Illustrations in story-books for three to five-year-olds should be:
(a) plentiful, clear, recognisable, pleasing to the eye;
(b) much more important than the text;
(c) very detailed to encourage the child to look intently;
(d) mostly funny caricatures and cartoon-type figures.

10. What is the most important prerequisite for a successful story session with nursery children?
(a) that the story is very short;
(b) that the adult tells, rather than reads, the story;
(c) that the story is accompanied by visual aids;
(d) that the adult likes the story herself.

Essay questions
11. (Suitable for students after approximately one year's training.)
How have you, during your training, tried to encourage children to love books?

12. Draw a plan, or a picture, of an ideal book-corner for a nursery school classroom, and list the types of book with which you would equip it.

Project
13. Visit some book shops near to college or your home. Concerning the children's department, collect information on:
(a) size of stock kept;
(b) methods of display;
(c) any sales promotion;
(d) current best sellers or latest publications;
(e) prominence of 'old favourites';
(f) numbers of children browsing, or adults looking at children's section;
(g) attitude of staff to children browsing or asking questions;
(h) titles and authors of new books which appealed to you (give reason for appeal);
(i) variety of simple reference books, poetry books, simplified vocabulary books for early readers.

Project
14. Make a simple first book for a child of approximately one year old, using improvised materials as far as possible, but incorporating all necessary features.

15. Accompany a child or group of children to a library. Write a short account of their reactions. How well are children catered for?

Suggestions for further reading

Joan Cass, *Literature and the Young Child*, Longman Group Ltd
Hazel Bell, *Situation Books for Under Sixes*, Kenneth Mason Publications Ltd
Alice Yardley, *Exploration and Language*, Evans Brothers Ltd
Joan Tough, *Focus on Meaning*, Unwin Education Books
Joan Tough, *Listening to Children Talking*, Ward Lock Educational Co. Ltd
Andrew Wilkinson, *The Foundation of Language*, Oxford University Press
Hilda J. Meers, *Helping Our Children Talk*, Longman Group Ltd
Schools Council, *Language Development and the Disadvantaged Child*, Holmes McDougall Ltd
Eileen Colwell, *Storytelling*, The Bodley Head Ltd
Dorothy Butler, *Babies Need Books*, The Bodley Head Ltd (hardback) and Penguin Books Ltd (new edition, limp)

Chapter 13
Social and emotional development

The newborn baby is an entirely self-centred creature. His emotions are few but extreme – rage or satisfaction – and in so far as he perceives other people at all, it is only in their degree of usefulness in administering to his needs.

Over the next seven years these two extreme emotions are refined and diversified and he becomes better able to handle and control them. His social development leads him to interact in an acceptable way with other people, and in the end to take his place in society on his own or as a member of a group.

The whole process is slow and gradual. There will sometimes appear to be reverses or periods of no progress, but these are perfectly normal; no aspect of learning or development proceeds at a uniform, uninterrupted rate. It must be borne in mind what a great deal of discovering the child has to do, both about himself and the world he finds himself in; moreover it all happens during a period of tremendous physical growth.

To set down ages and stages in this, as in any other aspect of young children's lives, is artificial. Likewise, generalisations can be foolish, even dangerous.

What we have to do is build up a picture of what, for many children, is *often the sequence of development*. For the purposes of clarity, we have divided the sequence into age bands.

Infancy

The newborn baby is entirely dependent on the person who looks after him – usually mother – for all his needs, food and comfort. Rage or contentment are clearly visible – and audible – and are mainly associated with feeding and elimination. Therefore he lives in a very sensuous and self-centred world.

By bringing pleasure and relief the mother or nurse becomes familiar and from early days the child realises, through his senses, the pleasure she takes in caring for him, her loving and sure handling of him and her voice. As soon as his eyes focus, he will see her eyes and her face and their relationship forms. With a normal, happy mother and baby these happenings bring about *bonding*. Midwives and obstetricians believe that this process is given a positive start by the baby's being placed into his mother's arms as soon after birth as possible. Some even place the naked baby on his mother's abdomen.

If bonding, or emotional attachment of mother to baby and baby to mother, does not take place in the early weeks (and there could be many reasons for this), all sorts of other things can go wrong. From the experience of this first relationship the child builds all his other relationships. From his mother's demonstrated love for him he begins to feel secure about himself. This knowledge is sometimes called self-image, or self-concept, and is not to be confused with conceit or inflated ideas of one's importance. If a child feels at ease with himself and secure in others' love for him, he is able to face life confidently and cope with challenges and limitations both within and outside himself.

This bonding process, then, becomes more established during the child's first months of life. By about six weeks the baby can recognise his mother as a separate person from himself, and will smile and respond to her. Play, encouraged by parents, makes him smile, kick and respond happily. By the age of three months, just the appearance of his mother often produces a joyful response. About this age he begins to chuckle, and at four months or so he laughs out loud.

The baby is thus already responding socially. His perception ensures that moving, changing sights, such as people, attract and hold his attention more than inanimate objects. From about three months, the father will elicit a special response, and soon after, the baby will welcome the attention of strangers, although still keeping his own special reactions for parents, brothers, sisters and familiar adults, such as grandparents. This distinguishing between familiar and strange adults shows us that his awareness of the world is widening.

Between about six and nine months he will make determined efforts to communicate by smiles, babbling and gestures. His ability to laugh at funny situations will play an important part in his later social life, as laughter is a useful safety valve. The baby of this age enjoys games with less familiar adults, and even deliberately tries to start them by dropping objects repeatedly out of his pram when out with mother. His understanding of speech, especially the word 'No' and tone of voice, influence his behaviour. Again, we see that his social development proceeds from his close family outwards.

His range of discernible emotions is widening too. Because he has developed **trust** of his parents, he can withstand a certain amount of delay, restraint, withdrawal of satisfaction, frustration. Weaning and toilet training, both of which he will experience in some measure before he is one, are built on this trust, leading to compliance with mother's expectations. Pleasure in giving pleasure to his beloved mother also aids the process. He may, at other times, display defiance, or jealousy, as for instance when father is taking too much of mother's attention away from him.

The mother's temperament and quality of care will be influential factors in his early social and emotional responses. But even at this tender age babies differ widely one from the other for no apparent reason. Some are friendly, happy and amenable from the first; others are fretful, demanding and unresponsive. It is undoubtedly true that certain personality characteristics are laid down at or, more accurately, before birth, some inherited from several generations back. The accommodation of these characteristics with the child's early environment – which includes most importantly the personalities of those looking after him – the interaction which takes place, and the modifying or otherwise of the characteristics, results eventually in the emergence of his adult personality.

This is why we say, rightly, that all babies – and all children and all people – are individuals and should always be recognised as such.

One to two

The importance of the baby's relationships with his parents continues into his second year, and will colour other relationships. Security, affection and trust are essential in his emotional background, and will provide the safe harbour from which he will increasingly sally forth to meet the world.

As he becomes more and more mobile, he will spend a great deal of time exploring his surroundings, but he still very much needs mother's presence around all the time, and will constantly return to her if puzzled or frightened.

Research in the past thirty years has alerted people who care for children to the important role of the mother in these early years. Not so long ago it was believed that the lack of such a background of consistent, loving handling by the same mother, or even the experience of an interruption in this relationship (such as in the case of a spell in hospital), could cause the child to grow up scarred for life. We now believe, however, that such damage may not be irreversible, and that skilled, sensitive handling of separation by all concerned can do much to minimise emotional damage. But it is thought, nevertheless, that handling by too many different people who are caring for the child (as for instance in homes of care) can result in little bond formation, whereas too few contacts with strangers can lead to later narrowness of outlook or shyness.

The relevance of this research to our discussion here is that ideally the under-two-year-old should be cared for by one or two consistent loving parents, but also be exposed to contacts with friends of the family.

During his second year, the child's sense of his personal identity begins to develop. Because of this, and aided by his growing acquisition of language, he begins to be interested in other children. He will not be able to play with them in any real sense, of course, but if put together with another child about his age, he will reach out, stare, touch, circle, possibly hand out temporarily a plaything, which will then quickly become the focus of a tug-of-war. There will probably be squeals and tears, and little talking, apart from frequent claims of 'mine'. Such early battles, trying as they are to mothers, are unavoidable and healthy because they are situations from which the child will learn. In such clashes, the child is asserting himself and his rights in the only way he is able. As adults, we control or hide such feelings, mutter darkly to ourselves or tell a friend later what we would *like* to have done. But a child of this age has no such outlet. He simply lashes out as the occasion demands. He *understands* adult restraints, although they may have little effect. However, he is quite easily distracted, which means that his aggression may soon die down.

It has been found that, limited though interaction is at this stage, companionship from the second year on has a stimulating effect on development generally.

Often during this period the child goes through a phase of refusing to conform in some way to the routines of his day; he may refuse to eat, sit at table, use the potty, or go to sleep at bedtime. This worries many mothers who previously took pride in their child's compliance. Because his growth rate has slowed down, his physical needs are changing. The comparatively new exercise and satisfaction of asserting his individual will, aided by growing language ability and the power of the negative, all combine to make this refusal a normal part of growing up.

Usually, the less fuss that is made, the sooner will the phase pass. If, however, his refusals are allowed to become the centre of pitched battles between himself and a fraught, tense mother, their once-happy relationship may be temporarily affected.

This relationship becomes more complex during his second year. Although the child loves mother and wants to please her, sometimes he hates her for thwarting him. Then he feels guilt and a torment of doubt about her continuing love for him. He cannot release this build-up of emotion as adults do, by words. (We call this mixed-up state of love and hate ambivalent feelings; they are present in most intense relationships – for example marriage. To accept this fact is to go a long way towards understanding a great deal of human behaviour.)

The child of this age can also be possessive of his mother. He may accept the fact that she has household tasks, but hates her to read a book, for instance, go by herself to the bathroom, or maybe make a fuss of another child. This is when he will appear demanding or draw attention to himself. Father will play a more active role in his life now, and he will enjoy Father's special rough and tumble, humorous or gentle tactics. From such experience he will learn about special male characteristics and qualities, which lays the foundations for understanding of the male role.

By the end of the second year he is no longer a baby. He is a confident young child who works hard at establishing and demonstrating his independence. However, he can easily return to baby dependence when frustrated or ill. There is a possibility that we may expect too much of him because he can appear so competent.

Two to three

These various trends continue into his third year. Particularly noticeable are the eagerness and unpredictability of his exploring, and his self-assertiveness. His own possessions mean a great deal to him; their positions at bedtime or around the home are an integral part of his security. His emotional base is still very much the home, and any weaning away from it should be gentle and gradual. He may be willing to stay an occasional night with grandparents or a favourite aunt.

As he becomes more and more aware of all the possible choices in his world, he may feel some confusion, and also change his mind and direction suddenly and frequently. He does not like adult interference in his schemes, and sometimes does not welcome friendly advances by adults. Sometimes he goes through a very shy or clinging phase, which can be a great trial to parents, particularly his mother.

This is the classic age of temper tantrums – the natural consequence of his self-assertiveness, exploratory impulses, inability to get inside the feelings of other people, or understand cause and effect. His rage and distress, when aroused, can be formidable. The overwhelming nature of them can be frightening to him.

Because his outlook on life is inevitably so self-centred and limited in understanding, he may think he is to blame for unhappy incidents such as his mother's temporary absence. Because he does not distinguish between reality and fantasy, he may have occasional nightmares or irrational fears.

With other children, he will still play side by side and although there will be more conversation, there will still be many clashes of will, snatching and grabbing. Given the choice, he will often choose to play alone.

Through his developing mental perception, he is observing and absorbing more and more about what is acceptable behaviour, and he learns this almost entirely from those within the family circle. Because he wants to feel accepted and loved, he will gradually learn to conform to these ideas, and so by the end of the third year he will be complying with many adult expectations.

Towards the end of this period one can also see tendencies which will be important in his adult personality – characteristics like leadership or submissiveness, gregariousness or detachment, dependence or independence.

Three to four

By this age the child starts to look at the world in a less self-centred way, and this stage sees the beginning of social relationships with his contemporaries. He is now aware of himself as a separate person, and therefore he can look with more interest at other people. He is interested in the actions and reactions of other children, and this forms the basis of real play. He will make friendly overtures to other children and want to sustain periods of play with them. He can, literally, give and take in a limited fashion, and can wait a short while, but, of course, he is still mainly concerned with getting his own way. However, he begins to learn that to acquire and keep companions, he sometimes has to compromise over this. He has greater emotional control, and also more 'know-how' about life and its limitations. Although there will still be occasional clashes with other children, clashes with adults will be fewer.

Jealousy, rivalry and bickering among brothers and sisters (siblings) are commonplace during this period, if not before. This can be another trial to parents, particularly, again, the mother who is often surrounded by apparent discord for hours each day, and it sometimes goes on for years. There is good and bad about every child's position in the family, and all, in a sense, are rivals for their parents' love. Within such a close-knit group in restricted premises there is bound to be friction. Through it, however, the siblings build their relationships from which they derive much happiness and security. Loyalty between family members in the face of criticism or threats from outside is also built up by such interaction. It is interesting to note how often childhood warring between two siblings grows into close enduring friendship and love in later life.

By this age the child can work out, through play, many of his aggressive feelings and distressing experiences. He likes rough and tumble play with an adult. This is particularly true of boys. Exasperating though it can be to mothers, especially just before bedtime, it is a normal and healthy testing out of his own strength, and outlet for exuberant spirits. He likes also to order his parents about in a playful way.

Adult patterns for acceptable social behaviour and harmony in the home are very important now. He needs practical, consistent demonstrations of affection, care, truthfulness and patience. The limits set on his behaviour in the home and the way these are put into practice should help him to conform, feel safe and be liked. He should be building up a good image of himself, but he cannot do this if overstepping the boundaries is linked with guilt. He will understand most logical explanations for limits, but will need constant reminders of abiding by them. Simple courtesies are learned from parents and mean little at first, but gradually the child will come to see them as signs of thoughtfulness to others.

During this stage the child may show curiosity about sex; children will explore one another's bodies and perhaps indulge in mutual genital manipulation; no emotions except sensuous pleasure are involved, and guilt is often only introduced by a worried parent.

Also during this stage, the child may invent an imaginary friend. This is an interesting, and often long-remembered development. It fulfils not so much a need for companionship as for someone on whom the child can project the other side of his personality. For instance, the 'friend' (one small boy's was 'Dob' who always had to be spoken to in a very gruff voice) may do all kinds of dreadful things, when the real child is feeling particularly good and conforming, while at other times the 'friend' may be a paragon of all the virtues. Thus the child is helped to handle his ambivalent feelings. Parents can play along with this fantasy without fear of rearing a neurotic, but, of course, it should not be carried to ridiculous extremes. When the child is emotionally ready to abandon the 'friend', he will.

Four to five

The imaginary friend will probably survive into his fifth year, but the four-year-old's own real life personality is by now well established. Through the examples around him, and his greater life experience, he has standards by which to judge his own behaviour and that of others. He will begin to rely on his own judgements.

He will alternate between dependence and independence, but will on the whole be self-confident and often boisterous. He is fairly amenable to reasonable adult demands, and fairly good at controlling his feelings. He can show patience if there is delay.

Four-year-olds are often happy to play together for long periods in groups. The groups frequently break up and form again, or there may be one pair of close friends within or outside it. Four-year-olds like to know that adults are dependably in the background, and while not liking the adult to interfere, they will turn to her for advice, approval or material help.

Nevertheless, they are essentially acting as individuals within the group. The first signs of genuine concern for others usually appear during this stage. A child will inform an adult about one of his group who is in trouble. On the other hand, four-year-olds are quick to condemn or reject a child they do not like.

Imaginary and imitative play flourishes, reflecting the child's observation of real life as well as the fulfilment of his desires. His heightened imaginative powers are evident, too, in his boasting about his family and possessions and the telling of tall stories. He constantly demands our praise and recognition: 'Watch how fast I can run!' and so on. He is asserting his own ability, and this 'showing off' as it is sometimes called, is a natural step to building skills and self-confidence.

Sometimes adults, particularly parents, are concerned at an apparent change which comes about in the child's behaviour between four and five. Boys may swear, shout, defy adults, show off ostentatiously. Girls may giggle secretively or become pert or insolent. Both may dawdle or talk among themselves to avoid complying with adult requests. There may be several explanations for this. The adults may not be acknowledging the child's need for greater independence as he is becoming more grown up. The child may be ready for more stimulation than home, play group or nursery can supply. The child may also be apprehensive about moving to 'big school' soon.

Five to six

This is the stage when the school years begin and it is a widening experience away from the family which will bring the child both happiness and unhappiness. He will welcome the new social contacts, but he will expect to be liked and valued by all, and if this does not happen, can feel hurt. Girls usually take to their new role more happily than boys; being eager to please the teacher, and being more mature as a rule, girls tend to get off to a good early start with literacy and numeracy skills. Boys often find the break from their mother more upsetting than girls. Some people think this may be because girls have much more practice than boys in learning about their future role in life, through close contact with their mother in the home, and are therefore more confident and independent.

Five-year-olds find apparent failure of any kind difficult to accept. They regard their contemporaries largely as rivals rather than friends, and as yet there is little real interest in team enterprises. Quarrelling and teasing can arise out of aggression, but some aggressive behaviour is inevitable as the child comes to terms with the outside and more grown-up world. Five-year-olds sometimes revel in destructive acts, through which they test out their own power and strength.

Five-year-olds will play in groups, but the groups are quite fluid. They are often happiest playing in pairs; if there are three, invariably one will be left out and hurt feelings will result, particularly among small girls who, by this age, are choosing 'best friends', who themselves change frequently. Separate boy and girl groups begin to form for play at about this age, with separate interests. Boys may appear outwardly more aggressive in play and conduct, but research has shown that this characteristic, in the early school days, masks greater anxiety and lack of self-confidence than girls experience.

Early school experience can be tiring and stressful, making for irritability or sullenness at home. Eager parents, interested in their child's new step, will frequently be disappointed or mystified at the lack of communication from the child about all that he has done. His 'cuddly' or comforter may still be much in demand at bedtime.

With skilful adult help, a group of children may stay together, perhaps for several days, and work for a common purpose. There will be many quarrels along the way; one child will appear content with a minor role, then suddenly demand a major one. Group leaders can be clearly identified by now. The children's developing sense of humour, growing out of a knowledge of what is real and what is ridiculous, will help to promote a happy atmosphere within a group of five-year-olds.

The five-year-old is still very much an individual, however. He can make deliberate independent decisions and put them into effect. In this sense, he has taken a big step towards becoming a self-directing person. He is still building up his own image of himself, and because he wants it to be a good one, he constantly asks questions and seeks praise about himself, his past, his abilities, etc. He cannot accept self-blame, although irrationally still feels guilty at things for which he is not to blame, thus revealing his muddled ideas on reality and fantasy. Despite his apparent move towards independence, he still needs his mother's support and companionship a great deal, especially in times of stress. He likes the familiarity of routine in the home.

Six to seven

By six, most children have become adjusted to the greater demands of school. Belonging to a group, and being accepted by their peers, means a great deal to them. They dread being rejected, and it is rare to find six-year-olds playing alone. Groups have grown bigger, and sometimes they become very over-excited, and play, including much 'horse-play', becomes uncontrolled. Sometimes a scapegoat is created. Six-year-olds often make up their own rules for group play as they go along. They can take part in organised games – for instance, party games, which involve competitiveness – but the games must allow each child to have his chance to shine. There is a good deal of rivalry and jostling for positions of influence in their social setting, and sometimes the strain brought about by this results in silly behaviour at home.

Changes of mood are very common in six-year-olds. They may be in turn dogmatic and impulsive. Some children of this age present entirely different personalities at home and at school. To all appearances, the teacher tends to have more influence than the parents, therefore the degree of co-operation with each varies, and can cause irritation at home. Fluctuating feelings make choices difficult, and sometimes six-year-olds let their parents down in a social setting.

They are highly imaginative, and although they enjoy fear and titillation of manageable proportions in stories, they may be a prey to imagined terrors, such as burglars breaking into their home. Nightmares accompany such fears.

They are very proud of their possessions, and only reluctantly allow others to play with or use them. They begin to be critical of their own achievements.

Although not generally outwardly affectionate, they do appreciate scope for happy activities and things of their own, as provided by adults. They can also usually be trusted not to hurt younger brothers and sisters if left in charge for a short period.

This stage probably sees the height of individualism. Sometimes adults assume a greater degree of maturity within the six-year-old than is really there, particularly if the child is well developed physically.

Age seven

The set of friends, though transitory, of which the six-year-old was aspiring to become an accepted member, now merges into a gang or club. With groups of boys, sometimes there is one shared predominating interest, nowadays often football. In other settings, it may be Cub Scouts, cowboys and Indians, space travellers, or secret societies with dens. Having friends with interests in common who like and respect one brings satisfaction and builds self-confidence at this stage. Girls will often stay together in a less formal way; sometimes a shared passing interest in, say, skipping or knitting is the reason for these groups. 'Best friends' are still important. The groups will invent and pay lip-service to rules, but individuals still find it difficult to apply the rules to themselves, and one child may quickly walk off in a huff if tackled by others, and be stubborn about admitting his wrong.

Seven-year-olds can also be very sensitive to teasing and being made to look silly in front of their peers. They will tell tales about each other because they like to feel righteous. This shows that they have adopted adult standards of what is acceptable behaviour. Brothers and sisters of this age will complain to parents of unfair treatment when they feel adults have deviated from these standards.

In their activities at home and at school we can see other typical seven-year-old characteristics – a striving towards perfection, through self-criticism which now becomes very marked. Children of this age can be very persistent in working towards their goal, and get angry at interference or interruption, especially by younger siblings. Gesell calls this 'the eraser age', meaning that the seven-year-old is forever rubbing out things he has written and drawn because 'I'm no good,' or 'It's rubbish,' – both common enough cries during this phase. At other times, however, the seven-year-old will be full of exuberance and enthusiasm for life. Moods change from exuberance to depression, brooding and preoccupied behaviour are very common.

About this age the child begins to feel genuine appreciation of others' efforts. Team games and competitive sports can now be enjoyed, although feelings may run high at times.

Sometimes a seven-year-old will fall in love for the first time. This is an interesting development, because it represents a move away from individuality and a recognition of the need for companionship. One small seven-year-old boy, who admired a girl twice his size, bestowed a ring case on her in the playground, assuring her that the ring would follow later. His gesture could be said to anticipate the more sophisticated, complex world of emotional and social experience which the child at seven is about to enter.

Moral development

Opinions differ on whether this can rightly be considered a separate aspect of children's development, or whether it is an integral part of the child's socio-emotional development, and a direct reflection of his parents' value systems.

Abstract notions of right and wrong are not easily grasped by children under eight. Situational factors, such as the intensity of a temptation, the likelihood of getting 'found out', the esteem of their group, are very powerful.

Although for many people there no longer exists the dominant moral influence of the Church, parents and society still deem it important that children be brought up both to know and follow certain rules of behaviour. The rules will vary according to the culture and traditions of their society.

Much will be absorbed and copied quite unconsciously by the child from a very early age. As the existence of rules of behaviour impinges on him, he will gradually modify his own behaviour to match them. This process we often call the development of 'conscience'. It frequently involves restraining his natural impulses to self-gratification. Later, the child will learn to make judgements about moral behaviour, and eventually to see the 'rules' as a positive framework for guidance in living, rather than a series of negative curbs.

Traditionally revered middle-class values in our society include honesty, courage, industriousness, compassion to weak and defenceless people and animals, enterprise, ambition and perseverance.

Adults who help the child gain control over his conduct through explanations are more likely to be successful than those who coax, bribe or threaten.

Exercise 13

Multiple-choice questions
1. Bonding between a mother and her baby means:
(a) emotional attachment;
(b) naked newborn baby being placed on mother's abdomen;
(c) their eyes looking at each other, for the first time;
(d) interaction between the two.

2. The older baby, six months and onwards, learns to withstand a measure of frustration, delay and restraint in the gratification of his desires, because he has developed:
(a) self-control;
(b) a smaller appetite;
(c) trust in his mother;
(d) wider interests.

3. Philip plays with one other child, usually Joanne, the same age as himself, for short periods of time. He seldom plays in a group. He likes his own way but will occasionally share or take turns in order to maintain play. He and Joanne often play 'doctors' and examine each other's bodies. When Joanne is not there, he often talks to an imaginary friend. His behaviour is characteristic of a child of:
(a) 1 to 2 years
(b) 3 to 4 years
(c) 4 to 5 years
(d) 5 to 6 years

Essay question
4. How does the environment of a good day nursery *or* nursery school help children between three and five to develop in social and emotional adjustment?

Observation
5. Observe a group of friends at the nursery. Note the number of children, ages, sexes, whether group is fluid or fixed, whether there is one obvious leader. Do they use language – discussion and compromise – to sustain the group, or action – show of strength, bullying, etc.? Are there frequent quarrels? How do they show their liking for each other?

Suggestions for further reading

Joseph Church, *Understanding Your Child from Birth to Three*, Fontana
Rudolf Dreikurs and Vicki Soltz, *Happy Children*, Fontana
Geoffrey Brown, *Child Development*, Open Books Publishing Ltd

Chapter 14
Difficulties in the pre-school years

Susan Isaacs, who made a detailed and valuable study of the social and emotional development of pre-school children, states:

> In the period from one to five years in particular, emotional difficulties occur so frequently that they may be looked upon as a normal phase of early childhood. Few, if any, children do not manifest some sort of difficulty, although these vary very much in degree and persistence.*

Because social and emotional development are so closely bound together, inner emotional difficulties will reveal themselves in disturbed behaviour. This being so common and normal a part of development, it is dangerous to label one facet of a child's behaviour as a 'problem', still worse to label the child a 'problem child'. Even if one does this only inwardly to oneself, it must inevitably colour one's attitudes towards and expectations of that child, and we know how most children live up to others' expectations of them. 'Naughty' is another word still used a good deal to and about children. We should be wary of branding the child with this. For one thing, it has a slightly wicked connotation which some children find attractive. More important, it is a vague, all-embracing word used to cover many different kinds of behaviour. Often it is behaviour which we, at that moment, with our superior knowledge of that situation and possible consequences, and sometimes – let us admit it – partly because of the mood we are in, find irritating or inconvenient. When three-year-old Darren suddenly smashes all the stickle bricks from the table where he is sitting, with a resounding crash on to the floor, to the shocked delight of his companions, he is not to know that a VIP visitor to the day nursery is expected in the room at any moment, nor that his nursery nurse is experiencing pre-menstrual tension *and* has just applied for a promotion. All he knows is that he has been waiting an interminable time for his dinner; he is hungry, bored and irritable. For the nursery nurse to round on this as 'naughtiness' is therefore irrational and unjust. This is not to say, however, that small children are never trying, nor a great test of our patience and self-control. It is inevitable that they should be so at times, when we consider that they are far from ready to meet all the demands that life makes on them. Their feelings are intense and rapidly changeable. They want instant gratification of those feelings, and lack, on the whole, the ability to control them if met with frustration or denial. They are surrounded by big, powerful adults who can dictate events, while they, the children, have to allow events to happen to them. Inner frustration will surface in one way or another. Sometimes their expression, and the consequences, give rise to guilt and emotional turmoil which, unless handled wisely, can perpetuate the undesirable conduct.

* Susan Isaacs, 'The Psychological Aspects of Child Development', p. 26, *Year Book of Education*, Section II, 1935.

The maintenance of a stable, consistent and happy atmosphere at nursery will go a long way towards reducing emotional and social difficulties. Surrounded by adults who care about him, and with absorbing activities to take part in, the child will gradually learn control and a measure of conformity.

If disturbed behaviour is very frequent, persistent, continues well after five, or suddenly manifests itself out of nowhere, there are certain questions we can ask ourselves:

1. Is there an upset in the home? For instance, has the father deserted or a new baby arrived?

2. How is the child's physical health? Is he sickening for something? Has he an undetected defect, such as hearing loss, which may make him appear unco-operative? Is apparent 'clumsiness' part of his difficulty?

3. Is he getting enough sleep?

4. Is he getting enough attention and affection at home?

5. Is he comfortable at nursery?

6. Is the pattern of his life a satisfying one? (or does he, for example, have too long a day at nursery, or too little contact with mother?)

7. Is he getting enough or too much stimulation? Is he bored?

8. Are we allowing him gradually to become more independent?

9. Are we expecting too much of him?

By endeavouring, without prying into the family's private affairs, to understand possible reasons for disturbed behaviour, we can begin to help the child.

Here *consistency between home and nursery* is vital, as in so many other matters. Inconsistent reactions to his behaviour will only confuse the child and increase his difficulties. Nursery staff and parents should all be pulling in the same direction, that is to help the child back to a happy, tranquil state of mind and reasonably conforming behaviour. Two-way information can be most helpful, provided the child is not aware that he is the focus of much attention and concern.

If parents are deliberately unco-operative and unapproachable, the nursery staff can only do their best, bearing in mind that, if the reasons for the disturbed behaviour lie entirely in the home, their influence will probably be greatly outweighed.

We should remember that most parents want to do, and indeed do, the best they can for their child. The fact that their best is not good enough, or that all their good intentions are rendered useless by circumstances in their personal lives, should not be held against them. Indifference, defensive attitudes or denials about difficult behaviour mask feelings of guilt, failure, anxiety, or fear that the child will lose his nursery place. Some parents need to offload their worries about the child to staff at nursery. Others are helped to handle their feelings of failure by nursery staff agreeing with them (out of the child's earshot) how difficult he can be, or telling the mother that he had a particularly trying day. Much can be done by tactful and friendly approaches.

Some common difficulties

Between toddler stage and approximately age seven, the following forms of behaviour are commonly seen from time to time:

1. tantrums;
2. destructive and aggressive behaviour and bullying;
3. negative, stubborn or defiant behaviour;
4. 'lying' and 'stealing';
5. withdrawal and shyness;
6. aimless activity and lack of concentration;
7. fears and anxieties;
8. jealousy;
9. sucking.

There are other difficulties which worry parents and nursery staff which could be described as *comfort-seeking behaviour habits*, such as thumb-sucking and masturbation. Sometimes these habits accompany the emotional states and difficulties listed above.

There are no magic formulas or glib solutions to any of these difficulties. All we can do here is to suggest possible underlying causes, general guidelines and a few practical tips gleaned from experience.

We also remind the reader that no two children react to the same approach in exactly the same way. Neither does the same highly commendable approach work as well for one adult as another. We must all be true to ourselves. All successful handling techniques rely on this, and equally on knowledge of the child, and a good relationship with him.

1. Temper tantrums. The classic stage for temper tantrums is the year between two and three. The child by now is fully mobile, is increasingly able to explore his environment and gratify his curiosity and his desires. Yet, while wanting to assert his developing personality and his will, he is conscious of apparently being frustrated at every turn. 'No' is all too familiar to him, as is having exciting-looking objects removed from his grasp or path. Physically, he attempts more than he is able to accomplish, in manoeuvring objects and so on. Although he can understand much more than he is able to express, he as yet cannot understand explanations about, for instance, why he may not help himself from the tempting sweet display in the supermarket – all within easy grabbing reach. His reaction on not getting his own way is often to throw himself on the floor, perhaps with arms and legs flailing, and scream until he is red in the face, by which time both he and mother are the centre of a part-sympathetic, part-critical crowd of onlookers. This, in itself, often complicates things, as does the problem of a trolley full of shopping to be dealt with somehow at the same time!

Children older than three often revert to these tactics in very 'fraught' moments, or if they have found in the past that they can get their own way by such means. Children of low intelligence may be specially prone, because they do not understand about limitations; but highly-intelligent children may also be given to such tantrums because they want to do so much more than their limited physical skills will allow.

Although it is much easier to say rather than do, the important thing is for the adult to keep calm and maintain an atmosphere of firm, patient affection. Do not give in to the child 'for the sake of a quiet life', but do not, either, turn the tantrum into a pitched battle between you; screaming back at him will do no good at all. The child is temporarily out of control and you must help him to regain that control. He will probably need to be removed bodily from the scene, away from staring or frightened children, or anyone who is likely to get physically hurt. Restraining the child, in a firm hold, from damaging property or himself will gradually have a calming effect on him, and will make him physically aware of your strength and resolve. If the tantrum lasts any time, he should not be left alone, so stay with him while these frightening, overpowering feelings last. When he has calmed down, quiet, comforting talk and a wash will all help him feel better. The nursery nurse will probably need to involve him in a quiet activity or chore she is doing so that he recovers his composure gradually, before being reinstated with the group. Do not refer to the episode again, and certainly do not adopt the attitude 'Miss P. doesn't love you when you do that'. The alarming experience he has gone through will be all the worse if you threaten to withdraw your friendly feelings towards him.

Prevention is always better than cure, and an observant nursery nurse can do much to foresee possible 'trigger-points'. Fortunately the two-year-old child is easily distracted by, for instance, something unusual you 'thought you saw' out of the window. Remove obvious and unnecessary frustrations from his environment, for example, treasured adult ornaments he must not touch. We all have to endure frustration in our lives, but the two-year-old's life abounds in it, so you need not fear that you are smoothing his path more than is good for him.

2. Destruction, aggressive behaviour and bullying. We all have aggressive feelings and impulses, particularly, the authors believe, boys and men. How far and in what ways we channel this aggression depends very much on the society we live in, and our early environmental influences. In wartime, for instance, we praised the young men who boasted about shooting down enemies; in peacetime, we condemn similar young men who vent their aggression on the football terraces. If a child has, from birth, seen arguments settled by physical blows or vehement abuse among those closest to him, this behaviour will probably be reflected in the child at the nursery. As civilised adults, we curb our destructive impulses – for instance, to throw a brick through a plate-glass window. We respect others' property rights; we can foresee consequences. Small children do not possess these adult attributes. Moreover, they need to destroy before they can create.

Boredom often leads to aggressive behaviour. It is small wonder that there are so many minor fights between children in ordinary primary school playgrounds – there is so little else to do. We should always ensure that small children's surroundings and routine give them enough stimulus. Variety in play material, the arrangement of the room, visits and visitors, new games introduced out of doors, all go a long way to prevent boredom. Older boys at the nursery or playgroup who have gone through all that the establishment has to offer, and also those at the top of the infants school especially need these stimuli.

Children with abundant physical energy, and often strength, need constant outlets if these are not going to be used for disruptive ends. An exciting garden, well equipped, and the opportunity to use it in an unhampered way, will use up a good deal of energy. Wet weather poses a problem for such children, and then they will require alternative vigorous activities such as movement and music-making and building with blocks. Play material which gives outlets for banging, cutting, pinching, tearing, destroying legitimately (such as woodwork, clay and dough, papier mâché, sand, painting, rag dolls) all channel destructive impulses, although needing careful supervision, especially where a potentially aggressive child is using tools or scissors. A home-made cardboard or wooden target figure on a pivot, to be aimed at with bean bags or something similar, is a popular toy for outside play. Play and cleaning jobs involving water can have a soothing effect on an aggressive child.

Sometimes an aggressive child is literally 'hitting back' at life which has been less than kind to him, and is making his mark and seeking attention. To let him see what a nuisance he is, or worse, how much he is disliked by one and all, will only satisfy his perverse impulse. The chances are that he will then go on making life more and more uncomfortable for everyone, living up to his bad reputation. Instead of taking a negative attitude to him and his behaviour, try to make him feel good about himself, by praising anything that can possibly be praised, and letting him help and take small responsibilities. Perhaps a disruptive six-year-old can be put in charge of collecting litter from the school field, or fetching the milk crate, so using his energy and love of power to the good of the community. Experienced staff recommend what they call 'catching' such a child first thing in the morning, by involving him straight away in an interesting, demanding activity.

Aggressive behaviour, although it will occur frequently in minor ways, cannot be tolerated incessantly or in severe forms. The child must realise that he is inflicting harm and hurt, and that you care enough about all the children to protect them from this. 'Hitting back', of course, cannot be recommended, nor can corporal punishment by the adult, although we are aware that when a child is punished in this way at home, our approach will seem weak and ineffectual. Learning to settle differences, or manipulate a situation through words rather than actions, is a very important part of the socialising process which all nurseries must work towards. Give reasons why a certain kind of aggressive conduct cannot be tolerated, and make it clear that you are condemning the deed, not the child. Although it often does not appear so, he badly wants to retain your liking for him. Take him to task quietly but firmly, away from other children. Shouting or emotional reactions on your part will only incite him to further unsocial behaviour; the presence of his friends around will encourage him to make the most of this attention. Where practicable, let him suffer the consequences of his actions, not as a punishment but rather as an unemotional matter of cause and effect. If he has deliberately 'flooded' the bathroom, supervise him calmly while *he* mops it up. He may think this fun at first, but the novelty will soon wear off, and he will probably think twice before doing it another time.

The emergence of both a bully and a victim figure must be quickly observed and steps taken; otherwise real harm could be done to both children, and trouble will arise in nursery/home relationships. Supervision outside must be very close, and possibly excuses found for keeping the children concerned in different parts of the outdoor area. The victim should be given opportunities to succeed and win praise in all sorts of activities, so that his self-confidence is boosted. The aggressor should be kept busy with all the various activities already suggested. Acts of kindness, sharing, etc., however small, should be noted and praised. Sometimes an aggressor will be helped by involvement with the nursery pet, but close supervision will be necessary. Incidents of bullying must be stopped and condemned, but soul-searching sessions of 'Why did you do it?', 'How would you like it if . . .?' or 'You're to wait here till you've said sorry' and so on avail little. The egocentric pre-school child cannot sufficiently think himself into another person's feelings; moreover the incident is past and forgotten as far as he is concerned. If there ever was a reason for his action (which is not always the case) he has probably forgotten it by now, or at any rate will not be able to put it into words. 'Sorry', if it is forced reluctantly out of a child, means little. What is worse, if he utterly refuses to say it, you have placed yourself in a position from which you will have to climb down – never a desirable course for an adult in charge.

3. Negative, stubborn or defiant behaviour. The child who exhibits this type of behaviour may be used to getting things all his own way at home, and be protesting about demands made of him at the nursery. He may be going through a self-assertive phase and feels he can best make his mark by negative gestures. Or negativism may mask fears and uncertainties.

The nursery nurse may be best advised to ignore his negativism over little matters. She should practise a positive approach in her voice and manner when requesting the group to do something. 'Now we're *all* going into the garden to hear a Topsy and Tim story.' Imply in your voice that you confidently expect everyone to participate in this delightful prospect.

If the child has objected to particular routines – for instance putting on his coat to play outside in winter or getting undressed for movement or PE – make the point of the exercise clear to him, not in a wheedling way but as a simple matter of fact. 'We must put our outdoor clothes on because it's so cold today.' Leave it at that. Do not make his refusal the focus of a scene, but let him experience the results of his action. If he sees everybody else having a good time outside, he will probably change his mind eventually and sheepishly join them – with coat. Do not make him feel he has given in.

Not making unreasonable demands on him, not blowing up a refusal into a confrontation between himself and you – all these will help. Giving him a choice of two definite alternatives often distracts him from the fact that he does not really want to do either. Try to find something he is interested in and encourage him to join in. Praise his efforts in group activities; if he wants to remain one of a group he will have to accept some orders.

We should remember that obedience as the Victorians practised it (and many cultures today still expect and obtain utter obedience from their children) was an end in itself. For us, it is only a means to an end. Our goal is for the child to derive the maximum benefit from the nursery, and become a social being.

4. 'Lying' and 'stealing'. We have put these words in inverted commas, because to use them in the usually accepted sense presupposes that young children can distinguish between truth and fantasy, yours and mine. We know from their enjoyment of stories and books which constantly step in and out of the real world (for example, engines that talk and have distinct personalities) that they cannot make such distinctions. Therefore, why should they not make up their own 'tall stories' about, for instance, seeing an alligator on the way to the nursery? Adults should never react sharply to this as telling lies, but enter into the spirit of the story, while letting the child see by their facial expression that it is a shared joke. This will help the child to know that it is only a joke, without demeaning him.

If tall stories and boasting persist well into the infant stage, it may be a sign that the child is not getting enough opportunity to succeed and win praise and admiration in other fields. Children also lie when they are afraid of the consequences of telling the truth, so that it may be a sign that we, or his parents, are being over-strict, or expecting too much of him. We have to help him understand, in a quite unemotional way, that it is important for us to feel able to believe him; otherwise we shall not know when he is telling the truth. Lying can also denote an escape from an undesirable world. Sometimes boasting about heroic acts and so on can represent what the child *would do* if the need arose, or what he would like to do. We should remember that there are many different kinds of truth, as well as untruths.

In the case of 'stealing', we should remember that moral principles of right and wrong are not really grasped until children are about seven or eight. We should also remind ourselves that the little child lives entirely in a here-and-now world, and that his feelings and impulses can be quite overwhelming. If he sees a lovely rosy apple in a friend's coat pocket, and he is feeling peckish, the fact that he can have three or four of his own at home that evening does not enter into it; he wants it there and then, and the temptation is overwhelming.

It is even greater for children who have little in the way of treats and personal possessions at home, particularly where they may be a division between 'haves' and 'have nots' at the nursery or school. Children who are experiencing emotional upsets, lack of affection or loneliness in their personal lives – and this applies particularly to the fives-to-sevens – may help themselves to tempting items as a form of compensation, much in the same way that we gravitate to the biscuit tin, refrigerator or chocolate box when we are feeling let down or miserable.

Parents are often unduly horrified and upset by the fact that their child is taking things. Emotive words like 'pilfering' and 'thieving' spring to mind, with an apparent future of juvenile delinquency. What the neighbours know or think about it also clouds the issue. It is important that if the child is taking things which do not belong to him, certainly for the five-to-seven-year-old, his parents and school staff should consider whether it may be a distress signal. The authors believe that children of this age should have a sensible amount of regular pocket money, freely and gladly given, as evidence of the parents' love for the child, and his growing independence. Pocket money should not be attached to chores like cleaning the car or doing the washing up; earnings for such tasks, if performed, can be extra. Some parents have been surprised to discover that, where punishments and deprivation of pocket money fail to solve the problem, extra love and attention, and possibly extra pocket money, help considerably.

If we know we have in our care a child who has this tendency, we should take sensible precautions not to leave tempting items in his path. Avoid asking the children to bring money to school whenever possible. Certainly never leave money around the room, or in an adult's desk. Snacks and special birthday presents, toys, etc. can be admired and then put on a high shelf for safe-keeping. If we find items belonging to other people, we should return them to the owner, explaining casually to the child. We should never 'frisk' children (parents could accuse us of physical assault if they chose), or turn the search for a missing item into a witchhunt, with a demand for confessions, and so forth.

As realists, we have to face the fact that regrettably there is a whole so-called grey area between the black and white extremes of honesty and dishonesty. How many people declare every penny of their earnings to the tax man, or return to a shop with excess change? How many of us exaggerate anecdotes slightly to make a better or funnier story? Then there is evidence in certain homes of items like tins of paint which have 'fallen off the back of a lorry', teaspoons, towels and ashtrays marked with name of public houses, hotels and transport companies in various parts of the world. This is to state facts, though not to condone.

Children are not deceived. They practise what we practise rather than what we preach.

5. Withdrawal and shyness. These two manifestations appear similar, but may be fundamentally different. A child may be severely withdrawn because of distressing circumstances or events in his early life; he has literally retreated, mentally and emotionally, from the possibility of further hurt and disappointment over relationships. Such a child may also withdraw physically, perhaps constantly to the book corner, home corner, or in small dens he finds or builds for himself. This is a very difficult child to help, and all approaches must be made exceedingly sensitively, gently and gradually. Forcing him to join in things, or badgering him with questions, will only make matters worse. Try to notice anything that seems to arouse his interest and this may lead into communicating with him and drawing him more out of himself and eventually into the group, but it will certainly not happen overnight. If withdrawal seems total, or persistent over a period of time, this child may need expert help, or it may be that he has started at the nursery too early.

Shyness is present in many of us, and to a certain extent can be hereditary. It may be a result of the child's not having mixed much with other children in the early years. It will be more helpful to this child to experience playing with other children on his home ground before being plunged into a larger group away from home. He should never be forced to join in something, or have attention drawn to his shyness, with, for example, apologies made for it. His mother may need to stay with him for a long time, even over a number of days, before he is able to be left happily at the nursery school. Direct close physical contact with strangers will paralyse him with shyness, so at first, contact needs to be oblique and indirect – a sideways, gradual drawing of him into activities, slowly merging into a warm, gentle relationship with adults and others. Praise will boost his self-confidence.

6. Aimless activity and lack of concentration. A child who flits from one group or activity to another can be a disruptive influence in a nursery group, and a trial to adults. Such a child may come from a high-rise flat where he is not allowed to run about or make a noise and where play opportunities are few. On the other hand, he may be over-indulged and overstimulated at home, so that his attention is constantly being distracted from one thing to another.

He will need to channel his energy into vigorous play for a good deal of the time, but he can also be gradually introduced to a more alternating pattern of vigorous, moving-around play, and quieter, relatively static activities. It will help him if a nursery nurse can sit with him, involve herself in his play, encouraging and praising the smallest sustained effort, endeavouring to extend his brief span of concentration in a gradual process. If he sees results achieved by, for instance, effort and time spent on a jig-saw, he may be more willing to settle next time. Strategic placing of this child near the adult at story, group or meal times may also have a calming, restraining influence on him.

7. Fears and anxieties. A child who is under pressure at home, perhaps by over-ambitious parents, or threatened domestic relationships, may appear generally anxious and 'nervy', afraid to accept the smallest new challenge. We can help by providing a happy and stable atmosphere at the nursery where he receives much praise, encouragement and affection.

Specific fears are very common, especially around three years of age. A fearful response to danger, real or apparent, and appropriate evasive action is part of our physical self-preservation mechanism, and is therefore a normal phenomenon. In dealing with young children's fears we should also remember the scale of the adult world as it appears to them. An Alsatian dog must appear as a large horse does to us, the sea an over-powering and endless expanse. Then, too, with our greater knowledge of the world we can rationalise and reassure ourselves that certain fears are groundless; we *know* that the dark corridor does not contain hobgoblins, nor is a clockwork spider really alive and threatening us. Young children are still finding out about such things.

Sometimes we actually *create* children's fears, for instance by squealing about a slow worm (legless lizard), looking frightened in a thunderstorm or, as parents, giving children the impression, through open quarrelling, that their home is about to break up.

To understand the reasons for and the intensity of children's fears is to go some way towards helping because then, clearly, we will not ridicule, tease, or force the child to 'face his fear'. A *gradual* facing and coming to terms with feared objects or situations will be necessary eventually, and often children set the pace themselves. A nursery pet can help a child with the fear of animals; singing songs about thunderstorms and rain can overcome, in a positive way, the distressing sound effects outside; water play and paddling pools can gradually familiarise a child with water as a non-threatening element. Masks or dressing-up clothes can help a child literally play out a fear. Funny books about ghosts or burglars can help to keep such subjects in proportion, although just before bedtime may not be the best time. One small girl who was terrified of fireworks but nevertheless watched a whole display, tightly clutching an adult's hand, was taken aback, then thrilled at an invitation to hold a sparkler for a few seconds. Her delighted recounting of this incident was proof enough that she had truly overcome her particular fear. Elements of fear in manageable (for small children) proportions can add much to the excitement of life.

8. Jealousy. Jealousy can arise at many times in a young child's life. Probably the classic occasion is when the child has to accept the arrival of a brother or sister. This can certainly give rise to deep-seated jealousy and we have tried to offer help over this in Chapter 4.

But other circumstances, too, can produce feelings of jealousy. A child with few possessions of his own can be very envious of peers with more. A child less intelligent, attractive or agile, or less obviously loved than his brothers or sisters may feel extremely jealous of them. Children without fathers can envy those with them.

Jealousy is often linked with lack of self-confidence and inner security. Therefore the adults caring for such a child need to bolster his confidence in himself. He needs a great deal of affection and opportunities to succeed and excel in all kinds of activities. If his jealousy is expressed in aggression, suitable play material can do much to channel these impulses into acceptable forms. A large rag doll can be thrown about and punished mercilessly; clay can be pounded, and nails hammered energetically. Baby doll play and looking after the nursery pet can awaken ideas of tender care. Books and stories about fictional children with similar feelings can help the child to see, in an indirect way, that his situation is not unique. This alleviates the guilt which may be complicating his jealous feelings. Mental notes can be made by staff of coveted things that other children possess, with a view to Christmas presents. Tactful approaches can be made to parents about the child's abilities and likeable characteristics, if it is the case that the jealousy stems from favouritism in the family.

9. Sucking. A baby has a natural instinct for sucking and it is essential for his survival. Besides being a means of getting food, sucking, or touching things with his lips, is a means of finding out the shape and texture of an article. It is also very comforting. As soon as a baby is able, he will put his hand or foot into his mouth to suck. Despite what people say, sucking does not cause a misshapen jaw or overcrowded teeth. From about six months, many babies will suck a thumb or two fingers as they go off to sleep and as this is a very comforting, soothing habit babies continue to do this, sometimes until they are three, four or even five years of age. Some children will, at the same time as sucking, stroke or pick at a small blanket or 'cuddly'. Others will just carry a blanket around with them. Other variations of these comforting habits are nailbiting, which is often a continuation of thumb-sucking, and masturbation. Of all these habits, masturbation (stroking and rubbing the genital organs) is the one which upsets adults most. But all babies find their genital organs and handle them in the same way as they find their hands or feet. The fact that masturbation is pleasant and comforting encourages the child to continue.

If these babyish habits continue well into the second and third years, one must ask oneself why the child is needing so much comfort. Does he need more stimulation or more demonstrated love? Is he happy? Are all his needs being satisfied? Perhaps a change in routine would help. Other than that it is best to leave him alone. As he gets older he will find other interests and satisfactions and should gradually drop the habit. If it disturbs you, then try distracting the child by giving him something different to do, or perhaps doing some activity with him. Nailbiting can sometimes be checked by giving the four-year-old a manicure set and helping him to smooth his nails so that there are no jagged edges to bite. Also oil around the nail will help to prevent jagged bits of cuticle forming.

If a baby admitted to the day nursery is used to sucking a dummy, or if a toddler still needs bottles, then care and judgement should be used to wean them gradually away from their comforters. The best method is to try to give them enough stimulation and care so that they no longer need the comfort of these things to suck.

Exercise 14

Multiple-choice questions
1. Your two-year-old suddenly throws a violent screaming tantrum because a friend's child has taken his favourite toy. You should:
(a) try to reason with him;
(b) effect a compromise between him and his friend;
(c) put him in a room on his own to 'cool off';
(d) remove him from the scene and remain with him until he has calmed down.

2. You are fairly certain that a child of six at your infant school is taking things that do not belong to him. You should:
(a) try to ascertain why he needs this consolation by talking casually with his parents;
(b) speak to him privately, explaining about right and wrong;
(c) send a note home to his parents saying he is pilfering;
(d) search all the children and their clothing next time it happens.

3. Julie, who is three years old, has a new baby brother. At nursery school she is by turns clinging, demanding, tearful and aggressive. Listed below are various ways of helping her. These are combined in four different approaches (a) to (d). Which approach do you consider might be the most effective?
 1. Ask many questions about the baby.
 2. Keep reminding her of what a big girl she is now.
 3. Begin a play project on babies and clinics.
 4. Give her extra affection and physical contact.
 5. Include her in attention to the baby when mother brings him to school.
 6. Make sure you read plenty of situation books about new babies to her.
(a) 1, 2, 3. (b) 2, 3, 4. (c) 3, 4, 5. (d) 2, 4, 6.

Essay questions
4. Describe a child of under seven you have known to experience behaviour difficulties. Were there explanations for his conduct, and how did you and/or other adults help him?
5. A child of three at the nursery seems either painfully shy or unusually withdrawn. What might be some of the possible reasons for this, and how would you try to reach him?

Suggestions for further reading

Martin Herbert, *Problems of Childhood*, Pan Books Ltd
John Gabriel, *Children Growing Up*, Hodder & Stoughton Ltd

Chapter 15
Play and development

What is play?

If we seek dictionary definitions of the word 'play', or think of adult forms of play, we gain an impression of an activity that is pleasant, light-hearted, even trivial – a pleasant contrast to 'work'. Yet these aspects of play are, for young children, only a very small part of its total significance.

Play *is* a child's work; in fact it is the business of childhood. Through play, the child will develop in body and mind. He will come to see some order in the confusing world around him. Because play seems to come naturally to children, and their enjoyment of it is so self-evident and spontaneous, it surely must be a natural way of integrating and exercising their curiosity, energy, vitality and capacity for learning in its widest sense.

Man has by far the longest period of immaturity (childhood) of all the animals. There is more that he must learn, therefore he is given longer in which to do so. It is through play that a great deal of this learning and preparation takes place. Think of how such attributes and abilities as perseverance, ingenuity, enthusiasm, co-operation, decision-making are all fostered during play.

We have seen in a previous chapter how small children cannot truly learn other than through first-hand experience; it is this same experience that we set out to offer them at nursery.

Play can be entirely undirected and unstructured, or it can be structured according to the child's evolving needs and developing powers. This is something that is sometimes difficult for parents to understand and recognise, but a good nursery is not simply a paradise of 'toys' on which the children are let loose. There should be provision for progression in every form of play, and this is where the expertise of the staff will ensure that the child is constantly moving forwards, but at his own rate.

With all new play materials, children pass through certain stages in their approach; first, they explore the material with their senses – and whole bodies, where possible. Then they experiment with it to find out its possibilities, potential and limitations. Later they imitate what they have seen other children do with it, or adults do with a similar substance. Ultimately, they play with it according to their own creative and original ideas.

Of course, the stages have little connection with the age of the child. A three-year-old, through frequent opportunity, may have passed through to the creative stage with sand play, whereas a five or six-year-old presented with clay for the first time will begin with the exploratory approach. Opportunity and discreet encouragement are key factors in children's working through the stages.

There are also definite stages through which children pass with regard to the social aspect of play. The very young child, or the child who has had little experience of mixing, will play first – with whatever materials – in a solitary way.

195

Later, he will act as a spectator to others' play, which will lead to parallel play, where he and another child play side by side with similar material, but still essentially as separate individuals. Then the child will begin to associate himself with the other child in a momentary or tentative way. Lastly he will involve himself fully in co-operative play with a group; he will give and take, share, take turns, submit and lead as the occasion demands.

Types of play

It is impossible here to do more than outline essentials about the various types of play we offer small children. There is a good deal of overlap between the different types, which makes categorisation somewhat artificial. The tables on pp. 200–213 are intended as starting points for further reading and discussion. They may also be used as a basis for re-examination of what play opportunities we provide, how we do it, and – most important – why.

Although nursery space and resources are assumed, and in some cases are essential, in what follows, a good deal is easily adaptable or improvisable by enterprising play group leaders and mothers at home in more restricted premises, and on a far slimmer budget.

Music and movement. Musical experience is one of those activities arranged by adults, and though it cannot be called 'play', it greatly enriches the life of young children. They are surrounded by it for much of the time on television and radio, but we can make it far more than 'audio-wallpaper' for them. We can transform music into another avenue of expression.

Enjoyment and participation by children and adults should be the keywords in all we do. Music for young children should not be regarded as either a spectator or performer art; rather it is an action art.

The adult does not need instrumental skills or a good singing voice herself. If she looks to her own creativity and tries hard to overcome any lack of self-confidence, she is well on the way to success. Intelligent use of a record player and tape recorder, for example, will also more than compensate for lack of skill in piano playing.

Music has been said to be a blend of mathematics and magic, and both strands have a part to play in the musical experience we offer young children.

Four main aspects of musical experience
(a) *Cultivating auditory discrimination through attentive listening*: activities here will include collecting sounds, using tape recorder (for example, all morning sounds: kettle boiling, Dad shaving, milkman delivering, etc.); matching sounds (in the environment and using tapes); making sound patterns, alerting children to intensity and pitch. Full use should be made of children's natural response to rhythm. Remember, our very bodies function to rhythm – heartbeat, etc. Simple time-beat can lead to definite rhythm. A climax will also be satisfying in our sound pictures;

(b) *Developing vocal skills*: activities here can include 'mouth' music, humming, singing individually, singing together (which entails discipline of stopping and starting, etc.). Remember, however poor you think your voice is, or however embarrassed you are to perform in front of another adult, the children will be impressed and will not laugh at you. When introducing a new song, first sing a couple of familiar ones, then sing the new one through twice or three times (if short). Do not separate or teach it line by line. If you like it and are putting it over well, the children will soon be joining in;

(c) *Developing instrumental skills*: activities here might include making instruments (for example, from shells, coconuts) and household junk (painted and filled squeezy bottle shakers, date-box and sandpaper scrapers, etc.), experimenting with these, using them as sound effects in stories and songs, playing *some* together with melodic music; being aware of commercial instruments and the most suitable buys for the nursery (big cymbals and xylophone?); encouraging children to join in songs, etc. with single notes of tuned instruments as appropriate; providing a music workship, or trolley, with pictures of adult instruments, etc.; letting children see and hear live instrumentalists, for example, a father who plays guitar? maybe get close enough to feel vibrations;

(d) *Adding to our repertoire of songs and music, and improving techniques*: there are many books of lively songs suitable for young children on the market today. Funny songs, rousing songs, gentle lullabies all have a place. We should make use of children's familiarity with TV jingles. Compose our own songs and musical phrases to accompany everyday actions like dressing, going upstairs, clearing bricks away, etc. because this can be fun. 'Children's' records can be evaluated, but tend to be limiting; we should make use of adult music – traditional, classical, modern, popular – which creates a mood, or is characterised by a strong beat.

Movement

Joy in music will lead quite naturally into movement and dance. Small children are rarely inactive, and response to beat and rhythm will be expressed in activity. Some children, in fact, are unable to stay still when music with a strong or 'catchy' beat is being played. We should welcome such a response and encourage spontaneity of expression.

Of course, music is not essential for children to enjoy movement. With a skilled adult to guide them, young children can move imaginatively, stimulated by experiences such as having watched snails moved, or a piece of machinery in action.

Children must have adequate space in which to move, and a prearranged signal – not a shout – will be needed to attract their attention for each fresh activity. Uniformity in how children move is not the goal; we should encourage individual experimentation and expression.

Creative movement brings the emotions into play – sadness, solemnity, joy. It helps children to gain control over their bodies, and develops body-awareness, which we now know to be of vital importance for many reasons. Co-ordination and control bring poise, grace and economy of movement. An uninhibited, joyful approach at this stage will lead naturally into creative dance and drama later on.

Fields of discovery. Children are born explorers. They explore through their five senses and through their bodies. Much of their exploring will be of play materials that we provide for them, but much will also be of objects they meet in their daily life. Some objects will be living, some inanimate. Some they will find on their own – in the nursery garden, on their way home, at Grandma's. Others we will deliberately bring into the nursery for them to look at, handle, manipulate, ask questions about.

Perhaps these processes can be better described as *investigation* rather than play. Such investigation performs the following functions:

(a) It satisfies and also feeds a child's curiosity and spirit of enquiry.

(b) It encourages powers of reasoning, memory, classification, association, problem-solving.

(c) It promotes language development through discussion, and through 'how', 'when' and 'why' questions and answers.

(d) It encourages use of reference books.

(e) It sharpens observation skills.

(f) It fosters ideas of caring, reliable tending, personal responsibility (e.g. for pets, plants).

(g) It teaches patience (e.g. waiting for bulbs to appear).

(h) It extends the child's knowledge and understanding of the world around him, including dangers (poisonous berries, etc.).

(i) It teaches respect for forms of life other than human.

(j) It builds a foundation for later formal scientific experimentation; in the same way, later recording, ordering and measuring of findings (mathematics) will also stem from this. Life is an increasingly complex technological society makes these aspects of education more and more important.

(k) It fosters a sense of wonder, and appreciation of patterns and order in the world around the child, and awareness of life cycles – birth and death.

If we are to care effectually for the environment of the present and the future, and find ways of making life on earth better for *all* mankind, then surely we need to give young children plenty of opportunity to begin developing these skills and attitudes as early as possible.

Starting points for investigation. We have to decide how much of the animate and inanimate world we can bring into the nursery, or take the children to visit. Here are some ideas:

(a) *keeping pets* (but *do* inform yourself fully *beforehand* on care and possible difficulties, health hazards, etc.), also wormery, aquarium;

(b) *gardening* activities (quick-maturing vegetables which can later be made into sandwiches or soups are especially good);

(c) keeping *plants and flower arrangements*;

(d) growing *spring flowering bulbs* indoors;

(e) taking children on frequent *walks*, particularly to see trees, wild flowers, ducks, animals, etc., fostering ideas on conservation;

(f) using natural materials in *displays* (e.g., leaves, bark, shells);

(g) using natural materials in *activities* (e.g., collage, leaf prints);

(h) making a *bottle garden*;

(i) making a *bird table* and observing activities on it, providing winter foodstuffs for birds, 'Christmas pudding' etc.;

(j) drawing children's attention to changing *weather, clouds, seasons, temperature*;

(k) keeping *seeds* and watching them germinate indoors;

(l) following up interest aroused by discovery of *beetle, snail* etc., in garden;

(m) keeping a *'discovery' table* ('things which work') with changing assortment of such items as bells, clocks, locks, taps, washers, pumps, syringes, egg-timer, springs, pendulums, cogs, levers, pulleys, springs, mirrors, magnets;

(n) organising walks to watch *work of all sorts* being carried out, for example, cranes at the docks, concrete mixer in the road;

(o) drawing children's attention to different means of *transport*, in books, pictures and real life; different sources of *power* (light, heat, water) and different types of *construction* (bridge, flats, tower, etc.);

(p) encouraging *inventiveness* in many different forms; junk modelling is a favourite means of expressing this.

The wider world. Children will find out more about the environment outside their home, nursery and school on various outings throughout the year (see page 281). But we can also bring into the school or nursery people from the world of work, service and entertainment to give children further information, understanding and insight. Such visitors might include a fire officer, police officer, farmer, road safety officer, dentist, music instrumentalist or puppeteers. Badges of office, tools of the trade and other visual aids that children can see and touch are particularly well received. However, a great deal can also be conveyed by simple talk and answering questions. The first-hand freshness and authenticity of the communicator make his words far more effective than any book, and such contact with new adults, in a familiar setting, builds confidence.

TYPES OF PLAY

1. Vigorous physical play, often on large or small equipment, mainly outdoors

Value	Provision	Role of the adult	Progression
Enjoyment Release of surplus energy Offers new freedom from tensions and restrictions Stimulus to: appetite, digestion, circulation, sound sleep, mental alertness, skin health Promotes: muscle tone, bodily co-ordination, manipulative skills, balance, control, body awareness, resistance to infection Develops such skills as: running, stopping and starting, hopping, aiming, climbing, swinging, steering, carrying Offers element of challenge and adventure Builds concepts of: height, width, speed, distance, spatial relationships Fosters social adjustment: levelling of abilities in new setting, sharing, collaborating Builds self-confidence. Stimulates intellectual curiosity, powers of observation, aesthetic awareness and sense of wonder (insects and birds,	A well and imaginatively-planned garden with paved area and grass, different levels, paths, trees, digging and growing areas, possibilities for dens and privacy, storage for equipment, easy access to nursery Large but manoeuvrable apparatus, such as: climbing frame, see-saw, rockers, rope ladder, trestle units and plank, hollow cubes, packing case boxes, tyres, barrels, space hopper Small apparatus such as: hoops, skipping ropes, balls, bean bags Wheeled vehicles such as: trucks, carts, scooters, tricycles, wheelbarrows	Exercise constant watchfulness in supervision for safety (of equipment and children). Undertake arrangement and rearrangement of apparatus. Encourage child in his activities, without directing or goading him to try feats beyond his capabilities. Inject new ideas. Maximise language opportunities (with children, not other adults). Introduce idea of fair play, and 'police' for bullying or dangerous quarrels. Train children in tidying away. Initiate ring games, singing games etc. as occasion demands. Sharpen your own and children's powers of observation. Keep informed of new equipment available; offer suggestions for new buys based on critical evaluation and consideration of your children in your available space.	Mastery of new skills. Tentative exploratory approach – simple repetition of newly-learned technique – individual interpretation and creative activity, e.g. skipping. Increase in co-ordination, control, economy of movement. Growth in confidence and acceptance of challenge, e.g. balance walking with adult help – with adults' reassuring presence – unaided. Growth in awareness of outdoor life, e.g. looks at birds with interest – ask questions and comments on characteristics – enthuses about making bird table, keeping records, using reference books. These developments also apply to all the following types of play { Passes through solitary – spectator – parallel – co-operative stages of play. Attention span lengthens. Increasing

Value	Provision	Role of the adult	Progression
changing seasons, rainbow, reflections in a puddle etc.) Feeds the imagination and leads into imaginative play.			language involved.
2. Play with basic materials.	**(a) Water**		
Enjoyment Fascination of primitive element Sensory experience Release of tension Outlet for aggression Soothing effect Language opportunities (very rich here) Encourages manipulative skills (e.g. pouring accurately) There is no right and wrong way, therefore endless scope. Link with imaginative play (e.g.. tea parties, bathing the doll etc.). Mathematical and scientific discoveries concerning: volume, capacity, gradation (big, bigger, etc.), floating and sinking, absorbency, changes, of objects when wet and dry, in textures, colour, shape, water	Play with paddling pool, water painting, hoses, etc. outside Equipment for washing dolls and dolls' clothes Suitable size water bath, preferably transparent Equipment for water bath: tubing, squeezy bottles, graded jugs and cups, beakers with holes, sponges, loofah, spoons and ladles, household articles such as colander, plastic dishes, lids, cotton reels etc., rubber ball, golf ball, table-tennis ball, bubble blowing equipment Protection for floor (newspapers on top of plastic sheet?) Protection for children, overalls on stand (number available can be way of restricting numbers) Table or similar nearby to hold categorised equipment Tepid water, sometimes coloured (vegetable colouring or	Site and plan water play for safety, comfort, accessibility of tap and sink. Supervise protection of children, looking out for wet sleeves, socks etc. Vary, perhaps limit equipment provided each day. Observe children closely for scientific discoveries, asking meaningful questions and giving extending suggestions. Maximise language opportunities. Intervene if play becomes over-boisterous. Constantly watch small children in paddling pool. Involve children in clearing away.	Early experience in the home: bathtime, paddling pool, household and garden chores. Formal water play at nursery. Simple pouring, filling, emptying, squirting, experimenting with properties of water. Child makes incidental scientific and mathematical discoveries; carries through simple tasks set. Structured water activities at infant school. Child carries out tasks based on capacity, conservation of quantity. Verbalises concepts learned. Experiments with ice, snow, etc. Works from formal workcards and records results. If given suitable opportunities, will progress from splashing in pool, through 'doggy paddle', swimming with armbands, on his own.

Value	Provision	Role of the adult	Progression
finds its own level, displacement of water, force and pressure, conservation (of quantity irrespective of shape of container), proportion, evaporation, syphoning, condensation, dissolving, properties of: cleansing, sustaining life, metal corrosion Categorisation (of equipment) Standard units of measurement	washing 'blue'), sometimes bubbly Opportunities to join in cleaning chores with water (washing furniture) and life-sustaining functions (watering plants, changing pets' water)		
(b) Sand			
Enjoyment Pleasurable link with seaside Outlet for aggression Opportunity to destroy legitimately Language opportunities Creativity Sensory experience Link with imaginative play There is no right and wrong way (see column 4) so endless scope Scientific discoveries concerning: properties and contrasts of wet and dry sand, weight, capacity, grains, moulding, imprints	Sandpit outside, away from trees, to afford children body contact Sand bought from builders' merchant (cheaper if fetched) Equipment for sandpit: variety of spades, buckets, cups, cartons, rake, shells etc. Sand container(s) inside for wet and/dry sand Equipment similar to that for sandpit For dry sand, also: funnels, colander, sieve, flour sifter etc. Protection for floor	Supervise children for safe and non-wasteful play (no throwing or removing it permanently). Supervise sandpit for foreign bodies, dangerous items, fouling by animals and litter. Check condition of equipment. Wash or replace regularly sand used indoors (sun and fresh air cleans outside sand). Maximise language opportunities, and inject new ideas. Involve children in sweeping up and caring for equipment. Observe stages children are at (exploratory play, through to creative building).	Exploratory play for texture, e.g. dry sand, trickling through fingers, patting. Experimental play for properties of wet and dry sand; sieving, pattern-making, digging, moulding. Creative play. Developing of manual dexterity, wrist strength and control to enable sand castles to be successfully turned out and form a base for complex imaginative play. 'Gardens', 'building sites', 'road layouts' also made, incorporating embellishments, other play materials, vehicles, etc.

Value	Provision	Role of the adult	Progression
(c) Clay and dough			
Enjoyment	Protection for children (aprons)	Site clay tables intelligently, near tap and sink, and supervise for undue mess (e.g. door handles, clothes, hair).	Exploratory play for feel of new substances.
Endless possibilities, no right and wrong way	Protection for floor and chairs		Experimental play for properties, e.g. elasticity of dough, retained imprint in clay.
Legitimate 'mucky' play	Tables and chairs of suitable height, to allow of banging and rolling with some force	Maintain clay by storing in grapefruit-sized balls, with small water-filled indentation. Place on brick or hessian rag inside airtight container, and cover with plastic sheet or damp rag. Inspect regularly, particularly before and after holidays. Keep in cool place. Well maintained, it will last indefinitely.	Accidental creativity – 'Look, I've made a snake!'
Emotional benefits: outlet for aggression (prodding, poking, cutting, banging)	Sufficient amounts of red and white clay (best bought in ready-to-use state from local pottery) and kept in perfect condition		Intentional creativity. Child comes to substance with preconceived ideas of recognisable object to be made.
Therapeutic effect of handling plastic material	Plain and different coloured dough, made about once a week		Elaboration of creative play.
Sensory experience	Equipment for each	Mix dough to preferred recipe (often three parts flour to one part salt, water, oil and colouring optional) but experiment with other sorts of flour. Keep in airtight plastic bag.	Child wants to – keep, dry, paint, varnish, take home, use clay pot.
Novelty of clay (too messy for most homes)	(a) Clay (keep equipment to a minimum): wire cutter, blunt knives, boards, spatulas.	Vary materials offered.	
Link with home of dough	(b) Dough: rolling pins, boards, flour sifters, patty tins	Introduce relevant and enriching vocabulary.	
Scientific discoveries about properties of both (elasticity, contrasts of wet and dry etc.)		Refrain from making objects or models 'for' child.	
Satisfies and externalises children's curiosity and preoccupation with bodily products, play with which is taboo		Value the doing more than an end product. Carefully dry older children's models, and	
Language opportunities (cool, moist, stretchy, etc.)			

Value	Provision	Role of the adult	Progression
		encourage painting, displaying, firing if possible.	

(d) Wood (wood can also be considered a creative and constructional play material)

Value	Provision	Role of the adult	Progression
Enjoyment Sensory experience Link (especially for boys) with father and grandfather Fosters manipulative skills and eye/hand co-ordination (e.g., banging in a nail) Language opportunities (names of tools, grains of wood, etc.) Emotional benefits: outlet for tension and aggression, satisfaction of making a noise legitimately, sense of power, sense of achievement Avenue of creativity, perhaps leading to adult interest Mathematical and scientific experience: length, breadth, angles, stress	Suitably-sized rigid woodwork bench Scaled-down real tools (toy tools break and cause accidents and frustration) such as: hammers, tenon saw, screwdriver, awl, vice, spanner Suitable storage for tools (e.g. on pegboard, with jubilee clips and silhouettes of appropriate tools) Assortment variously shaped and sized soft wood pieces Materials suitable for wheels (tins, lids, bottle tops etc.) Assorted nails and screws in transparent containers with lids	Plan and site woodwork bench intelligently so that it gives least disturbance to others (e.g., noise-deadening flooring underneath it, or piece of blanket nailed firmly on top. Consider siting it outdoors or in corridor). Supervise closely and constantly for safety (small numbers, spectators to keep well back, no distractions to allow children's concentration to wander). Intervene and offer help and suggestions where necessary, without 'taking over' play. Discuss work in hand with children and offer relevant and enriching vocabulary. Observe and cater for stage each child is at (just banging nails into bench or making preconceived models). Offer more advanced children opportunity to paint, display, use models.	Exploratory play for feel of wood, power of tools. Experimental play for properties of wood, own abilities. Accidental creativity; shape of wood triggers ideas of objects to make, e.g. aeroplane. Intentional creativity. Child comes to wood with preconceived ideas; selects appropriate pieces, nails etc., handles tools competently. Wants to paint and display or play with finished item.

Value	Provision	Role of the adult	Progression
		Value the 'doing' more than the end product. Train children in safe and correct method of handling and storing tools.	

3. Construction play (a) with large junk

Value	Provision	Role of the adult	Progression
Enjoyment Feeds imagination Language opportunities Encourages social play First-hand experiences in spatial relationships (next to, underneath, on top of etc.), also three-dimensional shape Sometimes takes place outdoors, involving all health benefits as set down in 1 Emotional benefits: outlet for vigorous action, sense of achievement, sense of power from making life-size models Link with group interests, e.g. robot, shop, and imaginative play	Sufficient time and space Large cardboard boxes (including TV and refrigerator packing cases) Sheets of corrugated cardboard Spools from paper bales etc. Sugar paper Newspapers Brown paper Materials, fabric as needed: string; strong glue; cellulose tape; paint; scissors Any other suitable discarded material 'Large junk' is also sometimes used to describe packing cases, tyres etc. used outside. See section 1.	Take up children's suggestions for constructions, or discreetly introduce ideas. Discuss practicalities with children. Sustain ideas begun. Introduce relevant vocabulary. Supervise for safe use of tools and materials. Use or display constructions as intended.	ALSO applies to (b) below: Exploratory play with shapes, objects, texture. Child haphazardly assembles pieces, may or may not fix them together. Inaccurate gluing, tearing, cutting. Accidental creativity. Shape, or juxtaposition of pieces triggers ideas of recognisable object, e.g. boat, train. Intentional creativity. Child selects appropriate pieces to carry out preconceived idea. Assembles, cuts, places, glues precisely, solving problems that arise as he works. Elaboration of creativity. Child

(b) with small junk items

Value	Provision	Role of the adult	Progression
Enjoyment Feeds imagination	Large assortment of household and other junk (sometimes	Initiate and maintain a successful system for collecting junk.	wants to dry, paint, keep, display, label, take home item

Value	Provision	Role of the adult	Progression
Promotes resourcefulness Embodies conservation principles (of using others' scrap to good purpose) Cheap to provide Involves parents and children in provision, thus fostering greater understanding and appreciation Link with group interest (boats, engines etc.) Language opportunities (names of containers, former contents, sources of origin, parts of models made etc.) Sensory experience Encourages small manipulative skills (fixing, gluing, etc.) Awareness of three-dimensional shape Experience in comparing, matching, sorting	called 'treasure') e.g. cereal packets, egg boxes – not polystyrene type (the particles are very dangerous if inhaled), lolly sticks, bottle tops, margarine tubs Strong glue Paste brushes Paper Paint Scissors Storage systems for all materials (e.g. wallpaper – covered large boxes with labels) so that there are separate categories, and children can select easily. Appearance of containers is also important to look of room Tables and chairs to work at Protection from glue (aprons)	Keep it neatly stored, throwing out useless or spoiled items. Discuss work with children, introducing relevant new vocabulary and suggestions where needed. Encourage, and offer help where necessary. Arrange attractive displays, where practicable. Use reference books whenever possible (e.g. to find out, with child, number of funnels on ship, or what a lighthouse looks like). Involve children in care and use of equipment, checking numbers of scissors returned, etc.	produced. Makes links with class projects. May be able to follow simple instructions from books, T.V. programmes, to make specific items.
(c) with blocks			
Enjoyment Sensory experience (blocks are clean, pleasant to touch, non-threatening) Emotional benefits: outlet for	Adequate time and space Sufficient large wooden blocks, made in geometric proportions (e.g. two shorts = one long) Sufficient small blocks varying	Site block play where children will not be disturbed by through traffic, or boisterous activities, and where they will give least disturbance (by noise to quiet activities).	Exploratory play. Baby bangs, throws, scatters, builds 'towers' of 2 bricks inaccurately placed. Early constructional play. Child lines up bricks on floor as

Value	Provision	Role of the adult	Progression
aggression, satisfaction of making loud but legitimate noise, and destroying	in shapes and sizes, colour, textures, grains of wood (possibly home-made from offcuts)	Check blocks for splintering and shortages.	roads, moves them as cars etc. Fills and empties truck, boxes. Builds towers of 3 and 4; enjoys crashing these down.
Feeling of power (especially of making life-sized models, walls to hide behind etc.)	Interlocking plastic bricks A corner, or at least a wall, against which to build	Discuss children's constructions with them, feeding in enriching vocabulary and ideas where relevant.	Later constructional play. Builds several towers, walls, houses, dens.
Encourages perseverance	Noise-deadening carpet or rug if liked	Remember that many children like to build for long periods on their own, undisturbed.	Complex constructional play. Child carries out preconceived ideas, e.g. airport, multi-storey car park. Uses vehicles, 'small world' people and accessories. Enters realms of fantasy play.
Fosters eye/hand co-ordination: balance, control, precision	Table where children can play with small bricks	Give adequate time warnings about dismantling constructions. Come to reasonable and individual arrangements about large or ambitious constructions.	
Develops muscle tone in: stretching, lifting, carrying	Accessibility of 'small world' – dolls, furniture, vehicles, animals, etc.		
Feeds imagination, often leading into imaginative play	Adequate and systematised storage facilities	Supply additional play aids as required, e.g. blanket for a roof.	
Language opportunities (names of shapes and constructions etc.)		Prevent deliberate untimely destruction by other children.	
Mathematical experience: height, weight, proportion, spanning, symmetry, three-dimensional shape		Involve children in clearing away (NB can be done to music). Make it a mathematical experience.	

4. Creative and imaginative play (a) Painting and visual arts

Value	Provision	Role of the adult	Progression
Enjoyment Avenue of expression Novelty for many nursery	Easels and/or tables Brightly-coloured paints of creamy consistency (mainly	Site facilities intelligently (in good light, with easy access to water and sink).	*Approach to paint and colour* Tentative at first, touches, may taste, paint hands etc. Holds

Value	Provision	Role of the adult	Progression
children Feeds imagination Language stimulation (colours, objects, etc.) Creativity Sense of achievement End product admired by adults Appeal of colour Experience in depicting and interpreting meaning of symbols on paper (foundation for later reading and writing) Control Emotional release (of frightening experiences, etc.) Fosters taste and personal preferences Perception of shape, spatial relationships Scientific discoveries about: textures, consistencies, mixing colours etc.	primary colours) Long-handled brushes, of different widths Paper of varying textures, shapes, sizes, colours (including textured paper like wallpaper samples) Non-spill paint pots Objects for printing (leaves, string, pastry-cutters, etc.) Non-fungicidal thickening agent for paint Washing-up liquid for bubble painting Candles for 'magic' painting Floor protection as needed Aprons on hooks Provision of drying rack or similar Space to display work Large chalks, board, chubby crayons	Maintain appeal of materials and equipment (no 'gunged up' easels or paint pots). Supervise children for protection. Talk to child about his work if he wants to, but not relentlessly, nor seeking representational likeness. Occasionally introduce different techniques using paint in a semi-directed way, e.g. marble rolling, butterfly painting. Involve children in clearing up. Allow children to take home paintings (put names on backs as soon as possible after completion). Arrange frequent displays of *all* children's work. Observe children's progress from exploratory stage to preconceived ideas stage.	brush like dagger in stiff arm. Blobs, scrubs, overloads brush, applies marks, lines, patches of colour. Superimposes colours, 'blocks' patches. Discovers symmetry in pattern. Suppler wrist facilitates deliberate and delicate brush strokes. *Symbolic representations* (a) Human figure. Random scribble. Oval emerges. Becomes big head (cephalopod) with features. Legs sprout from head. Legs blocked in to form body. Arms, ears, fingers, 'tent' dress with details. (b) House. Square, square with door and window in each corner, addition of 'strip' earth and sky, sun with radials, path, flowers, stairs; figure inside. *Age 6–7* – 'golden age of children's art'. Child is not aware of difficulties of proportion, perspective. Is uncritical. Fills page with flat and pleasing composition.

Value	Provision	Role of the adult	Progression
(b) Collage ('sticking' with a variety of materials)			
All the values listed for painting apply equally here ALSO Promotes resourcefulness Lends itself readily to group projects, current themes, etc. Sensory experience (comparison of textures) Invites judgements on suitability Encourages choice, personal preferences Involves small manipulative skills (using scissors etc.)	Supply of scrap materials, fabrics, wool, pasta, bottle tops, natural materials (bark etc.) Methodical and attractive system of collecting, storing, sorting materials Glue Paste brushes Scissors Protection for children Protection for table	Similar to that for painting ALSO Initiate themes for group collage work. Organise execution of large pieces (on floor, etc.). Sustain ideas and incorporate children's suggestions.	Similar to that for junk modelling. Child becomes increasingly selective of colours, textures, suitability.
(c) Dramatic play			
Enjoyment Role play Helps children project into feelings of others Helps children relive happy experiences (e.g., wedding), come to terms with unhappy ones (e.g., witnessing road accident) Language stimulus (boundless opportunities here) Encourages social co-operation	Adequate time and space Dressing up clothes (boys' as well as girls') Props (shopping bags, purses, jewellery, steering wheel, blanket) Masks Variety of puppets (sock, glove, finger, etc.) Storage for all the above (clothes should be hung up)	Set the scene and provide an encouraging atmosphere. Allow privacy if children require it. Give adequate time warnings. Allow play to spread outdoors if possible. Involve oneself through question and discussion. Keep clothes in good state of cleanliness and repair. Inject fresh ideas and fresh	Simple 'pretend' games from approx. 15 months onwards. Child substitutes one thing for another, e.g. soft toy for pillow. Imitative play on domestic themes (dolls' tea parties) or taking on role of animals. Simple role play with props, e.g. fireman with helmet. Re-enactment of observed incidents. Imaginary playmate. Sequences of actions, and more detailed role play; T.V. heroes.

Value	Provision	Role of the adult	Progression
Offers wish fulfilment and escape Involves small manipulative skills Exercises the imagination Sensory experience (textures and colours of dressing-up clothes) Outlet for tensions and aggression Insight for adult into thoughts and feelings of child		'props' to suggest new play. Supervise, and intervene when necessary for reasons of safety and noise level. Observe for signs of increasing co-operation.	Play moves away from domestic and familiar themes into realms of fantasy and escapism, e.g. space ship. Boy and girl groups often separate at about 5–6.
(d) Domestic play			
All the values listed for dramatic play apply equally here ALSO Link with home Greater knowledge of functioning of a home Mathematical experience (laying the table, etc.) Fosters social skills (e.g., being hostess)	Home corner, preferably large enough for sleeping and living areas, affording privacy and a sense of self-containment Bed and bedding Rug or carpet Table and chairs Cooker, saucepans, kettle Sink Cupboards Cutlery, crockery Cleaning equipment Telephones *NB*: Home corner may be temporarily converted into hospital, shop, hairdresser's, cafe, as	Similar to that for dramatic play ALSO Allow child to become involved in domestic chores of nursery (spring cleaning home corner, looking after nursery pets, plants, etc.)	Similar to that for dramatic play. Though remaining home-based, play sequences lengthen, become more complex and sophisticated. Roles are clearly designated and adhered to. Play sequences involve activities outside the home corner. Play can be highly verbal and laughter-producing.

occasion or current interest demands)			
(e) Dolls			
Enjoyment Avenue for projection into others' feelings Awakens ideas of caring, tenderness Outlet for tension and aggressions (e.g., if new baby is at home) Knowledge of baby care Knowledge of mother's role Mathematics involved in dressing dolls (comparative size, gradation, counting, pairs, matching, 1:1 correspondence, categorisation) Language stimulation Sensory experience (texture of dolls' clothes, etc.) Knowledge of principles of laundry	Variety of different dolls (large rag doll, baby doll, black doll) 3 matching size-graded dolls with identical clothes Variety of clothes for outdoor, indoor and night wear Doll's bed, pram Bath, soap, talc, bottle etc. Provision for washing doll's clothes Open dolls' house, and small-world dolls Road layout, farm, railway station etc. for small-world dolls	Observe intelligently children's play and reactions with dolls. Make the most of language and mathematical opportunities. Allow children to make dolls and dolls' clothes. Allow children to wash dolls and dolls' clothes. Encourage progression from simple handling and undressing, through to more complex and creative play. Involve children in systematic clearing and tidying away.	6 months–1 year. Cuddles, sucks, soft toy. Drops it out of pram for adult to retrieve. 1–2 years. Puts soft toy or simple doll in truck, box, pram and pushes or drags it around. Likes doll in bath or bed. Carries it round by arm or leg. May undress it, wrap in blanket. 2–3 years. Names favourite doll. Plays imitative games, tea-time, etc. Nurses doll, talks to it, puts it to bed. Undressing still easier than dressing. May scold and handle doll roughly. 3–4 years. Doll is often constant and necessary companion, especially at bedtime, unpleasant happenings. Doll is treated more as human being. Dressing is becoming easier. 4–5 years. Girls often keener than boys on doll play. 'Clinic', bath time, feeding, etc. sequences are popular. Also dolls' houses. 5–7 years. Teenage dolls are popular. 'Combat' male dolls liked by boys. Sequences become sophisticated. All accessories required. Girls may make material or paper dolls and clothes.

Value	Organisation and role of the adult	Progression
(f) Cookery. An adult-directed activity		
Enjoyment	Link it to an occasion, story, topical interest whenever possible (e.g., Shrove Tuesday, 'The Gingerbread Man', blackberries found in field.)	The adult will stage-manage and oversee progression in language used and understood, concepts learned and skills acquired.
Link with home	Involve children in shopping; discuss requirements, allow them to select items, proffer money, look after change.	
Sensory experience (feel, smell, taste)	Organise time, place, use of cooker, utensils, ingredients, etc. well beforehand.	
Emotional release (in beating, kneading, cutting, whisking)	Prepare illustrated recipe card, or find place in book.	
Satisfaction and pride in end-product	Select group (of approximately 4) and keep a record of who makes what.	
Language opportunities (names of utensils, origins of ingredients, descriptions of consistencies, etc.)	Pre-heat oven if necessary.	
	Make sure children go to toilet and wash hands, girls tie back long hair.	
Education in need for hygiene and home safety	Give clear instructions and demonstrate what you mean (e.g., 'cream the margarine').	
Social activity – working with a group towards joint goal, waiting turns, consulting with adult, handing round end products	Keep every child occupied all the time as far as possible, and let each have a turn at every process.	
	Supervise and give advice and suggestions and invite comments throughout.	
Social graces, contributing to special occasions (Christmas, school coffee morning, etc.)	Make the most of language opportunities (e.g., 'risen', 'golden brown', 'crunchy', etc.)	
	Involve all children in clearing up.	
Education in nutrition (emphasis on savoury and wholesome foods)	Give out or sell goods fairly, remembering 'sisters' or headteacher, and any visitors.	
Encourages concentration	Encourage cooking group to share experience with others.	

Value	Organisation and role of the adult	Progression
Scientific and mathematical experiences: shopping, standard units of measurement, passing of time, weighing, balancing, capacity and volume, counting, dividing, fractions, one-to-one correspondence, classification, judging, effects of heat, introducing air bubbles, absorption, changes in texture, pressure Link with reading: labels on goods, using recipe cards (left-to-right eye movement), seeing adults consult books, making own recipe cards, or pictures and records in class book	*N.B.*: 'Cooking' need not involve use of a cooker. Novelty sandwiches, bridge roll and cheese 'boats', peppermint creams, icing biscuits, etc. can all be made without a cooker.	

Exercise 15

Multiple-choice questions

1. Children of three to five are becoming silly, boisterous and very wet at the water-play equipment. You decide to:
(a) pack it all away for a few weeks;
(b) ban all those concerned from water-play for the rest of the term;
(c) protect them more completely with overalls, cuffs, wellington-boots, etc.;
(d) ascertain what was causing boredom, e.g., unchanging equipment, and try to remedy it.

2. Nursery children are showing little interest in clay at present. Your best course is to:
(a) try sitting at the clay-table yourself, and working a piece of clay;
(b) make a model for a small group to copy;
(c) substitute dough for it for the rest of term;
(d) organise a competition for the best animal model.

3. A child of eighteen months encounters a sandy beach for the first time. It would benefit him most if you:
(a) let him pat and prod it, run hands and feet over it as he chooses;
(b) make a series of sand-pies for him;
(c) teach him how to make sand-pies himself;
(d) pour sand repeatedly over his hands and feet to show him how lovely it is.

4. One of the following is a 'golden rule' for woodwork with young children.
(a) always nail a blanket to the woodwork bench to deaden noise;
(b) never provide real tools since they can cause so much injury;
(c) insist that children do not waste wood, but set out to make real models;
(d) ensure constant supervision.

5. Children gain a great deal from play with blocks. Which would you say is the most significant and unique contribution block-play can make to children's development?
(a) training in clearing away tidily;
(b) pleasure in destruction;
(c) knowledge of adult construction techniques;
(d) experience in three-dimensional shape and spatial relationships.

6. The most suitable doll for a two-to-three-year-old child would be:
(a) soldier doll, with equipment etc.;
(b) teenage doll, with appropriate outfits for different occasions;
(c) baby doll, with a few simple garments;
(d) walkie talkie doll.

7. The most valuable addition to imaginative play for two-to-three-year-olds would be:
(a) a uniform hat;
(b) jewellery;
(c) buttoned tunic;
(d) set of make-up.

8. Awareness of comparative size is necessary for formation of mathematical

concepts. Which of the following play materials would provide the most valuable experiences of this kind? Select from combinations (a) to (d) below.

1. Paints
2. Dolls
3. Woodwork tools
4. Paper
5. Dolls' clothes
6. Blocks

(a) 1, 2, 3. (b) 3, 5, 6. (c) 2, 3, 4. (d) 2, 5, 6.

Essay questions

9. Draw a plan of nursery garden and list features and equipment.

10. Imagine you are creating and equipping a moveable home-corner for a play-group. Cost must be kept to an absolute minimum.

11. Why is play with water so enjoyable for children? Describe some children of different ages you have seen playing with it, and say how you think they were benefiting.

12. Describe a cookery activity you have seen children take part in, remembering organisation, and the value of the exercise.

Project

13. From looking around in shops, decide on a suitable item as a fourth birthday present for a nephew, spending less than £2.

Observation

14. Observe children constructing something (out of blocks, wooden or cardboard boxes etc.), which they afterwards play with imaginatively. How did the idea arise? How many children took part? Is there a clear leader? Notice changes in direction as play proceeds. Record children's comments. Did an adult play any part?

15. Observe children painting spontaneously. Compare the approach, technique and skill of an older child with that of a younger child. What different opportunities are available, and how do children react to them?

16. Observe how children use large equipment for physical activity. Describe opportunities available to them and how they take advantage of these. Notice different approaches, and degrees of confidence and skill in such things as balancing, climbing, swinging, jumping.

17. Observe three different instances where children of varying ages were taking part in domestic play. How do you think each was benefiting?

18. Find out, in whatever way you like, what are the favourite play materials of the children with whom you are working. Conduct your study over a stated length of time.

Suggestions for further reading

Beatrice Harrop, *Apusskidu*, A. & C. Black Ltd.

Beatrice Harrop, *Okki – Tokki – Unga*, A. & C. Black Ltd

Marianne Parry and Hilda Archer, *Two to Five*, Macmillan Education Ltd

Kenneth Jamieson and Pat Kidd, *Pre-School Play*, Studio Vista Publishers

E. Matterson, *Play With a Purpose for the Under 7's*, Penguin Books Ltd

Donald Baker, *Understanding the Under 5's*, Evans Brothers Ltd

Catherine Lee, *The Growth and Development of Children*, Longman Group Ltd

Alison Stallibrass, *The Self Respecting Child*, Pelican Books

Alice Yardley, *Discovering the Physical World*, Evans Brother Ltd

Katherine Read, *The Nursery School*, W. B. Saunders Co Ltd

John and Elizabeth Newson, *Toys and Playthings*, Pelican Books

K. M. Chacksfield, P. A. Binns, V. M. Robins, *Music and Language with Young Children*, Basil Blackwell Ltd

David Evans, *Sharing Sounds*, Longman Group Ltd

Chapter 16
Children with special needs

The premature baby

In Great Britain about eight per cent of all babies born each year are premature. The international definition of prematurity is a baby weighing less than 2.500 kg (5 lb 8 oz).

In practice these babies can be divided into two main groups:

1. *dysmature* (light for dates): a baby born after thirty-seven weeks pregnancy weighing less than 2.500 kg (5 lb 8 oz).

2. *premature*: a baby born before thirty-six weeks pregnancy weighing less than 2.500 kg (5 lb 8 oz).
N.B.: By the end of the twenty-eighth week of pregnancy a baby has become 'viable'. This means although he may weigh less than 1 kg (approx. 2 lb) he is capable of a separate existence.

The causes of prematurity are not always known, as there are many contributing factors. The dysmature baby has suffered a reduction in his food and oxygen supply during pregnancy which may be due to failure or malfunction of the placenta. This could be caused by toxaemia of pregnancy or by a rapidly ageing placenta. Heavy smoking by the mother can also be a contributary cause. Another reason for dysmaturity could be a multiple pregnancy, where one baby takes most of the food at the expense of another baby.

The truly premature baby is more common in the lower socio-economic group and this may result from many factors, including poor general health in the mother, especially when this stems from poor nutrition. Lack of regular ante-natal care aggravates to the problem. Again, multiple births are often premature. Further, if there is any abnormality in the baby, he may be premature.

The proportion of premature babies who are subsequently found to be handicapped is higher than in full-term babies, despite the expert care they receive in special care units. So the best treatment is the prevention of prematurity and, of course, this is one of the main aims of good ante-natal care. First, it is necessary to ensure that the mother is as healthy as possible, by making sure that she has a good diet and by giving her advice about her general health. Secondly, it is necessary to examine mothers at intervals (so that if there are any signs of developing toxaemia it can be treated immediately) and to check that the baby is growing at the normal rate. If a mother does start to have her baby too early, then if at all possible the labour should be stopped.

The appearance of a premature baby will depend on its size, but the very tiny babies are extremely thin, because they have very little fat under the skin. They are wrinkled and have a worried look on their faces, like wizened old men. The

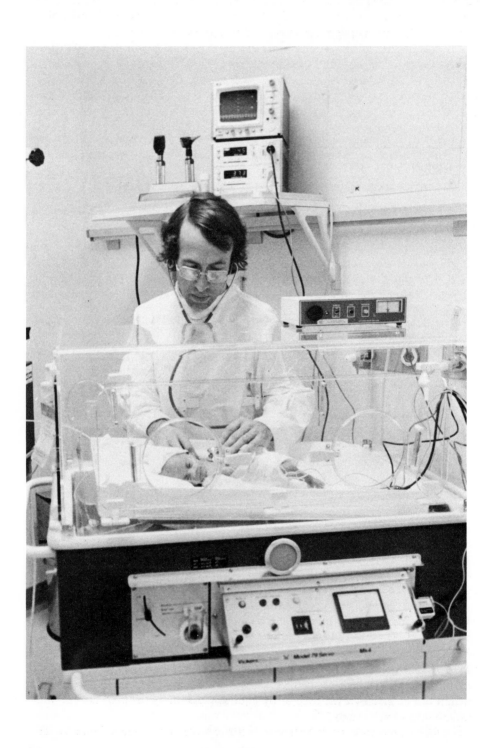

limbs of such a baby are thin but the abdomen is large and the head appears to be very large in proportion to the body. Fontanelles are large and easily palpable. There may be fine hairs on the body, and fingernails are very soft.

The dysmature baby's problems are mainly the need to 'catch up' with the normal baby by feeding and putting on weight, so if the baby is over about 2.350 kg (3 lb) in weight he has a very good chance of survival. The truly premature baby has problems, because he has missed the last few weeks in the uterus and the more weeks he has missed, the smaller he will be and the greater his problems. Towards the end of pregnancy a lot of development takes place to equip the baby for the outside world:

1. The respiratory centre in the brain matures.

2. The baby learns and practises the art of sucking and swallowing.

3. The heat-regulating mechanism centre in the brain begins to mature.

4. Fat is laid down under the baby's skin.

5. Calcium is being deposited in the bones.

6. Iron is being stored in the liver.

7. Antibodies against infection are being passed over from mother to baby.

So his problems can be as follows:

1. poor respiration (breathing) due to immature respiratory system;

2. inability to suck and swallow;

3. inability to regulate his temperature;

4. inability to keep warm;

5. soft bones owing to lack of calcium – this may lead to damage to the brain at birth as it lacks the protection of a hard skull;

6. anaemia owing to lack of iron;

7. poor defences against infection.

The majority of these babies are placed in an incubator and cared for in a special care unit for premature and sick babies. The incubator is a transparent box-like structure with 'portholes' so that the baby can be attended to without being taken out of it (see illustration, p. 218). Inside an incubator, the environment can be controlled and made to resemble the conditions in the uterus. Very warm, humid air with the correct amount of oxygen is supplied. The warmth enables the baby to be nursed without clothing, which might restrict his breathing. He is protected from droplet and airborne infection by being in the incubator, and strict hygiene measures are taken by doctors and nurses to minimise the spread of infection via their hands. He can be fed by means of a tube into his stomach, or fluids can be given into the veins. Iron, vitamins and possibly calcium can be given via the tube or by injection. Handling the baby is kept to a minimum to avoid trauma.

The larger premature baby with fewer problems may be nursed at home under the supervision of the doctor and health visitor. General care of this baby will be similar to that of the normal newborn baby, but extra special care must be taken over all aspects.

1. *warmth*: the room must be kept to 21°C (70°F) and some humidity may need to be supplied by putting bowls of water near the heat source;

2. *lightweight clothing* which will not restrict breathing or irritate baby's delicate skin;

3. *cleanliness and prevention of infection*: no visitors; one person to care for baby; hand washing; use of gown when attending to baby;

4. *care with feeding*: the baby is usually fed three-hourly with small feeds because he can become very tired from the effort of sucking. Some babies may need a special bottle so that the milk can be squirted into the mouth, e.g. a Belcroy feeder.

Because of the inevitable early separation, premature babies and their mothers often lack the feeling of belonging to each other (bonding) and this may lead to emotional problems. Efforts are being made to counteract this by giving the mother access to the special care unit so that she can sit beside her baby and put her hands in the incubator to touch him.

Premature babies are now sent home much earlier than was once the case, so that the mother will have closer contact. In the past the baby was not allowed home until he weighed 3.17 kg (7 lb) which could take months. Now, in many areas, there are specially trained health visitors called Premature Baby Visitors who can supervise the mother and baby by visiting daily. Because of this service, it is possible to send the baby home once he is out of immediate danger.

Children with handicaps

The definition of a handicapped child is one whose development is impaired by disease or injury. One in every twenty children born will have some abnormality or defect, but many of these will be minor ones, such as a birthmark, webbed fingers or toes or an extra finger. Others will be of a more serious nature such as cleft palate or spina bifida. The known causes of handicaps can be classified as follows:

1. an inherited defect – e.g., haemophilia;

2. injury to the foetus – e.g., deafness caused by rubella;

3. injury at birth – e.g., failure to breathe immediately after birth causes brain to lack oxygen, causes brain damage – cerebral palsy;

4. disease after birth – e.g., jaundice in new baby can cause brain damage – cerebral palsy;

5. injury after birth – e.g., head injury causing brain damage – mental deficiency;

6. severe deprivation – e.g., child never stimulated – mental backwardness.

Brief descriptions of some of the more common handicaps are given in the following charts.

HANDICAPS – CAUSES, DIAGNOSIS, TREATMENT, OUTLOOK

Condition	Possible causes	Diagnosis	Treatment	Outlook
Visual defects (a) *Blindness* vision 3/60 or less, so may have some sight but not enough to learn by sighted methods	hereditary; rubella in pregnancy; congenital syphilis; optic nerve tumour; cataract; glaucoma	usually detected very early when a baby shows: no early eye-to-eye contact; slowness to smile; no response to visual stimulation; *delayed* development	early diagnosis; stimulation of other senses and education to make use of them, e.g., hearing touch smell	cannot be cured
(b) *Partially sighted* vision 6/18 or less when corrected by spectacles; may be nystagmus (rapid involuntary movements of eyeball)	hereditary; rubella in pregnancy; infection; refractive errors due to shape of eye; astigmatism; albinism	'clumsy' child; 'rolling ball' test available at 9 months, but not very accurate; vision test at 2 years or $3\frac{1}{2}$ years; may be squint	correction with unbreakable spectacles or contact lenses to best possible sight; large-print books; stimulation of other senses	cannot be cured; vision can be improved with use of spectacles
(c) *Strabismus (Squint)*	hereditary; astigmatism (irregular-shaped eye); rarely – brain damage	may be very obvious from 3 months; 'cover' test; eye turns in or out	early diagnosis to prevent deterioration of sight; orthoptics – eye exercises; black patch on good eye to make 'lazy' eye work; spectacles; surgery	variable; many can be completely corrected if diagnosed early.

Condition	Possible causes	Diagnosis	Treatment	Outlook
Hearing defects *(a) Deafness*	hereditary; rubella in pregnancy; brain damage caused by (a) lack of oxygen at birth (b) jaundice after birth; meningitis; repeated ear infections	usually detected early in life when a baby: does not respond to noises; looks startled when someone stands over him (did not hear him coming); stops making his own noises (no pleasure if he cannot hear); fails routine hearing test at 7 months; does not develop speech	early diagnosis; hearing aid for any residual hearing; speech therapy – always talk face to face; home tutor to show mother how to help; special tuition at school; child learns to lip read and to use sign language	cannot be cured; ability to speak normally depends on: (a) amount of residual hearing (b) how early the diagnosis is made (c) child's intelligence (d) level and value of tuition
(b) Partial hearing (1) may be unable to hear high pitched sounds such as 's'; may be unable to hear low tones	(1) as above	failure of routine test at 7 months; poor speech	early diagnosis; hearing aid; speech therapy	(1) cannot be cured but child can overcome problem with specialised help
(2) may be periodic deafness	(2) catarrhal and sinus problems, including enlarged adenoids	test should be repeated at intervals, especially if speech problems	may need drainage of middle ear, and/or removal of adenoids	(2) may be completely cured

Condition	Possible causes	Diagnosis	Treatment	Outlook
Speech defects, e.g., Stammer Stutter Garbled speech	hearing loss; emotional tension (may be associated with cerebral palsy and/or mental retardation); lack of stimulation; cleft lip and palate	from 3 years; inability to make himself understood; frustration – expressed in temper tantrums	hearing test – correct hearing loss as possible with hearing aid; speech therapy; relaxation; music therapy; bubble blowing; rarely – drugs for relaxation	with help most children can overcome the problems
Cleft palate and/or *Cleft lip* opening dividing upper palate and lip into two or three sections	failure in facial development in 3rd month of pregnancy cause not known	if lip *and* palate: obvious at birth palate only should be detected at examination immediately after birth; feeding problems	plastic surgery – lip repaired in first 6 weeks; palate at about 18 months; meanwhile removable dental plate is made to cover gap in palate during feeding may need to be spoon-fed because of difficulty with sucking; teeth may be irregular – orthodontist; speech may be affected – speech therapy	usually surgery effects a complete cure

Condition	Possible causes	Diagnosis	Treatment	Outlook
Autism (Alone) child retreats from the normal relationships of life into a world of his own; ignores everything and everybody; may be highly intelligent	25% associated with brain damage; others not known	withdrawn; does not respond to mother or anyone else; unable to appreciate or to interpret the sounds of speech; no speech	early diagnosis; speech therapy; special schooling tailored to child's ability; development of one-to-one relationship	if detected early then good possibility of normal development
Cerebral palsy varies from 'clumsiness' to complete paralysis	hereditary (rare) brain damage at birth due to: (a) lack of oxygen (b) bleeding into brain brain damage after birth due to: (a) jaundice (b) injury (c) convulsion	may be obvious at birth; birth history; development delay Three types: (a) spastic – unable to relax muscles (b) athetoid – unable to control movement (c) ataxic – poor balance and difficulty in eye/hand co-ordination (clumsy)	*complete* assessment as early as possible; may have other problems such as deafness or epilepsy; may have very low or very high intelligence physiotherapy; hydrotherapy; speech therapy; drugs to relax muscles; crutches, leg irons, wheelchairs, etc.	no cure, but some problems can be overcome
Spina bifida ('Split spine') vertebrae fail to unite	thought to be	obvious at birth;	surgery – may have to	without surgery to

Condition	Possible causes	Diagnosis	Treatment	Outlook
Spina bifida – cont. and protect developing spinal cord; this prevents proper development of nerves in area	hereditary; recent research has indicated poor maternal diet prior to conception, especially in lack of folic acid and vitamin B	protruding spinal cord causes lesion on back; varying degree of paralysis of lower part of body, depending on site of lesion	have several operations; physiotherapy	repair opening in back and protect spinal cord from infection child will die; result of surgery depends on degree of abnormality present varies from weakness in legs to complete paralysis of legs
Hydrocephalus (Water on the brain) cerebro-spinal fluid collects in the brain instead of circulating	often associated with Spina bifida; brain tumour; meningitis; may be congenital, of unknown cause	enlarging head; baby – fontanelles remain open and sutures may open to accommodate increasing size; older child – headaches due to increasing pressure on the brain	following early diagnosis, introduction of a tube containing a valve to allow fluid to drain into the bloodstream	early stages can be controlled, late diagnosis – brain damage due to increasing pressure
The Muscular Dystrophies a progressive degeneration of the muscles;	precise cause not known			no cure;

Condition	Possible causes	Diagnosis	Treatment	Outlook
The Muscular Dystrophies – cont. several types, e.g. (a) Duchenne	sex-linked hereditary, i.e. passed on by a normal 'carrier' mother to 50% of her sons	from about 3 years, increasing difficulty in walking; frequent falls, walks on toes blood tests; muscle biopsy	physiotherapy; surgery to lengthen Achilles tendon to keep child walking as long as possible; leg-irons or crutches may be used; wheelchair from about 10 years	muscles gradually grow weaker; starts with leg muscles then, when child chairbound, other muscles deteriorate; heart and respiratory muscles affected last, causing death in early adulthood
(b) Limb-girdle Facio-scapulo, etc.	hereditary	increasing muscular weakness but much less severe than 'Duchenne', and onset may be delayed until adulthood	physiotherapy	as above, but disease develops more slowly, and may affect different muscles initially
Haemophilia failure of the blood to clot following an injury	hereditary; sex-linked (see Duchenne Muscular Dystrophy); defective production of the 'clotting' factor in the blood	excessive bleeding following injury; baby: excessive bruising; child: bleeding into joints as child becomes more mobile, leading to eventual deformity; bleeding from any organ, e.g., kidney	transfusion of whole blood or of missing factor as soon as any injury occurs	cannot be cured, but can now live reasonably normal life provided missing factor is given as soon as possible after any injury; any operative treatment hazardous
Heart defects faulty development of heart during foetal life;	rubella in early pregnancy;	if severe, diagnosed at birth:	surgery to correct deformity;	outlook much improved in past 10 years or so;

Condition	Possible causes	Diagnosis	Treatment	Outlook
Heart defects – cont. *or* failure of ductus to close at birth	drugs in early pregnancy; mostly unknown	'blue' baby, breathing problems; less severe; usually found at 6-week developmental check when heart sounds are abnormal; slow weight gain; chest infections	may be a temporary relief operation at birth, with main surgery postponed until child is older	children who survive birth and surgery usually live a normal life
Epilepsy abnormal electrical discharge from the brain, causing fits *Petit Mal* – mild *Grand Mal* – severe	hereditary; brain damage due to injury; brain tumour; sometimes associated with low mental ability; in most cases unknown	Petit Mal – occasional momentary fits; child looks blank and loses concentration Grand Mal – convulsive fits with loss of consciousness and bladder control	investigations for any underlying cause; drugs to control fits	no cure; control of fits usually possible
Cystic fibrosis mucus glands secrete abnormally sticky mucus which clogs digestive and respiratory systems; sweat glands secrete very salty sweat	hereditary; actual cause not known	newborn may have blocked intestine; repeated chest infections; stools offensive – contain unabsorbed fat;	physiotherapy to keep chest clear; pancreatic enzyme given with meals (because this enzyme cannot get to intestine as tubes are blocked with mucus)	no cure; 20% children die in first year; otherwise gradual deterioration to death in early twenties

Condition	Possible causes	Diagnosis	Treatment	Outlook
Cystic fibrosis – cont.		slow growth; sweat test	antibiotics for chest infections	
Coeliac disease inability to absorb gluten because of missing enzyme, leading to: (1) inflammation of intestinal cells which produce mucus (2) interference with absorption of fats	hereditary; unable to make a necessary enzyme	failure to thrive; retarded growth; poor appetite; pot belly; stools – pale, large and offensive (contain excessive fat)	gluten-free diet; (gluten present in flour and many common foodstuffs)	normal outlook, provided child stays on diet
Asthma wheezing and breathlessness	probably allergy – inherited sensitivity which may cause asthma, eczema or hay fever	attacks of 'wheezing' which gradually become more incapacitating	physiotherapy; drugs; 'Spinhaler'; hospital for acute attacks	variable sometimes disappears spontaneously as child grows up, but can be life-long and cause increasing incapacity; barrel chest
Mental handicap children with a low intelligence quotient (normal = 100) who have				

Condition	Possible causes	Diagnosis	Treatment	Outlook
Mental handicap – cont. difficulty in coping with normal life (a) *Educationally subnormal* (slow learners) I.Q. 50–80 approx.	mostly unknown; may be: hereditary; deprivation; brain damage due to: (a) lack of oxygen at birth (b) jaundice (c) meningitis (d) injury – accidental, child abuse; conditions such as Down's Syndrome (*see below*)	may not be detected until child reaches school age; slow physical and mental development; poor speech; poor powers of concentration; poor progress at school	recognition and assessment as early as possible; child treated according to mental age; small classes with individual attention to enable child to work at his own pace	no cure; training may enable child to cope with normal life – this depends on level and value of tuition
(b) *Severely subnormal* I.Q. below 50	as above	usually obvious at birth; excessive delay in all aspects of development; may have other defects; poor control of bowel and bladder (often life-long incontinence); susceptible to chest infections	as above, plus extra training in social skills, care and protection	no cure; will need life-long care and protection
Down's Syndrome (Mongolism)	hereditary (extra chromosome)	diagnosed at birth; typical appearance –	as above	no cure

Condition	Possible causes	Diagnosis	Treatment	Outlook
Down's Syndrome – cont.		broad, flat face, slant eyes; retarded development; may have heart defect; intelligence varies from educationally subnormal to severely subnormal		
Phenylketonuria	hereditary; inability to use phenalynin (a protein) leads to build-up in brain, causing damage	at birth – routine Guthrie blood test is abnormal	diet reducing amount of phenalynin	provided child remains on diet whilst brain is developing he will grow into normal adult; if not, child will become severely subnormal
Microcephaly	not known	at birth: abnormally small head; fontanelles close early; child becomes increasingly mentally and physically retarded	physiotherapy; training in social skills	no cure; increasing mental subnormality because of pressure on growing brain
Maladjusted (Emotionally disturbed child) poor behaviour due to emotional or physical disturbance	unstable home life; physical, emotional or social deprivation	may be: (a) obsessive (b) disruptive (c) solitary	child guidance (parent guidance); sometimes removal from home if severe deprivation	variable; some recover, others grow up to be deviants; may develop mental illness

A congenital disease is one which originates before birth, so it may be either inherited or a result of injury in the uterus. Some handicapping conditions are predictable during pregnancy (see page 34), so some affected babies will be aborted. Better ante-natal and post-natal care could prevent some conditions, such as cerebral palsy. However, many handicapped children come from the lower socio-economic groups, which suggests that an improvement in living standards, especially housing and nutrition, could reduce the numbers more than any specific care.

Although all babies are examined at birth by a midwife and a doctor, and during the first two weeks of life, many of these handicaps are not obvious and are therefore not detected at this time. Some defects can be found by using special tests. For example, all babies have a blood test for phenylketonuria, a rare inherited disease which, if not treated within the first two weeks of life by putting the baby on a special diet, leads to mental handicap. Another test commonly carried out on newborn babies is that which detects congenital dislocation of the hips. This is a condition which, if treated early enough, can usually be completely cured.

The majority of handicaps only become obvious as the baby grows and often developmental assessments during the first five years of life reveal that the baby is not progressing as he should. In other cases the parents of the child suspect there is something wrong and take him to their doctor. In many areas there are diagnostic units where the child can be examined by various consultants, and investigations can be carried out to discover the nature of his handicap and either cure it or alleviate some of the associated problems. Otherwise the child may be referred to a paediatrician at a local hospital.

The effect on the family

Discovering that their child has a handicap is a terrible shock to most parents. Despite the fact that a mother's first question after her baby is born is often 'Is he all right?', mothers and fathers expect their babies to be normal and fortunately this is usually the case. If the defect is obvious at birth, then the mother should be told immediately, so that acceptance and adjustment will occur as early as possible. Usually the father is present, so that both parents can be told together. They will need to be told again after the initial shock is over, so that plans can be made as early as possible about the baby's future. Similarly, should a handicap be detected later in a child's life, his parents should be told as soon as possible.

Reaction to the fact that a child is handicapped can range from a rejection of the child to a complete refusal to believe that there is anything wrong at all. Fortunately, most parents do eventually accept their child as he is and do their best to help him. But nearly all parents ask themselves 'Why should this happen to me?' and there may be a tendency for one parent to blame the other, especially if the disease is hereditary. The arrival of a handicapped child can cause much marital stress, and the ability to cope will depend on the maturity of the parents and the strength of their marriage. Another factor in the acceptance of the handicap is the child's position in the family. If the parents already have a normal child, then it will be easier to accept a handicapped child.

It is difficult to understand how a mother can reject her own child, unless we are aware that we are animals and it is usual for animals to reject the abnormal. If, for instance, a mother cat has a litter containing a deformed kitten, she will ignore it and concentrate on the healthy kittens. In fact she will allow the kitten to die.

Sometimes the child is not rejected, but the handicap is. The parents ignore the handicap altogether and expect the child to behave like a normal one and to achieve the same standards. This can place a tremendous strain on the child.

Over-protection is another parental reaction to a handicapped child and can bring problems both for the child and for his brothers and sisters. They will resent the attention given to the child.

Brothers and sisters may be embarrassed about a handicapped child and will not bring friends home. Family friends and relatives often keep away, because they do not know how to deal with the situation; consequently the family may become isolated. Conflicting medical opinions as to the degree of handicap and frequent visits to hospital with long waiting periods can be physically and emotionally exhausting. Many families lack the financial and emotional resources to cope.

The care of the child places a burden on all the family; the mother in many cases is unable to work because of the demands of this child. Holidays are difficult, because the child may need special facilities. The child may be incontinent, which causes endless washing and cleaning. Babysitters are difficult to get. In such circumstances even everyday chores such as shopping for food may become an insoluble problem because of the necessity of caring for the child.

The majority of parents eventually come to terms with their child's handicap and many handicapped children have special qualities which contribute to family life. It should be remembered that this is a child (first) with a handicap (second) because his physical, mental and emotional needs are exactly the same as those of a normal child. Handicapped children and their families benefit if they are able to attend a day nursery, nursery school or playgroup and mix with normal children. Under the guidance of trained staff, with space to play and a variety of play materials, their experience can be widened and confidence can be gained.

Education for the handicapped child

It is the responsibility of the local education authority to assess these children and plan their education as early as possible. In many areas special day schools are provided for children with specific handicaps or a special class is provided in a normal school.

In the case of some rarer handicaps, such as blindness, there are not enough affected children in one area to justify a day school, so there are a few boarding schools scattered over the country in which specialised teaching can be given. There are also residential schools for children with other handicaps whose parents are unable to cope at home. Alternatively, in many areas, home tutors are available to visit the house and assist parents in the care and education of their child.

In the past a handicapped child was nearly always placed in a special school, but since 1954 the principle has been laid down that no handicapped pupil should be sent to a special school who can be satisfactorily educated in a normal school. This principle was reinforced by the Warnock Report, which reiterated the need for disabled children to enjoy a normal school life. The report was incorporated into an

Education Act to take effect from 1st April 1983. By that date, however, there was little evidence to suggest that many educational authorities were in a position to implement the Act fully.

Some head teachers have always tried to assimilate handicapped pupils into their schools, but their efforts have often been limited by the suitability of the school buildings and the need to engage extra staff (often nursery nurses) to cope with the physical care of the children. In areas where education authorities have been sympathetic and helpful it should be possible to extend the system quickly to cope with larger numbers of disabled children. But in other areas, where a policy of segregation was formerly pursued, it is bound to take time and a great deal of money to change attitudes and to modify school buildings so that they can accommodate children in wheelchairs.

It is also obvious that some children, such as the severely subnormal, must remain in a special school because of the degree of physical care needed. Many are incontinent and have to be fed. Other children, such as the deaf, still need specialised tuition which may be difficult to organise in a normal school. There are advantages and disadvantages to both special and normal schools for a child, so each side should be considered carefully when a decision is being made about an individual child.

1. Special schools

Advantages

(a) The ratio of adults to children is laid down in the Education Act and ensures that classes are small.
(b) This means that each child can work at his own pace.
(c) Staff may have special training and experience.
(d) Emphasis is on mutual care and support.
(e) The child has an opportunity to excel when surrounded by children with similar disabilities.
(f) The building will be adapted to the children's needs, e.g.:
  (i) toilet facilities for disabled in wheelchairs, encouraging maximum independence;
  (ii) ramps instead of stairs for physically handicapped.
(g) Special equipment and facilities may be available, e.g., heated swimming pool with hoists.
  (i) Some schools have residential hostels attached so that children can be weekly boarders.

School nurses, physiotherapists and speech therapists are usually on the premises, ensuring that regular treatment and any necessary medical attention are available without too much loss of schooling.

Disadvantages

(a) Child grows up surrounded by handicapped people so that his social life is restricted.
(b) He may be so protected that he cannot cope with normal adult life.
(c) Segregation leads to ignorance about the needs of handicapped people by general public.
(d) School is usually some way from home, so travelling makes a long day for child.

(e) Because of distance, school friendships are difficult to sustain at home.

(f) Special schools are costly to maintain.

2. Normal schools

Advantages:

(a) Mixing with normal children benefits both normal and handicapped children and adults – normal people become aware of others' needs. Handicapped children are stimulated more.

(b) Child's social life is widened.

(c) Child's day is shorter because less distance involved.

(d) Most parents prefer to have their child in normal school.

(e) Child can go to same school as brothers and/or sisters.

(f) The ratepayer is saved the expense of maintaining a special school.

(g) A larger school has a larger staff, so a wider spread of subjects to study.

Disadvantages:

(a) Lack of any special facilities, e.g., toilet.

(b) Lack of specially-trained teachers and helpers.

(c) Medical treatment may not be available on the spot.

(d) School buildings may be unsuitable (too many stairs).

(e) High ratio of children to adults.

(f) Child may have to strive very hard in order to keep up with work and appear normal.

Help available

Parents need a good deal of support and encouragement if their child is severely handicapped. The family doctor, health visitor and local authority social worker can all provide that support and also put the family in touch with other agencies which may offer specific help.

1. Free transport. This is provided to and from school.

2. Residential homes. These are for children under five years old whose parents cannot cope with them.

3. Attendance allowance. This is a weekly sum of money for adults and children over the age of two years who are severely handicapped, either physically or mentally, and need to be looked after for six months or more. There is a rate for day attention and a higher rate for those who need constant attention day and night.

4. Invalid care allowance. This is a weekly allowance for a person of working age unable to work because he or she is needed at home to care for a disabled relative. This is only available to married women if they are unsupported by their husband.

5. Mobility allowance. If a child aged five years or over is unable, or virtually unable, to walk, then a monthly sum of money is paid to enable him to be taken out.

6. Car tax. Since December 1978 recipients of the mobility allowance have been excused car tax for their vehicles (in the case of a child, the parent or guardian's vehicle which is used to take him out).

7. Car badge scheme. Parents of a physically handicapped child can obtain a badge for their car which entitles them to free parking.

8. The local authority social service department. This department may provide any or all of the following free:

(a) telephone;

(b) incontinence pads;

(c) disposable nappies;

(d) laundry facilities;

(e) night sitters;

(f) home helps (there may be a charge for this service).

9. Housing. The local housing authority may provide a specially-adapted council house for the family. If the family owns a house, the social services department may make money available for alterations to the house, for example the installation of a lift and/or ramps instead of steps, or a shower instead of a bath.

10. The family fund (Joseph Rowntree Memorial Trust). This is a trust fund set up to help disabled children and their families. The aim is to fill in the gaps of statutory care, so help depends on individual needs, e.g., provision of a washing machine for parents of an incontinent child.

11. Appliances. Wheelchairs, crutches, glasses, hearing aids and other appliances are provided free under the National Health Service.

12. Voluntary organisations:

(a) Many parents of children with specific handicaps have formed their own societies for mutual help and support and collect funds for research into their children's disease. One example is The Muscular Dystrophy Association.

(b) The local Red Cross Society, Women's Royal Voluntary Service and others will often give specific help to handicapped children and their families, for example holidays.

13. Genetic Counselling Centre. This is a special centre where advice on hereditary diseases is available to parents and relatives.

The deprived and disadvantaged child

This child has been denied one or more of the fundamental rights of childhood, which are normally supplied in a happy family life. We believe those rights to be:

1. a stable home;

2. a well-organised, loving mother;

3. a supportive father who provides for the child's material needs, such as protection, clothing, adequate diet and play space;

4. fresh experience to stimulate language and mental growth, which is allowed to proceed at its own rate;

5. recognition and an encouraging atmosphere;

6. contact with other children and adults.

Because one or more of these rights has been denied and a basic need left unfulfilled, there is a chance that the child will develop in an uneven, unbalanced way. His personality may present obvious gaps, or even be scarred for life. Because the first four years are critical and a period of tremendous growth and development, all children should enjoy '*an abundant environment*', as Willem van der Eyken calls it.

We sometimes separate, as in this chapter, the various aspects of deprivation into material, social, environmental, intellectual, cultural, educational and linguistic. We have to do this to identify problems and needs, but it is an artificial practice; one 'lack' invariably goes alongside, or creates, others, as we hope to show further in this chapter.

Some people draw distinctions between the various terms used, for instance claiming that 'disadvantaged' refers to the inner condition of the child, resulting from an outer deprivation. Other people regard it as a matter of degree or severity, deprivation referring to the most basic and urgent 'lacks'. 'Under-privileged' is another term employed, usually to describe children lacking in material things.

It is possible, even easy, to become too bogged down by these various terms. It is dangerous to bandy them about indiscriminately, to label children, to make judgements (that deprivation is the 'fault' of the parents) and certainly to make spoken reference to such terms in front of children or parents.

One other fact needs to be borne in mind while considering this subject. Deprivation is not confined to low-income groups. One meets examples of deprivation in all classes and kinds of families. It is easy to recognise material deprivations – if, for instance, a child wears obvious hand-me-down clothes or looks undernourished. But the invisible, difficult-to-recognise forms of deprivation are usually more serious and lasting in their effects.

Material, environmental and social deprivation

1. Manifestations and reasons. Unemployment, poverty and mismanagement of money; shared or inadequate facilities for washing and cooking; poor housing; poor clothing; poorly-balanced diet; inadequate medical care, including preventive measures; lack of cleanliness, space, play material, protection. The 'typical' deprived child looks pale, undernourished, often has a runny nose and never seems to be really fit. The term 'inadequate parents' is often used to describe parents who reflect the social ills listed above. The term is also applicable to alcoholics, criminals, battering husbands and wives, prostitutes, drug addicts, glue-sniffers and inciters of crime (for example, mothers who train children to shop-lift). It is not possible to deal fully with this subject here, but you should make a point of reading some of the abundant literature, both non-fiction and fiction, on social problems such as these.

2. Possible effects. Ill-health (physical and mental) and lack of resistance to disease, undiagnosed defects, infestation; road and other accidents; becoming a social outcast; fatigue owing to cramped sleeping arrangements; apathy and lack of response to stimuli; depressed height and intelligence (through poor, low-protein diet in early years); envy and resentment of others with more; over-boisterous, aggressive or attention-seeking behaviour at nursery or school; lack of concentration and physical co-ordination.

3. How the nursery nurse can help. The nurse must understand the child's difficulties and make allowance for the child arriving late, in a dirty, ill-clad or unkempt state. He may need nursery clothes, bathing, possibly first-aid of some sort. He may need additional food, or rest. He will need space and opportunity for vigorous play, and also help in care of play materials.

It is vital that the nursery nurse acts in a tactful manner, both with child and parents. The child is an individual and has his pride. Parents may need to be referred to other social agencies for help in coping with their problems, but this must never be done in a patronising or condemnatory manner. The nursery nurse may be able to suggest ways in which parents can help a child, for example, a different bedtime arrangement. The child needs to be helped to feel good about himself, so praise and encouragement, one-to-one, are beneficial. Care must be taken that the child does not sense criticism of his background, making for divided loyalties.

Emotional deprivation

1. Causes:
(a) Child has been deprived of mother's care and love (this is called maternal deprivation) either through death or separation.
(b) Child has been rejected, is unwanted or unloved (because he is handicapped, illegitimate, 'wrong' sex, or parent is, irrationally, unable to feel love for him).
(c) Child has experienced seriously unsatisfactory family relationships (absent father, parent mentally ill, violence in the home, etc.).

2. Possible effects. Any one of these causes may result in the child's needing to go into substitute care (residential home, fostering, adoption). Adoption and long-term fostering arrangements often work out successfully and may supply the child with more emotional and material benefits than he would have had in his natural home. But disturbed arrangements and long-term care in a residential home can result in the child's growing up with little sense of his own identity, individuality or personal worth. Through lack of personal involvement by parents in his all-round development, his past and his future, he may experience problems of personality, language or learning.

For a child who stays within his family unit, but experiences any of these three causes of emotional deprivation, there is a danger that if he has never known continuing personal love and involvement from one person close to him, he may be unable to give it himself. He may grow up with warped or idealised concepts of the opposite sex which may lead to immature and indiscriminate choice of friends and marriage partners later. He may withdraw from relating to others, to protect himself from further hurt. He may mistrust adults, and in particular those who represent authority. He often indulges in attention-seeking behaviour, of an obsequious, clinging, or anti-social nature. He often lacks concentration, frequently needs reassurance and encouragement to meet new challenges. The insecure young person may drift from one job to another, or hit back at life which has been less than kind to him, and make his mark by vandalism or hooliganism.

3. How the nursery nurse can help. This child needs adult interest, concern and affection, even when he appears to reject it in a most unlovable way. He needs to build up a good self-image, and so he must be praised not just for results, but for effort and progress – for *him* – whether it be a small act of kindness, one minute longer of concentration, one little bit of co-operation. If nothing else presents itself, then a brightly coloured jumper or well-brushed hair can be the focus for compliments. The nursery nurse should always stress the positive. If the child is withdrawn he will need very gentle approaches, on a one-to-one basis. Casual showing of books, or an invitation to help the nursery nurse with chores, can provide the occasion for gradually building up a good relationship. Such a child should never be forced to mix or join in or contribute in front of others. Wild behaviour, although it cannot be permitted in nursery, must be understood, and acceptable alternatives provided as outlets for aggression, such as woodwork, blocks, clay, water.

Intellectual, cultural and educational deprivation and disadvantages

This is a confusing and controversial area.

1. Recognising the different facets:
(a) On a straightforward level, a child who has been denied the opportunity to develop mentally at his natural rate because of lack of stimulation in the home (for instance, if he has been kept in a cot, or one room most of the time, or if his parents are deaf and dumb or of a very low intelligence) is disadvantaged *intellectually*.
(b) So, too, is the child who is subjected to a bombardment of over-stimulation, either from too much, or unsuitable television, or from ambitious parents with unrealistically high expectations.
(c) Both children could also be said to be *educationally* disadvantaged, because they will not be able to benefit to the full from the education system. But neither will children who travel around a great deal with their parents – it could be abroad with Service personnel, or around the country with rising company executives, motorway labourers or gypsies. Also educationally disadvantaged are those children who evade much schooling (through parents' convictions, or truancy) or who have very poor schooling (fortunately rare today).
(d) Another category of educationally disadvantaged children is those with perceptual or learning difficulties, or physical handicaps such as poor co-ordination, or those who have lengthy spells in hospital. They will need special care and attention if they are to cope happily in a normal nursery or

infants school, where they are usually kept until accurate assessments of their difficulties can be made around seven years of age.

(e) Much controversy exists over cultural deprivation. 'Culture' here is sometimes used to mean middle-class values and attitudes concerning behaviour, linguistic ability, books, music, etc. In this sense, many thousands of children may be 'culturally deprived'.

More precisely, if controversially, the term is also used with reference to children from backgrounds of different ethnic or national cultures from the British. Certainly these children may be at a disadvantage educationally in our schools, but it would be more sensible to say they are culturally 'different'; their culture may be a rich and lively one which can contribute greatly to their own and other people's lives.

(f) Linguistic deprivation may exist in any one of these cases, if the child is not talked to and listened to and encouraged to communicate in his early years. We may also use this term in referring to a child who has been confused in his attainment of one language by the use of two by the adults around him in his early years.

2. Possible effects:

(a) The under-stimulated child may appear lifeless, incurious, deceptively unintelligent. He will not reach the normal milestones of mental development (memory, small problem solving, etc.) at the usual times. He may also be slow physically.

(b) The over-stimulated child may be jumpy and 'nervy', over-anxious about things he does, tense, a poor sleeper. He may stammer. He may easily become over-excited or distracted. He may feel himself a failure in his parents' eyes, and thus unloved. He may suffer from nightmares or irrational fears. He may play highly imaginative or imitative games which tend to get out of control and frighten other children.

(c) Children who miss continuity of formal schooling, for whatever reason, are likely to have learning problems which could cause them to 'drop out', or make their mark on society in a different way. They have difficulty in forming relationships which may make them into 'loners'.

(d) A child with perceptual or learning difficulties may be unable to cope with quite simple forms of play, domestic tasks or memorising. Only very close observation will reveal the nature and extent of his difficulties. Because he cannot keep pace with other children, he may resort to boisterous, 'silly' or otherwise unacceptable behaviour. On the other hand, he may be excessively quiet and retiring, so that his difficulties can be easily overlooked. Sometimes a child who will later be termed 'educationally subnormal' looks noticeably dull, with lack-lustre eyes and open mouth; but, again, he may be possessed of a lively personality and animated manner which masks the extent of his lack of understanding.

Lack of co-ordination results in a child being 'clumsy'. He will be constantly falling over, or knocking into, spilling or dropping things. He may not be able to hop, skip or hold a pencil, and thus appears 'different' and possibly laughable to other children.

A child who has undergone long hospital treatment may have missed out whole chunks of everyday learning and social experience. He is therefore at a disadvantage in comparison with nursery or infant children who, we confidently assume, know all about such things as family meal times, involving as they do shopping, cooking, laying table, social conversation. Such a child's physical co-ordination and muscle tone could also be poor, through lack of exercise.

(e) Conventionally accepted standards of beauty in the environment – nature, art, music, books, poetry, creativity etc. – which most nursery staff take pains to introduce to their children, will be alien and uninviting to these children. They may as a result build up an anti-school attitude. This resistance may accentuate the difference between such a child and his more conforming peers.

(f) Lack of competence and confidence in expressing himself in one language often leads the child into behaviour problems arising from frustration and isolation, and also learning difficulties.

3. How the nursery nurse can help

(a) Stimulation in the form of play materials, discussion points, stories, songs etc., must be introduced gradually to the under-stimulated child, with clear explanations and interaction by the adult. Games which foster mental alertness can be enjoyed, and praise will motivate the child further.

(b) The child who has been over-stimulated requires from the nursery nurse calm, stability, exposure to child-like rather than sophisticated pastimes and pleasures. He requires boosting in his own eyes if he has been made to feel 'slow'.

(c) The child who is destined to miss continuity of schooling is not yet an educational problem, but the disruptions in his life so far may have left him needing special care, an emphasis on one-to-one relationship, an encouragement to mix with other children.

(d) Children at an educational disadvantage because of handicap or long spells in hospital need special individual attention and encouragement, much praise for the things they *can* do, play materials, constructional and creative, which will let them experience success of all kinds, especially in large and small muscular skills, preferably within small groups. Good relationships with parents can help a great deal. Body awareness, leading to greater control and co-ordination, can develop from use of large and small apparatus for vigorous physical activity, and also from swimming. Music and rhythm, too, can be employed effectively to develop these qualities and break down barriers set up by feelings of inadequacy.

(e) This child must be accepted for what he is, and points of contact sought in subjects that are of genuine interest to the child, so that he can make his contribution to the group.*

(f) While understanding his frustration and the forms it may take, the nursery nurse must give this child outlets, first to vent his frustration, and secondly to build his self-confidence. Suitable forms of self-expression are painting,

* N.B.: See following section on child from minority ethnic group.

dressing up and music. She has also to build up his grasp of English, which can only be done within a warm relationship. Words concerning the child himself, parts of the body, clothes, etc., are an obvious starting point, and much playful repetition in the form of games, finger plays, action rhymes, will reinforce this beginning. Hearing himself on tape can intrigue and encourage this child. Play with basic materials is good for vocabulary building. All forms of dramatic play, particularly puppets, foster language. Visits outside the nursery can widen the children's experience of good, interesting vocabulary, as do stories and pictures. (See chapter on Intellectual Development and Language.)

The child from an ethnic minority group

In recent years the needs of these children have been overshadowed by racial tensions and politics. The many thousands of ethnic minority group children growing up in Britain today require specially sensitive and informed care if they are to benefit to the full from the British educational system, and grow up socially adjusted, with a positive cultural identity.

The background

The great majority of these children will have been born in Britain, of parents and maybe grandparents who have been settled here for years. Some adults no longer consider themselves 'Jamaican' or as hailing from some specific region. There will be a marked difference in the degree of adaptation to a western way of life visible in these families, compared with more recently arrived families such as Vietnamese, Cypriot or Chilean.

Life in Britain once held out great promise for all such people. In fact the British government in the 1950s invited people from the West Indies and the sub-continent of India – comprising India, Pakistan and Bangladesh – because there was a shortage of workers to fill less attractive jobs.

Others, like the Ugandan Asians or the Vietnamese, were political refugees. Confidence in British education and career training inspired ambition for their own and their children's futures. Some of these hopes have been fulfilled; others have been sadly dashed.

Many people are deeply ignorant of the cultural and even geographical backgrounds of these groups. It is impossible here to do more than touch on specific cultural differences, but it is of the utmost importance that all those who work with ethnic minority group children should read and find out all they can. Much prejudice springs from ignorance and an unwillingness to understand. To give one small example, the custom of common law marriage, changing of partners and the acceptance of illegitimate children found among some Caribbeans is an inheritance from slave trade days, when marriage among slaves was inconvenient to plantation owners, but children in large numbers were welcome as a future work force.

Each ethnic group should be considered in its own context. Making assumptions, stereotyping and generalising are to be avoided. When considering one large group, such as the Caribbean peoples, it should be remembered that each island has its own distinctive character.

Cultural background will, to a greater or lesser extent, continue to be reflected in the home, in attitudes towards marriage and other unions and offspring, in religious faith and practices, in language and folklore, in dress, cooking, music and entertainment and in the pattern of the day. The young child, therefore, has the difficult task of coping with a second culture which begins outside his front door and continues to be reinforced at nursery, school and wherever he goes. Cross culture, as it is known, can make for confusions and even identity crises later on.

Factors affecting his parents' circumstances. These will affect the child. Some such factors could be:

1. language difficulties – understanding and being understood;

2. loss of extended family;

3. stress of adaptation (to white faces, different food, clothes, etc.);

4. need for the mother to work;

5. unemployment, poverty, loss of self-respect, especially having to accept state benefits;

6. barriers put up by others to practising their own life-style;

7. prejudice and intolerance;

8. fear of officialdom;

9. ideas and practice on child-rearing, e.g., discipline, which differ from those of their adopted society.

Factors such as these may lead to some of these *problems*:

1. physical or mental illness or depression;

2. unsatisfactory child-minding arrangements;

3. home accidents;

4. absenteeism owing to the child's being used as an interpreter (large families exacerbate this).

There may be particular *health problems*:

1. illness resulting from first-time exposure to disease (e.g., T.B.);

2. inadequate ante-natal care stemming from lack of knowledge, lack of communication, or modesty, which may cause premature or difficult births, even handicap;

3. anaemia caused by a diet deficient in iron, protein and/or vitamin B12 arising from an inadequate vegetarian diet; this is seen among Rastafarians;

4. specific illnesses of a hereditary nature which may affect certain groups, e.g., sickle cell anaemia in people of African extraction;

5. rickets caused by lack of vitamin D, owing to unsuitable diet or screening of available sunlight from skin (by darker skin, traditional clothes or indoor life);

6. damage to eyes and lead poisoning from the use of *imported* lead-based Asian cosmetics.

Contact with parents

Friendly contact with and acknowledgement of parents will help the child to settle within the group, but sometimes language barriers and other factors, such as working mothers and shy and modest Asian mothers who tend to stay within the home, make it difficult for nursery staff to get to know them.

Smiles and welcoming attitudes transcend some of these difficulties. First steps in this direction can lead to encouraging the mother or parents to spend some time in the nursery so that they are fully informed on the child's day. They may at first feel it is presumptuous to involve themselves in any way, as they usually have a high regard for the competence and status of the nursery staff. They may feel surprise, even disappointment or disapproval, concerning the play, particularly messy kinds, which takes place; they thought they were giving their child a head start in *formal* education, but this appears to be something quite different. Inability to communicate on both sides increases misunderstandings.

Care must be taken that friendly approaches are not made in a patronising way. Allowances must be made for the fact that limited communication can result in reasonable requests sounding like bald statements or demands. Tolerance should also be shown towards those parents who do not want involvement in the nursery; they may badly need this break from their children, or perhaps they do not like children in large numbers. Some parents may be reluctant to focus on their ethnic group identity by contributing to ideas of nursery staff.

To avoid misunderstanding and muddles, any regulations or announcements in written form from the school should be translated into the parents' first language if they do not possess much English. Older brothers and sisters at school nearby can also help here.

Helping the child

If possible, there should be more than one child of an ethnic minority group in a class or group. This will reduce the possibility of his feeling so different, or even being overloaded with attention, as, for instance, can happen when a beautiful little Indian girl, dressed enchantingly, enters an all-white Anglo-Saxon class.

Certain groups may need specific help and may include:

1. Children of West Indian origin. Children may need special guidance in handling and caring for play materials or books, as these are generally lacking in their homes.

They find a great deal of choice bewildering, as they are not encouraged to be self-regulating at home. Strict discipline and sometimes corporal punishment at home can mean that soft-spoken restraints and explanations about behaviour limitations go unheeded at the nursery; sometimes the children even regard the adults as 'soft' or weak.

West Indian children can be lively, boisterous and responsive. Their feeling for music and rhythm often makes it physically impossible for them to remain still when music is being played.

2. Children of families from the Indian subcontinent. Religious faiths govern many families' lives; Moslems will not eat meat of the pig. Hindus will not eat meat. Taboos must be respected. This needs to be borne in mind in the selection of stories, rhymes, playground games and so on, as well as the more obvious business of menu planning. English food offered may seem to Asians very bland and unappetising, and cheese may be quite unknown to them.

If girls are brought up to be exceedingly modest, getting undressed for movement, paddling or P.E. can be distressing to them. Sikh children should never remove metal bangles.

Boys may not take kindly to being treated the same as girls. In the home a boy, particularly the eldest, is treated as someone very special. In the nursery, often the boys come in for less attention than the pretty little girls, thus creating a difficult reversal of roles. The inferior status of women may also affect boys' attitudes to teacher or nursery nurse.

Asian children may appear very quiet and dependent on adults, as they are encouraged to be submissive within the family. Choices, again, can be confusing. Another point to bear in mind is that, in many Asian cultures, extreme politeness is very evident in social contacts; this is sometimes seen by other groups as stupid or funny.

Names can be puzzling – boy and girl Sikhs, for instance, with the same first name. However, the second name Singh is given to a boy, and the second name Kaur to a girl.

Young Chinese children may be involved in the family business if there is one, because this is their way of life – that all contribute to the family income. If the business is catering, hours for bedtime may be different, later, and in school hours, children may appear tired.

Vietnamese children arriving with their families in recent years have had to undergo problems of temporary accommodation and enforced moving around. Parents and grandparents may have suffered terrible hardship in their journeys to Britain, which may have left psychological scars. Unemployment has hit these families particularly badly. Although some are of Chinese extraction, even in multi-racial communities, they often seem to be very isolated.

Language

The process of becoming bi-lingual, which many ethnic minority group children undergo, must be regarded in a positive light. It is an enrichment to their lives, a bonus, not a problem. It is now appreciated that children must be competently established in their mother-tongue before they embark on second language learning: it is essential for concept formation. To this end, a good deal of mother-tongue work is being done in nurseries and schools, and parents and other visitors are being brought in to read stories so that children will see that their mother-tongues are recognised and valued.

A great deal of English will be absorbed by the child simply by being in a place where English is spoken. The fact that he is not talking does not mean he is not absorbing. Other children may ignore a non-English speaking child, therefore the child is very much dependent on concentration by the adult. A warm, accepting relationship with the child must come first, through smiles and possibly touch, although here it must be remembered that touch is unwelcome to some cultures.

All points of contact with the child should be made into language opportunities – greeting him in the morning, commenting on his clothing, demonstrating with pictures and objects the talking points or interest of the day. The adult should look the child full in the face, let him see her mouth working, and use accompanying facial expressions and gestures. She should express herself clearly, simply, and in short sentences. Newly introduced words should be fed into later conversations to aid memory. Stories with illustrations, finger plays and action rhymes (but beware of confusion caused by fingers being presented as, for example, 'five little ducks') all consolidate language skills. They encourage the child to join in the fun, yet do not make undue demands on him or make him self-conscious.

Understanding and using inflection, which is so important in the English language – for instance to express disapproval or sympathy – may be difficult for children to grasp. Inflection does not have the same importance in all languages as it does in English, and can be used quite differently in some. Special one-to-one times with a friendly, skilled adult will help to offset the possible confusion of the enriching language experiences that will be offered to English children.

A multi-cultural approach

This aims to give *all* children and adults equal importance and acceptance in each other's eyes, but at the same time recognises the richness of what different cultures can contribute.

The materials presented to children at nursery and school reflect the kind of society they live in. Discrimination is still evident in some books and illustrations, where ethnic types are either caricatured or represented in a foolish or pathetic light. The extreme images projected by some third world relief charities, and, at the other end of the spectrum, the glossy pictures of travel agents, are not suitable for nursery use either. It is desirable to offer books and pictures which show a wide variety of cultures and race, in a positive light, in everyday situations. Such books might, for instance, have a central character who is black, and is depicted as interesting, brave, creative and wise.

A truly multi-cultural approach should be reflected in many nursery items. They might include 'home corner' equipment, such as frying pans for chappattis (tawa) and chopsticks; dressing-up clothes such as shalwar, kameez, saris; black and brown dolls correctly dressed; pictures on jig-saw puzzles; and posters and other items for inclusion in displays. This is just as important in all-white areas as it is in multi-ethnic areas, if a positive, informed, prejudice-free attitude is to be promoted.

Far better than choosing a specific multi-cultural theme for display or project work – 'India', for instance – would be to choose a theme of general interest. Food is a good example to which all mothers can contribute – items used in Indian or Pakistani cooking, West Indian cooking, English cooking and so on. A project on 'Babies' – of all colours and types – is another good idea, and one which promotes a positive self-image. The same applies to weddings, when these are in the air. The children themselves can do cooking with an adult; one can buy packets of chappatti mix, for instance. Fruit for 'snack' time does not always have to be apple or orange; banana or mango make a welcome change.

Direct contact with ethnic minority group children by nursery or school staff is usually warm, loving, accepting. But prejudices about their backgrounds still exist and are often discernible when adults talk together. 'You wouldn't think he was a Pakistani' is a give-away remark, as is, 'If only they didn't eat that smelly food.'

Staff must take an interest in the whole family and their lives. Holidays taken in the country of origin should be prepared for and regarded afterwards as enrichment for the child, family and nursery group, rather than as a disruptive 'nuisance', or a time when the child will forget his English and 'undo all the hard work we've done.' Staff must face up to their own prejudices, try to discover where they originate, and change them. The overriding consideration is that every child has a right to be acknowledged and valued for himself, as an individual.

Children from travelling families

Travellers comprise many different groups of people – Romanies or 'true gypsies', 'didikois', 'tinkers', fair and showground people and semi-settled families. They have been in Britain for about a thousand years and have married widely into the host community. Linking most of them is the Romany dialect, and some social characteristics. The largest numbers of travelling families are to be found in south-east England, the Lincolnshire fens, Hereford and Worcester, and the north-east.

Their occupations include tarmacadaming, scrap-metal dealing (although this was hit by the recession), roofing, tree-felling, hopping, mucking (bagging and selling bulk manure), seasonal field work, such as fruit-picking, second-hand car trading, bric à brac, carpet-selling at markets, and fortune-telling at shows such as Appleby, Cambridge, Epsom and Stow. Traditional craft articles like hand-made pegs and brushes have largely been replaced by factory-produced plastic goods.

Since the 1968 Caravan Site Act, local authorities are required to provide up to fifteen official sites. But there has been a general reluctance to conform and there is frequently opposition from local residents. If sites are not provided, travellers park their trailers and lorries on public land which often leads to conflict. Council-controlled sites tend to be placed in depressed areas which have no other planning value, as, for example, under motorways or next to railways. Gypsies are the only group of people against whom a criminal charge of trespass can still be brought. The quality of official sites is generally not good. Although they now have baths, showers and flush toilet facilities, they are still often dismal and depressing places. There is little safe play space for children. Scrap in the process of being sorted is often lying around and, unlike the débris of former years, the discarded rubbish of today will not rot away. Some can be burned, but this often causes a nuisance to nearby residents. With his life-style of moving on, the traveller has no great concern for anything he leaves behind him. Large dogs often roam the sites, to protect precious possessions in trailers. Many travellers who have moved out into houses in the last ten years or so have been unable to pay overheads and have become mobile again. Private sites are usually in good locations but are acquired only after much effort. These are invariably attractive, well-kept and controlled.

Travellers live in close-knit extended families. One family may have up to six caravans, grandparents and unmarried children living in one, and married children in others. There is great loyalty between family members; respect for grandparents and dead ancestors, pride and protectiveness towards a new baby, watchfulness between older and younger siblings. It is virtually unknown for old people to be placed in residential homes. Travellers' isolation from the host community increases their dependence on one another. Quarrels can quickly arise when many relations are living at very close quarters in difficult circumstances. Moving to where they can earn a living is the most important thing in their lives, so interruption of children's schooling is unavoidable. Living in a twilight culture, they are often characterised by evasiveness, particularly about past and future happenings. Many adults are illiterate. Some parents want their children to receive schooling to help them progress in life. Others fear that schooling will make their children 'soft' and they see education, particularly secondary schooling, as irrelevant to today's world.

They cherish their traditional songs, but also like much modern cult music such as rock and roll. Romany and Shelta (originating in Ireland) are retained in dialect form and some travellers' groups are making determined efforts to preserve and revive these as complete languages. Children are brought up to perform chores in the home and on site from earliest days. There are usually distinct sex roles in work performed. Because of their traditional occupations they are often curious, discriminating and resourceful in putting materials to good use. In the home – the trailer – they are usually extremely tidy and clean. Their money is spent on shiny cars, luxurious trailers, china, brass, jewellery, gold, perhaps horses. Some dress their daughters in high quality velvet dresses and patent leather shoes.

They are robust people, used to tough conditions and difficult circumstances. The children may have a high tolerance to pain. Health care from the state, such as ante-natal care, is, like education, unavoidably fragmented. Record-keeping and communications are both difficult, but most families are happy to use medical services when they need them. As in non-travelling families, there will inevitably be a percentage who are smelly, infested and inadequately clothed.

Travellers still experience some prejudice and hostility from settled society, but where positive steps have been taken to break down barriers, there is much more tolerance. Where decent sites have been established, the travellers no longer pose a threat to the community. Pubs and cafés are no longer allowed to display signs saying 'No gypsies'. Travellers' children are usually well able to cope with taunts from their non-travelling peers.

Efforts have been made to provide appropriate schooling for travelling children since early last century. In recent years, some imaginative schemes have been initiated, either taking teachers and travelling classrooms to where they were required, or gathering children from an area to a special unit. Some authorities have designed their own reading schemes.

The child at five will have had little of the pre-school experience of settled five-year-olds, which obviously puts him at a disadvantage. Some voluntary societies have taken playgroups into travellers' sites to help here. Where there are no specific learning difficulties, travelling children usually progress normally at school. Numeracy, particularly, comes easily. Spoken language is functional only and needs to be developed and elaborated in school. Concentration span can be limited. Children cannot be expected to cope if they are pitchforked into a completely strange situation. Ways have to be found to 'build bridges' to reach them, but not at the expense of their rich, colourful culture and life-style. Teachers' expectations of them must be made plain. A one-to-two ratio of help has often been found to be most productive in developing pre-literacy skills.

There is much apprehension from parents about entering the school environment. It stems from fear of the unknown and feelings of inadequacy due to illiteracy. They may be reluctant to let their children go on school visits because of their protectiveness. But when parents can be encouraged to become involved in their children's education the results can be most rewarding.

Abused children

These are to be found in all social classes. They are children who have received serious physical abuse from a parent or foster parent. At one time these children were called 'battered babies' but now they are usually referred to as cases of non-accidental injury or concealed parental violence (CPV).

There has been a progressive increase in these cases in the past twenty years. The exact number of children killed or injured is not known. The most widely quoted estimates for Britain indicate that between 2400 and 4600 children are seriously injured each year. The estimates of the number of deaths from these injuries range from 100–750 each year. The commonest injury from this sort of violence is bruising, especially on the face. There may be black eyes or bruising around the mouth caused by forced feeding with a bottle. Some children are found to have cigarette burns, others are admitted to hospital because of fractured skulls, or fractures of the arms or legs.

Bleeding into the brain has been found in some cases, where violent shaking has caused the jelly-like brain to bang violently against the hard skull. This can cause mental retardation or cerebral palsy.

Few people could fail to feel deep anger towards the parents when faced with a badly injured child, but evidence suggests that most of these parents love their child and are desperately in need of help. They are reacting to the whole circumstances of their lives.

The underlying causes of child abuse, however, are a study in themselves and they are many and complex. Apart from unsatisfactory living conditions and lack of money, many of the parents have acute problems of insecurity, inadequacy and possibly psychological damage during their own childhood. The isolation caused by new types of housing, especially high-rise flats and the separation from other members of the family, who in earlier times might have lived close at hand, and helped out in a crisis, also plays a part.

Investigation of a family where children have been ill treated does, in fact, often reveal that the parents themselves were neglected and badly treated by their own parents. Because of this they have grown up feeling unloved and unworthy of love. This can lead to difficulties in all their personal relationships, especially in marriage. In addition, these people have not had good models from which to learn about being a parent. Children learn by example and, if they grow up in a stable home with loving parents, the pattern is passed on to them. Even though children from a stable home may rebel against their parents in their teens, when they in turn become parents, they usually repeat the pattern of their own childhood. Similarly, children who have uncaring, neglectful parents tend to repeat that pattern when they, too, are parents.

Many of the unfortunate, abused children have young parents who have this sort of background and in addition are living in poor housing and poverty. There is nothing new in this – in Britain there has always been an underprivileged section of the community. However, in earlier times that section tended to be set apart, socially and geographically, from the rest of the population. Nowadays, when shops, magazines and colour television reflect the comfortable life-style and enviable luxury of better-off people, those who are struggling with poverty realise the great disparities, and understandably resent them. It does not matter that the pictures they may see are grossly exaggerated; they merely emphasise to the less able members of our society their inadequacy, frustration and inability to compete. They feel they are failures in today's affluent society. And with the pressures they have to bear, it is natural for the parents to become short-tempered and irritable and their children become the nearest convenient targets for their anger. Often the mother is pregnant or has had a baby recently, so that she is not physically fit. She may be overwhelmed by all the responsibility and the worry.

Usually an abused child is a 'wanted' baby and when he is born is showered with affection. But he will be expected, in return, always to respond lovingly. The parents have little idea of a baby's abilities or of his needs, and are liable to make unrealistic demands for obedience and to have high expectations of his progress. When the baby is wakeful at night, refuses food or cries, it is interpreted as ingratitude and a rejection of the parents' love.

Sometimes it becomes apparent why one child in a family is being abused – he may have been a premature baby or had a difficult birth, so that there was early separation of mother and baby and bonding did not occur. Other typical abused babies are handicapped or they are those babies whose early days were marred by constant crying, possibly because of feeding problems or colic.

Obviously, prevention is the best cure for this social disease, but measures which would help most must come from society at large. Ensuring that good housing is available to all and the abolition of family poverty would solve many problems, because these two factors – unsatisfactory housing and a very low income – are often the last straw to inadequate parents. Educating young people so that they understand themselves, the role of parenthood and the needs of children may also help to prevent some of these cases.

In Britain progress has been made in identifying families whose children are at risk and offering early help and support. Research suggests that picking out mothers likely to react to stress with violence during the ante-natal or early post-natal period may well be possible. These mothers could then be given extra help whenever stress is likely to occur. For example, a home help during the early weeks of a baby's life will enable the mother to care for and get to know her baby without the stress of coping with her home. Other help could be a day nursery place or nursery school place for the child for part of the day. In addition, if the parents have someone they can trust and to whom they can talk about their problems, it may act as a safety valve – health visitors, NSPCC Officers and social workers can all fulfil this function. When families lived in a close community, Grandma used to do this.

Many authorities have set up a life-line for these parents, similar to that offered by the Samaritans, so that they can ask for help when things get too much for them.

Social work departments keep a register of children considered to be 'at risk'. When a child is found to be injured in suspicious circumstances certain procedures are followed. First, contact is made with the keeper of the register to establish whether the family's name appears there, so that all agencies involved can be alerted. Secondly, if the child is not already in a hospital accident department, he is taken to a hospital, general practitioner or clinical medical officer for a complete examination. It may be necessary to carry out a complete skeletal X-ray to see if there are any healed broken bones as well as to check the extent of the present injury. If it is felt necessary, the child is either admitted to hospital or taken to a 'place of safety'. Lastly a case conference is called as soon as possible to exchange information and to decide on the best possible plan of action.

When a child has been abused, the aim of any treatment of the parents is to prevent a recurrence of the violence and also to keep child/parent relationships going, in an attempt to lessen the harmful effects. The child may be placed in a day nursery, or possibly in a residential nursery, under a 'care order'. In all cases efforts are made to keep parental links and the aim is eventually to return the child to his family, if at all possible.

The gifted child

A gifted child is more than just 'very bright'. Giftedness implies exceptional intellectual abilities, either of high intelligence, or in one particular sphere of activity – for instance music, ballet, art, sport. Less easily discernible, the special ability may be for creative thinking or innovation.

Recognising the gifted child

It is difficult to recognise gifted young children, for several reasons. The performance skills that are conventionally examinable have, on the whole, not yet been learned. We have, therefore, either to compare the child with his peers – a controversial and unfashionable pastime – or arrange for him to be tested by an educational psychologist. This course may produce an untrue picture of the young child, who may be affected by, for instance, hunger or discomfort in a strange situation. When they are tested, usually at seven, gifted children score approximately 140 or above intelligence quotient.

Gifted children are comparatively rare, and there are no national statistics on them. They are produced by parents of all social classes and all levels of intelligence; sometime they are found in families where one would least expect them.

In the nursery or the home, we may observe one or more of the following characteristics:

1. Extreme liveliness, often associated with less need for sleep than usual

2. Early mobility, linked with curiosity.

3. Advanced language development, and use of quite long and complex sentence constructions. Also frequent and searching questions, of the 'how' and 'why' variety.*

4. Advanced manipulative skills, often shown in problem-solving.

5. Marked interest in topics usually associated with older children, e.g., prehistoric monsters, makes of motor cars.

6. Complicated imaginary games, with or often without props.

7. Response to music – melody or rhythm – or marked artistic talent.

8. Reading as young as two and a half or three.*

9. Understanding of mathematical ideas.*

10. Complete concentration on the task in hand; perseverance.

11. Initiative and originality.

12. Marked independence.

Writing – of letters, words or figures – is seldom learned at such an early age; it is too tedious for a quick brain.

Coping with a gifted child

Potential and performance can be two very different things. The child's gifts require recognition, understanding and skilful nurture. With these he can grow into a well-adjusted, happy individual who can contribute enormously to society – perhaps even change the course of history.

There may be problems and pitfalls. A toddler who is always on the go, exploring and investigating, particularly if he can find ingenious ways of reaching forbidden items, or 'escaping' from his place of safety, can exhaust a mother or nanny. It is worse if he cannot be relied on to settle down early to a good night's sleep. The adult may feel she is failing, or else may feel exasperated that, despite

* Middle class children can be deceptively advanced in their language development, denoting background encouragement rather than exceptionally high intelligence.

all her well-intentioned efforts, the child refuses to respond conventionally. Without reassurance and practical help, such a mother may even fear for her own sanity, or her fitness to be safely alone with so demanding a creature. She must be helped to see that her child *is* different, and has different needs. Tranquillisers from her doctor, or supposed words of comfort about this being 'just a phase' that he will grow out of, are little help. What she does need is a husband and/or reliable child minder to relieve the pressure sometimes in the day, and certainly during a long spell of disturbed nights. If there is an older child, he could be found a nursery or playgroup place. The toddler himself will need such extra outside stimulation at two or two-and-a-half; by the age of three, many typical nursery activities will be too babyish for him. Questions must be listened to and answered, interests followed, however tiring or trying this may be at times.

The child's 'differentness' may set him apart from his peers, whose company and interests hold little appeal for him. Yet older children will not accept him as an equal. At the playgroup or nursery he may evoke dislike because he appears superior, or else may try to organise the people there – including adults!

He must be helped to get along with his peer group, however uphill a struggle this is for the adults. Not only could failure here result in many years of miserable schooling for the child, but it could also instil anti-social attitudes for life.

His interests should be taken into account. He could be assigned an appropriate aspect of a group activity or project. For instance, if a model castle is being made out of junk material, perhaps he could research on vital facts and statistics for its construction and use. Freshly stimulating play material must frequently be presented to him. Home-made games, puzzles, etc., as well as improvised and borrowed materials, can supplement manufactured ones. New tasks can be set and lines of enquiry followed up, using basic materials such as sand and water.

At the same time as extending such a child's intellectual capacities, and working towards his social integration, the adult must recognise that the child's physical and emotional needs are as important as those of any other child. The stage these are at may even be characteristic of a younger child. For instance, his physical co-ordination may be poor. Parents, particularly, need help in being patient and acknowledging that his development may well be uneven. It may irritate them to watch a classic temper tantrum, staged after a narrow defeat at chess. It may also annoy them to find that common sense by no means always accompanies giftedness.

There are still some parents and teachers who regard gifted children as a nuisance, or even a threat. Some parents are ill-equipped to nurture their child's gifts. They may have little liking for music or mathematics themselves, or fear that their child is the 'wrong' sex to possess such a talent. They may play down their child's giftedness for any of the foregoing reasons, or else because they fear he will grow up conceited.

At the infant school, the child may find the activities and work tedious. He *may* even be held back in his progress in, for example, reading, because it is inconvenient to the class's programme. Frustrated and bored, he may develop anti-school attitudes very early. He may become excessively withdrawn, or indulge in disruptive or aggressive behaviour. He may take on the role of the class clown. He may attempt to hide his giftedness in order to be accepted more freely by the group. In an extreme case, he may have to attend the Child Guidance Clinic, and/or become one of life's misfits.

Joining with a group of older children to pursue his particular interest – for example playing an instrument – can ensure his active co-operation for at least a number of sessions per week. The Association for Gifted Children offers half-day activities and short courses. Total segregation at an early age is not thought, in our society at least, to be in the child's best interests. Other aspects of his development may be neglected in such a rarefied atmosphere, and it has been known for the gift itself to wither and die.

Rushing him through the infant school curriculum only delays his boredom with school. Mentally demanding activities must be found for him, and here one can draw on the experience common to the group as a whole and let him go further. But he does require individual attention to 'extend' his powers and should not be expected to work on his own for long periods.

Wisely handled, a gifted child can bring great joy, indeed excitement, to all who know him.

Exercise 16

Multiple-choice questions
1. The official definition of a premature baby is:
(a) a baby weighing less than 2½ kilos (5½lb);
(b) a baby born two weeks early;
(c) a delicate baby;
(d) a baby born too rapidly.

2. What is the best attitude a family should adopt towards a handicapped child?
(a) treat him as a normal child, making allowances for his handicap;
(b) indulge him, to compensate for his handicap;
(c) make him the central concern of the whole family;
(d) be light-hearted about the handicap and make fun of it sometimes.

3. You are told that a child in your nursery group suffers from maternal deprivation. This means:
(a) the child's mother goes out to work;
(b) the child misses his mother when separated from her;
(c) he lacks material possessions;
(d) he and his mother have been separated for a long period of time.

4. You are told that the four-year-old child of a newly arrived Asian family is to join your English nursery group the following Monday. By way of preparation, would you:
(a) find out all you can about the family's background, and casually mention the newcomer to the other children;
(b) prepare a project on Asia;
(c) arrange a welcome party the first day so that the child will be the centre of attention;
(d) tell the other children that black people *can* be nice.

5. You are told that a child in your group at nursery is a gifted child. Which approach would you adopt?
(a) treat him just the same as all the others;
(b) play down his giftedness, for fear of making him conceited;
(c) treat him with the same care you show to all the children, but take steps to extend his special gifts;
(d) hope it's just a passing phase because he doesn't fit in with your plans for the other children.

Essay questions
6. Deprivation and disadvantage occur among children from all strata of society. Explain how this can happen among higher income groups.

7. How would you, as a nursery nurse in a nursery school, endeavour to make your group a happy and effective multi-cultural society?

8. What would lead you to suspect that a five-year-old child was being abused by his parents? How would you deal with the child at school, and what services could you call upon to help the family?

Suggestions for further reading

Helen Featherstone, *A Difference in the Family*, Basic Books
Mary Crosse, *The Pre-Term Baby*, Churchill Livingstone
Bowley & Gardner, *The Handicapped Child*, Churchill Livingstone
Mary D Sheridan, *The Handicapped Child and his Home*, The National Children's Home
Lesley Webb, *Children with Special Needs in the Infant School*, Fontana Books
Peter Wedge and Hilary Prosser, *Born to Fail?*, Arrow Books
Lorna Bell, *Underprivileged Under 5's*, Ward Lock Educational Co. Ltd
Mia Kellmer Pringle, *The Needs of Children*, Hutchinson & Co. Ltd
Edited by James Loring and Graham Burn, *Integration of Handicapped Children in Society*, Routledge & Kegan Paul Ltd
Ivor Morrish, *The Background of our Immigrant Families*, Unwin Educational Books
Christopher Reiss, *Education of Travelling Children*, Macmillan Ltd
Mary Waterson, *Gypsy Family*, A. & C. Black Ltd
Calendar of Religious Festivals, Commission for Racial Equality (Shap Mailing, 7 Alderbrook Road, Solihull, West Midlands)
The Multi-Racial Playgroup, PPA Publications (Alford House, Avelina Street, London, S.E.11)
Robert Jeffcoate, *Positive Image*, Chameleon Books
Children's books:
Petronella Breinburg, *My Brother Sean, Dr. Sean, Sean's Red Bike, Sally-Anne's Umbrella*, Bodley Head Ltd
Ezra Jack Keats, *The Snowy Day, Whistle for Willie, Goggles*, Picture Puffin
Sean Lyle, *Pavah is a Sikh*, A. & C. Black Ltd
Madeline Blake, *Nadha's Family*, A. & C. Black Ltd
Fiction:
Harper Lee, *To Kill a Mocking Bird*, Heinemann Ltd
Semi-fiction:
George Lamming, *In the Castle of My Skin*, Longman Group Ltd
Autobiography:
Camera Laye, *The African Child*, Fontana Books

Chapter 17
The single-parent family

About one in eight families today is a one-parent family, five out of six headed by a woman. Single parents include unmarried mothers, widows and widowers; deserted, separated and divorced fathers; deserted, separated and divorced mothers. Of these, the last is by far the largest group.

Single-parent families have become a social problem in that they are the fastest-growing group living at poverty level in Britain. It is, in the main, not the single-parent status that brings problems to parents and children alike, but the attendant money problems. Only about half single-parent families earn their main income; the rest live on social security. Society is still geared to a two-parent family unit and those who differ from the norm suffer many inequities. For example, fifty per cent of *two-parent* families rely on the earnings of both parents to maintain living standards.

Unmarried mothers

Most vulnerable of all are the unmarried mothers, many of them under twenty, and even under sixteen. Despite relatively freely available sex education and contraception, every year some 56,000 unmarried women become pregnant (see page 23). They have the difficult task of deciding whether to go through with the pregnancy or have it terminated. Most authorities have a counselling service to help them. Sometimes shame, worry, fear of parental reaction, or ignorance causes them to leave it too late for there to be a choice in the matter. Some young girls effectively hide the fact of their pregnancy until the birth itself, sometimes with tragic results.

In the months of pregnancy, the girl has to think about whether or not she is going to keep the baby. Many factors weigh heavily in the making of this decision: What is the attitude of the baby's father? Is she likely to get any financial or moral support from him? How will she support the child financially? Who will care for him? What is the attitude of her parents? Where will she and the baby live? What about her disrupted social life and chances of finding happiness with another partner? Is she capable of giving the child a good enough start in life, and the unselfish care he will need?

No official pressures will be brought to bear on the mother to make this decision during her pregnancy, nor at the time of birth. Although some mothers ask not to see the baby they have decided to part with, it is generally thought advisable that all mothers should see and hold the baby they have produced. It is the natural culmination of a natural process, and may give the mother a precious memory to hold on to in the future.

If circumstances at home are difficult, she may go to a mother and baby home for a few weeks before the birth. In some cities there are schoolgirl mother and baby units where the girl can continue her studies up to the time of birth, while also learning child care. Afterwards, she can remain there until her sixteenth birthday, keeping the baby with her, and caring for him under the guidance of teachers and nursery nurses. Regular ante-natal care is vital for these mothers, as statistics show them and their babies to be greatly at risk.

There is a great shortage of normal babies free for adoption, so there will be no problem in finding suitable and delighted parents. The mother will have to give her final consent when the baby is a few weeks' old. If she keeps the baby, it will be a hard struggle for her to do her best by him, and retain much life of her own. Her mother may still have a full-time job and not be willing to stay at home for the grandchild's sake or to resume baby-rearing at this stage in her life. Her father, too, may resent the constraints on his freedom and money. Sometimes the sense of social isolation, the added responsibilities and insistent demands of a baby are too much for the young mother and she becomes physically or mentally ill. Worse, she may neglect or ill-treat the baby, and in extreme cases the baby may be removed from her and placed in care. Often, however, the girl's parents give all support they can and the baby is brought up almost as another sibling. There may be an abundance of adults in his life. To be fatherless does not now carry the social stigma it once did.

A marriage ends through death

Although sad, the death of an old person is easier to accept than that of a marriage partner and young parent. We have come to think of death as happening mainly in old age, in hospitals or old people's homes. This puts death outside our everyday experience, where it happened at one time. Death as shown on television is not 'real' and is no preparation for the death of someone we know. The first death we encounter at close quarters is always traumatic.

When a husband or wife dies, the remaining partner may turn in on himself in his grief and become isolated. He may, with the best of intentions, wish to protect the child or children from the harsh facts and from the rituals of burial and evidence of grief. It is now generally believed that this is unwise and that grief should be shown and shared, not suppressed.

Young children will watch the surviving parent and other adults to see how they are reacting. They should not sense that death is a taboo subject, and if they ask bald questions such as 'Where is she?' 'When will she come back?' they should be given answers that are true to what the parent knows and believes. To raise false hopes, or evade the facts will bring uncertainty, confusion and heartbreak. It is not easy to give answers that satisfy, especially as research tells us that children under three cannot understand death at all, children of five to seven can understand it only as a temporary event, and that it is not until children are approximately seven and upwards that they begin to appreciate the finality of death and its connection with illness, hospitalisation, accidents and so on.

Adults with religious convictions will probably give answers of reassurance and the expectation of eventual reunion with the loved one. In all cases, the person who has died should be spoken about and remembered positively, with thankfulness for past happy times. Grief is a normal process that seems to follow a set pattern of shock, disbelief, denial, anger, guilt, self-recrimination, depression, idealisation of the dead person and finally acceptance. These same stages of grief may follow other serious losses in people's lives, such as miscarriage, desertion, robbery, removal by imprisonment. Former societies had set rituals and accepted periods of mourning, which may have helped, and which are missing today.

When a parent dies, the key role he or she played in the child's whole world has ended, so besides sorrow and bewilderment, there is often the need for great readjustments all round. If death was preceded by prolonged illness the surviving partner is also probably exhausted and suffering great strain.

If children meet with death in the keeping of pets, this will in some measure help them to understand the inevitability of the birth, life, death cycle, and sensitive handling of this experience will influence attitudes in the future.

The lone mother

The parent who finds herself deserted, separated or divorced, and committed to coping with a child or children, has some immediate decisions to make. A time of shock, anger, grief and hurt is not a good time to take decisions which will set patterns for the future, but many of these decisions cannot wait. She will probably make many mistakes in the months and years to come and will learn from them. She should try to avoid situations which lead to further pain or nostalgia.

There are usually pressing financial considerations, chief of which is often whether the mother will work full-time, part-time, or not at all and resign herself to living on state benefits. These are still an inadequate provision on which to bring children up, and yet a job will probably leave little spare income after child care and basic living costs have been met. At home, she may feel depressed and socially isolated; at work, the stimulus and companionship she receives may be offset by feelings of guilt, exhaustion and lack of energy left over for her child, or any social life of her own.

General problems facing the lone parent are many. She lacks the moderating effect of a second parental opinion on day-to-day decision-making, discipline of the children, and so on. She may try to involve the children in all family decision-taking, but inevitably situations arise when she has to have the final word. She may play on the sympathy of the children and thus bind them to her with feelings of responsibility. She may try to make up for their emotional loss in material terms and over-indulge the children. Feelings of rejection may make her depressed and bitter and turned in on herself. She may be hypersensitive to other people's opinions and attitudes towards her, her children and her status. She may worry that her children have been irrevocably influenced by a pattern of unsuccessful marriage. She may become desperate for a break from her intense situation, yet feel guilty about leaving the children. The whole family may be denied holidays and outings, which makes life that much more dreary and humdrum. At its worst, her situation may break down altogether and the children be taken into care. This is the biggest worry of many struggling single parents.

The lone father

The lone father has much the same problems and pitfalls to face. In some ways his lot is easier; his earning power will almost certainly be greater, in fact about forty per cent greater, thus enabling him to employ child care help. Society does not appear to expect him both to bring up the children single-handed and do a job of work, whereas lone mothers seem to be expected to cope with the dual role. Relatives, friends and neighbours are likely to be supportive and sympathetic. In other ways, however, his lot is much harder. Any uncertainty about whether or not the mother will return will complicate feelings and decisions.

If he decides to remain in work, although this will be better for his pride and self-respect, he may have to pass up chances of overtime, shift work, bonuses, maybe promotion, if it involves a move and he is dependent on neighbours for help. He is unlikely to get the chance of a part-time job. Employers, particularly of manual workers, often lack sympathy for a man in his position and unpunctuality, time off for children's illnesses, etc., will probably not be tolerated. He may live with feelings of constant pressure about his responsibilities, and anxiety about the next crisis or a breakdown in his helping arrangements. Unless he can secure a day nursery place for a pre-school child, child-minding costs will eat up a large portion of his earnings. At day nursery the child will have to share one adult with several other children; the father may worry about this happening at a time when the child is most missing his mother. It will also mean a very long day away from home for the child. If the father advertises for a housekeeper, the accommodation he can offer her will be limited and not self-contained. She herself may be a single parent with child, thus completely changing the make-up of the household and demanding further adjustments from all. If the child is at school, the long summer holidays present a great problem.

If he opts for the full-time 'mother' role, he may find it completely foreign to him and realise how little he understood the organisation of running a home. He may master the obvious tasks, such as cooking and basic cleaning, but the ironing, for instance, may pile up uncontrollably and be 'the last straw' in his coping. His expendable income will certainly drop and this will affect the diet of his family and thus possibly their health. He feels wide open to criticism by others. Special occasions like Christmas and birthdays can be particularly painful, when money is short, the former organiser of such events has gone and other families are affirming their togetherness.

The effects of family break-up on the children

These effects can be many and varied, but the great increase in divorce in recent years has meant that at least a child need not feel alone in his situation today. In fact, the very terms 'break-up', broken marriage', etc. may in time be replaced by phrases without these overtones of failure and regret, as changing partners becomes more accepted. This has come about since the 1969 Divorce Reform Act, where, in divorce proceedings matrimonial *offences* are replaced by the concept of irretrievable breakdown of marriage.

Immediate effects on the child will depend greatly on what has preceded the break; prolonged bitter conflict may leave the child shaken and insecure. The end of conflict can bring relief, but also guilt about the relief. In most cases there will initially be sorrow at the departure, bewilderment, hurt, a feeling that in some obscure way the departure was the child's 'fault'. He will need much physical contact and reassurances of love from the remaining parent. He will also need to know that there are other adults who love him and would care for him if the remaining parent, too, were removed from the scene.

Behaviour disturbances may arise; at home, or at the nursery or school he may become 'wild', clinging, or start wetting or soiling himself, become withdrawn, suffer nightmares, do less well at school work, lack concentration, present minor physical ailments, or refuse to go to school. Sometimes these symptoms do not appear until some time after the initial event, when the adults wrongly assume that he has 'settled down'. However, it is a mistake for any adult to *expect* the child to show any of these signs of disturbance, or to label him 'a single-parent child' or, worse, 'a typical single-parent child'.

At home, the degree of closeness to the remaining parent and involvement in more household tasks and similar activities may bind the child in an intense emotional situation. If the absent parent has access to the child, such visits may be fraught with difficulties, such as one parent's anger, resentment and possessiveness. A father may not have money or means to take the child anywhere suitable, and the visits may become arid stretches of time, with the child feeling disorientated. He may be 'wooed' with gifts. He may ask unanswerable questions about the reasons for the marriage break-up, court decisions on custody, the date of the next visit and so on. There may be tearful partings, leaving the child in an upset state for the coming week. Division of loyalties can be very painful. On the other hand, children are often far more resilient than we give credit for, and may seem to take in their stride this divided state of affairs, and even adapt to 'ready-made' brothers and sisters in the second marriage.

Help available to lone parents

1. Finance. Lone parents may qualify for any of the following payments, depending on income:
(a) maintenance from spouse
(b) National Insurance benefits (see page 289)
(c) Family Income Supplement (F.I.S.)
(d) Single-parent family benefit
(e) free prescriptions, dental treatment and spectacles
(f) Supplementary benefit
(g) Child's special allowance
(h) additional tax allowance
(i) free school meals, uniform grants, educational maintenance allowance
(j) free legal aid
(k) rent and rates rebates
(l) grants from charities
(m) extra single payments for essential household equipment
(n) help with fuel bills
(o) TOPS training allowance, if taking Training Opportunities (Form TSND 103)

2. Social Services. These may provide through a social worker:
(a) information on money, housing, etc.
(b) support to anxious and isolated parents
(c) advice and arrangements concerning adoption
(d) help to pregnant girls
(e) arrangements for mother and baby placements
(f) day nursery placements
(g) Home Aids (formerly known as Home Helps)

3. Other agencies. These include:
(a) Citizens Advice Bureaux
(b) National Council for One Parent Families
(c) Gingerbread (a self-help group)
(d) Council for Voluntary Service
(e) youth counselling agencies
(f) Cruse (for widows and their families)
(g) Citizens' Rights Office (London)
(h) Child Poverty Action Group
(i) Family Conciliation Services
(j) Marriage and Family Guidance
(k) social clubs
(l) Families Need Fathers
(m) Women's Aid Federation
(n) local self-help and church-based community housing schemes

Exercise 17

Multiple-choice questions
1. One of 'your' parents has just experienced the death of her husband. At first she appears stunned; later she expresses to you anger that this could have happened, and guilt about not sufficiently appreciating him during their married life. Would you think that:
(a) she needs to see a psychiatrist;
(b) she is neurotic;
(c) she ought to snap out of it and think of other things;
(d) all reactions are natural stages in the grieving process.

2. One of 'your' parents asks your advice on what to tell her six-year-old son about the recent death of his elderly grandfather. You suggest:
(a) Grandad is ill in hospital and will be back some time;
(b) Grandad has stopped living because his body was old and worn out;
(c) Jesus called Grandad to be an angel in heaven;
(d) say nothing and hope he does not ask.

3. Single parents have become a social problem because:
(a) they are a fast-growing group living at poverty level;
(b) they sponge off the state;

(c) they can't bring up their children properly;
(d) they take up an unfair amount of council housing.

4. A father of two young children calls at your house to say his wife has left him suddenly and he is desperate. Your most helpful action on that day would be:
(a) to offer to move into his house and take over the household;
(b) to offer to let the children sleep at your house;
(c) to find out his long-term plans;
(d) to suggest he contacts a social worker.

Essay questions
5. A seventeen-year-old friend comes to you and says she is pregnant and does not know what to do. How would you help her think through the options open to her?

6. A four-year-old in your class is obviously being greatly disturbed by the breaking up of his parents' marriage. What might all the adults at school do to help the situation?

Discussion topic
7. What does it mean to each different member of a family when it breaks up? You may like to translate this into role play.

Suggestions for further reading

Judith Hann, *But what about the children?*, The Bodley Head Ltd
Judith S. Wallerstein and Joan Berlin Kelly, *Surviving the break up*, Grant McIntyre
Anne Hooper, *Divorce and your children*, George Allen & Unwin Ltd
Victor George and Paul Wilding, *Motherless Families*, Routledge & Kegan Paul Ltd
Relevant D.H.S.S. leaflets

Chapter 18
Accidents and first aid

Prevention

Accidents in the home or on the streets are among the commonest causes of death in young children of under seven years of age. Every year out of every 100 000 children approximately ten will die as a result of an accident in their homes, seven will die because of road accidents and about 6000 children will require hospital treatment following an accident of some kind. Many, if not all, of these accidents could be prevented with forethought, and much physical and mental misery could be avoided.

Children in the birth to four years age group are most prone to home accidents, and there are several reasons for this:

1. Children under four years lack experience and knowledge of what is dangerous and do not always understand verbal warnings.

2. Children of this age are natural explorers – impelled by their own curiosity.

3. Children put things in their mouths because this is how they explore and feel things.

4. Children have a poor sense of taste.

5. Children are vulnerable to adults' carelessness.

6. Children copy adults' actions.

7. Many adults under-estimate a child's reach and ability.

All adults in charge of children should examine the furniture and fittings in a child's surroundings and use their imaginations – and their knowledge of a child's ability – to detect potential hazards. Those hazards should then be tackled in some way. It is better to make the environment as safe as possible than to rely on saying 'No' or 'Don't touch'. Over-protection and constant warnings often cause children to become over-timid and unable to fend for themselves. As in all aspects of child-rearing, emphasis on the *positive* is always better than the negative.

Adults should themselves act safely at all times, especially when in charge of children, remembering that children will imitate their actions. For example, when crossing the road you should always use the proper crossing place, even if it means extra walking. Taking a chance and dashing across a road may be safe for an adult who can judge the speed of traffic, but could be fatal to a child who copies that action.

Good housekeeping and general tidiness will help to reduce accidents, and children should be taught to put away their toys and clothes. This habit is learned primarily by good example.

Children under seven should *never* be left alone in a house, not even for a minute when they are apparently safely asleep. There are many grieving parents who know, too late, how necessary this rule is. All dangers are multiplied many times when adults are absent.

We cannot discuss all eventualities here, but the following are some of the commonest accidents which happen to children (and in many cases cause their deaths) and routine preventive measures.

Cause	Prevention
Inhalation and ingestion of food – choking	
Baby left in pram or cot with bottle.	Babies should always be nursed when drinking from a bottle.
Baby vomits and inhales vomit.	Put baby on tummy or side to sleep, so that if he vomits he cannot inhale. Bring up baby's 'wind' before putting him down to sleep.
Child chokes on large piece of food.	Cut food into small pieces. Encourage child to chew properly. Never leave him alone when eating. Always make child sit down when eating – don't let him walk around.
Child inhales peanut.	Do not give young children peanuts.
Inhalation of other objects	
Small beads or toys in baby's mouth.	Do not give very small toys. Check eyes, etc. on fluffy toys.
Baby left in pram or cot with dummy.	Avoid using a dummy.
Suffocation	
Plastic bib flaps up over face – forms seal.	Do not use thin plastic bibs.
Plastic bag placed over head.	Destroy plastic bags when finished with. Never leave within reach of children.
Baby buries head in soft pillow.	Pillows are not necessary for a baby. Use 'safety' pillow made of foam rubber for older child.
Cat gets into baby's cot or pram – smothers baby.	Use a cat net. Discourage cats from getting on beds or entering bedrooms.
Child gets in refrigerator and closes door which cannot be opened from inside.	Remove doors from old refrigerators. Ensure refrigerator has magnetic catches on door which will open from inside.
Burns	
House on fire.	Never leave child alone in house.
Child plays with matches.	Keep matches away from children.
Portable heater tipped over.	Use fixed heater and fixed guard.
Clothes airing near fire ignite.	Do not leave clothes to air too close to fire; supervise it.

Cause	*Prevention*
Cigarettes left burning.	Make sure cigarettes are out before discarding.
Child's clothes are set alight when he leans over fire.	Use a fixed guard on all fires. Use non-flammable materials for clothing. Do not put mirrors or children's possessions on mantelpiece.
Child plays with bonfire.	Never leave a bonfire unsupervised.
Child plays with live electric plug.	Disconnect plugs from kettles and irons, etc. when not in use. Use short flex.
Iron pulled from ironing board.	Never leave iron, ironing board in position if child alone in room.
Scalds	
Hanging tablecloth pulled by child – hot tea pours on head.	Avoid use of tablecloth.
Child pulls saucepan handle – contents tip on child.	Use a guard for the cooker. Turn saucepan handles inward so that they do not overhang.
Adult drinks hot tea whilst nursing baby. Tea tips on child.	Always put baby down when drinking tea.
Child climbs in bath containing very hot water.	Always put cold water in bath first.
Child burnt or scalded by hot water bottle.	Do not use boiling water. Use a cover on bottle. Check rubber bottles before each use for wear and tear.
Falls	
Baby left on bed, settee or table – falls off.	If you have to leave the baby for a moment, put him on the floor.
Toddler climbs and falls.	Give child somewhere safe to practise climbing under supervision, e.g. firmly-fixed low climbing frame with rubber mat or grass underneath. Teach child how to come downstairs backwards. Use a stair gate. Put ladders away when finished using. Make sure clothing and shoes are safe for climbing.
Child falls out of window.	Safety catches on all windows, or window guards.
Child falls from pram or cot.	Use safety harness in pram. Put child in a bed once he starts climbing rails of cot.
Child falls from top bunk bed.	Use a guard. Children under five should not sleep in top bunks.

Cause	Prevention

Child falls or trips over:
    discarded toys;
    untied shoelaces;
    dressing up clothes;
    loose carpet;
    rugs on slippery floors.
	Keep home tidy.
	Check shoelaces.
	Cut them short.
	Fasten carpets securely.
	Do not polish under rugs.

Poisoning Child takes tablets prescribed for adult.	Keep tablets and medicines locked up. Take unused drugs back to chemist. Do not take tablets in front of children – they may think these are sweets and try to get one.
Child drinks bleach, disinfectant, detergent or weedkiller.	Keep these things in a locked cupboard. Never put other liquids in lemonade bottles.
Child drinks alcohol.	Keep bottles locked up. Never leave glasses with dregs within reach of children.
Child sucks painted surface containing toxic substances.	Use lead-free paint on all surfaces.
Child eats berries or leaves from poisonous plants.	Remove these hazards from garden. Watch child when out on walks. Warn child.
Drowning Falls in bath.	Never leave child alone in bath. Use non-slip mat in bath.
Falls in goldfish pond, swimming pool.	Make sure these are guarded.
Electric current Child pokes something in plug.	Use safety plugs with shuttered holes.
Bleeding Child plays with scissors, knives, pins, needles, razor blades, etc.	Keep all these away from children.
Toddler walking with drink in glass trips and breaks glass.	Make children sit down to drink. Use plastic cups.
Toddler falls against patio doors.	Use 'safety' glass.

Road safety

A great many children are killed or injured on quiet roads within a few hundred yards of home. So all roads must be considered dangerous to children under the age of seven years, and they should always be accompanied by an adult when away from their own home. The skills needed to cross a road must be acquired and practised.

They do not come naturally. We all know from our work with children that their ability to concentrate is limited and they are easily distracted. They have no experience to fall back on when trying to judge speed and distance accurately. Words such as 'mind where you are going' and 'look out' mean nothing to a small child. In addition, their view of the road is limited by their size. They do not have the advantages of an adult, who can see over parked cars and can also be seen by drivers.

Training for road safety must be approached like any other learning process:

1. *Protection from danger* – keep doors and garden gates secure. Do not allow a child to play in the road. Hold his hand, or (preferably) use harness and reins when walking out.

2. *Talk to him about the road* when you are out, pointing out features so that he becomes familiar with the language of road safety.

3. *Show by example* – always cross the road correctly and tell the child why you are doing this.

4. *Repetition* – teach the child the Green Cross Code as follows:
(a) Find a safe place to cross, then stop.
(b) Stand on the pavement near the kerb.
(c) Look all round for traffic and listen.
(d) If traffic is coming, let it pass. Look all round again.
(e) When there is no traffic near, walk straight across the road.
(f) Keep looking and listening for traffic while you cross.
    Repeat and use the code every time.

5. *Gradual independence* – let the child tell you and show you the Green Cross Code. Let him cross alone whilst you watch. Show him safe places to cross, with the lollipop lady, zebra or pelican crossings, subways, etc.

It is a good idea for children of three and over to join the 'Tufty' club organised by the Royal Society for the Prevention of Accidents. Details can be obtained from the Road Safety Officer employed by your local authority. The Road Safety Officer will also come and talk to groups of children and/or parents about road safety and provide many colourful posters.

Note: Safety in the car – see page 279, 'Travel by car'.

Fire

When fire occurs it can cause panic amongst adults as well as children, therefore it is best to be prepared in advance. Most institutions have an established fire drill and practices are carried out at random intervals to test procedures. You should know what is expected of you and proceed in a calm manner so that the children will follow your example. If you are in a private home, make sure you know all the exits and try to plan ahead what to do in the event of fire. It is a sensible precaution to keep a coil of rope in an upstairs room as a last means of escape.

Your first duty is to get your children out of the building to a place of safety quickly, however small the fire. Do not delay – it is not your job to fight the fire. But you should raise the alarm and close doors and windows as you go out, because air circulation helps to fan the flames. Remember that smoke and fumes can be as lethal as actual flames.

Should you be trapped in a room, close all doors and stand by a window so that you can be seen from outside and wait for help. Usually the fire brigade will be there within minutes of an alarm, so do not throw children out or jump unless the fire is overwhelming you.

First aid

All accidents, however trivial, are accompanied by some degree of shock, and most children are very frightened when they are hurt. Fear increases shock, so it is important that the adult in charge should keep calm and appear to be in control, even if she is quaking underneath. A hurt, frightened child needs comfort and support and this is also the treatment for shock.

Sit or lie the patient down, hold his hand or cuddle him and tell him it is going to be all right. This must be the *first* action, whatever the injury and fortunately most mothers and nursery nurses do this instinctively. It is no use expecting a small child to report accurately on what happened, as he will not be able to tell you properly. Use your own observation and make a quick examination whilst you are comforting him. Is he pale or flushed? Is he bleeding? Is one of his limbs at an unnatural angle?

Potentially fatal conditions

The main purpose of a first-aider is to save life, so it follows that any condition threatening life must be dealt with first. There are four main causes of death following an injury:

1. shock – treat with comfort, reassurance and rest;

2. bleeding – treat by raising the affected part and by putting pressure on the bleeding point;

3. asphyxia – treat by using mouth-to-mouth resuscitation;

4. heart stops – treat by giving heart massage (this applies *only* to a trained first-aider).

In nurseries and schools there should always be someone available who is trained in first aid, because if a child needs mouth-to-mouth resuscitation or heart massage it must be started within four minutes to be effective. All these conditions need medical aid urgently, so send for an ambulance immediately – don't waste time.

Other conditions

The other purposes of first aid are to prevent the injury becoming worse and to aid recovery. Often the best way is to do nothing apart from treating shock and sending for an ambulance. Too much interference can sometimes make the injury worse.

1. Unconsciousness (for any reason). If the child does not respond to his name, he is unconscious. Extend head by raising back of neck.
(1) Check whether he is breathing – put your ear to his mouth and listen.

If he is breathing:
(2) Turn him almost on to his tummy with his head on one side. This is known as the recovery position and it prevents his airway being blocked, either by his tongue falling to the back of his mouth or by the child's own saliva or vomit collecting in the back of his throat.

Stay with him to support him and keep him in this position. Talk to him gently, because he may be able to hear you. (Hearing is the last sense to be lost in unconsciousness.)
(3) Send for medical aid.

If he is not breathing:
(2) Start mouth-to-mouth resuscitation.
(3) Send for medical aid.

2. A blow on the head:
(1) Comfort child.
(2) Cold compress can be put over injured part.
(3) Allow child to rest but watch his condition.
(4) Inform parents.
(5) Medical aid is needed if any of the following conditions is present:
    (i) any unconsciousness, even if only momentary;
    (ii) vomiting; (iii) confusion.

3. Fainting. Put child in the recovery position and observe as with any unconscious person.

4. Cuts and wounds. Large gaping cuts or wounds which bleed a lot will need hospital treatment.
(1) Stop bleeding:
    (i) Raise the injured part.
    (ii) Place a pad over the wound and apply firm pressure. If the wound is gaping, press edges together before applying pad. The only exception to this is a head wound where you suspect that there may be a fracture under the wound. In this case press edges of wound together only.
(2) apply a dry, sterile pad and bandage firmly – if blood comes through this dressing, add another pad and bandage.

(3) If a foreign body is present in the wound, leave it alone unless it is easily removed. It is rare for a wound to bleed heavily if a foreign body is present, because it acts as a plug. In this case leave it alone and cover loosely with a sterile dressing.

(4) Get medical aid.

Small cuts and wounds, grazes and scratches which do not require medical attention should be treated in the following way:

(1) Wash well with soap and water.

(2) Dry and leave exposed to the air.

(3) It may be necessary to apply a dressing for psychological reasons, but this should only be temporary and should allow air to circulate. Wounds heal much better when exposed to air. If the child is playing in a sandpit or mud, etc., then a temporary dressing may be needed to protect the wound from contamination.

Antiseptics and antiseptic cream should *never* be used in first aid work. This is in accordance with modern views and practice.

5. Cat and dog bites. Treat as any small cut or wound. Refer to medical aid.

6. Insect stings:

(1) Remove sting if present.

(2) Treat as any small cut or wound.

(3) Medical aid is needed if sting is in the neck or face area, or if there is excessive swelling.

NB: When treating any break in the skin, the first-aider should enquire whether the patient is protected against tetanus. If he is not, then the patient or his parents should be advised to seek medical aid. Most children under five will have protection, because it is included in the routine immunisations. If the older child had a 'booster' immunisation before entering school, then he also is protected.

7. Nose bleed:

(1) Sit child down with head slightly forward.

(2) If child will co-operate, make him blow his nose in order to remove clots and mucus.

(3) Pinch the nose just below the bony prominence for three minutes (by the clock). This will control the bleeding.

(4) Sponge the child's hands and face and remove bloodstained clothing as quickly as possible.

(5) Encourage child to sit quietly and try to avoid blowing his nose for the next hour.

8. Bruises. These are due to bleeding under the skin and this is controlled by the increasing pressure of the skin, so that no first aid is necessary. However, a cold compress (cottonwool squeezed in very cold water) can be applied and the injured part elevated. If bruising is extensive, suspect further injury underneath and get medical aid.

9. Squashed fingers. Treat as for bruising.

10. Fractures, dislocations and sprains. Usually these are preceded by a fall, blow or twist. There is immediate pain and there may be swelling. Movement will be painful and difficult. No first-aider is qualified to differentiate between a sprain and a fracture so all these injuries should be treated as a fracture.
(1) Keep patient still.
(2) Call an ambulance.

11. Burns and scalds:
(1) Reduce heat immediately by immersing the affected part in slowly-running cold water for ten minutes – do not remove clothing or burst blisters.
(2) Cover with a sterile cloth and bandage.
(3) Medical aid will be necessary if blisters or a reddened area larger than a 10p piece are present.

12. Poisoning:
(1) If patient is unconscious and breathing – place in the recovery position.
(2) If patient is conscious – give nothing to drink unless poison is corrosive, when sips of milk or water can be given. DO NOT MAKE CHILD VOMIT.
(3) Get medical aid immediately.
(4) Save any tablets, liquids, containers and vomit so that the poison can be identified.

13. Foreign bodies:
(a) lodged in eye:
     (i) sand or dust – can be lifted from white of eye with a piece of moistened cottonwool;
     (ii) if embedded – apply sterile eye pad and get medical aid;
     (iii) if corrosive – wash continuously with water until medical aid arrives.
(b) lodged in ear or nose: do not attempt to remove foreign body. Get medical aid.
(c) lodged in throat: hold child head downwards and slap sharply between shoulder blades, or try to hook foreign body out with fingers. Mouth-to-mouth resuscitation is necessary if breathing stops.
(d) splinters – remove with sterilised needle; treat as any wound.

Mouth-to mouth resuscitation

All adults in charge of children should learn how to perform mouth-to-mouth resuscitation by practising on a dummy. The method used is as follows:
(1) Tip the child's head right back by placing one hand under the back of the neck and the other on the forehead. This will give a clear airway and may be all he needs to enable him to start breathing. Check before proceeding.
(2) Keeping your hand under the neck to maintain position, pinch the nostrils with the other hand.
(3) Take a breath in and then, covering the child's mouth with your own to make a seal, breathe into the child. Watch the child's chest rise.

(4) Remove the mouth and take another breath.

(5) Repeat this action about twenty times a minute.

(6) If the chest does not rise, the airway must be blocked, so check for any obstruction before continuing.

First aid box

The Health and Safety (First Aid) Regulations 1981 provide guidance on the provision of first aid boxes as follows:

1. Boxes or other containers should be clearly marked with a white cross on a green background.

2. They should contain only the following items:
(a) card giving general first aid guidance;
(b) individually wrapped, sterile adhesive dressings;
(c) sterile eye pads with attachment;
(d) triangular bandages;
(e) safety pins;
(f) a selection of individual sterile medicated wound dressings, to include standard dressings Nos. 8, 9, 13 and 14 B.P.C. and ambulance dressings Nos. 1 and 3 B.P.C. (amounts according to number of employees).

3. Soap and water and disposable drying material should be available. If not, sterile water in 300 ml containers.

Useful additions which can be kept near the official box are:
crêpe bandage; tweezers; needle in a cork; pad and pencil; large piece of clean linen; scissors; first aid book.

Keeping a record

Always remember to make a note of all the details of the injury and treatment given as soon as possible, because it is so easy to forget details. Be sure to date and time your note, as you may be asked about the incident at any time in the future. In nurseries and schools there will be an official accident book for this purpose so make sure you know where it is kept. Always report accidents to the head of the school or nursery. Parents should also be informed, and if the child needs to go to hospital try to get one of the parents to accompany him, not only because it comforts the child, but also because the hospital authorities may need to know the child's medical background and obtain consent for the child's treatment. In an emergency this may not be possible and in this case the head of the nursery or school can act *in loco parentis* (in place of the parent). She should know who the child's general practitioner is so that he can be contacted if necessary.

If a child arrives at nursery or school with an injury such as bruising, do remember the possibility of child abuse. If possible, detain the mother and ask for an explanation. Do this in a discreet and tactful way, because children do have accidents and parents feel very guilty, even if it is not their fault. Any suspicions should be reported to the head of the school or nursery, out of the child's hearing. Arrangements are then made for a complete medical examination to check for other injuries.

Exercise 18

Multiple-choice questions

1. Which of the following is the accepted treatment for shock?
(a) wrap patient in blankets to keep him warm;
(b) give patient a hot cup of sweet tea;
(c) make him tell you what happened;
(d) lie patient down, hold his hand and comfort him.

2. A child comes to school with a swollen ankle. Would you:
(a) put a bandage on it, and tell him 'it's just a sprain';
(b) put a cold compress on it;
(c) take him to the hospital for an X-ray;
(d) take the child home and advise his mother to take him to hospital.

3. Which of the following is the best treatment for a nose-bleed?
(a) put a cold key down the child's back;
(b) hold child's wrists under a cold-water tap;
(c) sit child, lean his head forward and pinch his nose;
(d) lie child down with his head back.

4. A child has swallowed some berries. Which action would you take?
(a) give him milk to sip;
(b) leave him, but watch his condition;
(c) take him to hospital with a sample of the berries and leaves;
(d) give him salt-water to make him sick.

5. Which of the following is the best immediate treatment for a bleeding hand?
(a) hold hand above head and apply pressure over the wound;
(b) apply a tourniquet around the wrist;
(c) cover wound with a pad and dressing;
(d) clean wound with disinfectant and apply a dressing.

Essay questions and project

6. Why are accidents in the home one of the commonest causes of death in young children? How can these accidents be prevented?

7. How would you treat a child suffering from each of the following accidents?
(a) a wasp-sting on the lip;
(b) a piece of glass in the foot;
(c) a fall from a height, causing a head injury.

8. Imagine you have three children under five years of age. Look around your own home and list the potential hazards, noting how you would make them safe.

Chapter 19
Travelling with children

We believe that children today should grow up as part of the family, and part of the world in which they are going to live. However, the broadening influence of travel is more to the benefit of older children and adults; young children prefer the continuity and comfort of home and, for the under-sevens generally, as far as holidays are concerned, they will be happier on a local beach than in Majorca. However, parents' needs must be considered too, and often desperation for sunshine or a complete change is felt by the mother or father and must take precedence over small children's requirements. The child need not suffer. In fact he may have a wonderful time, and the whole family benefits.

Apart from holidays, there will be other circumstances when children have to travel – for instance to accompany a father who is in the armed forces or doing other work abroad.

All travel with children needs to be planned in advance. The longer and more ambitious the journey is, the more thought and preparation will be involved.

Modes of travel will depend on time available, finance, preference of adults, and circumstances. It may happen – for instance, in an emergency or after a sudden change of plan – that a journey must be undertaken at quite short notice. This makes it doubly important for a nursery nurse who intends to become a nanny to know what preparations are advisable before setting out, and the difficulties that could arise. 'Nanny' is often put in sole charge of a child or two; she may even be taken on expressly to look after them while travelling.

We shall deal with specific types of travel and the needs of the different age groups in this chapter. Some general advice applies in every case, however. Try to arrange the journey so that there is the least possible disturbance to the child's routine, and, if possible, so that he has some familiar things around him during the journey, and when he arrives. Try to adopt a calm and confident attitude towards the event yourself. Tension, flustered or fussy behaviour on your part will be sensed by the child and make the journey miserable for both of you. Plan to be self-sufficient; you *may* receive offers of help, but do not count on it!

Travelling with a young baby (up to ten months)

If you are going abroad, you will need to obtain information from your doctor or travel agent about health matters such as immunisation, vaccination and standards of hygiene at your destination. Any immunisation should be carried out some time before the journey. You will need to know whether the milk and water will be safe to drink and whether the baby's milk will be obtainable. It may be necessary to take with you dried milk and sterilising tablets. Babies going to live in tropical countries may need a milk with a lower fat content. Consult your health visitor about this. If the child is on solid food, you need to know if the local food will be suitable; if not, you may have to take stocks of tinned food. The

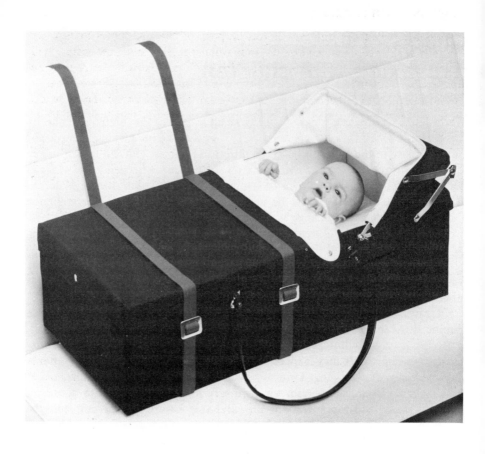

position will be rather different if the purpose of the journey is to take up long-term residence, in which case the baby will gradually have to get accustomed to local food. Whether suitable food and drink is available will also depend on whether the place where you will be staying is to be a hotel or private home.

With a small baby, travelling is fairly simple and straightforward. The only real burden – literally! – is the amount of luggage required, which is out of all proportion to the size of the infant.

As well as minimum disturbance to routine, minimum handling will also benefit the baby. A pram which can be divided into a carrycot and wheels is invaluable here, as the baby can 'stay put' whenever and however he is being moved about.

When planning for his needs, bear in mind that unexpected delays are possible. His food should stay the same, and no changes should be made as the journey draws near. Bottles can either be made up as wanted, or made in advance and refrigerated before being packed in an insulated bag to keep cold. If the baby is being weaned, however, he should become used to tins or jars of baby food *before* the journey. Most babies will accept these foods at room temperature, but the jar can be stood in hot water if preferred. It is safest to feed straight from the jar or tin, and throw away any uneaten remains.

List of baby's requirements

either:

1. several sterilised bottles with teat and screw-on cap;

2. vacuum flask of hot boiled water;

3. milk powder and scoop;

or

1. sterilised bottles containing teat and feed made cold in insulated bag;

2. vacuum flask of hot water (for heating bottle to correct temperature when ready);

3. container to stand bottle in;

also

4. rusks for older baby;

5. bottle containing cool boiled water;

6. jars or tins of food, tin opener, plastic spoon;

7. bag containing baby's toilet requisites (excellent plastic 'duffle' bags, with space for talc, etc., and a separate zipped pocket for soiled nappies, can be bought in baby shops);

8. disposal nappies;

9. plastic pants, if needed;

10. spare set of clothing, including jumper or cardigan;

11. 2 damp flannels or 'wet wipes';

12. tissues;

13. familiar toy;

14. clothing should be in several thin layers so that it can easily be adjusted according to temperature.

Emergency sterilising of a bottle can be carried out by cleaning it and then filling it to overflowing with boiling water – obtainable in cafés and restaurants where tea-making urns are used.

Requirements for stay at destination

These will be dictated by your knowledge of the situation, but you will certainly need sterilising equipment. You will need to find out whether the cows who supply the local milk are tuberculin tested, and whether the milk has been pasteurised. If the quality of the local milk is suspect you should use powdered milk instead. As a general rule, boil all water and milk before use for the under two year old.

Travelling with a child from 10 months to 2 years

This can be the most difficult age, because toddlers dislike change. If they become tired or miserable, they regress in behaviour and need to be treated like babies. When wide awake and in good spirits they want to be active, independent, noisy and self-assertive.

More than ever, the principle of trying to stay within their routine is important. If the child is used to a nap in the morning, afternoon or both, then means must be found for this. A combined pram and carrycot will still be useful at this stage; although a pushchair is easier to manoeuvre, a pram is a comfortable and familiar place for the child to sleep, and at other times, is useful for holding luggage.

Meals should be light and plain – the sort of food he normally has at home. No extra sweets or snacks should be given, but a drink of cool water or unsweetened fruit juice and an apple, might be a good idea from time to time.

If the child is using a potty, then his own familiar one should be taken along. Familiar toys are just as important.

Requirements

1. bottles as for baby, if child still has bottle feeds;

2. toilet articles as for baby;

3. several spare pairs of pants;

4. spare jumper;

5. potty;

6. familiar toys;

7. mackintosh or plastic tablecloth (useful for beds and underneath feeding chairs);

8. apples;

9. drinking water and/or fresh fruit juice;

10. harness with reins.

Travelling with an older child – 2½–7 years

At this age, the child can understand a little of what is in store, if you talk with him beforehand about the journey and together look at suitable children's books about travel. A child of six or seven may well enjoy looking at a simple map or travel brochures.

If possible, the journey should be broken up by stops for stretching legs, going to the toilet and perhaps having picnics, etc. If this is not possible, or even in between stops, the child will need a good deal of amusing if he is not to become restless or bored. Give him his own bag or case containing favourite toys, books and drawing materials. Perhaps a comic or two may be bought specially for this journey, adding to the sense of occasion. The adult in charge should be careful to space out any little treats of this kind to break the tedium.

A damp flannel or 'wet wipes', and spare jumper and pants are still a wise precaution.

At this age the child will enjoy chatting to an interested adult and commenting on all his new and exciting experiences. There are also many simple games which two can play, while just sitting quietly – for instance, 'I spy' and an easy version of 'twenty questions'. If you can see the scenery from the window you can soon think up more 'spotting' games.

Travel by car

A journey by car is probably the commonest and least stressful way to travel with children, because most children are used to car travel. Luggage is easier to manage, timing can be arranged to suit the travellers (during the night can be quite convenient) and you are not dependent on outside factors, except traffic and weather conditions.

A *baby* can stay in a carrycot on the back seat, anchored by a safety strap.

A *toddler* should be in his own car seat, safely strapped in the back.

Older children should always sit in the back restrained by safety straps. A booster cushion can be used to elevate the child so that he can see out of the window, and to make an adult seat belt safe for him to use. If there is more than one child, an adult should sit with them (probably between, to prevent squabbling) and organise a few games. You will not have to worry about annoying strangers, so singing games are ideal, with your own adaptations, if you like. However, children must understand that squealing and horseplay are not allowed, as they can distract the driver and be dangerous. Keeping several children happy on a long journey can be quite demanding. For this reason there should always be in addition to the driver another adult looking after the children. If the two can take turns with the driving, so much the better. The journey should be broken up into spells of approximately two hours, but stopping places will need to be carefully chosen for safety. Adequate ventilation will make conditions more pleasant, and children's car locks should, of course, be present on the doors.

Travel by train

This can be a novelty and quite exciting to a small child. It is better to book in advance to avoid last-minute panics, and also to travel mid-week and avoid the rush hours. If the journey is very long, overnight travel may be a good idea and sleepers can be booked. The corridor lets one stretch one's legs and visit the toilet and will help to break the monotony. A meal or snack on the train can also be exciting for a toddler or older child, and is probably easier than taking a packed meal.

Travel by coach

There will be little chance to get at your luggage, or to move around or go to the toilet during coach journeys. There will not be much space for belongings and toys; activities, too, will be limited. But you will have a good vantage point to watch the passing scenery and there will probably be plenty to interest a young child.

Travel by ship

It is as well to ask in advance exactly what provision there will be for a baby or toddler, especially for meals and washing. On a long journey, a nursery kitchen is available for making up feeds, while any special food or milk can be ordered in advance if sufficient time is allowed. There will be facilities for the adult to do washing, and most probably a laundry with nappy service. This service, and buying disposable nappies on board, will, of course, involve some expense. There is usually a special early evening meal for toddlers, and stewards will act as a baby alarm so that adults can eat together later. On a large liner there will also be a crèche and trained nursery nurses, but such facilities may be crowded, depending on demand. A cot will be provided, but a pram will be useful for going on deck.

Travel by air

This has the advantage of getting you to your destination quickly, and many airlines are extremely helpful to adults with babies and children, provided they are informed in advance. For airline purposes, all children under two years of age are called babies, and are allowed to travel at 10 per cent of the adult fare. No seat is provided, but on request the accompanying adult(s) will be given a bulkhead seat, which allows plenty of leg room as there are no passengers in front. A 'skycot' is also provided. This is a small cot suspended from the bulkhead. The baby has no luggage allowance, but all his travel needs are free of charge, and usually this is generously interpreted.

A baby under one year will travel happily under these conditions, but if the child is a lively, active toddler between one and two it could well be worth considering whether to pay the child's fare of 50 per cent so that he may have a seat of his own, and a normal luggage allowance and normal meals.

If you let the airline know beforehand they will probably allow an adult who is travelling with young children to board the plane first, and they will provide help to settle the children in their seats. On take-off some children may be frightened at the extra noise and strange sensation. They should be told about this before the actual flight, if they are of an age to understand. The ears tend to pop because of changing pressure. This can be eased by swallowing, or, for a baby a drink of fruit juice in a bottle will help.

Many airports have nurseries where changing and feeding can be done conveniently and in privacy.

Visits with children

Nursery nurses working in private families and in day care and nursery education will appreciate the stimulation that comes from visits – outings undertaken for their own sake. Apart from the obvious benefits of fresh air and exercise, and a welcome break from normal routine, a visit offers valuable opportunities to broaden children's horizons. A city child, for instance, can see life on a farm; another child may perhaps travel on a train for the first time. Excellent incidental teaching can easily arise from such topics as road safety, conservation of the countryside, kindness to animals, dealing sensibly with litter, respecting property, and showing appreciation. There are bound to be many talking points which will later lead on to follow-up activities and books.

Sometimes a visit like this just happens spontaneously, inspired by a lovely day, or perhaps the arrival of an interesting ship at a nearby dock, or workmen at a local building site. At other times, a visit will be organised well in advance, needing arrangements about transport, packed meals, etc. As a general rule, the younger the children, the shorter and less ambitious should be the outing, particularly the travelling time.

In every case, the permission of the head of the establishment is required, and also, of course, the permission of the parents. Care must be taken that domestic and other arrangements at the nursery or in the family are not disturbed, and that all the staff concerned with the children is kept informed about the plans.

Adequate adult supervision must be provided – preferably not more than four children to one adult and fewer than this if the children are very young. If a large group is going, mothers can often be invited too; they will need to be reliable people who will understand what the staff hope the children will gain from the outing and co-operate with them. Badges with names of children and school are a good idea, and each child must be clear about whose group he is in.

The children can be told a little of what is to happen. For example, if they are going to the zoo, a few animal songs or poems can be introduced. However, one of the benefits of an outing is the freshness and directness of impact that the experience will make on the children, so do not overdo the preparatory talk.

Where an outing involves travel, take along spare clothes, damp flannels, plastic bags, first aid kit and other 'accident' provision. If a coach is being hired, it is best to make enquiries from several firms about prices, as these can vary considerably, and cost should be kept as low as possible, so as not to embarrass any parents. It is also wise to find out about parking facilities at your destination, picnic sites, and alternative arrangements in case of wet weather. Admission charges to public places are usually reduced for parties of children, and sometimes waived altogether.

During the visit, the children must be closely supervised, and number of children studying any one aspect of the place you are visiting should be kept very small. In this way there will be enough viewing space, opportunities to answer questions and take up comments, and there will be less chance of children getting over-excited. Provide for regular visits to the toilet, and a comfortable break for a meal, if you are having one. Keep a careful eye on the picnics that individual children have brought, as these can vary from a huge feast to almost nothing. For this reason, many nurseries and schools like their kitchen to provide a standardised picnic for everyone. You should, in any case, have previously discouraged the bringing of sweets and sticky foodstuffs, and also glass bottles and tumblers. Arrangements about spending money should also have been made clear in advance. If children are bringing money it is wise to stipulate a small maximum sum, and allow only one fixed time for spending it. Money easily gets lost, causes jealousy, and encourages children to dart off in the direction of an ice-cream van, or disappear into a shop, causing delays to one's schedule, worry to the adults, and possibly breaking up the group.

The adult should see that periods of walking are alternated with resting and periods of concentration and listening alternated with periods of vigorous exercise. Otherwise the children will become overtired, fractious or bored.

If the visit is a success, and visits usually are, most children will want to talk eagerly about it to others when they return, or during the next few days. While enthusiasm lasts, this is a good time to make a display of their mementos on a related subject – for instance castles – while sometimes a group or class 'book' is made. Each child should be encouraged – but not forced – to contribute. A display of this nature frequently attracts much interest from parents and affords a valuable opportunity for friendly contacts and conversation. This is a way of showing appreciation for parents' co-operation over outings, and probably ensures it also for next time.

Exercise 19

Multiple-choice questions
1. Which would be the most suitable choice of an outing for nursery school age children?
(a) an all-day trip to the seaside；   (c) a guided tour of a factory；
(b) a coach-tour to a stately home;   (d) an afternoon at the local park.

2. The most suitable breakfast for a child before starting a journey would be:
(a) bacon, egg, and fried bread;
(b) nothing at all;
(c) fresh fruit-juice, cereal with sugar and milk;
(d) dry toast only.
3. After a visit with infant children interest in follow-up work seems totally lacking. Which course of action would you take?
(a) insist that each child draws a picture;
(b) insist that each child contributes to a class book;
(c) organise an exhibition for parents, hoping this will motivate the children;
(d) drop any ideas of follow-up work altogether.

Essay questions
4. You are required to accompany a six-month-old baby and a three-year-old child on a car journey lasting four hours. Describe how you would plan the journey and entertain the children en route.

5. You are a nanny to a family of two children, John aged two and a half years and Emily aged five years, and have to take them on a two-week farm holiday in Wales. The journey will be by train, taking one and a half hours. Describe the preparations. How would you help to make the holiday an enjoyable experience for both children?

Chapter 20
The government and the welfare state

Britain is a parliamentary democracy, which broadly means that all adults have a voice in government, either directly or through their elected representatives. Therefore it is very necessary for everyone to understand how the parliamentary system works.

Although the Queen, as monarch, is the constitutional Head of State, her powers are limited and the actual business of policy-making and government is carried out by the House of Commons and the House of Lords. Political power is held largely by the House of Commons although the House of Lords – whose members include hereditary peers, bishops, the law lords and various worthy people who have been made 'life peers' in recognition of their ability or their service to the country – may suggest amendments to proposed laws or even slow down their passage. In the Commons each Member of Parliament (M.P.) has been elected to represent the interests of the people living in his area (or constituency). The country is divided into more than six hundred constituencies and every person over the age of eighteen, who is on the electoral roll, is eligible to vote for a representative in a general election, held at least every five years.

Most potential M.P.s belong to specific political parties, though some choose to be independent. When an election is announced, each party publishes a manifesto setting out the policy it will follow if it comes to power. Leaflets are delivered to voters' homes on behalf of the various candidates, describing their particular policies and aims. Meetings are held in each constituency so that candidates may explain their party's standpoint and try to gain votes, and vigorous campaigns are run in all the media. After the general election the leader of the party with the largest number of elected members is invited by the Queen to become her Prime Minister and to form a government. The second largest party becomes the official Opposition. Its role is to offer constructive criticism of government policy and to hold itself in readiness as a possible alternative government.

Proposals for new laws are brought before the two houses in the form of Bills. After discussion and debate they are put to the vote and, if passed by a majority in both houses, become Acts of Parliament and are entered in the statute book. Statutes are the country's written laws.

An important duty of the Prime Minister is to appoint other ministers to take charge of government departments such as the Department of Health and Social Security, the Department of the Environment, the Ministry of Agriculture, Fisheries and Food, etc. These ministers must be members either of the House of Commons or the House of Lords. Each government department is staffed by permanent civil servants whose job is to implement the various Acts of Parliament.

Central government also passes on some of its functions to local government, which makes local bye-laws, provides essential services, including policing and the local courts. Local government comprises local authorities, which may be county, city, or urban district councils and consist of councillors who are elected in local polls, which are similar to national polls. The local authorities employ professional administrators and officers who organise such local services as education, social services, environmental health, housing, highways and town and country planning. To finance these operations rates, which are local property taxes, are collected from local householders and businesses, and each local authority also receives a grant from central government.

The national income needed for the whole range of government activities, and for M.P.s' salaries, etc. is raised from taxes, which include direct taxation such as income tax, motor vehicle tax and estate duty, and indirect taxation – for example, value added tax, duties on alcoholic drinks and tobacco and customs duties.

This very simplified description of how Britain is governed serves to emphasise the following points:

1. Our right to vote gives us some small influence on our government and, as responsible citizens, we should use our votes to try to elect the best possible Parliament and local authority.

2. None of the services we get from the government is free. We all pay directly or indirectly for these services. It is true that some people pay more than others and that some people need to make greater use of the services but that is the hallmark of civilisation – the strong should help look after the weak.

3. We are governed by our consent, which means that people must respect and obey the laws in order for our parliamentary system to function.

The most far-reaching Acts of Parliament in modern times have been those which formed the foundations for the welfare state. Although in the past, attempts were made to aid people in distress, especially poor families with young children, the welfare state that exists in Britain today did not come into being until after the Second World War. Before the war many people felt that if a family was destitute it must be its own fault. They argued that if help was too readily available then families on very low incomes would only take advantage of it and would not try to help themselves. However, it was eventually realised that poverty could arise from events beyond a person's control. Therefore help given at the right time and in the right amount could prevent unfortunate families from sinking irrevocably into destitution, and give them the hope and the means to keep on trying.

Much of the assistance available to poor people before the war was given by charitable institutions and by kindly, well-meaning individuals, so the degree of help varied widely from area to area. But in 1942 Sir William Beveridge produced a report recommending a comprehensive national insurance system and the formation of a Health Service. In his report he described the five evils which lay in the path of a better society – want, disease, ignorance, squalor, and idleness. He said that all members of a society should be free from these evils.

This concept marked the final stage of development of the social and health services started at the beginning of the century. The report was followed by several acts of Parliament which laid the foundations of the services we enjoy today:

1944 *The Education Act* (took effect from 5 April 1945)
This provided for free education from a statutory five to fifteen years according to age, ability and aptitude, in a system of public education organised as a continuous

process in three stages – primary, secondary and higher (for those who wished to go on beyond fifteen). Until this time free education had been largely elementary and from five to fourteen years only.

1945 *The Family Allowances Act*
This provided an allowance for each child in a family, other than the first child. The allowance is now called child benefit and all the children of a family are now entitled to it.

1946 *The National Health Service Act* (took effect from 5 July 1948)
This provided free medical care for all, whether they paid contributions or not. From 1951 charges were made for dental treatment, prescriptions, spectacles and some appliances, although children and some special categories of patient are exempt.

1946 *The National Insurance Act* (took effect from 5 July 1948)
This scheme paid certain financial benefits in return for fixed weekly contributions from employed persons and their employers – for example, unemployment benefit and sickness benefit.

1948 *The National Assistance Act* (took effect from 5 July 1948)
This provided financial assistance for those whose needs were not met by National Insurance or any other source. It also provided residential accommodation for the aged, infirm and homeless. These arrangements are now known as social security benefits.

1948 *The Children Act*
This Act was designed 'to make further provision for the care and welfare, up to the age of eighteen years and, in certain cases, for further periods, of boys and girls when they are without parents...'

Since 1950 many more Acts of Parliament were passed which modified and changed the provisions of the original acts, in an attempt to make good any deficiencies and to ensure that the various provisions and services continue to meet the changing needs of British society.

Today, the following services are available to everyone who lives in Britain:

1. Health
The main changes which have occurred since the 1948 Act are these:

1967 *The Family Planning Act*
This made contraceptive advice freely available to all. Previously this was (officially) confined to women with medical problems. This has since been amended so that all family planning aids are free, either from family planning clinics or the family doctor (GP).

1968 District nurses were allowed to treat people on Health Premises, thus paving the way for the health centre treatment room.

1968 *The Abortion Act*
This made the induction of abortion legal under certain conditions.

1973 **Reorganisation of the Health Service.** Originally the Health Service was divided into Hospital Services and General Practitioner Services, each with their own management, and Community Services which were managed by the local authority. With the reorganisation all three sections were unified and came under the management of Regional Boards, which were divided into Area Health Authorities. These authorities were subdivided into districts which were in turn subdivided into units. With this reorganisation came the growth of health centres, which had been proposed in the 1948 Act but were slow to develop. The reason for their growth was the new concept of a primary health care team working together to achieve the optimum health of the community they serve. A team consisted of a general practitioner (family doctor), health visitor, midwife and district nurse. It was obviously better for them to work from the same premises. Previously the general practitioner had worked independently, and there had often been an overlap with the work of other disciplines.

Regional health authorities

A second reorganisation was accomplished in 1982–83, aimed at reducing the number of administrators and making the service more efficient. The Area Health Authority tier of management was abolished, and the country was divided among regional health authorities. Each region was subdivided into several small district health authorities. Each district consists of approximately ten smaller management units. The composition of each unit varies in different districts, but might typically comprise one hospital and a group of community workers, such as health visitors or, in some districts, all the community services may be in one unit.

General practitioner (GP)

Everyone can register with a general practitioner and receive free medical treatment, except where prescription charges are applicable. All hospital services are free, although some state hospitals have a few private beds for which charges are made.

Primary health team

In most areas the GP is part of a primary health team usually working from a health centre and providing many services:

(a) health visitors – who visit all families, especially those with children under five years of age, to advise on health matters including the prevention of illness;
(b) midwives – who care for mothers before, during and after the birth of their babies; now that most births take place in hospitals, community midwives are mostly concerned with ante-natal clinics and classes and also visit mothers and babies at home after discharge from hospital until the baby is 10 to 14 days old;
(c) home nurses – who care for sick people in their own homes at the request of hospitals and general practitioners;
(d) child health clinics;
(e) immunisation clinics;
(f) ante- and post-natal clinics;
(g) ante-natal classes for parents;
(h) family planning clinics;
(i) a treatment room staffed by qualified nurses.

Other optional services could include physiotherapy, speech therapy, dental services, hearing assessments, social workers, abortion counselling service, infertility clinics, etc., although many of these are also available in the local hospital.

Free drugs and medicine
These are provided for:
(a) children under sixteen years of age;
(b) pregnant women;
(c) mothers of children under one year;
(d) people suffering from certain medical conditions;
(e) people on low incomes;
(f) people receiving family income supplement or supplementary benefit;
(g) people receiving retirement or war-disablement pensions.
All other patients receive drugs at reduced costs.

Dental care
This is free for:
(a) children under seventeen years (except dentures, if a child is working);
(b) children up to eighteen years, in full-time education;
(c) pregnant women;
(d) mothers of children under one year;
(e) people on low incomes, receiving family income supplement or supplementary benefit.

Dental care is provided at reduced cost for all others.

Ophthalmic services
Eye tests are free and spectacles are provided at reduced cost, but are free for people on low incomes.

Free hospital services
These include: general, children's, orthopaedic, eye, maternity, and mental hospitals; the services of consultants, registrars, housemen (doctors), nurses, physiotherapists, radiologists, occupational health therapists and medical social workers; in-patient and out-patient treatment; ambulance service and VD clinics.

People on low incomes may have their fares paid for visits to hospital.

School health service
This provides the services of:
(a) school doctor – school medical inspection;
(b) health visitor/school nurse – hygiene inspections, hearing and vision tests, etc.;
(c) dentist – dental inspections;
(d) audiometrician – hearing tests;
(e) ophthalmic services – eye test and provision of spectacles;
(f) nutritionist – advice on diets;
(g) chiropodist – foot clinics;
(h) speech therapist – speech clinics;
(i) family welfare visitors;
(j) family guidance service.

2. Social services:

The 1948 Children Act was administered by Children's Officers from the Children's Department of the local authority. In 1970, following the Seebohm Report, the Local Authority Social Services Act required local authorities to set up a Social Services Committee and to appoint a Director of Social Services and a staff of social workers. The present Department of Social Services is an amalgamation of the existing Children's Department and departments for welfare services to the elderly, handicapped and mentally disordered. The duties required of it are:

(a) provision of social workers to work with individuals and families needing help with personal problems;

(b) child care under the various acts of Parliament, e.g., Children Acts, Children and Young Persons Acts, Nursery and Childminder Regulations and the Adoption Acts (see below);

(c) welfare services for the elderly, the handicapped, the chronically sick and those suffering from a mental disorder;

(d) provision of residential accommodation for the elderly and disabled;

(e) provision of home helps and meals-on-wheels for people in need;

(f) delegation of any or all of these responsibilities to a voluntary organisation with subsequent support, for example, WRVS meals-on-wheels service run with a grant from Department of Social Services.

Under the Child Care Acts social workers:

(a) supervise children in day nurseries and playgroups;

(b) supervise children in private foster homes;

(c) work with families in trouble; try to prevent a break-up leading to children being taken into 'care'; they do this by giving guidance to parents and involving other agencies and methods will vary from area to area;

(d) if concealed parental violence is suspected, investigate and convene case conferences with other workers involved, such as health visitor, probation officer, police and N.S.P.C.C. officers, to pool knowledge and make the best plan of action for the family; also to keep a central register of children known to be at risk of CPV;

(e) arrange and supervise adoptions;

(f) take children into care when parents are unable to look after them, either temporarily or permanently;

(g) take children into care when subject to a court order, usually because the child needs care and protection because of an offence committed (or likely to be committed) against him or because the child himself has committed an offence;

(h) accommodate and maintain children in care and look after their interests; 'care' may be with friends, relatives, foster parents or in a community home or voluntary home.

3. Education:

(a) nursery schools;

(b) primary schools;

(c) comprehensive schools;

(d) special schools for handicapped children;

(e) hospital schools;

(f) home teachers;

(g) evening classes;

(h) colleges of further education;

(i) colleges of higher education;
(j) universities.

Staff
Teachers and lecturers; nursery nurses; ancillary helpers; school inspectors; school welfare officers.

Subsidies and grants (at the discretion of the local authority)
(a) free school meals for children of low-income families;
(b) school meals for all children;
(c) free milk for all children;
(d) uniform grants;
(e) fares paid for primary school children if they live more than 3.2 km (2 miles) from their school;
(f) fares paid for secondary and further education students if they live more than 4.8 km (3 miles) from school or college;
(g) grants for further and higher education;
(h) transport to and from school for handicapped children;
(i) educational maintenance allowance;
(j) school health service;
(k) student grants.

4. Finance

There are three different *kinds* of cash benefit which may be claimed by all eligible adults in Great Britain:

(a) *National Insurance (N.I.) benefits* These are dependent upon payment of N.I. contributions in the past. Unemployment benefit is one example.
(b) *Means-tested benefits* These are dependent on assessment of present income and savings. For instance, from November 1983 if you have £3,000 or more in savings you cannot claim.
(c) *Non-contributory benefits* These are dependent on meeting certain conditions. A woman can, for example, claim maternity grant when she is twenty-six weeks pregnant, as certified by a doctor or midwife.

The benefits listed below are keyed (a), (b) or (c) according to these categories.

Child benefit (c) A weekly sum payable to mothers for each child in the family from birth to the time of leaving school.

Child's special allowance (c) A weekly amount paid for each dependent child of a divorced woman on the death of her former husband, if he was helping to support them.

Death grant (a) A sum of money to help pay funeral expenses.

Employment rehabilitation scheme payment (c) A weekly allowance for people over nineteen years who have been sick or injured or who are handicapped in some way, and are taking part in an employment rehabilitation scheme.

Family income supplement (F.I.S.) (c) A weekly allowance paid to a family whose parent is employed at least thirty hours a week, but on a low income.

Free milk and vitamins (c) Parents on low incomes may claim free milk and vitamins for children under five years of age.

Guardian's allowance (c) A weekly allowance paid to an adult who undertakes the care of an orphan.

Industrial death benefit (c) An extra allowance for widows and children of workers who die in industrial accidents or from industrial diseases.

Industrial disablement benefit (c) This is similar to industrial injuries benefit and is calculated according to the severity of disablement.

Industrial injuries benefit (c) A weekly allowance paid to a person whose work has caused certain specified illnesses or injuries.

Invalidity benefit (a) A pension which replaces sick benefit after twenty-eight weeks. This allowance depends on the age of the claimant.

Job search and employment transfer scheme payment (c) A sum of money to help in the search for a new job.

Maternity allowance (a) A woman normally in full-time employment is entitled to a weekly allowance for eighteen weeks, ending six weeks after the birth of her baby.

Maternity grant (c) A lump sum to help with the expense of having a baby.

Mobility, attendance and invalid care allowance (c) Cash help for handicapped people. See page 234.

Non-contributory invalidity pension (N.C.I.P.) (c) A weekly sum for a person of working age who has been unable to work for at least six months and who does not qualify for invalidity benefit. (Married women can claim only if they are unable to do normal household work.)

One-parent benefit (c) Lone parents can get extra money for the first or only child.

Redundancy payments (c) A lump sum, the amount of which depends upon the number of years' service in the same firm.

Sickness benefit (a) A weekly sum paid after eight weeks' sickness, which is increased if there are dependants. Employees get a statutory minimum sick pay from their employers for the first eight weeks' sickness in any tax year.

Supplementary benefit (b) Any person over sixteen, not in full-time employment and with insufficient money to live on, may apply for this benefit.

TOPS training allowance (c) A weekly allowance for a person over nineteen years who has been away from full-time education for at least two years and who wants to take part in a Training Opportunities Scheme (TOPS) to learn or update a skill.

Unemployment benefit (a) A weekly payment for fifty-two weeks, for unemployed persons, with increased payments for dependants.

Widows' benefits (a)
(i) An allowance for twenty-six weeks following the husband's death, if the widow is under sixty years of age.
(ii) A widowed mother's allowance which commences after the first twenty-six weeks, if there are dependent children.
(iii) A widow's pension following (i) or (ii), if a widow is over forty years of age.

Workmen's compensation supplement (c) An addition to the other industrial benefits.

Youth Opportunities Programme allowance (c) A weekly sum for unemployed school leavers who want to receive work experience or vocational training.

5. Housing. Local housing authorities are responsible for:

(a) the provision and maintenance of council houses, to rent, for people who need homes;
(b) the provision of accommodation for homeless families;
(c) encouragement and help to housing associations who provide cost-rent houses and flats, and co-operative or co-ownership housing;
(d) the provision of mortgages to home-buyers who cannot get loans from other sources;
(e) the provision of grants and loans to home-owners to improve and modernise their houses;
(f) rate and rent rebate scheme for people on low incomes;
(g) the provision of specially adapted homes for the disabled.

6. Environmental health. Environmental health inspectors are responsible for:
(a) provision of clean air, water and food;
(b) noise abatement;
(c) pest control;
(d) removal of rubbish and sewage;
(e) inspection of housing and condemning of unfit houses.

7. Other services in the community:

Free legal aid This is means-tested, so that the amount granted will depend on a person's income.

Law centres These exist in some areas to provide free legal advice.

Free library Provided by local authorities.

Police

Fire brigade

Probation officers Social workers, attached to courts, who work with criminal offenders. They also undertake reconciliation work in cases of broken marriage.

Citizens Advice Bureaux A general advisory service which helps people, especially those with legal, matrimonial or housing problems.

School crossing patrols By an Act of Parliament of 1954, a school crossing patrol can stop traffic if the patrol-person is wearing a uniform or emblem approved by the Secretary of State.

8. Voluntary services. There are many of these and they vary from area to area. Some examples are:

Women's Royal Voluntary Service Branches of this service often help families in need, by providing second-hand items of clothing, etc.

British Red Cross Society This society operates a loan service of walking-aids, wheelchairs, bed-pans and other nursing equipment.

National Society for the Prevention of Cruelty to Children (NSPCC)   The society's workers are trained in preventive work and help families and children in distress.

Marriage guidance clinics   This is a service for people who need help with their marriage problems.

Gingerbread Club   An organisation which helps one-parent families.

Exercise 20

Multiple-choice questions
1. Family Income Supplement is:
(a) money paid weekly to one-parent families;
(b) a weekly sum of money for all children;
(c) a weekly tax rebate;
(d) a weekly sum of money paid to families with low incomes.

2. Which of the following officials is responsible for visiting all families with children of under five years of age?
(a) health visitor;   (c) housing officer;
(b) environmental health officer;   (d) social worker.

3. A social worker visits:
(a) all families with children under five;
(b) all families with a handicapped member;
(c) all families which have problems and seek help;
(d) all families living on social security.

4. Karen is an unmarried mother of sixteen bringing up her son of three months in her parents' home. For which of the following benefits may she be eligible? Select from combinations (a) to (d) below.

    1. One-parent benefit   5. Guardian's allowance
    2. Supplementary benefit   6. Sickness benefit
    3. Rate and rent rebate   7. Maternity allowance
    4. Child's special allowance   8. Lump sum payment for special needs
(a) 1, 2, 8. (b) 2, 3, 4. (c) 1, 6, 7. (d) 1, 4, 5.

Essay questions
5. Describe briefly the service provided by the state to help prevent the break-up of families which have young children.
6. Who would you approach for help for a one-parent family experiencing difficulties? What statutory services are available to this family?

Project
7. Find out about the different voluntary societies in your home area. Describe one in detail.

Suggestions for further reading

Winifred Huntly, *Personal & Community Health*, Baillière, Tindall & Cassell
Phyllis Willmott, *The Consumers' Guide to the British Social Services* (Pelican Original), Penguin Books Ltd
Brian Meredith Davies, *Community Health & Social Services*, English Universities Press Ltd
DHSS Leaflets from Social Security Offices
N. J. Smith, *A Brief Guide to Social Legislation*, Methuen & Co Ltd
A. E. Leeding, *Child Care Manual for Social Workers*, Butterworth & Co Ltd
P. J. North, *People in Society*, Longman Group Ltd

Chapter 21
Looking after other people's children

Professional responsibilities

The nursery nurse's first responsibility is to the child or children with whom she works. But she is also responsible and answerable to her employer.

In private work, she will be dealing direct with that employer. In public sector work, authority lies with her head teacher, ward sister or officer-in-charge. To her, she owes punctuality, reliability, co-operation, conscientiousness and loyalty. If she is seriously at odds with her superior over measures concerning children's well-being, she must privately, and as disapassionately as possible, voice her views to the person in charge. Trivial day-to-day sources of irritation should be played down as much as possible in the interest of maintaining a good working relationship and relaxed atmosphere. Tensions and sulks will quickly be conveyed to children and be manifested in their behaviour.

The nursery nurse also has certain responsibilities to herself. Besides concentrating on functioning as well as she can in the present, she ought to think of her future and seize every opportunity to continue her professional growth. The availability and quality of in-service courses open to her varies greatly from one area and time to another. But caring for children is a field which is constantly changing and evolving, and she must try to keep pace.

She also owes it to herself to try and 'switch off' from work concerns when she is off duty. Although this is never completely possible, especially when she may be dealing with tragic or deeply worrying circumstances, she must remember that a haggard, overwrought, exhausted nursery nurse is no good to anybody.

A vital feature of a nursery nurse's professionalism is confidentiality. She will find herself, in almost every job, privy to highly personal information about the backgrounds of her children. Newcomers to this position can find the temptation to share a 'tasty' piece of gossip or scandal irresistible. In doing so, they may betray the trust placed by parents in the nursery or school, and perhaps undo years of patient work spent in establishing good relations. They may also be instrumental in the stigmatising or ostracising of a child or family. Instead of an improvement in the situation, which is the aim of the nursery staff, there may be a worsening of it. Other families will be deterred from confiding or trusting in that nursery staff.

Depending on circumstances and individuals, the nursery nurse will meet many styles of management in her superiors. Some managers make most policies and decisions themselves and expect their staff to carry them out. Others prefer most issues to be debated by their staff and agreed by majority decisions. Many try to combine the best of both these styles, reserving the ultimate power of veto or implementation on certain matters.

Trade unions and professional organisations

There are several trade unions to which nursery nurses may belong. These are:

N.A.L.G.O., N.U.P.E., C.O.H.S.E. (for nursery nurses in hospitals) and A.C.T.S.S., a subsidiary of T.G.W.U., Britain's largest union.

Many people are afraid of trade unions because they do not understand their purpose, which is to serve and protect their members. Unions should be the servants, not the masters, of their members; they can strive and negotiate for better conditions of work, pay and status. A union can only be effective if its members unite and co-operate. By belonging to a union, nursery nurses have the right to be directly involved in furthering and improving their conditions of service and, consequently, their careers. They also have union backing and support whenever the need should arise. If employees are happy with their conditions of work, and are assured of support of this kind, they usually do a better job and serve their 'clients' most effectively.

There are at present two professional associations to which nursery nurses can belong. The first is the National Association of Certificated Nursery Nurses. It was formed in 1948 but has not in general been a large or forceful pressure group. Its aim is to improve the status of nursery nurses by encouraging a good standard of training, consulting and liaising with local authorities on all aspects of child care and development, and working with the unions at local level. It has representatives on many official bodies, chiefly the National Nursery Examination Board of England and Scotland, the National Association of Nursery Matrons, the National Association of Maternal and Child Welfare, and the National Association of Nursery Nursing Tutors. Social and educational meetings are held at local branches throughout the country. Seminars are held and newsletters circulated. Student nursery nurses qualify for membership at a reduced rate. In recent years moves have been made to encourage more nursery nurses to join this association, as a means of influencing central and local government on pay and conditions.

In 1982 a new organisation which is also a registered trade union, the Professional Association of Nursery Nurses, known as P.A.N.N., was formed. It arose out of concern on the part of many nursery nurses over the taking of strike action when in conflict with local or central government policy, and thus harming children. Their main standpoint is 'the force of argument rather than the argument of force', and giving priority to professionalism. Like N.A.C.N.N., P.A.N.N. disseminates information, and supports research and reform in child care. Student nursery nurses may take out free membership of P.A.N.N. Day Nursery Officers may also belong to the National Association of Nursery Matrons. P.A.N.N. is also a registered Trade Union offering legal and insurance benefits to its members, and, like its sister, The Professional Association of Teachers, can negotiate with local authority employers.

Nursery nurses, being warm, caring, amenable people, are seldom the raw material of political activism. But if they are not to be exploited and if their status in society is to be duly recognised, raised and rewarded, as was so strongly urged in the 1981 Brierley Enquiry into the N.N.E.B., it is necessary for them to be vocal and make their concerns known.

Teamwork

Nursery nursing is a multi-disciplinary field of activity, which gives it special breadth, interest and variety. But it demands flexibility and sensitivity to changing situations. In an ideal setting, there is no set hierarchy, but each member representing different disciplines within the same team gives of her best as she sees fit, and acknowledges and reacts to the special contributions made by others.

As an example, a nursery nurse working in a children's hospital ward may play a valuable role in providing companionship, play activities and general understanding support to the childen. She may be asked to run a crèche for the young children of visiting parents. Through her well-trained eyes and ears she will be quick to observe changes in children's physical or emotional well-being. She will share this information with the nurses who are there to carry out treatment as prescribed by doctors and consultants. She may also work alongside and complement hospital school teachers, the play therapist and possibly the medical social worker if there are problems at home. Both her role, and her interaction with others, make her an important member of a smoothly running team.

Working with parents

More and more today, in all types of establishments for the under-sevens, nursery nurses are called on to work with the parents of children in their care. Sometimes they will initiate and organise such contacts; in other cases they will share in and support efforts begun by others.

It has long been appreciated, and research in the last thirty years has borne this out, that parents and nursery or school staff must all pull in the same direction. They must agree on the approaches used, so that the child may derive maximum benefit from the establishment he is attending, with its rich store of materials, opportunities and trained personnel. Any divisions of loyalties because of disagreements, lack of respect, misunderstandings or aloofness will adversely affect the child's progress and well-being.

The involvement of parents in nursery or school life varies tremendously, according to people and circumstances. But it ought to begin, in the case of an oldest child in the family, when the parent comes to discuss the child's admission. A warm, accepting and welcoming tone must be set. Many parents still have feelings of unease, even failure, dating back to their own schooling. In the case of admission to day nursery, they may feel they have failed as parents, or reveal hostility, defensiveness or indifference towards 'authority'. Ways must be found to break down this 'them and us' mentality. Preliminary visits to the establishment by the child, before he begins regular attendance, are now common. They are a widely accepted way of minimising the pain of separation from the parents and the strangeness of the surroundings, and they also help the parents to feel reassured and part of the establishment. Often a parent will stay half a day at first, not always because the *child* seems to require it!

In due course parents may find themselves invited to take part in activities such as sewing, with or for the children; fund raising; running a National Savings Bank, lending library, or book club; repairing books or equipment; laundering; helping to run a mother and toddler club, a mothers' group or a more formal parents' association; helping with sports, P.E., swimming, cooking, outings, chess or reading. Special occasions such as harvest festival, school birthday, Christmas parties, plays and services are always well attended by parents. They may also be asked to open days or evenings, coffee mornings and visits by a doctor or photographer. A parent may be invited in to share a special job, talent, skill, such as playing an instrument, with a group. Fathers are especially welcome because of the missing male figure from many single-parent families.

Some nursery establishments run a home-visiting scheme where younger siblings of nursery children are introduced by nursery teachers to worthwhile play and language activities. More spontaneous home-visiting may occur when a child is taken ill or there is special information to be imparted.

Some day nurseries have official mother-and-child placements which gives a mother the chance to be there regularly and absorb the nursery atmosphere and see how it is run. Sometimes a member of staff works with a parent on a one-to-one basis, helping with child care and housekeeping skills. Either can be of real help to a very young or unsupported mother.

With most parental involvement schemes, a low-key, small beginnings, informal approach is best. Most parents dislike being organised, making far-reaching commitments, being patronised, or made to feel that they are being improved, 'got at' or 'done good to'. One of the most successful and longest running mothers' clubs in the authors' experience was held at a well-nigh inaccessible nursery school in a depressed industrial area. Here the head teacher, who had set up the club, faded out as soon as the mothers were able and willing to run it themselves and choose speakers and events *they* wanted. She remained on the best of terms with them and conveyed all kinds of information about matters such as road safety and dental hygiene through strategic placing of displays and by casual chat. Toddlers were welcomed into the school and allowed to join older brothers and sisters.

Where there is a good relationship between the home and the nursery or school not only do children perform more happily and well, but the activity generated can become a real focal point in a community, a source of help, companionship and support between parents, and the starting-point of further self-help ideas.

Provision for the under-sevens

You will find children under seven (and mainly under five) being looked after by a variety of people, including nursery nurses, in many establishments, and for a variety of reasons.

Working mothers
More than half Britain's working women are mothers, and a small but steadily increasing proportion of these are mothers of under-fives. Inflation, an increase in marriage breakdown, greater educational attainments and job opportunities, a desire to improve one's standard of living and a need for companionship are all influencing this trend.

Contrary to many older people's beliefs, there is little evidence to prove a link between working mothers and juvenile delinquency, truancy, vandalism and under-achievement at school.

For *some* women, it is not true that they are the best people to look after their children for these first impressionable years. Moreover, a contented woman is more likely to raise a well-adjusted child than one who is tense, resentful or frustrated. The quality of time spent together is much more important than the quantity.

However, substitute care depends on good organisation, good health, and the unfailing reliability of a number of people. A mother's feelings of fatigue, strain and guilt are never far away, especially when things go wrong.

Britain lags behind many European and other countries in the pre-school provision for children of working mothers.

Only families with pressing social or health needs will be granted a day nursery place. There are not enough registered child-minders. Nursery schools and classes are unevenly distributed (almost non-existent in rural areas), have long waiting lists, and do not pretend to cater for the schedules of working mothers. Full-time nannies are beyond most people's means. Grandmother, if she lives nearby, which is not usual today, may well have a job herself, or else be unwilling to be permanently tied. Playgroup hours are even less compatible with a working mother's timetable than are those of a nursery school.

The mother who needs or chooses to work, and also the stay-at-home mother who seeks peer companionship or wider play opportunities for her child, therefore need to be fully informed about what provision is available to them. In this chapter we outline the various types of pre-school facilities and describe them briefly.

Pilot schemes and new approaches are constantly being tried in an attempt to meet more adequately the needs of today's small children and their families. Facts and figures are valuable pointers, but in the nature of things they soon go out of date.

We have made only passing references to voluntary and community schemes. This is from lack of space only, and in no sense underestimates the immense contribution these make. The personal concern, close relationships, and freedom from red tape and officialdom which characterise voluntary schemes are often exactly what is most needed by the families they are serving.

Nursery nurses (or nursery officers or nursery assistants, as they are known in some jobs) working in the public sector are paid in accordance with the National Joint Council scale. There is no such prescribed scale for nursery nurses working in the private sector; here, it is negotiable by individuals. All public employees must have a written contract of employment (job description) and guidance on grievance procedure.

Provision for children from birth to seven

	Day nurseries	
	Day (family) centres	Authority responsible – local
	Registered child minders	Social Services Department
	Residential homes	
	Foster parent placement	
Public Sector	Hospitals	Authority responsible – District Health Authority

Nursery schools	
Nursery classes	Authority responsible – Local
Nursery centres	Education Authority
Infant schools	
Special schools	

	Private nurseries	
	Crèches	Approval, liaison and consultation
	Playgroups	with local Social Services
Private	Playbus	Department necessary
Sector	Adoption	

Mother and toddler clubs
Private work (nannies)

Day nurseries

The expansion of day nurseries was a wartime measure to free women to work in factories and in the service industries. After the war, many were closed, and since then, growth has been confined to socially needy areas.

A day nursery is staffed by a nursery officer-in-charge (N.N.E.B. and/or S.R.N. trained), a deputy, and trained nursery nurses – who are termed 'nursery officers' – on a ratio of one adult to five children, not including the officer-in-charge. Several domestic staff will also be employed, as the children (aged from six weeks to five years) can take breakfast, lunch and tea on the premises, and, of course, there is a good deal of laundry and cleaning involved. The children are divided into 'family groups' of between six and eleven children, covering the total age span and keeping members of real families together. A separate baby room may be provided, but mothers are not encouraged to leave babies under nine months. Some children may stay at a day nursery for several years; others remain there only months or weeks during a temporary domestic crisis.

Day nurseries open from about 7.30 a.m. or 8.0 a.m. until 5.30 p.m. or 6.0 p.m., although few children are likely to be there for the whole day. Nurseries stay open all the year round except for Bank Holidays, and in some cases, one extra day. Some children attend part-time, others attend for a long day, although there is a good deal of flexibility.

A good day nursery offers children first-class physical care, including medical inspections, and the services of various professional people such as audiometrician, speech therapist, etc. It also offers stability, security, and linguistic and intellectual stimulation. Although nurseries commonly accept more children than they were intended to, priority has to be given to working single parents, children with physical or mental handicap, impoverished or severely-strained home environment, ill or handicapped parents. Many of these children might be subjected to concealed parental violence (C.P.V.) if the day nursery did not take away some of the strain. Sometimes the relief offered to, for instance, a very young mother or harassed lone father is sufficient to keep the family together and functioning reasonably well. Parents pay only minimal costs for meals taken – nothing else – and many parents apply and are eligible for free meals. It is therefore an expensive form of local authority care, but can be regarded as a preventive measure, and infinitely less expensive than residential care.

Because many of the children come from troubled backgrounds, disturbed behaviour is inevitable, and, at its worst, this *can* give rise to another unfavourable environment for the child. However, dedicated staff can work wonders in maintaining a homely, happy atmosphere in which the children settle and often blossom.

Contacts with parents are of vital importance, if all the chief influences in the child's life are to be working towards the same ends. But such contacts can be difficult. Feelings of failure and guilt are sometimes masked by feigned indifference or even aggression. Some parents can be involved with nursery activities; others will be happy to leave their children in expert hands. Single and working parents do not find it easy to attend nursery functions.

Day Care centres

Attempts have been made in recent years to extend the services offered by day nurseries, because it is argued that to help a child in isolation is superficial and ineffectual. Rising figures of child abuse have added urgency to the need for more prevention and rehabilitation.

It is almost impossible to generalise about day care centres, as they vary so much. In some areas, this pattern of care is being introduced, and day nurseries will probably be phased out eventually, as deliberate policy on the part of the Social Services Department. Elsewhere, day centres are set up by voluntary agencies in response to local needs – for instance, if there are many families with young children in bed and breakfast accommodation. Several different services will be offered on the same campus, including possibly medical attention, and a meeting place for the handicapped. Some day centres are set up jointly by the Social Services Department and the local health authority.

Family Centres are another attempt to support whole families in difficulties. At the centre in the London borough of Camden, day care for children for up to seven days a week is offered, as well as parent units. The teaching at family centres is aimed at helping the adults to be more adequate and interesting people, as well as parents; help with budgeting, cooking, diet, household chores, appearance and leisure skills might all be included. At Camden there are also home visits by centre staff, to give parents a better insight into their children's needs, for instance in play and language stimulation. Some family centres have an assessment unit.

Child minders

For many thousands of working mothers, using the services of a child minder is the only realistic arrangement. It can also be the best, as hours can be fixed to suit the mother. Moreover, the child minder often lives near the mother's home, and for the child the surroundings are probably familiar and remind him of his own home. Thus it is less demanding and stressful than day nursery for most children under three. There is also the advantage that when the child starts school, he can continue to use the same child minder before and/or after school.

Anyone who looks after an unrelated child for more than two hours a day for money must register as a child minder and conform with regulations laid down in the Nursery and Child Minders Act, which became law in 1948. Its provisions were later amended, and loopholes tightened up in the Health Services and Public Health Act of 1968. The standards set by local authorities for registered minders vary enormously, but few minders are registered to take more than four children. Social workers visit at intervals to supervise the child minder, and the health visitor visits 'her' children and gives advice on home safety, play, language stimulation, menu planning, etc.

It is a hard-working, long day for a child minder, and she will not earn a great deal of money. She will be advised on what to charge her clients by the D.H.S.S., but out of this money she will have to pay for meals, toys, equipment, outings, wear and tear on her home, as well as additional heating and lighting costs. Steps are being taken in various areas by the D.H.S.S. and health visitors to provide more support and in-service training for registered child minders. The B.B.C. ran a very good series of programmes on this subject. Access to playgroups, toy libraries and other resources can also improve the lot of the child minder and her charges. Day fostering/sponsored child minding schemes have been started by a number of authorities, particularly to meet the needs of children who are considered 'at risk'.

We must add a note on unregistered child minders, of whom there are large, unknown numbers. Some slip into child minding, and are ignorant of the laws governing this work. Others evade the law, in order to take more children and earn more money. It is very difficult for social workers and health visitors to track down such practice. Sometimes space and facilities are hopelessly inadequate, but large numbers of babies and children are minded; horror stories are not uncommon. Naturally, in such a cramped situation, emphasis will be laid on quietness, sleep and 'tidy' activities. Children who spend several years in such an atmosphere are likely to grow up with retarded language and stunted intelligence.

Before we condemn such practice, however, we should appreciate that where it is rife, the women concerned are responding to a local need which the state is not meeting.

Residential care

Children whose parents are not able to look after them permanently or, more likely, temporarily, for reasons of physical or mental illness, death, eviction, accident, alcoholism, imprisonment, or who have been parted from their parents by Court Order, because of assault or neglect, are taken into residential care. Such care used to come under the auspices of the Home Office, but is now administered under the social services. All residential work calls for a particular kind of dedication from those who are involved.

The homes used often to be large, soulless places, offering sanctuary to orphans and illegitimate children, who might stay there many years. The care they received was often tainted with a Victorian aftermath of rescuing unfortunates from immoral backgrounds; there was much emphasis on godliness and cleanliness, and children were supposed to appreciate all that was being done for them.

Post-war government studies and generally-accepted research findings about the potentially damaging effects of institutionalisation have led to great changes in the last thirty or so years.

For psychological reasons, and also financial ones – residential care being very expensive for local authorities – social workers try to prevent the break-up of families whenever possible. Where separation is unavoidable, the period of time a child spends in care is kept as short as is compatible with home circumstances, and all staff involved will be working towards the rehabilitation of the family.

Children over five will probably be placed in small family group homes of about six children of varying ages up to sixteen. The house may be council-owned on an estate. There will be a house mother and sometimes a house father, who may or may not have had some kind of formal training for this job.

Alternatively, children in care may be fostered out. The under-fives, particularly if they have been subjected to parental violence, or if they are handicapped, may be placed in residential nurseries. There has been a marked increase in recent years in parental violence to children, usually small children. It is of vital importance that such children are handled with the utmost sensitivity, skill and care. Trained nursery nurses' knowledge of children and observation skills will be invaluable in many different ways, not least of which may be court involvement, and judgements involving a child's wellbeing and future.

Besides local authority homes, several voluntary bodies such as Dr. Barnardo's, National Children's Homes, etc. also fund and administer residential children's homes, but their approach, too, has changed and diversified greatly over the years. Frequently, they now offer preventive and support services such as family (day) centres, playgroups and holiday schemes for handicapped children.

Fostering

Fostering is a form of residential care. It can last for a few days or several years. Since the Children Bill of 1975, foster parents can now apply for the custodianship of a child – a sort of halfway stage between fostering and adopting – which safeguards the child from his natural parents changing their minds. Adoption can follow custodianship.

Babies who are going to be adopted are fostered out to registered foster parents for approximately six weeks.

Long-term fostering with infants is most likely to be successful. The more disrupted and traumatic a life an older child has experienced, the more difficult will be his settling in. Other difficulties he may encounter are the jealousy and resentment felt towards him by the natural children of the family, and unrealistic expectations about his adjusting process by the foster parents. Counselling by social workers can go a considerable way towards avoiding disenchantment and breakdown.

Foster parents, who undergo careful screening, particularly of motives, before they are accepted, need endless patience and selfless love. They will be paid only enough to cover the child's food, clothing and pocket money. This, of course, is to ensure that no unscrupulous couples take it on purely for money. Recently, appropriate monetary recognition has been shown to foster parents who take on older and difficult children (teenage truants, bedwetters, etc.). Local authorities are usually short of registered foster parents.

Where a child is accepted naturally, fully and happily into a foster family, it can make the crucial difference and greatly improve his chances of growing up as a well-adjusted, happy individual.

Adoption

There is a great shortage of normal healthy babies who are free to be adopted. This is because contraception and abortion have reduced the number of unwanted babies born, while the social stigma of keeping an illegitimate baby has diminished. Adopting couples often have to wait a year or two before a baby becomes available.

There are voluntary adoption societies, as well as local authority adoption services. As far as the state is concerned, adoption is easily the cheapest way of looking after children who are not kept by their natural parents. It is, incidentally, illegal to arrange adoption privately for money.

Some 'adoptable' babies are orphans or have been totally rejected because they are handicapped or of mixed (coloured) parentage, but most are illegitimate. Since the Children Bill of 1975 there is a shorter interval of time during which the natural mother can revoke her decision, thus reducing the tensions and heart-break of hopeful would-be adopters.

Since adopted children are clearly so much wanted, there is every chance that, provided adoption takes place early in their lives, the arrangement will be highly successful.

In the past, adoption agencies tried to 'match' children and parents for colouring, intelligence and background. This was obviously to minimise embarrassment and disappointment, but today it is thought to be a mistake. After all, natural parents cannot predict exactly what their children's hair colour or intelligence quotient will be!

Before an adoption can be approved, the couple's home will be visited by a social worker to see that adequate standards of cleanliness, space, economic security, etc. are assured. But most important will be the couple's own relationship, and attitude towards the forthcoming child. Adopting a child to rescue an ailing marriage would bring happiness to no-one. One enthusiastic and one reluctant partner could also bode trouble.

Some of the issues the couple will have to think and talk over will 'be their attitudes to illegitimacy, and so-called 'bad blood', their own capabilities as parents, their views on how and when to tell the child he is adopted, their possible reaction if he later wishes to trace his natural parents, which he is now legally able to do.

Hospitals

Many sick children are kept in hospitals today for only very short stays, compared with the practice of a generation ago. The reasons are partly financial and partly psychological, based on what we know about the harm that can be caused when children are separated from their families, and another factor is improved surgery and medication. The exceptions, of course, are seriously ill children, orthopaedic cases, and children requiring specialised treatment. The unrestricted access which allows their families to visit them freely has also greatly changed the lot of children in hospital, and life on the wards. Many hospitals run a playgroup and schooling is provided in hospital for all school-age children.

Some district authorities employ nursery nurses to work with babies and children in hospital. We can find them in maternity wards, special care wards, ear, nose and throat wards and children's hospitals. With the babies, they will help with feeding, changing and general duties, as well as supporting and teaching the mothers. With older children, nursery nurses may be employed at night in a general surveillance capacity, or during the day to offer companionship, play, and educational opportunities. Some hospitals employ nursery nurses as play leaders or workers. Nursery nurses in hospitals may have close contact with the children's parents who are often encouraged to remain involved with the physical handling and emotional care of their children.

Nursery schools

Because statutory schooling in Britain begins at five, the position of nursery schools in the education system has always been vulnerable. No child has a *right* to a nursery school place, and long waiting lists are common.

Rachel and Margaret McMillan, working in the slums of Bradford and Deptford in the early twentieth century, pioneered the idea of the nursery school. Their work, beginning as a rescue operation, soon evolved into a source of mental and spiritual stimulation for the parents concerned as well as the children.

Ever since those days, expansion has been sporadic. Nursery schools are usually among the first victims when government spending has to be cut.

In recent years, many headmistresses have seen the role of their nursery schools as forming the heart of a local community – a base for neighbourhood schemes.

Undoubtedly a good nursery school can enormously benefit a child physically, socially, emotionally and intellectually in the opportunities and expertise it offers. It can provide not only a good start for later schooling, but a good start for life.

Nursery schools are administered as part of the state primary school system and are the responsibility of the Department of Education and Science which works through the local education authorities. They are housed in separate buildings from infant and junior schools, and have their own head teacher. They are staffed by qualified teachers and nursery nurses. A nursery school might comprise two or three classes of twenty to twenty-five three to five-year-olds, each class attached to a teacher and nursery nurse team.

Hours of opening will probably be from 8.45 a.m. or 9.0 a.m. to 3.30 p.m. School holidays are the same as for primary schools. A subsidised mid-day meal is available; education/care is free. Some children attend full-time but many more part-time.

Among her many other tasks, the nursery school head must select from her waiting list a balance of boys and girls, a 'spread' of birthdays among her intake. She must weigh the relative needs of, for instance, children with behaviour difficulties or language retardation, with the needs of children who lack safe play space or stimulation in the home. She will receive many referrals from doctors and health visitors. In order to benefit those children with special needs, she must also keep a balance of 'normal' children.

There will be a pattern to the nursery school day, but it will consist mainly of free play and informal group activities. Foundations for later '3R' work will be laid down in many different ways, but formal reading, writing and number work has no place at this stage.

The nursery nurse will carry out the programmes that the class teacher puts in hand, supporting and complementing her all the way.

Nursery classes

These are attached to infant schools, and are administered by the infant head, although the nursery teacher often enjoys a degree of autonomy. Hours, holidays and staffing are the same as for the nursery school.

Most nursery expansion in recent years has been in the form of nursery classes or units built on to existing schools, for obvious reasons of economy.

It is often possible for the nursery children to enjoy P.E. on the exciting infant school apparatus, and to take part in special festivals and occasions, all of which makes for an easy transition for the child at five.

Combined approach to nursery provision

The Plowden Report in 1967, and later the Halsey Report in 1972, both recommended that the two be combined in an as yet unknown form. This was made financially possible in the ensuing Urban Programme, and the nursery centre was the result.

Its aims are to avoid duplication and overlap between what is provided by social services and education departments; to combine the best of both; to create enough flexibility to meet all children's needs; to cut capital and running costs by centralising pre-school resources in each area.

There are now more than thirty nursery centres, mostly funded and administered by local authorities, but in some cases by a charitable trust or independent body, as for instance at the Thomas Coram Children's Centre in London. Social services and the local education authority share the external administration, but it is not always shared in the same way. There may be one nursery head (teacher) overall, with a matron (N.N.E.B.) as her deputy, or two such trained people may be heads of their own departments within the centre. Trained nursery teachers and nursery nurses make up the staff, but may be employed by one or both authorities.

The day will be longer, so that early opening or late closing can meet different families' needs. Therefore the staff usually work in shifts. Many children attend part-time for as little as two and a half or three hours, but some others may be there as long as ten hours (extended day provision). The children are usually expected to remain at the centre from their time of admission until reaching five, but some may be there only temporarily during a domestic crisis. In any case, their length of day may change during their period of attendance at nursery centre, depending on their own needs and their family's circumstances. The nursery centre is usually open all the year round except for statutory holidays. The teaching staff mostly enjoy the same number of weeks' holiday as their counterparts in nursery schools, but it may have to be staggered throughout the year and not more than three weeks taken at a time. N.N.E.B. staff usually have five weeks' holiday.

There are usually good links between the nursery centre and health visitors and social workers, which makes for a more effective and comprehensive service to the community. Many nursery centre personnel have made great progress with parental involvement, and offer a parents' room, 'drop-in' centre, or other facilities. Through such contacts, much indirect teaching of child care can be transmitted to parents.

All the nursery centres built so far are close to housing estates in socially needy areas. This naturally makes for an intensification of problems among the intake. It was found early on that a completely 'free flow' of all ages and kinds of children in the building and grounds did not work well and the under-threes are now segregated to an extent, that is to say they are given a geographical secure home base within the building, although patterns of grouping throughout vary greatly. A child who attends a centre for a long day may meet up to one hundred children and be expected to relate closely to several different adults, all in the course of a day. This fact, and also the open-plan design and noise level of some centres, can make great demands on the child.

Other experimental avenues in joint approach are extended hours at the nursery school, and introducing teachers into day nurseries.

Infant schools
Depending on prevailing educational policies and population trends, the 'rising fives' will sometimes be found in infant schools. Generally speaking, children at school will be in the five to seven age range.

The delight and relief many mothers experience when their children reach the statutory school age, and they feel free to earn some money, is often short-lived. Five-year-olds are easy prey to the many new infections they meet. Child minding arrangements are still necessary at times. Moreover, even if the child remains completely fit, he will badly need love, support and attentive care from his mother at the time of taking this big new step in his life.

Infant schools are part of the state primary school system. They may be separate from junior schools, and have their own head teachers, or they may be part of a junior mixed infant (J.M.I.) school.

Most children attend the school in whose catchment area they live. Sometimes the nearness of several schools makes choice possible, provided there are vacancies. Children pay for optional mid-day meals; some will be eligible for free dinners.

Grouping of children within infant schools may be based on either age bands, or family grouping. Numbers within a class may vary between about fourteen and nearly forty.

Play and creative activities form a proportion of the day's programme, but in the main will now be structured so that they more obviously lead the children into literacy and numeracy skills.

Teaching of these skills will include some formal approaches and a good many informal ones. Children will be allowed a degree of choice; there will be active learning, movement, and work performed by groups of children. There will also be opportunities for art, music and physical exercise. The day's programme may be loosely timetabled, or all activities may be integrated. Even the most apparently informal approach, if the teacher knows her job, is based on a great deal of organisation, preparation and record-keeping.

For some excellent further reading on the functioning of the modern Infant School, see Cynthia Mitchell's *Time for School*, Penguin Education Press.

Ancillary workers in infant schools may be known as general assistants, general assistant/secretaries, welfare assistants, and nursery assistants. Some will have been trained, either as nursery nurses, or on short in-service courses, others will not.

Sometimes a nursery nurse is employed to help a handicapped child cope at ordinary infant school. If the Warnock Report is implemented, this trend could grow. Generally speaking, the employment of nursery nurses as full-time assistants to teachers is patchy throughout Britain.

Special schools
(See Chapter 16, Children with Special Needs.)

Private nurseries
These are set up in private individuals' houses and offer their services to any parents who can affort to pay for their three- to five-year-olds to attend. Charges made have to cover all overheads, staff wages, children's meals, etc. Private nurseries do good business in areas where there is inadequate state provision, and where there are opportunities for better paid women's jobs. Therefore they are often to be found in pleasant residential districts and country towns.

Premises and facilities must be inspected and approved by social service personnel and a fire prevention officer and environmental health officer must see the kitchen. If the person in charge has neither a N.N.E.B. nor S.R.N. qualification, one person on her staff must be thus qualified. Sometimes a nursery is registered to take children under three, in which case the ratio of adults to children must be higher than the normally stipulated one to six.

Keeping of records is compulsory, and the nursery will be visited regularly by social service staff and the health visitor to see 'her own' children, to safeguard against any negligence or exploitation of children and parents.

Crèches
This French word meaning cradle is still used to describe a private nursery in factory, shop or other business premises which offers child minding facilities to children of employees (or in the case of shops, customers). It is interesting to note that Robert Owen, the social reformer, saw the usefulness of this idea and put it into practice at his New Lanark mills as long ago as the early nineteenth century.

In this century and in Britain it has been an idea which has been slow to evolve, but it has been adopted by employers of large numbers of women, for example, those who work in hospitals. In some areas workers, students and teachers have pressurised employers into providing facilities for their children. But some trades unionists have resisted the idea, fearing that the existence of a crèche will act as an unfair hold on the employees.

At best, a crèche can offer care superior to that of many child minders. It can mean a shorter day for the child than if he were being taken to child minder or day nursery, and mother is at hand in case of emergency.

At worst, it can be merely child minding by unqualified staff. The children may also miss the neighbourhood atmosphere and neighbourhood friends.

Playgroups

Playgroups first appeared on the British scene in the early 1960's. Mrs. Belle Tutaev, who had started a voluntary group in London, was overwhelmed by the response which her letter to a national newspaper on the subject brought forth. The resulting loose association of playgroups evolved into the Pre-school Playgroups Association. By 1975, there were one third of a million children in such groups.

Eventually the movement gained government recognition and now receives financial aid. This is paid to P.P.A. nationally, some of the money going to each of the eleven regions in England and Wales.

Although there is no overall pattern of funding playgroups, most receive local authority help. It may be in the form of rent-free premises (schools, halls, etc.) or the means to bulk-buy play equipment. Some social service departments pay for socially needy children to attend playgroups.

Some playgroups are run by charities like N.S.P.C.C. and Save the Children, but most are run by groups of mothers.

Groups vary tremendously. They may be home-based or community based. They may consist of six or twenty-four children. The children are aged three (very occasionally two) to five. There is a paid supervisor. If she is not an ex-teacher or nursery nurse, she will be expected to attend recognised playgroup courses. The supervisor will involve other mother helpers, sometimes one or two 'regulars', sometimes several on a rota basis.

Some groups are essentially informal. Some are highly organised, and own a mass of bought and improvised equipment which all has to be stored away at the end of each session, and the premises left in a suitable condition for the Brownies or Karate Club who may be using it that evening. Although a group may function every morning, the same children will be encouraged to attend only two or three times a week, as there is often great demand for places.

Playgroups operate on a low budget. Fees for each session – usually paid termly – in 1983 were between 50p and £1.50, depending on area and overheads. Equipment, breakages, rent, electricity, edible snacks (one-third of a pint of milk per child can be obtained free) and the supervisor's pay must all be met out of playgroup funds. Social events to raise money are frequently occasions for neighbourhood co-operation and fun. Fathers can contribute a great deal to the success of a playgroup.

The original aim of P.P.A. was to provide stop-gap pre-school provision, and to continue to support and press for nursery schools for all. Since then, its aims have widened considerably, but parent involvement has always been of paramount importance.

Despite some professional jealousy from nursery education personnel, and the accusation that governments have encouraged the playgroup movement *at the expense of* nursery school expansion, playgroups have undoubtedly brought much benefit to children, and much satisfaction, growth in understanding and self-confidence to mothers. Lonely, or new-to-the-area mothers can find friends and a useful role, without taking on too onerous a commitment, or being frightened off by a school-like atmosphere.

P.P.A. have taken playgroups into remote rural areas. Save the Children have taken playgroups into travellers' sites. Local needs are catered for. In Hammersmith, for example, there is a playgroup that specialises in preparing non-English-speaking children for school at five.

Standards of play are variable, but all playgroups prepare children for the break with mother, and all offer children the chance to mix with their peers.

Opportunity Playgroups are for handicapped young children. These may be organised by P.P.A. or voluntary agencies.

Playbus

In Britain in 1979 there were one hundred playbuses. These specially equipped buses often result from the efforts of community-conscious individuals – students or volunteer workers with other organisations. There is no overall pattern of funding, but once started, Playbus schemes usually attract finance and practical help from local authorities, P.P.A., and associations such as Adventure Playgrounds and Fair Play for Children.

Buses are bought from bus companies or commercial vehicle dealers. They cost between £500 and £1000, and considerable further expense is involved in renovating them and adapting them to their future use. The outer appearance of the bus is important, and the colourful and imaginative manner in which it is decorated helps to give it a sort of 'Pied Piper' appeal to children whenever they see it.

This novel and lively first impression, combined with a Playbus's mobility and flexibility, has produced an effective community resource. The original idea of a Playbus was to take playgroups to areas where pre-school provision was inadequate. By working with parents, Playbus staff – drivers/social worker and assistant(s) – would then gradually wean the groups away to permanent premises and a self-sufficient organisation. There have been great successes here, and mothers who probably would not have been confident enough to initiate a playgroup of their own have become happy and capable playgroup leaders.

The functions of Playbuses have widened considerably over the years, and now many are to be found involved in work for the community with a variety of different groups and age bands. The Bristol Playbus, for instance, takes part in holiday play schemes for primary age children, gives puppet shows, provides accommodation for Asian mothers learning English, and is constantly seen around the city on Saturdays, providing attractions at fêtes, carnivals, and so on. This trend towards community, rather than exclusively pre-school, work is likely to develop in the future.

There is a National Playbus Association, and each Playbus has its own committee, unless run solely by a local authority, as happens in Wandsworth and Edinburgh.

A few large manufacturing companies have shown interest in financing and equipping Playbuses. The firms gain from good advertising and the community benefits from extra facilities.

Mother and toddler clubs
These are sometimes offshoots of playgroups, although they can also be set up by health visitors at health centres, by teachers at secondary schools, or can arise independently. In some areas, they can receive a grant under Urban Aid, but they are not at the moment statutorily controlled; as the mother is present, she is responsible for her child, therefore registration is not necessary.

They form part of the support network for mothers of pre-school children who often experience social isolation.

Private work (nannies)
During the nineteenth century, and later, English nannies became a byword for propriety, hygiene, discretion, and firm handling tempered by love. A nanny might stay with 'her' middle or upper-class children for many years, and was often closer to them than their parents, maybe even remaining with the family after the children had grown up.

Changed social conditions today have meant that nannies are more commonly employed by mothers who are also professional or business people, or are public figures. Few houses today can offer 'staff quarters' which the nanny of old would have enjoyed, and so some nannies may lack privacy or time off. Living as one of the family is quite common, and so are nannies employed on a day-time basis. A nanny may be required for a year or so only, or else she may choose to move on. She may be offered chances of travel abroad. Each nanny position is unique. A nanny works in triangular interaction with the parents and the child or children. How successfully she handles this situation will depend on her maturity, skills, diplomacy, sensitivity, good humour and stickability.

Her employers' expectations of her will be influenced by their experience of previous nannies, and possibly those of their own childhood, their knowledge – or lack of it – about her training course, the age difference between them and the nanny, and their views on child-rearing practices, such as toilet training and discipline.

Ideally these, and many other matters, should be discussed at interview, and further explored during a week-end stay at the home before the nanny accepts the position. Points to be discussed and settled include the salary and salary review, leave, duties (how many and what household duties?), hours, sickness arrangements, use of car, freedom to entertain other nannies and their charges, or personal friends and permission to join a pre-school club. Very important is the question of how National Insurance and tax contributions are to be paid. A contract of employment should be drawn up, agreed and signed by both parties. A trial period, and agreement on procedure for termination of employment, may be suggested.

The nanny should be prepared for feelings of loneliness and homesickness at first, lack of professional support and guidance (as enjoyed by new nursery nurses at day nursery, for example), the constraints of twenty-four hour care and the charge of a sick child, both of which may be completely new to her. She should also expect a process of adjusting to living under the roof of another family, one which may be different from her own in every way, socially and culturally. If this family has not employed a nanny before, it will take a little while for the complementary roles of mother and nanny to evolve and establish themselves to the satisfaction of both.

If there is not enough discussion and explanation and too little attempt to 'match' the nanny and family at an early stage, misunderstandings and disappointment may creep in, perhaps with resentment on both sides. The nanny may feel an intruder, or the parents may feel alienated from their child. The nanny may feel that she is exploited and her skills and training are not being used to the full. A bad atmosphere may build up, creating tension, confusion and unhappiness for the child. The nanny may resign sooner than she intended, leaving in her wake a disturbed child and a disgruntled employer. This sequence of events does nothing to raise the reputation and status of nursery nursing.

Many nursery nurses, however, enter this work well prepared, with a mature, sensible attitude. They enjoy the process of widening their horizons, stay with 'their' families as long as is appropriate, and remain life-long friends. A good nanny offers her charges above all companionship, stability, stimulation and affection.

Exercise 21

Multiple-choice questions

1. You are told that a child at nursery has just come out of care. This means:
(a) he is not now being looked after by anyone;
(b) he has just come out of hospital;
(c) he had been battered at some time;
(d) he has spent a period in a residential or foster home.

2. People accepting payment for minding other people's children should be registered as child-minders because:
(a) they will get more money;
(b) it will make them more caring people;
(c) they can take more children;
(d) they are required by law to do so.

3. CPV usually stands for:
(a) a strong white glue used in junk modelling;
(b) Committee of Parent Voters;
(c) Council for Pre-School Vaccination;
(d) concealed parental violence.

4. The most senior person in a day nursery should have the title:
(a) nursery officer-in-charge;
(b) sister;
(c) matron;
(d) supervisor.

5. A crèche is:
(a) the French name for nursery school;
(b) another name for a state day nursery;
(c) a private nursery in shop, factory or other work premises;
(d) a person who does baby-minding.

6. Margaret McMillan was:
(a) late wife of a former Conservative Prime Minister;

(b) proprietress of a firm which publishes children's books;
(c) matron of a famous day nursery in the London slums;
(d) one of the founders of nursery education.

7. Only one of the following statements about the Playgroup Movement is true:
(a) Playgroups are funded solely by Social Services.
(b) Playgroups are funded by local education authorities.
(c) Playgroups arose voluntarily because of lack of nursery provision.
(d) Playgroup leaders must be trained teachers or nursery nurses.

8. The main aim of the Playbus Movement was to:
(a) make playgroups seem more fun;
(b) bring about cheaper playgroups;
(c) create jobs for the unemployed;
(d) take playgroups into areas where there were none.

Essay questions
9. What are the essential differences between a day nursery and a nursery school?

10. How does the Playgroup Movement serve the community?

11. What qualities do you think are most needed by nursery nurses taking up residential work?

12. A friend comes to tell you that she is thinking of starting child-minding. What advice would you give her?

Project
13. Find out what facilities exist in your home locality for your child of three. Imagine that you are a single mother. Where do you think you would place your child?

Discussion topic
14. All mothers of under-fives should stay at home to make the most of these first impressionable years.

Suggestions for further reading

Elizabeth Bradburn, *Margaret McMillan*, Denholm House Press
Marion Dowling, *The Modern Nursery*, Longman Group Ltd
Ivonny Lindquist, *Therapy through Play*, Arlington Books
Lesley Webb, *Purpose and Practice in Nursery Education*, Basil Blackwell Ltd
Joan Cass, *The Role of the Teacher in the Nursery School*, Pergamon Press Ltd
Marianne Parry and Hilda Archer, *Pre-School Education*, Macmillan Education Ltd
Lesley Webb, *Making a Start on Child Study*, Blackwell's Practical Guides, Basil Blackwell Ltd
Jerome Bruner, *Under Five in Britain*, Oxford Pre-School Project
Lesley Garner, *How to Survive as a Working Mother*, Penguin Books Ltd
Elsa Ferri, *Combined Nursery Centres: A New Approach to Education and Day Care*, Macmillan Ltd

Chapter 22
Child observations

These are a necessary part of N.N.E.B. Certificate Courses and form part of the final assessment. They usefully combine the theoretical and practical aspects of the course. Students through their observations gain an ever-increasing insight into and understanding of the development, make-up and behaviour of children, so that they can more fully meet their needs.

The committing to paper of what students see, hear and notice serves to:
(i)   provide a point of sustained focus amid all the distracting activity at the nursery;
(ii) encourage attention to detail;
(iii) imprint it on the student's memory for later reference in discussion, examinations and, most important, in future careers.

Content of observations

The N.N.E.B. requires that some fifty to sixty written observations be submitted at the end of the two-year course. These should cover the whole age-range of birth to seven, should be carried out in a variety of settings in addition to practical placements, and should include:

1. Characteristics of physical growth and development
(a) appearance;
(b) size;
(c) skills;
(d) co-ordination.

2. Development of communication skills
(a) non-verbal and verbal;
(b) language and speech;
(c) reading and writing;

3. Development of cognitive skills
(a) memory;
(b) understanding;
(c) thinking and reasoning.

4. Variety of emotional expression and behaviour revealed in different experiences
(a) new baby;
(b) starting school;
(c) separation.

5. Social development and relationships
(a) social interaction;
(b) types of play;
(c) socialisation – differing cultures and customs.

6. Specific activities related to
(a) creative arts;
(b) growing independence;
(c) daily living (e.g., washing, dressing, etc.)

7. Wider learning capabilities
(a) five to seven year old child;
(b) gifted child.

8. Development patterns (preferably through the long-term observation of an individual child).

Observations both of individual children and groups of children are required. The former will highlight norms of development, individual characteristics and evidence of progression and regression. The latter will focus on interaction between children.

Techniques of observing

The N.N.E.B. does not dictate *how* these observations are to be tackled, but acknowledges that there is a variety of differing approaches and hopes students will explore many of them.

1. Students may work from *prepared schedules* which focus their attention on aspects of children/play/situations that tutors wish them to study.

2. Students may, in *time sampling observations*, focus on one particular child for a few minutes each day over a given period of time or, alternatively analyse what each child in a group is doing during a particular period of time, for example at the beginning and end of the day.

3. Students may focus on *one particular aspect of behaviour*, for instance aggressiveness.

4. Students may record *stages in the development of independence*, such as walking, dressing and feeding.

5. Students may *report verbatim* (word for word) children's conversations, discussion and questions.

Recording and interpreting

Much of what the student commits to paper will be in straightforward, descriptive narrative. But graphic representation, line drawings, sketches, flow charts and tape recordings are all equally acceptable, and make a refreshing change.

The interpreting of what the student records is an essential part of observation work. It will come gradually with familiarity, understanding and the experience of being involved herself and watching other skilled adults involved with children. Temptations for the beginner are to make judgements, to jump to glib conclusions,

Favourite play materials in the classroom

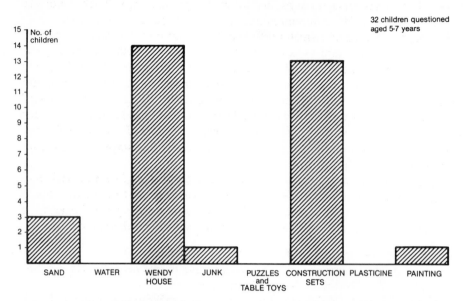

or to make sweeping generalisations. A student will often reveal her growing insight into children by stating at the end of the observation what she has learned from this incident. Sometimes a more relevant comment is to link the significance of what she has witnessed with something taught or discussed at college, or read privately. Disparities between theory and reality can make interesting discussion points. The N.N.E.B. stresses that these child observations should be followed up by discussion between students and staff of the practical placement and/or college supervisor. This will extend the student's understanding of the child concerned, introduce explanation and analysis of his behaviour and invite suggestions for possible lines of future action regarding the child. The supervisor may also comment on the student's method of recordings and suggest possible alternative or future observations.

Here are some extracts from first and second year students' written observations.

Playtime for Esther (See Contents of Observations Notes 1 and 2a).
I watched Esther Rose, who is a lovely five-month-old baby. She has brown hair and deep blue eyes.

I watched her as she played on the floor. Her mother laid her on her stomach while she went to find some toys. Esther pushed herself up on to her hands and turned to see where her mother was. She gurgled happily when her mother came back with a basket full of her favourite toys.

'Hello Esther,' her mother said with a smile, as she sat down in front of the baby. In reply Esther smiled. 'Ow w w . . . . ,' she said in a high-pitched voice. Her mother began to sort out Esther's toys.

'Here's a bunny rabbit, look Esther, look.' She shook the toy in front of the baby and then put it down near her. Esther's eyes widened.

'Oooo,' she said sharply. She followed each toy and accepted a teething ring with coloured keys on it, when it was handed to her. She put the ring into her mouth and began to bite on it. 'Mmmmmmmmmmmm.......,' she said contentedly.

Her mother picked up a small fluffy dog. 'Oh look! Here's Esther's favourite!' The baby turned her head to look at what her mother was holding. The dog was placed in front of her and Esther fixed her eyes on it. She dropped the teething ring and she tried to reach for the toy. She kicked her legs as she tried with all her strength to reach the toy. Her mother encouraged her. 'Come on Esther, look!'

Esther's brow puckered and she pursed her lips. She squealed with frustration and her mother moved the toy to within touching distance. Esther picked it up, looked at it carefully and put it straight to her mouth. She stayed contented for several minutes.

Both mother and baby seem to enjoy these playtimes. Esther, I have noticed, likes the feel of the carpet on her bare feet. She also likes to be talked to constantly. She is usually a happy baby. Her mother says she gets a lot of satisfaction and enjoyment from her baby. Both parents are in their mid-thirties. Esther is their only child.

Breastfeeding (See Contents of Observations Notes 6b and c).
I watched as a skilled nursery nurse helped a mother to feed her baby. He was three days old and was born with Down's Syndrome.

I noticed his rooting reflex as he turned his mouth to his mother's nipple. I could see the strong sucking movements as he fed. He was pressing with his lips and sucking well behind the nipple. I was told he sucked well for a new baby with this condition, but he did drop off to sleep several times and had to be gently rewoken. His eyes were closed as he fed and he wriggled his feet and hands contentedly.

Young child eating
Andrew, twenty-three months, picked up the spoon in his right hand, the fork in his left and began to tackle his meal of cheese flan, peas and boiled potatoes. He handled his spoon and fork rather well and found no difficulty in getting the peas on to his spoon, using the fork to push the peas on to it. When he came to the flan, he attempted to make the pieces smaller by raising his spoon and banging at the flan until the pieces were eventually broken down.

Birthday boy (See Contents of Observations 3, Notes 3, 4 and 5).
On the 17th of January I had a lovely opportunity to observe Mark, who had just celebrated his fifth birthday, talk about it at Assembly.

Mark and three other 'birthday' children stood in front of the assembled Infants School. Mark stood by the teacher fiddling with his jumper, twisting it around his finger then letting it go.

The teacher asked him if he had lots of presents. 'Yes, I had Dukes of Hazzard', he answered, his eyes wide open, looking straight in front of him. The teacher asked him if he had the real Dukes of Hazzard. Mark giggled. 'No, it's a game.' His face crinkled into a smile and his head went back.

Mark was asked if he had a party and who had been invited. He looked puzzled. His finger went on his lips and his eyes turned upwards. 'Er, I had a cake. It was a five.' His face showed bashful delight at the memory. 'Ben came and Damien – er – Michael and Victoria', his eyes darting round the group of children as he spoke.

The teacher asked what else he had had for tea. 'Hula hoops and Skydivers, sausages on sticks and sandwiches.' He put his fingers together and splayed them out, bending them backwards and forwards. His face coloured and he shifted from one foot to the other.

The teacher commented on how nice it all sounded and, when the other children had shared their birthday details, together they blew out the candles on the school 'birthday cake.' Mark's face exploded into a grin, pride in the occasion written all over his face.

He was clearly shy and uneasy in front of all the other children at first. He needed much coaxing by the teacher to describe his party but once he had 'remembered', the words flowed as he relived the excitements of the day.

Firework follow-up (See Contents of Observations Notes 6a and 7a).
Sasha is six years old, with fine shoulder-length blonde hair, brown eyes and rather a long face. She is very friendly towards me and is one of the livelier members of the class.

Today we were doing some follow-up work on Bonfire Night. The object of the exercise was to put a blob of glue in the middle of the paper and spread it out to make a small circle. You then took a cocktail stick and dipped it into the paint – first yellow, and let the paint drip on to the glue, and then do it with red paint. You then took a clean cocktail stick and made spikes out from the centre of the blob. When these dry they look like fireworks exploding into the sky.

'I'm doing it like this,' said Sasha as she wiped a blob of glue on to the paper. She giggled.

'Is this O.K., Andrea?' she asked, not looking up.

'Yes, that's very good,' I replied.

She could not get the paint to drip off the stick so I told her to dip it back into the paint. She put it into the glue instead. She was holding the stick delicately in a finger and thumb pincer movement.

'Mine won't go like yours,' she said, frowning.

'But you shouldn't try to do it exactly like mine because you must have ideas of your own,' I told her.

She carried on, with her tongue out. She put her left hand on the paper to steady it. When she had finished she looked at mine again and then at her own. She stood up quickly, scraping her chair loudly. She picked up her picture, folded it neatly in half and then screwed it up.

'Oh, Sacha, that was silly,' I said.

'Well I'm starting again because it wasn't very good,' she said indignantly. So she did!

From this incident I realised my mistake in giving her the impression that she had to copy an adult's example exactly. She obviously compared the two and was discontented with her own efforts. On the other hand, it may have been partly attention-seeking behaviour and a way of 'spinning out' her time working with me.

First day at school (See Contents of Observations Nos. 2b, c and 4b).
Hamish is a child from a traveller's family and it was his first day at school. He had not been to playgroup or nursery, and had previously socialised only with children on the caravan site.

The children were playing with items of their own choice. When asked what he would like to do he replied 'Draw.'

He sat down at the table and I gave him some paper and a selection of thick wax crayons. He picked up one of the crayons and peered at it suspiciously. He put it on the palm of his hand and prodded it with his index finger. He then picked it up and held it closely in front of his eyes in order to further examine it. He eventually slammed it down on the table and said 'Pens,' pointing at some felt tips. He added, 'I have pens at home.' He started to draw on the paper, making marks which seemed to resemble capital and lower case letter A's. He also seemed to enjoy making dots on the paper. After a few moments he turned the paper over, explaining, 'Use other side.' He was fully absorbed in his work and concentrating intently.

Later in the morning, the children had to copy their names from their name cards. I noticed Hamish looking blankly at his card. I went over and guided his hand so that he wrote his name. When he saw the results and I explained that it was his name, he looked up and gave me a beaming smile.

My teacher explained later that Hamish is unlikely to have met crayons, or indeed many other play materials, at home. His integration within the group may be a very gradual process.

His use of language was not as advanced as others in the group. He spoke in single words or short phrases only. He seems keen to learn new skills at school.

A find on a shopping expedition (See Contents of Observations Notes 3a, b, c).
It is a bright, sunny day. Nicholas, aged three-and-a-half and I are going to the local shops. I notice a snail shell on the ground so I draw Nicholas's attention to it. He picks it up, looks at it frowning and says, 'What is it?'

'It's a snail shell; it's where the snail used to live,' I explain.

'Is he there now?' asks Nicholas, peering inside the shell.

'No, not any longer,' I reply.

'Is he a Daddy now?' he then asks. 'He will have to have a big shell.'

'How big do you think?' I enquire.

'See that flower over there?' says Nicholas, pointing to a dahlia.

'Well, it's not as big as that, but I think it will be as big as that one there,' he says, pointing to an aster.

'And the little boys will be as big as . . . as . . .' He looks around, then crouches down on the floor and points to a stone . . . 'as big as that stone there.'

Nicholas looks thoughtful for a moment, then says, 'Do you think a snail can be as big as a house?'

'I don't think so,' I replied. 'Do you?'

Nicholas laughs. 'No,' he says. 'It will be *very* big!'

He suddenly remembers the sweets we are going to buy and starts to talk about these.

Nicholas was using his everyday experience of the generations, comparative sizes etc. and applying it to this newly-discovered object, as soon as he understood it had once been a living creature. He was also seeking suitably-sized objects round about him and using his imagination. Attention to one topic of conversation is usually very short at this age.

Playtime conversation (See Contents of Observations Notes 2, 3 and 5).
The children were excited at being back at school. Stephen (six) and Wayne (seven)

had brought their toy cars into the playground and were quietly looking at them together. Stephen touched Wayne's car and he immediately said, 'Get off Stephen, that's mine.'

Stephen looked upset and the teacher came over to the couple. Wayne looked up at her and said, 'We're playing. Tomorrow Stephen's bringing his tractor.'

Stephen said, 'I'm happy with my car. Daddy bought it for me.'

Wayne said, 'Let's make a motorway. You put your car over there, Steve.'

Stephen replied, 'I rode on the motorway yesterday.'

Joy (six) came up to the boys and asked, 'Can I play?'

The boys replied, 'No.' Joy looked cross and immediately hit Wayne. The teacher came over and Joy cried, 'He wouldn't let me play, so I hit him.'

In this observation, we can see infant-age children using language in a variety of ways. Wayne was protecting his own property and pleasure. He also reported on present experience to the teacher. He projected into the future. Stephen reflected on his feelings and seemed to be explaining their cause. Wayne asked Stephen to co-operate with him on a play theme. He then directed Stephen's actions. Stephen reported a past experience, seeing the relevance of it to this game. Joy tried to initiate a play relationship, then needed to justify her behaviour to the teacher.

Suggestion for further reading

Lesley Webb, *Making a Start on Child Study*, Basil Blackwell Ltd

Answers to Exercises

Exercise 1   (page 20)
1(b), 2(d).
Exercise 2   (page 30)
1(b), 2(d), 3(a).
Exercise 3   (page 42)
1(c), 2(d), 3(b), 4(b), 5(b).
Exercise 4   (page 50)
1(c), 2(c), 3(d).
Exercise 5   (page 65)
1(a), 2(c), 3(b), 4(c), 5(c).
Exercise 6   (page 87)
1(c), 2(b), 3(d), 4(c), 5(a).
Exercise 7   (page 104)
1(c), 2(a), 3(c), 4(c), 5(d).
Exercise 8   (page 116)
1(c), 2(c), 3(b), 4(a), 5(b).
Exercise 9   (page 132)
1(c), 2(d), 3(d), 4(a), 5(b).
Exercise 10   (page 144)
1(b), 2(d), 3(c).
Exercise 11   (page 153)

1(d), 2(c), 3(c).
Exercise 12   (page 169)
1(c), 2(a), 3(a), 8(d), 9(a), 10(d).
Exercise 13   (page 181)
1(a), 2(c), 3(b).
Exercise 14   (page 193)
1(d), 2(a), 3(c).
Exercise 15   (page 214)
1(d), 2(a), 3(a), 4(d), 5(d), 6(c), 7(a), 8(d).
Exercise 16   (page 254)
1(a), 2(a), 3(d), 4(a), 5(c).
Exercise 17   (page 261)
1(d), 2(b), 3(a), 4(d).
Exercise 18   (page 274)
1(d), 2(d), 3(c), 4(c), 5(a).
Exercise 19   (page 282)
1(d), 2(c), 3(d).
Exercise 20   (page 292)
1(d), 2(a), 3(c).
Exercise 21   (page 310)
1(d), 2(d), 3(d), 4(a), 5(c), 6(d), 7(c), 8(d).

Index